MW00800922

REALWRITE

realtime ©

Computerized Shorthand Writing System

LESSON BOOK

SECOND EDITION

ROBERT W. MCCORMICK
CAROLEE FREER

PEARSON
Prentice Hall

Pearson Education LTD.
Pearson Education Australia PTY, Limited
Pearson Education Singapore, Pte. Ltd
Pearson Education North Asia Ltd
Pearson Education Canada, Ltd.
Pearson Educación de Mexico, S.A. de C.V.
Pearson Education – Japan
Pearson Education Malaysia, Pte. Ltd

PEARSON
Prentice Hall

10 9 8 7 6 5 4 3 2
ISBN 0-13-118052-5

This textbook is dedicated to my wife, Rose, and my children, Tara, Erin and Nicole, for their love, patient endurance, understanding, support and sacrifice.

-R. W. McCormick

This textbook is dedicated to my husband, Richard, and my children, Jennifer and John, who have provided me with their patience, understanding, and love.

-Carolee Freer

TABLE OF CONTENTS

UNIT 2

Lesson Five

Lesson Six

Lesson Seven

Lesson Eight

Unit 2 Review

UNIT 3

Lesson Nine

Lesson Fourteen

Lesson Fifteen

Lesson Sixteen

Unit 4 Review

UNIT 5

Lesson Seventeen

Lesson Forty-Eight

Unit 12 Review

INDEXES

INTRODUCTION

The Theory

In the early 1900s, when the original machine shorthand theory was first used, it proved to be an adequate system for writing the spoken word. However, with the advent of computers in the later 1960s and early 1970s, it became necessary to differentiate the vowel pronunciations for Computer Aided Transcription (CAT). This was accomplished by using the long and short vowels in writing different words.

Now, as court reporting and machine shorthand writing advance into the twenty-first century with concepts of realtime writing and instantaneous video transcription, it is absolutely necessary that machine shorthand theory adapt to the changing technology. This adaptation of theory to reflect the mode of transcription is necessary because so many of our English words sound alike but are spelled differently and because so many sound-based words are in potential conflict with each other.

Thus the *Realwrite/realtime* theory, the first theory of its kind, was created solely for the realtime writing and immediate transcription by computer. The theory is a rule-based theory; that is, it is based on a series of principles or guidelines. We all know that without rules in our society, life would be chaotic. The same is true for sports, games, driving a car, flying a jet airliner, and writing shorthand. You will follow a series of rules that will guide you in your writing outlines. However, the theory is flexible enough to allow for individual formatting and personal likes and dislikes.

The most important thing you can do as a beginning student is to literally "learn" the system, commit it to memory, practice it as you would practice anything at which you want to do well like golf, tennis, or a musical instrument. But, also, enjoy learning the system. It won't be long before you will find a very rewarding and successful career using your skill.

The Books

The Realwrite/realtime computerized shorthand writing system is presented in a series of textbooks and supplementary materials. It is important to use the entire series of texts as one unit because each book is an integral part of the entire system.

The series is made up of the following books:

Realwrite/realtime LessonBook	48 lessons containing basic theory
Realwrite/realtime DrillBook	24 drills to accompany the basic theory lessons and a series of drills on basic and advanced phrases
Realwrite/realtime NoteBook	12 exercises to accompany the LessonBook and DrillBook containing Realwrite notes for read back and transcription

As a beginning student, you will start with the *LessonBook*. Each lesson contains an assignment from the *DrillBook*. At the end of every four lessons and two drills you are given an assignment from the *NoteBook*. This completes a unit, after which you will be given the opportunity to show how well you learned the theory by completing a unit exam.

This is how the books correlate to each other:

LessonBook lesson	*DrillBook* drill	*NoteBook* exercise	Unit exam
1 & 2	I		
3 & 4	II	A	1
5 & 6	III		
7 & 8	IV	B	2
9 & 10	V		
11 & 12	VI	C	3
13 & 14	VII		
15 & 16	VIII	D	4
17 & 18	IX		
19 & 20	X	E	5
21 & 22	XI		
23 & 24	XII	F	6
25 & 26	XIII		
27 & 28	XIV	G	7
29 & 30	XV		
31 & 32	XVI	H	8
33 & 34	XVII		
35 & 36	XVIII	I	9
37 & 38	XXIX		
39 & 40	XX	J	10
41 & 42	XXI		
43 & 44	XXII	K	11
45 & 46	XXIII		
47 & 48	XXIV	L	12

Equipment and Setting up the Shorthand Writer

For true realtime writing, you should be working with an adequate computer setup which includes a court reporting software package. Some shorthand writers may require a disk or cassette tape in order to record what you write. Some student models may be "paper-less," and/or "disk-less" models, and only write true to the screen. Your setup will vary accordingly. Your software or hardware vendor will assist you in how to make the proper connections between your shorthand writer and computer.

For now, you will be more concerned with getting paper into your shorthand writer, setting it up, and beginning to write. Listed below are the steps for setting up your writer.

1. Place the shorthand writer on the stand (tripod):
   a. extend the three legs of the tripod to their fullest position
   b. pull up the center bar to its furthest position (loosen knob)
   c. place base of shorthand writer on top of center bar so that notch fits into slot
   d. turn the tripod counterclockwise until it clicks into place
   e. move the writer and tripod to make sure they are firmly in place and will not fall

2. Place paper in the shorthand writer:
   a. pull the paper-holder drawer all the way out
   b. place a pack of paper inside the drawer
   c. take the top fold of paper and place it directly underneath the rubber roller
   d. force the paper underneath the rubber roller until it comes out the top
   e. move the silver paper holder forward and place the paper underneath it
   f. push the pack of paper inside the shorthand writer, leaving the drawer out
   g. pull up two or three folds of paper and place them in the drawer
   h. make sure that the paper folds naturally and falls into the drawer automatically

3. Sitting at the shorthand writer:
   a. sit straight back in a comfortable chair with both feet flat on the floor
   b. place the writer directly in front of you between your legs, or with legs together, place the writer on your left or right side
   c. adjust the height of the writer by loosening the knob that holds the bar
   d. the height of the writer should be such that your forearms are parallel with floor
   e. place fingers in a curved position over the keyboard
   f. elbows should be close the body
   g. readjust the height of the machine if necessary

4. Writing on the shorthand writer and reading back:
   a. strike keys quickly, sharply; do not hold keys down or press them slowly
   b. use the "rounded" parts of your finger tips, not the flat part
   c. when reading back, pull an extra fold of notes out and place the notes on top of writer
   d. after reading back, place notes back in tray on their natural fold

5. Removing notes:
   a. when finished writing, lift up the pack of written notes from the tray
   b. "tear" off the last unwritten fold on the "cutting edge" of the silver paper holder
   c. remove the paper from under the writer
   d. holding the silver paper holder forward, pull out the last fold from the rubber roller

6. Removing shorthand writer from tripod:
   a. locate the tripod release lever underneath the writer
   b. push the lever with the index finger to release the tripod
   c. turn the tripod clockwise while pulling it away from the writer
   d. release the center bar knob, push the center bar in, and fold the legs of tripod

Always hold the shorthand writer with both hands or place in on a solid, flat surface. Make sure that the legs of the tripod are fully extended. Severe damage will result if it is dropped or falls. Refer to your owner's manual or instructor for proper preventative maintenance on your shorthand writer.

Keyboard Chart

On the following page you will find a keyboard chart. Tear out and fold the chart and place it near your shorthand writer as you learn your theory. Begin now by going to Lesson 1. Good luck!

UNIT 1
LESSON ONE

Review

Review the procedures in the *Introduction* that explain how to set up your shorthand machine. Also review the correct procedures for putting paper into the steno writer and how to sit correctly. Posture is very important when learning to write.

Keyboard Arrangement

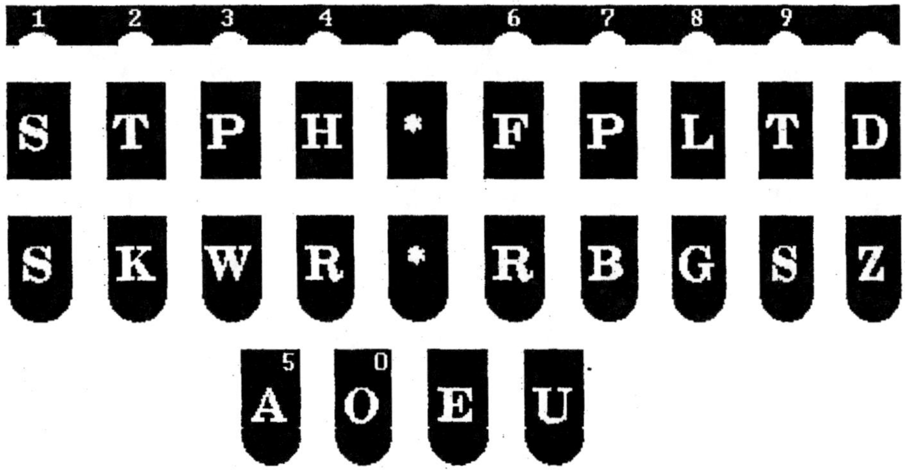

You will notice that the shorthand machine keyboard is arranged in such a way that there are consonant letters appearing on the left side and the right side and that there are vowels at the bottom of the keyboard. The left side is known as the "initial" side, and the right side is called the "final" side. The numbers at the top of the keys are referred to as the "number bar."

There is a reason for this. Most English words can be divided into one or more syllables containing a beginning consonant, a vowel, and an ending consonant. The keyboard is arranged to write words or syllables of words as you hear them, not a letter at a time, but a sound at a time.

For example, if you were to write the word TOP on a regular computer keyboard, you would write the T, then the O, and then the P; this would take three strokes or movements. On the shorthand machine, it would only take one movement: the consonant T on the left side together with the vowel O and the final P on the right side.

You will also notice that some of the letters of the alphabet are not on the keyboard. Any letter that is not on the keyboard will be written by combining other letters to represent them.

For example, the letter D on the initial side is represented by stroking a combination of the T and K together. What may appear to the untrained person as pure nonsense will make complete sense to the trained court and realtime reporter.

It is most important to remember that ALL combinations of letters begin with the hands in the home position. The keys should be depressed quickly and sharply. Immediately after depressing a key or combination of keys you must return to the home position. Do not depress and hold the key down but hit it and return immediately to the home position.

In this lesson you will learn to depress the home position keys and some of the reaches for individual letters. These letters will be taught again in later lessons. Your goal in this first lesson is to get the "feel" of the machine and get used to putting your fingers in the proper position on the keyboard.

Home Position

Home position

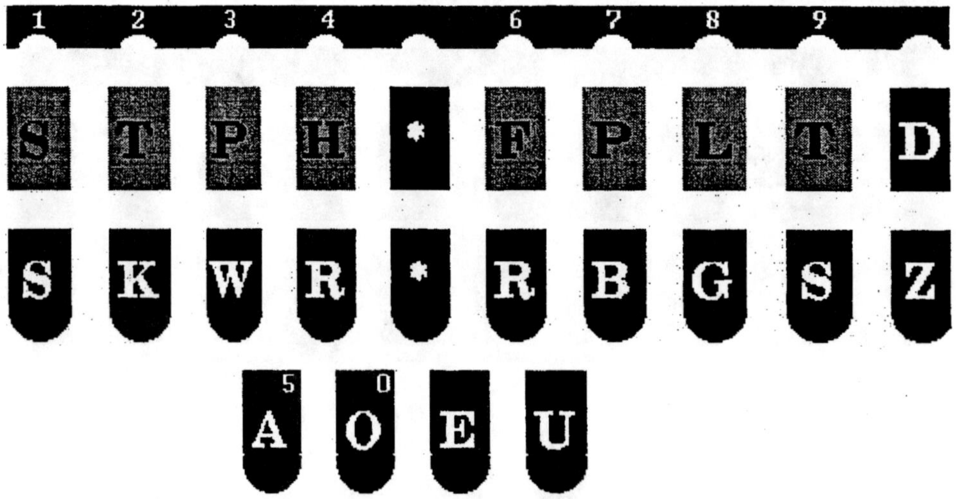

With the left hand, place your

small finger over the letter **S**
ring finger over the letter **T**
middle finger over the letter **P**
index finger over the letter **H**

place your left thumb
over the vowels **A** and **O**

With the right hand, place your

index finger over the letter **F**
middle finger over the letter **P**
ring finger over the letter **L**
small finger over the letter **T**

place your right thumb
over the vowels **E** and **U**

Practice striking some of these home position keys now. It is not necessary to learn the keys yet. You will be learning them in future lessons. It is important for you to get the "feel" of the keyboard. It is important for you to learn to strike the key and immediately let go. It is important for you to return to the home position every time you hit a key. Write each letter separately.

☞ *practice the following:*

Look at the keyboard chart. Read the letter or have someone read the letter to you. "Feel" in your mind which finger you would use to strike it. Strike each letter quickly and sharply.

left hand:

S S S S	T T T T	P P P P	H H H H	S T P H	S T P H
S S S S	T T T T	P P P P	H H H H	S T P H	S T P H
S S S S	T T T T	P P P P	H H H H	S T P H	S T P H
S S S S	T T T T	P P P P	H H H H	S T P H	S T P H

right hand:

F F F F	P P P P	L L L L	T T T T	F P L T	F P L T
F F F F	P P P P	L L L L	T T T T	F P L T	F P L T
F F F F	P P P P	L L L L	T T T T	F P L T	F P L T
F F F F	P P P P	L L L L	T T T T	F P L T	F P L T

left hand:

S T P H	S T P H	S T P H	S T P H	S T P H	S T P H
S T P H	S T P H	S T P H	S T P H	S T P H	S T P H
S T P H	S T P H	S T P H	S T P H	S T P H	S T P H
S T P H	S T P H	S T P H	S T P H	S T P H	S T P H

right hand:

F P L T	F P L T	F P L T	F P L T	F P L T	F P L T
F P L T	F P L T	F P L T	F P L T	F P L T	F P L T
F P L T	F P L T	F P L T	F P L T	F P L T	F P L T
F P L T	F P L T	F P L T	F P L T	F P L T	F P L T

You have been learning to strike each letter separately. In the following lessons you will be asked to return your fingers to the home position and to depress the entire home position at once. In other words, you are to strike the S T P H with the four fingers of your left hand all at the same time along with the F P L T using the four fingers of the right hand.

☞*practice striking the STPH all together*

STPH STPH STPH STPH STPH STPH STPH STPH STPH STPH STPH STPH
STPH STPH STPH STPH STPH STPH STPH STPH STPH STPH STPH STPH
STPH STPH STPH STPH STPH STPH STPH STPH STPH STPH STPH STPH

☞*practice the FPLT all together*

FPLT FPLT FPLT FPLT FPLT FPLT FPLT FPLT FPLT FPLT FPLT FPLT
FPLT FPLT FPLT FPLT FPLT FPLT FPLT FPLT FPLT FPLT FPLT FPLT
FPLT FPLT FPLT FPLT FPLT FPLT FPLT FPLT FPLT FPLT FPLT FPLT

☞*practice striking the STPH-FPLT at the same time*

STPH-FPLT STPH-FPLT STPH-FPLT STPH-FPLT STPH-FPLT STPH-FPLT
STPH-FPLT STPH-FPLT STPH-FPLT STPH-FPLT STPH-FPLT STPH-FPLT
STPH-FPLT STPH-FPLT STPH-FPLT STPH-FPLT STPH-FPLT STPH-FPLT

Although this may feel cumbersome to begin with, you will learn to write the home position quickly and comfortably as time goes on. Learn the home position well because it is from this position that you will learn hundreds of combinations that will allow you to gain remarkable speed and accuracy in your chosen profession of verbatim realtime writing.

Lesson Practice

Read from left to right then down to the next line. Look at the keyboard chart as you strike the letters. Think of which finger you would use to strike it, strike the letter quickly and sharply, then return to the home position.

☞ *practice the following:*

Write each letter separately with the left hand:

S S T T P P H H   S S T T P P H H   S S T T P P H H   S S T T P P H H
S S T T P P H H   S S T T P P H H   S S T T P P H H   S S T T P P H H
S S T T P P H H   S S T T P P H H   S S T T P P H H   S S T T P P H H

Write each letter separately with the right hand:

F F P P L L T T   F F P P L L T T   F F P P L L T T   F F P P L L T T
F F P P L L T T   F F P P L L T T   F F P P L L T T   F F P P L L T T
F F P P L L T T   F F P P L L T T   F F P P L L T T   F F P P L L T T

Write the home position together using both left and the right hands:

STPH-FPLT   STPH-FPLT   STPH-FPLT   STPH-FPLT   STPH-FPLT   STPH-FPLT
STPH-FPLT   STPH-FPLT   STPH-FPLT   STPH-FPLT   STPH-FPLT   STPH-FPLT
STPH-FPLT   STPH-FPLT   STPH-FPLT   STPH-FPLT   STPH-FPLT   STPH-FPLT

Remember to write quickly and sharply. Tap the home position instantly. Do not depress the keys and hold them down. Tap the home position as quickly as possible.

Comprehensive Practice

Practice the home position until you can write it quickly and smoothly. When you are finished, check your notes for accuracy. This can be done by reading your paper notes or by looking at the notes on your video screen if you are using realtime. Strike all eight keys STPH-FPLT all at the same time.

☞ *practice the home position using the left and right hand:*

STPH-FPLT   STPH-FPLT   STPH-FPLT   STPH-FPLT   STPH-FPLT   STPH-FPLT
STPH-FPLT   STPH-FPLT   STPH-FPLT   STPH-FPLT   STPH-FPLT   STPH-FPLT
STPH-FPLT   STPH-FPLT   STPH-FPLT   STPH-FPLT   STPH-FPLT   STPH-FPLT

Additional Practice

Each lesson contains a section entitled *Additional Practice*. These sessions are meant to complement and supplement the material that you learned in the lesson. They are necessary in order to learn the complete theory. Not only do they allow you to practice what you learned in the lessons, but they also contain new information which will be essential in the lessons that follow. Do not overlook this *Additional Practice.*

All *Additional Practice* sessions are contained in the *Realwrite DrillBook* or *Notebook* which accompany the *LessonBook.* Make sure that you learn all short forms, words, and phrases from the *DrillBook.*

Go to the:	Do the following:
Realwrite DrillBook (recommended)..................	Read over and study Drill I (Lessons 1 & 2)
Realwrite NoteBook (optional)..................	Read and transcribe the notes from Exercise A, Lesson 1

UNIT 1
LESSON TWO

Warm up and Review

Review the procedures in the *Introduction* that explain how to set up your shorthand machine. Review the correct procedures for putting paper into the shorthand machine and how to sit correctly. Review the home position.

☞ *practice the home position using the left and right hand:*

STPH-FPLT	STPH-FPLT	STPH-FPLT	STPH-FPLT	STPH-FPLT	STPH-FPLT
STPH-FPLT	STPH-FPLT	STPH-FPLT	STPH-FPLT	STPH-FPLT	STPH-FPLT
STPH-FPLT	STPH-FPLT	STPH-FPLT	STPH-FPLT	STPH-FPLT	STPH-FPLT
STPH-FPLT	STPH-FPLT	STPH-FPLT	STPH-FPLT	STPH-FPLT	STPH-FPLT

Explanatory Notes

Rules are numbered according to the order of presentation within the lessons. For example, the first rule in Lesson 1 is Rule 1.1, the fifth rule in Lesson 22 is Rule 22.5.

It is important for you to learn each new rule. The rules are the basis for the theory; and the theory rules make up the foundation for your writing careers.

The initial side of the keyboard refers to the left side; the final side refers to the right side.

The fingers of the hands are referred to as the small finger, the ring finger, the middle finger, and the index finger.

In this textbook you will see some symbols that are used for ease of reading and dictation. One of these symbols is the hyphen (-). If the hyphen appears before a letter or combination of letters (-PB) it means to use the final side of the keyboard. If a hyphen appears after a letter or combination of letters (PW-), or there is no hyphen (W), use the initial side.

For example, R means to write the R on the initial side using the left hand; however, -R means to write the -R on the final side using the right hand.

Any word that is divided by a slash (/) means that the word is written in more than one stroke. The concept of strokes will be explained in greater detail in future lessons.

While learning some of the basic theory, you may be asked to write the home position after a series of strokes. The initials (hp) mean to write the home position STPH-FPLT.

New Letters A and Long A

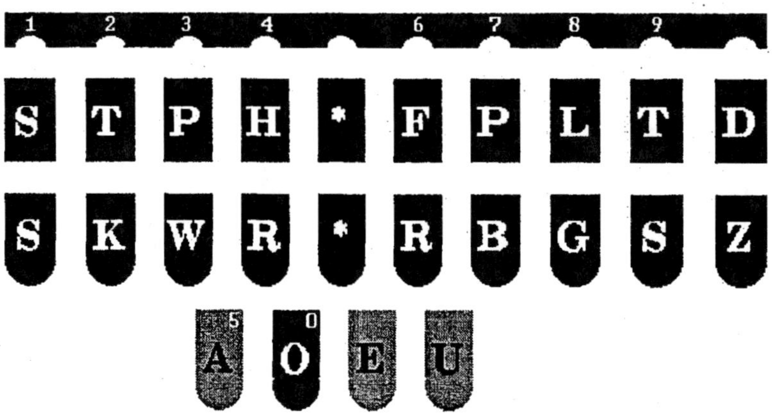

2.1 The vowel A is written with the left thumb.

With your fingers in the home position, strike the letter A quickly and sharply with your left thumb. Look at the keyboard chart when learning the positioning of each new letter. Strike each letter quickly and sharply.

After striking each letter three times, strike the home position (hp). Remember, the home position (hp) is the STPH-FPLT all written together. Repeat the exercise as outlined.

☞ *practice the following:*

A A (hp)	A A A (hp)	A A A (hp)	A A A (hp)	A A A (hp)
A A (hp)	A A A (hp)	A A A (hp)	A A A (hp)	A A A (hp)
A A (hp)	A A A (hp)	A A A (hp)	A A A (hp)	A A A (hp)

Learn the A-position thoroughly. Whenever you see the letter A or hear the sound of A, you should automatically write the letter A with your left thumb.

It will be important to distinguish a regular vowel sound from a long vowel sound. The distinction is necessary in order to write words as they are pronounced. For example, the word "rack" has a short "a" while the word "rake" has a long "a" sound.

Generally, a long vowel contained in a word sounds like the vowel itself. In later chapters you will learn how these sounded vowels are used to make a distinction in writing outlines.

Long vowels are formed on the shorthand machine by writing the vowel you want to make long, together with the two opposite vowels. This is known as the "Double-Opposite Rule." Later you will learn of one exception to the rule for the vowel O.

2.2 The long A is written by striking the A key with the left thumb, together with the E and U keys using your right thumb. (Long A = A + EU)

All three keys are written together. This is your first lesson in combining two or more letters to represent a single letter or sound. It is important that you strike all letters at the same time, using both the left and the right thumb.

Strike the E and U keys together using the flat of your right thumb. Strike all three keys together (A-EU) quickly and sharply, letting go immediately.

Looking at the keyboard chart, practice the following vowels and vowel combinations. In these initial sessions you are practicing not so much for the "sound" as you are for the "reach" of the vowels and vowel combinations.

☞ *practice the following:*

long A

A-EU A-EU A-EU (hp)   A-EU A-EU A-EU A-EU (hp)   A-EU A-EU A-EU (hp)
A-EU A-EU A-EU (hp)   A-EU A-EU A-EU A-EU (hp)   A-EU A-EU A-EU (hp)
A-EU A-EU A-EU (hp)   A-EU A-EU A-EU A-EU (hp)   A-EU A-EU A-EU (hp)

A and long A

A A A (hp)   A-EU A-EU A-EU (hp)   A A A (hp)   A-EU A-EU A-EU (hp)
A A A (hp)   A-EU A-EU A-EU (hp)   A A A (hp)   A-EU A-EU A-EU (hp)
A A A (hp)   A-EU A-EU A-EU (hp)   A A A (hp)   A-EU A-EU A-EU (hp)

Learn these keys thoroughly now! Practice this drill until you can write the A (A) and the long A (A-EU) without looking or thinking where your thumbs go.

New Letters B- and -B

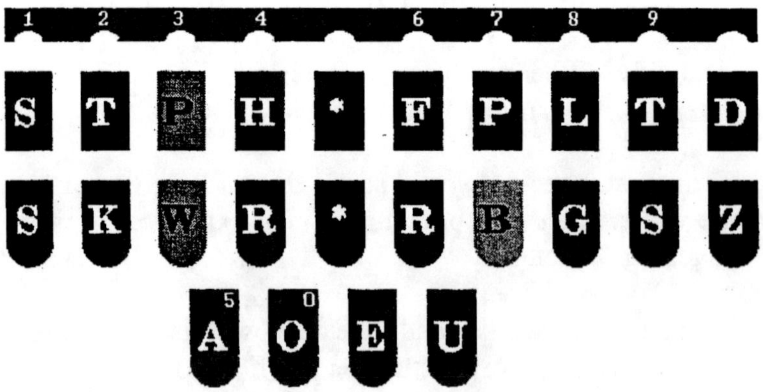

2.3 The initial side B is written by striking the P and W keys together using the middle finger of the left hand. (B = P + W)

Strike the P and W keys together by hitting the crack between the two keys, using your middle finger. Immediately return to the home position. This is your first combination of letters to represent a letter not on the keyboard.

It is important for you to learn these combinations thoroughly so that you can instantly write and r back the PW- as the initial B. From now on, any time that you see the PW together, you should instar think of the initial letter B.

Look at the keyboard chart as you write.

☞ *practice the following:*

initial B-

PW- PW- PW- (hp)	PW- PW- PW- (hp)	PW- PW- PW- (hp)	PW- PW- PW- (hp)
PW- PW- PW- (hp)	PW- PW- PW- (hp)	PW- PW- PW- (hp)	PW- PW- PW- (hp)
PW- PW- PW- (hp)	PW- PW- PW- (hp)	PW- PW- PW- (hp)	PW- PW- PW- (hp)

Learn this combination thoroughly before going on. Practice it again, saying and thinking initial "B' you write each PW.

2.4 The final side -B is written by moving the middle finger of the right hand down from its ho position P to strike the letter -B.

Hit the key quickly and sharply and immediately return to the home position.

☞ *practice the following:*

final -B

-B -B -B (hp)	-B -B -B (hp)	-B -B -B (hp)	-B -B -B (hp)	-B -B -B (hp)
-B -B -B (hp)	-B -B -B (hp)	-B -B -B (hp)	-B -B -B (hp)	-B -B -B (hp)
-B -B -B (hp)	-B -B -B (hp)	-B -B -B (hp)	-B -B -B (hp)	-B -B -B (hp)

New Letters C- and -C

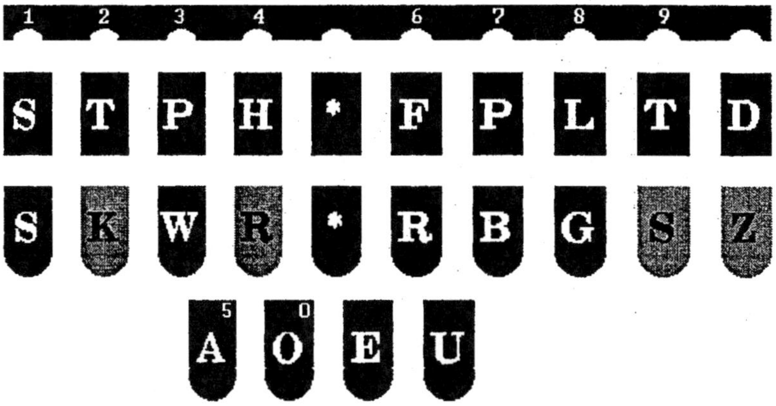

The initial letter C in the English language has two distinct sounds. The soft C sounds like the letter S in the word "cent" and the hard C sounds like the letter K as in the word "cat." Therefore, since you using a phonetic/alphabetic shorthand system (a system based upon sounds as well as spelling), you use the S or K for the sounds of C, depending on the sound.

In addition, there are times when you will have to write the alphabetic letter C and there will be other instances when you will use the C with another consonant to make a distinction between two outlines.

For now, you will learn the initial and final C as "letters" rather than "sounds" in order to complete the learning of the alphabet and the keyboard arrangements.

2.5 The initial side C is written by striking the K and R keys together using the ring and index fingers of the left hand. (C = K + R)

Strike the keys quickly and sharply, immediately returning to the home position.

☞ *practice the following:*

initial C-

KR- KR- KR- (hp)	KR- KR- KR- (hp)	KR- KR- KR- (hp)	KR- KR- KR- (hp)
KR- KR- KR- (hp)	KR- KR- KR- (hp)	KR- KR- KR- (hp)	KR- KR- KR- (hp)
KR- KR- KR- (hp)	KR- KR- KR- (hp)	KR- KR- KR- (hp)	KR- KR- KR- (hp)

2.6 The final side -C is written by striking the final side -S and -Z keys together using the ring and small fingers of the right hand. You must move your right hand from the home position and strike the last two bottom keys using your last two fingers. (-C = -S + -Z)

Taking your fingers off the home position to reach the -SZ, it requires a shifting of the hand. Once you have shifted your hand position and hit the -SZ, immediately return to the home position.

Look at the keyboard chart while writing.

☞ *practice the following:*

final -C

-SZ -SZ -SZ (hp)	-SZ -SZ -SZ (hp)	-SZ -SZ -SZ (hp)	-SZ -SZ -SZ (hp)
-SZ -SZ -SZ (hp)	-SZ -SZ -SZ (hp)	-SZ -SZ -SZ (hp)	-SZ -SZ -SZ (hp)
-SZ -SZ -SZ (hp)	-SZ -SZ -SZ (hp)	-SZ -SZ -SZ (hp)	-SZ -SZ -SZ (hp)

Practice the -SZ for the -C until you can write it without hesitation.

Lesson Practice

As you read the letters on the page, look at the keyboard chart. Do not look at your machine or the paper coming out of your machine. Learn the lettering position so that you can write the letters without hesitation.

☞ *practice the following:*

A and long A

A A A (hp)	A-EU A-EU A-EU (hp)	A A A (hp)	A-EU A-EU A-EU (hp)
A A A (hp)	A-EU A-EU A-EU (hp)	A A A (hp)	A-EU A-EU A-EU (hp)
A A A (hp)	A-EU A-EU A-EU (hp)	A A A (hp)	A-EU A-EU A-EU (hp)

initial B-

PW- PW- PW- (hp)	PW- PW- PW- (hp)	PW- PW- PW- (hp)	PW- PW- PW- (hp)
PW- PW- PW- (hp)	PW- PW- PW- (hp)	PW- PW- PW- (hp)	PW- PW- PW- (hp)
PW- PW- PW- (hp)	PW- PW- PW- (hp)	PW- PW- PW- (hp)	PW- PW- PW- (hp)

final -B

-B -B -B (hp)	-B -B -B (hp)	-B -B -B (hp)	-B -B -B (hp)	-B -B -B (hp)
-B -B -B (hp)	-B -B -B (hp)	-B -B -B (hp)	-B -B -B (hp)	-B -B -B (hp)
-B -B -B (hp)	-B -B -B (hp)	-B -B -B (hp)	-B -B -B (hp)	-B -B -B (hp)

initial C-

KR- KR- KR- (hp)	KR- KR- KR- (hp)	KR- KR- KR- (hp)	KR- KR- KR- (hp)
KR- KR- KR- (hp)	KR- KR- KR- (hp)	KR- KR- KR- (hp)	KR- KR- KR- (hp)
KR- KR- KR- (hp)	KR- KR- KR- (hp)	KR- KR- KR- (hp)	KR- KR- KR- (hp)

final -C

-SZ -SZ -SZ (hp)	-SZ -SZ -SZ (hp)	-SZ -SZ -SZ (hp)	-SZ -SZ -SZ (hp)
-SZ -SZ -SZ (hp)	-SZ -SZ -SZ (hp)	-SZ -SZ -SZ (hp)	-SZ -SZ -SZ (hp)
-SZ -SZ -SZ (hp)	-SZ -SZ -SZ (hp)	-SZ -SZ -SZ (hp)	-SZ -SZ -SZ (hp)

Comprehensive Practice

In this exercise you will be writing individual letters and then combining these letters together in one stroke. For example, you will see the letters PW-A-B. This means you should write the PW, then the A, then the B, and then combine the three letters together and write BAB. This one stroke combination of letters may or may not form a word. That's not important at this time. What is important is your fingering technique, how you write the individual letters.

After writing the individual letters and then the combination, you should immediately return to the home position and write the home position (STPH-FPLT) in one stroke, depressing all the keys together at the same time. You should repeat this exercise ten times for each combination.

Remember to read the combinations first, look at the keyboard chart, then write the combination.

READ (the combination) -- **LOOK** (at chart) -- **WRITE** (the outline)

Write each of the following combinations as follows:

1. Write the individual letters (PW-A-B).
2. Write the one-stroke combination of the letters (PWAB).
3. Write the home position (STPH-FPLT).
4. Repeat the exercise ten times.

☞ *practice the following, writing each combination at least ten times:*

	write the individual letters	write the combination	STPH-FPLT	repeat
1.	PW-A-B (pronounced B, A, final B)	PWAB	home position	10X
2.	PW-AEU-B (B, long A, final B)	PWAEUB	home position	10X
3.	KR-A-B (C, A, final B)	KRAB	home position	10X
4.	KR-AEU-B (C, long A, final B)	KRAEUB	home position	10X
5.	PW-A-SZ (B, A, final C)	PWASZ	home position	10X
6.	PW-AEU-SZ (B, long A, final C)	PWAEUSZ	home position	10X
7.	KR-A-SZ (C, A, final C)	KRASZ	home position	10X
8.	KR-AEU-SZ (C, long A, final C)	KRAEUSZ	home position	10X
9.	PW-A (B, A)	PWA	home position	10X
10.	KR-A (C, A)	KRA	home position	10X

When you are finished writing, take a look at your notes. Are your letters cleanly written? Did you make any errors? If you did, circle the errors in your notes with a pen. Go back and practice the letters that you made a mistake writing until you can write them perfectly.

It is most important that you learn the letters thoroughly before going on to the next lessons. Your homework exercise will help reinforce what you learned in this lesson.

Additional Practice

Go to the:	Do the following:
Realwrite DrillBook (recommended).........	Write and practice Drill I (Lessons 1 & 2)
Realwrite Notebook (optional)..................	Read and transcribe the notes from Exercise A, Lesson 2 and Drill I

UNIT 1
LESSON THREE

Warm up and Review

Look at the keyboard chart. Try writing the letters without thinking. Memorize the position for each letter. Memorize where your fingers go, saying the letters as you are writing them.

☞ *practice the following:*

A and long A

A A A (hp)	A A A (hp)	A-EU A-EU A-EU (hp)	A-EU A-EU A-EU (hp)
A A A (hp)	A A A (hp)	A-EU A-EU A-EU (hp)	A-EU A-EU A-EU (hp)
A A A (hp)	A A A (hp)	A-EU A-EU A-EU (hp)	A-EU A-EU A-EU (hp)

initial B- and final -B

PW PW PW (hp)	-B -B -B (hp)	PW PW PW (hp)	-B -B -B (hp)
PW PW PW (hp)	-B -B -B (hp)	PW PW PW (hp)	-B -B -B (hp)
PW PW PW (hp)	-B -B -B (hp)	PW PW PW (hp)	-B -B -B (hp)

initial C- and final -C

KR KR KR (hp)	-SZ -SZ -SZ (hp)	KR KR KR (hp)	-SZ -SZ -SZ (hp)
KR KR KR (hp)	-SZ -SZ -SZ (hp)	KR KR KR (hp)	-SZ -SZ -SZ (hp)
KR KR KR (hp)	-SZ -SZ -SZ (hp)	KR KR KR (hp)	-SZ -SZ -SZ (hp)

The Asterisk (*) Key

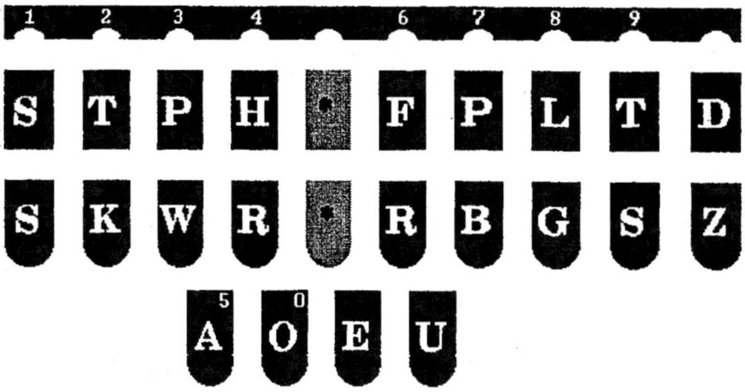

The asterisk or star key is used for two purposes. First, whenever you make a misstroke or mistake in writing, immediately hit the star key. In reading back your steno notes, the asterisk will stand out and tell you to ignore the stroke before the asterisk. If you want to ignore more than one word, hit the asterisk as many times as necessary to equal the number of words you want to ignore.

If you are using a computer you may be writing in realtime. Realtime writing occurs when everything you write on your shorthand machine is transcribed immediately and appears on a monitor. The asterisk is used to delete strokes in realtime writing. Every time you hit the asterisk or star key the word will disappear. If you want the last five strokes deleted, you would hit the star key five times.

The asterisk key is also used in realtime writing to tell the computer to do certain special functions. You will learn these special computer commands in later chapters. Do not use the asterisk to form short forms or for resolving a conflict between two outlines. Do not use the asterisk to indicate a paragraph. You will learn other rules in later chapters to perform these functions.

3.1 If you make a misstroke while writing on your shorthand machine, strike the asterisk or star key to delete the preceding outline.

Strike the key using the index finger of the left or right hand by extending the finger to the middle key and depressing it quickly and sharply. The number of times you hit the star key should equal the number of outlines you want to delete from your notes.

You might note that both the upper and lower keys located in the center of the machine are connected, therefore, both of them will write the asterisk or star.

New Letters D- and -D

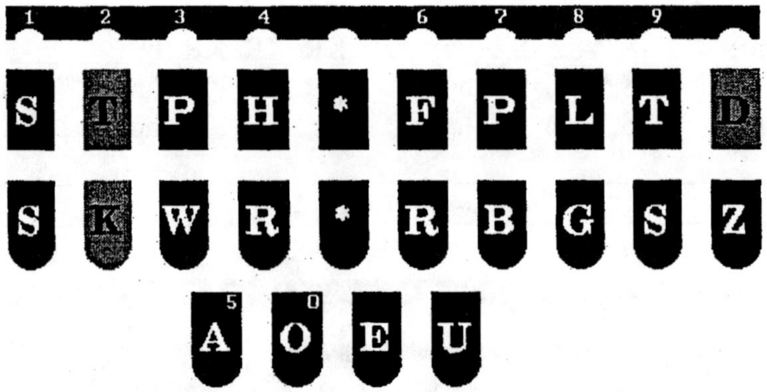

3.2 The initial side D is written by striking the T and K key together using the ring finger of the left hand. (D = T + K)

Strike the T and K key together on the left side of the keyboard by hitting the crack between the two keys. Immediately return to the home position.

☞ *practice the following:*

initial D-

TK TK TK (hp)	TK TK TK (hp)	TK TK TK (hp)	TK TK TK (hp)
TK TK TK (hp)	TK TK TK (hp)	TK TK TK (hp)	TK TK TK (hp)
TK TK TK (hp)	TK TK TK (hp)	TK TK TK (hp)	TK TK TK (hp)

Remember to keep your eyes on the chart. Learn the position of the letters so that you can strike them without hesitation.

3.3 The final side -D is written by extending the small finger of the right hand from the home position -T over to the -D.

☞ *practice the following:*

final -D

-D -D -D (hp)	-D -D -D (hp)	-D -D -D (hp)	-D -D -D (hp)
-D -D -D (hp)	-D -D -D (hp)	-D -D -D (hp)	-D -D -D (hp)
-D -D -D (hp)	-D -D -D (hp)	-D -D -D (hp)	-D -D -D (hp)

New Letters E and Long E

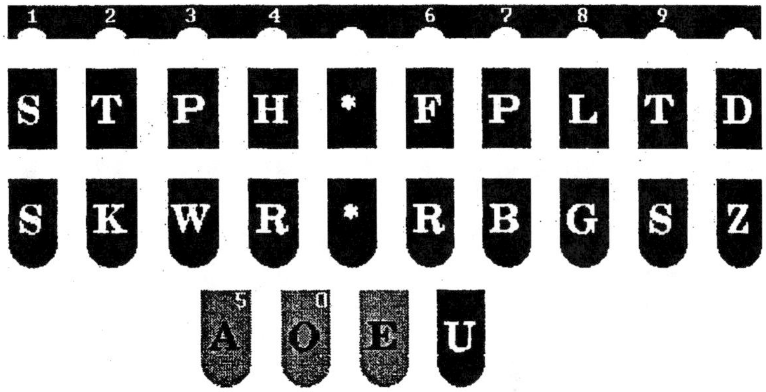

3.4 The vowel E is written with the right thumb.

With your fingers in the home position, strike the letter E quickly and sharply with your right thumb.

☞ *practice the following:*

short E

E E E (hp)	E E E (hp)	E E E (hp)	E E E (hp)	E E E (hp)
E E E (hp)	E E E (hp)	E E E (hp)	E E E (hp)	E E E (hp)
E E E (hp)	E E E (hp)	E E E (hp)	E E E (hp)	E E E (hp)

Remember the "Double-opposite Rule" for forming long vowels. Strike the two opposite vowels along with the vowel you want to make long. This rule applies for making the long E.

3.5 The long E is written by striking the E key with your right thumb together with the A and O key using your left thumb. (Long E = AO E)

Strike the A and O keys together using the flat of your left thumb. Strike all three keys together quickly and sharply, letting go immediately. Keep your eyes on the keyboard chart.

☞ *practice the following:*

long E

AO-E	AO-E	AO-E (hp)	AO-E	AO-E	AO-E	AO-E (hp)	AO-E	AO-E	AO-E (hp)
AO-E	AO-E	AO-E (hp)	AO-E	AO-E	AO-E	AO-E (hp)	AO-E	AO-E	AO-E (hp)
AO-E	AO-E	AO-E (hp)	AO-E	AO-E	AO-E	AO-E (hp)	AO-E	AO-E	AO-E (hp)

E and long E

E	E	E (hp)	AO-E	AO-E	AO-E (hp)	E	E	E (hp)	AO-E	AO-E	AO-E (hp)
E	E	E (hp)	AO-E	AO-E	AO-E (hp)	E	E	E (hp)	AO-E	AO-E	AO-E (hp)
E	E	E (hp)	AO-E	AO-E	AO-E (hp)	E	E	E (hp)	AO-E	AO-E	AO-E (hp)

Number Bar

The long bar located above the home position keys is referred to as the number bar. To write a number, hit the crack between the number bar and a home position key.

New Numbers 1 and 9

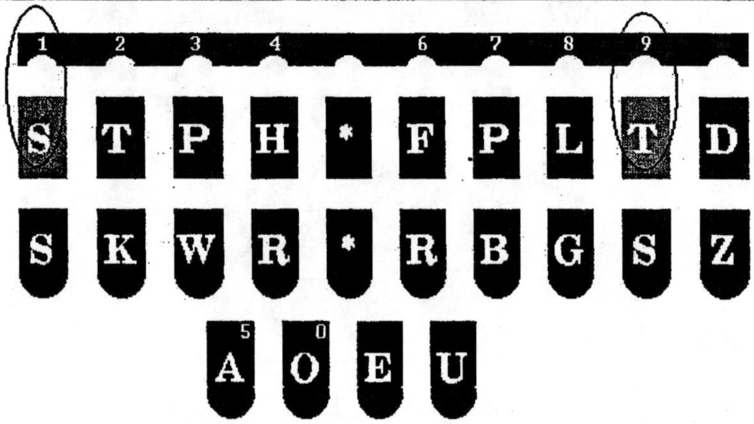

3.6 Write the number 1 with the small finger of the left hand. Hit the crack between the home position S and the number bar, using the top and flat part of your finger to depress both key and bar at the same time.

☞ *practice the following:*

1 1 1 (hp)	1 1 1 (hp)	1 1 1 (hp)	1 1 1 (hp)	1 1 1 (hp)	1 1 1 (hp)
1 1 1 (hp)	1 1 1 (hp)	1 1 1 (hp)	1 1 1 (hp)	1 1 1 (hp)	1 1 1 (hp)
1 1 1 (hp)	1 1 1 (hp)	1 1 1 (hp)	1 1 1 (hp)	1 1 1 (hp)	1 1 1 (hp)

Get the "feel" of what fingers to depress and then memorize their location on the chart.

3.7 Write the number 9 with the small finger of the right hand. Hit the crack between the home position -T and the number bar, using the top and flat part of your finger to depress both key and bar at the same time.

☞ *practice the following:*

9 9 9 (hp)	9 9 9 (hp)	9 9 9 (hp)	9 9 9 (hp)	9 9 9 (hp)	9 9 9 (hp)
9 9 9 (hp)	9 9 9 (hp)	9 9 9 (hp)	9 9 9 (hp)	9 9 9 (hp)	9 9 9 (hp)
9 9 9 (hp)	9 9 9 (hp)	9 9 9 (hp)	9 9 9 (hp)	9 9 9 (hp)	9 9 9 (hp)

Lesson Practice

Remember to READ the sound, LOOK at the chart, and WRITE the outline. Memorize the location. Do not hesitate. Write quickly and sharply and return to the home position.

☞ *practice the following:*

initial D-

TK TK TK (hp)	TK TK TK (hp)	TK TK TK (hp)	TK TK TK (hp)
TK TK TK (hp)	TK TK TK (hp)	TK TK TK (hp)	TK TK TK (hp)
TK TK TK (hp)	TK TK TK (hp)	TK TK TK (hp)	TK TK TK (hp)

final -D

-D -D -D (hp)	-D -D -D (hp)	-D -D -D (hp)	-D -D -D (hp)
-D -D -D (hp)	-D -D -D (hp)	-D -D -D (hp)	-D -D -D (hp)
-D -D -D (hp)	-D -D -D (hp)	-D -D -D (hp)	-D -D -D (hp)

short E

E E E (hp)	E E E (hp)	E E E (hp)	E E E (hp)	E E E (hp)
E E E (hp)	E E E (hp)	E E E (hp)	E E E (hp)	E E E (hp)
E E E (hp)	E E E (hp)	E E E (hp)	E E E (hp)	E E E (hp)

long E

AO-E AO-E AO-E (hp)	AO-E AO-E AO-E AO-E (hp)	AO-E AO-E AO-E (hp)
AO-E AO-E AO-E (hp)	AO-E AO-E AO-E AO-E (hp)	AO-E AO-E AO-E (hp)
AO-E AO-E AO-E (hp)	AO-E AO-E AO-E AO-E (hp)	AO-E AO-E AO-E (hp)

number 1

1 1 1 (hp)	1 1 1 (hp)	1 1 1 (hp)	1 1 1 (hp)	1 1 1 (hp)	1 1 1 (hp)
1 1 1 (hp)	1 1 1 (hp)	1 1 1 (hp)	1 1 1 (hp)	1 1 1 (hp)	1 1 1 (hp)
1 1 1 (hp)	1 1 1 (hp)	1 1 1 (hp)	1 1 1 (hp)	1 1 1 (hp)	1 1 1 (hp)

number 9

9 9 9 (hp)	9 9 9 (hp)	9 9 9 (hp)	9 9 9 (hp)	9 9 9 (hp)	9 9 9 (hp)
9 9 9 (hp)	9 9 9 (hp)	9 9 9 (hp)	9 9 9 (hp)	9 9 9 (hp)	9 9 9 (hp)
9 9 9 (hp)	9 9 9 (hp)	9 9 9 (hp)	9 9 9 (hp)	9 9 9 (hp)	9 9 9 (hp)

Comprehensive Practice

Write each of the following combinations as follows:

1. Write the individual letters (PW-A-B).
2. Write the one-stroke combination of the letters (PWAB).
3. Write the home position (STPH-FPLT).
4. Repeat the exercise ten times.

☞ *practice the following, writing each combination at least ten times:*

write the individual letters	write the combination	STPH-FPLT	repeat
1. PW-E-B (pronounced B, E, final B)	PWEB	home position	10X
2. PW-AOE-B (B, long E, final B)	PWAOEB	home position	10X
3. KR-E-B (C, E, final B)	KREB	home position	10X
4. KR-AOE-B (C, long E, final B)	KRAOEB	home position	10X
5. PW-A-D (B, A, final D)	PWAD	home position	10X
6. PW-AEU-D (B, long A, final D)	PWAEUD	home position	10X
7. PW-E-D (B, E, final D)	PWED	home position	10X
8. PW-AOE-D (B, long E, final D)	PWAOED	home position	10X
9. TK-A-B (D, A, final B)	TKAB	home postion	10X
10. TK-AEU-B	TKAEUB	home position	10X
11. TK-E-D	TKED	home position	10X
12. TK-AOE-D	TKAOED	home position	10X
13. TK-E-B	TKEB	home position	10X
14. TK-AOE-B	TKAOEB	home position	10X
15. TK-A-D	TKAD	home position	10X
16. 1 9 1 9 1 9 1 9 1 9			10X
17. 9 1 9 1 9 1 9 1 9 1			10X

When you are finished writing, take a look at your notes. Are your letters and numbers cleanly written? Did you make any errors? If you did, circle the errors in your notes with a pen. Go back and practice the letters that you made a mistake writing until you can write them perfectly.

It is most important that you learn the letters thoroughly before going on to the next lesson. Your homework exercise will help reinforce what you learned in this lesson.

Additional Practice

Go to the:	Do the following:
Realwrite DrillBook (recommended).............	Read over and study Drill II (Lessons 3 & 4)
Realwrite NoteBook (optional).....................	Read and transcribe the notes from Exercise A, Lesson 3

UNIT 1
LESSON FOUR

Warm up and Review

☞ *practice the following:*

short A
A A A (hp) A A A (hp) A A A (hp)

long A
AEU (hp) AEU (hp) AEU (hp)

initial B-
PW PW PW (hp) PW PW PW (hp)

final -B
-B -B -B (hp) -B -B -B (hp) -B -B-B (hp)

initial C-
KR KR KR (hp) KR KR KR (hp)

final -C
-SZ -SZ -SZ (hp) -SZ -SZ -SZ (hp)

initial D-
TK TK TK (hp) TK TK TK (hp)

final -D
-D -D -D (hp) -D -D -D (hp) -D -D -D (hp)

short E
E E E (hp) E E E (hp) E E E (hp)

long E
AOE AOE AOE (hp) AOE AOE AOE (hp)

number 1
1 1 1 (hp) 1 1 1 (hp) 1 1 1 (hp)

number 9
9 9 9 (hp) 9 9 9 (hp) 9 9 9 (hp) 9 9 9 (hp)

New Letters F- and -F

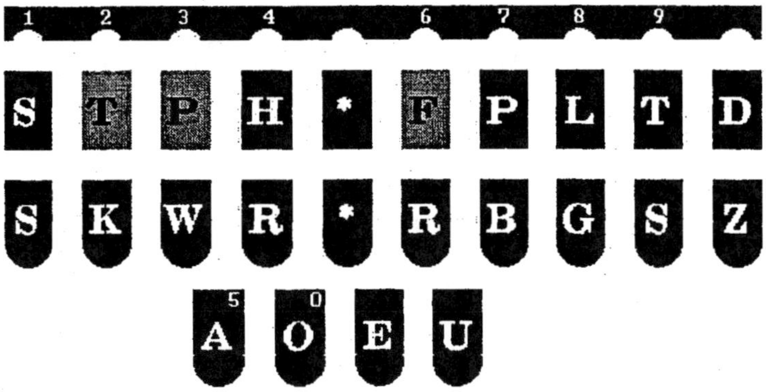

4.1 The initial side F is written by striking the T and P keys together using the ring and middle fingers of the left hand. (F = T + P)

Remember to hit both the T and the P key together, do not hold the keys down, depress them quickly and sharply.

☞ *practice the following:*

initial F-

TP- TP- TP- (hp) TP- TP- TP- (hp) TP- TP- TP- (hp) TP- TP- TP- (hp)
TP- TP- TP- (hp) TP- TP- TP- (hp) TP- TP- TP- (hp) TP- TP- TP- (hp)
TP- TP- TP- (hp) TP- TP- TP- (hp) TP- TP- TP- (hp) TP- TP- TP- (hp)

4.2 The final side -F is written by striking the home position F key with the index finger of the right hand.

☞ *practice the following:*

final -F

-F -F -F (hp) -F -F -F (hp) -F -F -F (hp) -F -F -F (hp) -F -F -F (hp)
-F -F -F (hp) -F -F -F (hp) -F -F -F (hp) -F -F -F (hp) -F -F -F (hp)
-F -F -F (hp) -F -F -F (hp) -F -F -F (hp) -F -F -F (hp) -F -F -F (hp)

New Letters G- and -G

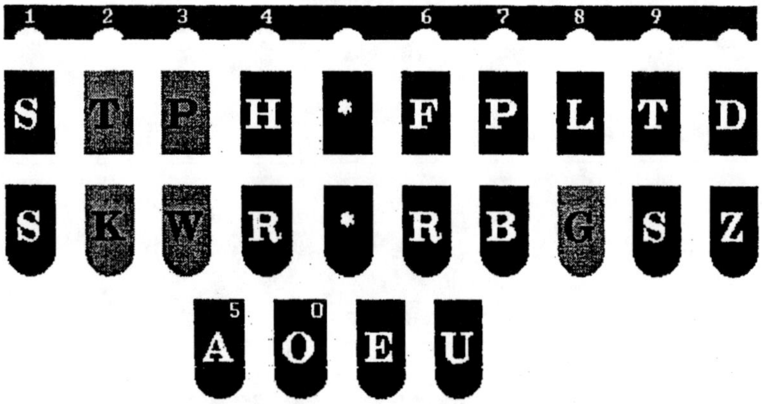

4.3 The initial side G is written by striking the D keys (TK) together with the B (PW) keys using the ring and middle fingers of the left hand. (G = TK + PW)

Strike the TK and PW keys together by hitting the crack between the four keys. Hit all four keys together. Immediately return to the home position.

☞ *practice the following:*

initial G-

TKPW- TKPW- TPKW- (hp) TKPW- TKPW- TKPW- (hp) TKPW- TKPW- TKPW- (hp)
TKPW- TKPW- TPKW- (hp) TKPW- TKPW- TKPW- (hp) TKPW- TKPW- TKPW- (hp)
TKPW- TKPW- TPKW- (hp) TKPW- TKPW- TKPW- (hp) TKPW- TKPW- TKPW- (hp)

4.4 The final side -G is written by extending the ring finger of the right hand from the home position -L down to the -G.

☞ *practice the following:*

final -G

-G -G -G (hp)	-G -G -G (hp)	-G -G -G (hp)	-G -G -G (hp)	-G -G -G (hp)
-G -G -G (hp)	-G -G -G (hp)	-G -G -G (hp)	-G -G -G (hp)	-G -G -G (hp)
-G -G -G (hp)	-G -G -G (hp)	-G -G -G (hp)	-G -G -G (hp)	-G -G -G (hp)

New Letters H- and -H

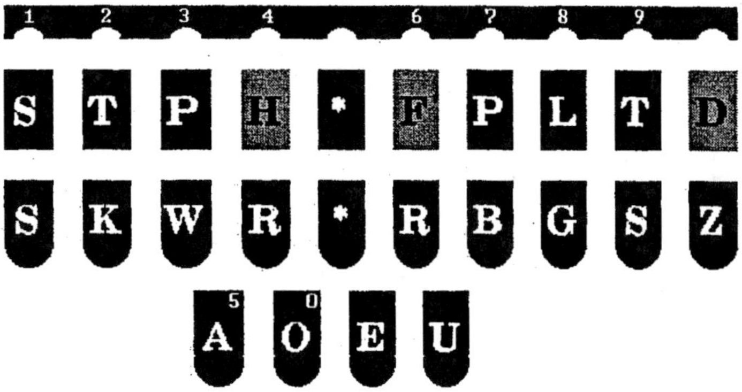

4.5 The initial side H is written by striking the home position H key with the index finger of the left hand.

☞ *practice the following:*

initial H-

H- H- H- (hp)	H- H- H- (hp)	H- H- H- (hp)	H- H- H- (hp)	H- H- H- (hp)
H- H- H- (hp)	H- H- H- (hp)	H- H- H- (hp)	H- H- H- (hp)	H- H- H- (hp)
H- H- H- (hp)	H- H- H- (hp)	H- H- H- (hp)	H- H- H- (hp)	H- H- H- (hp)

4.6 The final side -H is written by striking the final side -F and -D keys together with the index and small fingers of the right hand. (-H = -F + -D)

Strike the two keys together, immediately returning the small finger to the home position.

☞ *practice the following:*

final -H

-FD -FD -FD (hp)	-FD -FD -FD (hp)	-FD -FD -FD (hp)	-FD -FD -FD (hp)
-FD -FD -FD (hp)	-FD -FD -FD (hp)	-FD -FD -FD (hp)	-FD -FD -FD (hp)
-FD -FD -FD (hp)	-FD -FD -FD (hp)	-FD -FD -FD (hp)	-FD -FD -FD (hp)

Lesson Practice

Learn the proper positioning for each letter without looking at your machine. Look at the keyboard chart. You will learn to look away from the chart later.

☞ *practice the following:*

initial F-

TP- TP- TP- (hp)   TP- TP- TP- (hp)   TP- TP- TP- (hp)   TP- TP- TP- (hp)
TP- TP- TP- (hp)   TP- TP- TP- (hp)   TP- TP- TP- (hp)   TP- TP- TP- (hp)
TP- TP- TP- (hp)   TP- TP- TP- (hp)   TP- TP- TP- (hp)   TP- TP- TP- (hp)

final -F

-F -F -F (hp)   -F -F -F (hp)   -F -F -F (hp)   -F -F -F (hp)   -F -F -F (hp)
-F -F -F (hp)   -F -F -F (hp)   -F -F -F (hp)   -F -F -F (hp)   -F -F -F (hp)
-F -F -F (hp)   -F -F -F (hp)   -F -F -F (hp)   -F -F -F (hp)   -F -F -F (hp)

initial G-

TKPW- TKPW- TPKW- (hp)   TKPW- TKPW- TKPW- (hp)   TKPW- TKPW- TKPW- (hp)
TKPW- TKPW- TPKW- (hp)   TKPW- TKPW- TKPW- (hp)   TKPW- TKPW- TKPW- (hp)
TKPW- TKPW- TPKW- (hp)   TKPW- TKPW- TKPW- (hp)   TKPW- TKPW- TKPW- (hp)

final -G

-G -G -G (hp)   -G -G -G (hp)   -G -G -G (hp)   -G -G -G (hp)   -G -G -G (hp)
-G -G -G (hp)   -G -G -G (hp)   -G -G -G (hp)   -G -G -G (hp)   -G -G -G (hp)
-G -G -G (hp)   -G -G -G (hp)   -G -G -G (hp)   -G -G -G (hp)   -G -G -G (hp)

initial H-

H- H- H- (hp)   H- H- H- (hp)   H- H- H- (hp)   H- H- H- (hp)   H- H- H- (hp)
H- H- H- (hp)   H- H- H- (hp)   H- H- H- (hp)   H- H- H- (hp)   H- H- H- (hp)
H- H- H- (hp)   H- H- H- (hp)   H- H- H- (hp)   H- H- H- (hp)   H- H- H- (hp)

final -H

-FD -FD -FD (hp)   -FD -FD -FD (hp)   -FD -FD -FD (hp)   -FD -FD -FD (hp)
-FD -FD -FD (hp)   -FD -FD -FD (hp)   -FD -FD -FD (hp)   -FD -FD -FD (hp)
-FD -FD -FD (hp)   -FD -FD -FD (hp)   -FD -FD -FD (hp)   -FD -FD -FD (hp)

Comprehensive Practice

Write each of the following combinations as follows:

1. Write the individual letters (PW-A-B).
2. Write the one-stroke combination of the letters (PWAB).
3. Write the home position (STPH-FPLT).
4. Repeat the exercise ten times.

☞ *practice the following, writing each combination at least ten times:*

write the individual letters	write the combination	STPH-FPLT	repeat
1. PW-A-B (pronounced B, A, final B)	PWAB	home position	10X
2. PW-AOE-D	PWAOED	home position	10X
3. KR-A-B	KRAB	home position	10X
4. KR-AOE-D	KRAOED	home position	10X
5. TK-E-D	TKED	home position	10X
6. TK-AOE-D	TKAOED	home position	10X
7. TP-A-F	TPAF	home position	10X
8. TP-E-F	TPEF	home position	10X
9. TP-AEU-F	TPAEUF	home position	10X
10. TP-AOE-F	TPAOEF	home position	10X
11. TKPW-A-G	TKPWAG	home position	10X
12. TKPW-AOE-D	TKPWAOED	home position	10X
13. TKPW-A-B	TKPWAB	home position	10X
14. TKPW-E-D	TKPWED	home position	10X
15. H-A-D	HAD	home position	10X
16. H-E-D	HED	home position	10X
17. 9 1 9 1 9 1 9 1 9 1		home position	10X
18. H-A-FD	HAFD	home position	10X
19. TKPW-A-FD	TKPWAFD	home position	10X
20. PW-A-FD	PWAFD	home position	10X

When you are finished writing, take a look at your notes. Are your letters and numbers cleanly written? Did you make any errors? If you did, circle the errors in your notes with a pen. Go back and practice the letters that you made a mistake writing until you can write them perfectly.

It is most important that you learn the letters thoroughly before going on to the next lessons. Your homework exercise will help reinforce what you learned in this lesson.

Short Forms and Phrases

In your practice of individual letters, you have learned to put the letters together. In some cases, these combined letters form words. This concept of writing individual letters to make up sounds is how the high-speed court reporter is able to write quickly and accurately.

Court reporters also use a series of "short forms" or shortcuts to write words. These are also called "abbreviations," "briefs," or "arbitraries." The *Realwrite DrillBook* contains a number of words and short forms that are necessary for you to learn.

Listed below are some short forms that are necessary for you to learn. Practice writing these outlines now! As you hear the words, write the outlines. As you see the outlines, read the words.

☞ *practice the following*:

a	AEU[1]	about	PW-
did	TK- (-D)[2]	of	-F
he	HAE	be	-B
if	TP-	had	H- (FD)
about a	PWAEU	if a	TPAEU
did a	TKAEU	had a	HAEU
he did	HAED	he had	HAEFD
if he	TPE	had he	HE
did he	TKHE[3]		

[1]The article "a" is always written as a long a (AEU); the prefix "a" is always written as a short a (A).
[2]Letters in parentheses are short forms that will be used in phrases, for example "he did" HAED.
[3]The DHE (TKHE) is used for "did he" to avoid a conflict.

Additional Practice

Go to the:	Do the following:
Realwrite DrillBook (recommended)	Write and practice Drill II (Lessons 3 & 4)
Realwrite NoteBook (optional)	Read and transcribe the notes from Exercise A, Lesson 4 and Drill II

UNIT 1 REVIEW

After each unit (four lessons of new material) you will be given a Unit Review. The purpose of this review is to allow you the opportunity to go back and learn thoroughly everything that was presented in the *LessonBook*, *DrillBook*, and *NoteBook*. This Unit Review is very important.

Lesson Review

1. Go back to each lesson and learn each new rule thoroughly.
2. Go back to each lesson and write the Lesson Practice.
3. Go back to each lesson and write the Comprehensive Practice.
4. Read back all paper or electronic notes and transcribe a portion of your review.

Review of Writing Rules

2.1 The vowel A is written with the left thumb.

2.2 The long A is written by striking the A key with your left thumb together with the E and U key using your right thumb. (Long A = A EU)

2.3 The initial side B is written by striking the P and W keys together using the middle finger of the left hand. (B = P + W)

2.4 The final side -B is written by moving the middle finger of the right hand down from its home position P to strike the letter -B.

2.5 The initial side C is written by striking the K and R keys together using the ring and index fingers of the left hand. (C = K + R)

2.6 The final side -C is written by striking the final side -S and -Z keys together using the ring and small fingers of the right hand. You must move your hand from the home position and strike the last two bottom keys using your last two fingers. (-C = -S + -Z)

3.1 If you make a misstroke while writing on your shorthand machine, strike the asterisk or star key to delete the preceding outline.

3.2 The initial side D is written by striking the T and K key together using the ring finger of the left hand. (D = T + K)

3.3 The final side -D is written by extending the small finger of the right hand from the home position -T over to the -D.

3.4 The vowel E is written with the right thumb.

3.5 The long E is written by striking the E key with your right thumb together with the A and O key using your left thumb. (Long E = AO E)

3.6 Write the number 1 with the small finger of the left hand. Hit the crack between the home position S and the number bar, using the top and flat part of your finger to depress both key and bar at the same time.

3.7 Write the number 9 with the small finger of the right hand. Hit the crack between the home position -T and the number bar, using the top and flat part of your finger to depress both key and bar at the same time.

4.1 The initial side F is written by striking the T and P keys together using the ring and middle fingers of the left hand. (F = T + P)

4.2 The final side -F is written by striking the home position F key with the index finger of the right hand.

4.3 The initial side G is written by striking the D keys (TK) together with the B (PW) keys using the ring and middle fingers of the left hand. (G = TK + PW)

4.4 The final side -G is written by extending the ring finger of the right hand from the home position -L down to the -G.

4.5 The initial side H is written by striking the home position H key with the index finger of the left hand.

4.6 The final side -H is written by striking the final side -F and -D keys together with the index and small fingers of the right hand. (-H = -F + -D)

Review DrillBook and NoteBook Applications

1. Review Drills I and II from the *Realwrite DrillBook* (recommended).
2. Review Exercise A from the *Realwrite NoteBook* (optional).

Unit Evaluation Number One

Unit Evaluation Number One will cover all material from the following: *Realwrite LessonBook*, Lessons 1-4; *DrillBook*, Drills I and II.

UNIT 2
LESSON FIVE

Warm up and Review

Read from left to right. Practice each line until you can write without hesitation.

☞ *practice the following:*

short A
A A A (hp) A A A (hp) A A A (hp)

long A
AEU (hp) AEU (hp) AEU (hp)

initial B-
PW PW PW (hp) PW PW PW (hp)

final -B
-B -B -B (hp) -B -B -B (hp) -B -B-B (hp)

initial C-
KR KR KR (hp) KR KR KR (hp)

final -C
-SZ -SZ -SZ (hp) -SZ -SZ -SZ (hp)

initial D-
TK TK TK (hp) TK TK TK (hp)

final -D
-D -D -D (hp) -D -D -D (hp) -D -D -D (hp)

short E
E E E (hp) E E E (hp) E E E (hp)

long E
AOE AOE AOE (hp) AOE AOE AOE (hp)

initial F-
TP TP TP (hp) TP TP TP (hp)

final -F
-F -F -F (hp) -F -F -F (hp) -F -F -F (hp)

initial G-
TKPW TKPW (hp) TKPW (hp) TKPW (hp)

final -G
-G -G -G (hp) -G -G -G (hp) -G -G -G (hp)

initial H-
H H H (hp) H H H (hp) H H H (hp)

final -H
-FD -FD -FD (hp) -FD -FD -FD (hp)

number 1
1 1 1 (hp) 1 1 1 (hp) 1 1 1 (hp)

number 9
9 9 9 (hp) 9 9 9 (hp) 9 9 9 (hp) 9 9 9 (hp)

New Letters I and Long I

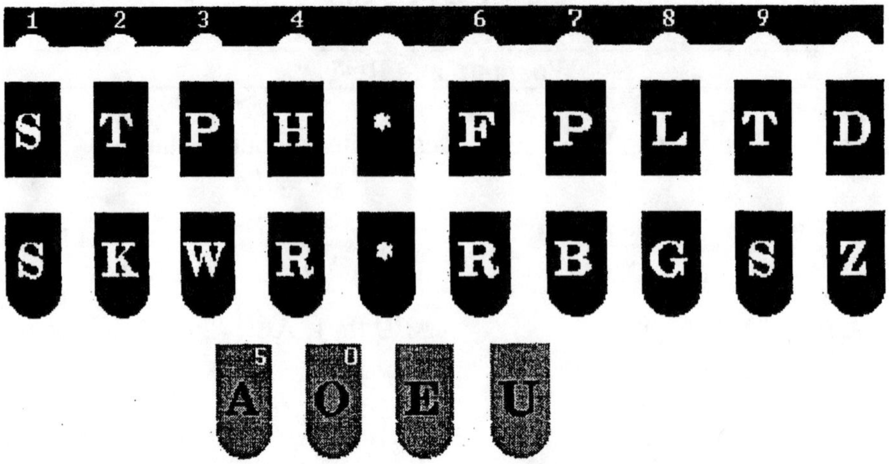

5.1 The vowel I is written with the right thumb by combining the letters E and U together in one stroke. (I = E + U)

☞ *practice the following:*

short I

EU EU EU (hp)	EU EU EU (hp)	EU EU EU (hp)	EU EU EU (hp)
EU EU EU (hp)	EU EU EU (hp)	EU EU EU (hp)	EU EU EU (hp)
EU EU EU (hp)	EU EU EU (hp)	EU EU EU (hp)	EU EU EU (hp)

Remembering the "Double-Opposite" vowel rule, the long I is written with all of the vowels together.

5.2 The long I is written by striking the AO keys with your left thumb together with the EU key using your right thumb. (Long I = AO + EU)

☞ *practice the following:*

long I

AOEU AOEU AOEU (hp)	AOEU AOEU AOEU (hp)	AOEU AOEU AOEU (hp)
AOEU AOEU AOEU (hp)	AOEU AOEU AOEU (hp)	AOEU AOEU AOEU (hp)
AOEU AOEU AOEU (hp)	AOEU AOEU AOEU (hp)	AOEU AOEU AOEU (hp)

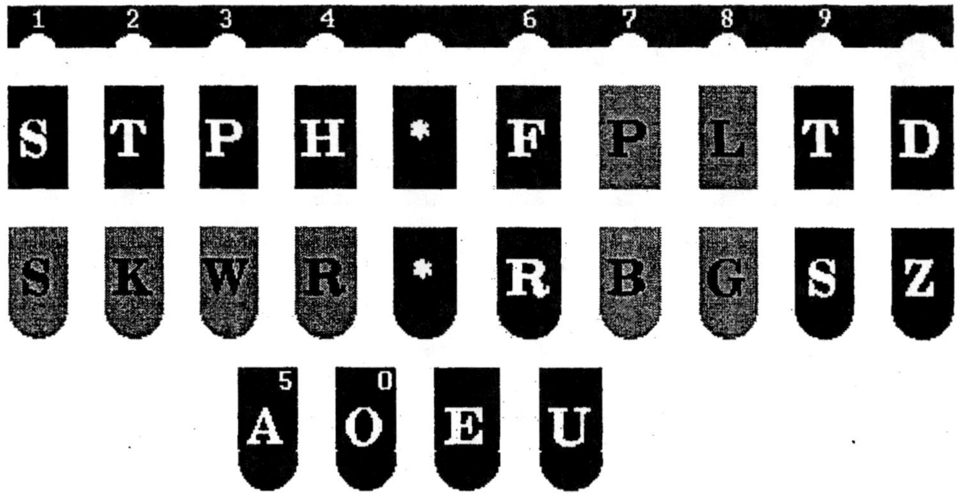

5.3 The initial side J is written by striking the four keys SKWR together using the small, ring, middle, and index fingers of the left hand. (J = S + K + W + R)

Strike all four keys together quickly, immediately returning to the home position.

☞ *practice the following:*

initial J-

SKWR- SKWR- SKWR- (hp) SKWR- SKWR- SKWR- (hp) SKWR- SKWR- SKWR- (hp)
SKWR- SKWR- SKWR- (hp) SKWR- SKWR- SKWR- (hp) SKWR- SKWR- SKWR- (hp)
SKWR- SKWR- SKWR- (hp) SKWR- SKWR- SKWR- (hp) SKWR- SKWR- SKWR- (hp)

5.4 The final side -J is written by striking the -PB and -LG keys together using the middle and ring fingers of the right hand. (-J = -PB + -LG)

Strike the -PB and -LG keys using the top flat portion of your fingers. Strike all four keys together quickly, immediately returning to the home position.

☞ *practice the following:*

final -J

-PBLG -PBLG -PBLG (hp) -PBLG -PBLG -PBLG (hp) -PBLG -PBLG -PBLG (hp)
-PBLG -PBLG -PBLG (hp) -PBLG -PBLG -PBLG (hp) -PBLG -PBLG -PBLG (hp)
-PBLG -PBLG -PBLG (hp) -PBLG -PBLG -PBLG (hp) -PBLG -PBLG -PBLG (hp)

Remember to keep your eyes on the chart to learn the proper position. After learning the proper position for the letters, try to memorize where your fingers need to go in order to write the letter.

New Numbers 2 and 8

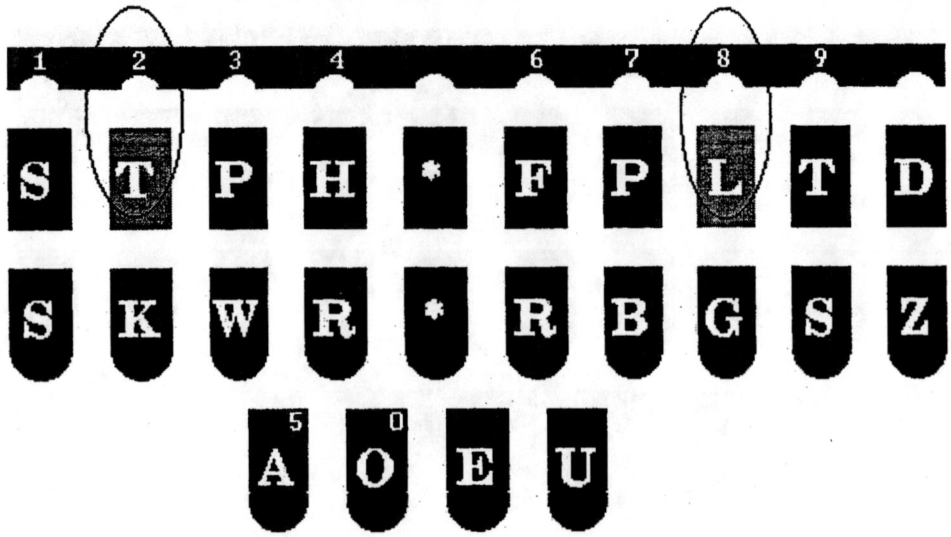

5.5 Write the number 2 with the ring finger of the left hand. Hit the crack between the home position T and the number bar, depressing both key and bar at the same time.

Use the top and flat part of your finger to depress both key and bar at the same time.

☞ *practice the following:*

2 2 2 (hp)	2 2 2 (hp)	2 2 2 (hp)	2 2 2 (hp)	2 2 2 (hp)	2 2 2 (hp)
2 2 2 (hp)	2 2 2 (hp)	2 2 2 (hp)	2 2 2 (hp)	2 2 2 (hp)	2 2 2 (hp)
2 2 2 (hp)	2 2 2 (hp)	2 2 2 (hp)	2 2 2 (hp)	2 2 2 (hp)	2 2 2 (hp)

5.6 Write the number 8 with the ring finger of the right hand. Hit the crack between the home position -L and the number bar, depressing both key and bar at the same time.

Use the top and flat part of your finger to depress both key and bar at the same time.

☞ *practice the following:*

8 8 8 (hp)	8 8 8 (hp)	8 8 8 (hp)	8 8 8 (hp)	8 8 8 (hp)	8 8 8 (hp)
8 8 8 (hp)	8 8 8 (hp)	8 8 8 (hp)	8 8 8 (hp)	8 8 8 (hp)	8 8 8 (hp)
8 8 8 (hp)	8 8 8 (hp)	8 8 8 (hp)	8 8 8 (hp)	8 8 8 (hp)	8 8 8 (hp)

Lesson Practice

After learning the proper positioning by looking at the chart, try to look away when you write the letters and numbers. Try to memorize the proper fingering for each letter, combination, and number. It is important to learn the basic lettering now so that you do not have to hesitate. Hesitation slows you down. It should become an automatic response.

☞ *practice the following:*

short I

EU EU EU (hp)	EU EU EU (hp)	EU EU EU (hp)	EU EU EU (hp)
EU EU EU (hp)	EU EU EU (hp)	EU EU EU (hp)	EU EU EU (hp)
EU EU EU (hp)	EU EU EU (hp)	EU EU EU (hp)	EU EU EU (hp)

long I

AOEU AOEU AOEU (hp)	AOEU AOEU AOEU (hp)	AOEU AOEU AOEU (hp)
AOEU AOEU AOEU (hp)	AOEU AOEU AOEU (hp)	AOEU AOEU AOEU (hp)
AOEU AOEU AOEU (hp)	AOEU AOEU AOEU (hp)	AOEU AOEU AOEU (hp)

initial J-

SKWR- SKWR- SKWR- (hp)	SKWR- SKWR- SKWR- (hp)	SKWR- SKWR- SKWR- (hp)
SKWR- SKWR- SKWR- (hp)	SKWR- SKWR- SKWR- (hp)	SKWR- SKWR- SKWR- (hp)
SKWR- SKWR- SKWR- (hp)	SKWR- SKWR- SKWR- (hp)	SKWR- SKWR- SKWR- (hp)

final -J

-PBLG -PBLG -PBLG (hp)	-PBLG -PBLG -PBLG (hp)	-PBLG -PBLG -PBLG (hp)
-PBLG -PBLG -PBLG (hp)	-PBLG -PBLG -PBLG (hp)	-PBLG -PBLG -PBLG (hp)
-PBLG -PBLG -PBLG (hp)	-PBLG -PBLG -PBLG (hp)	-PBLG -PBLG -PBLG (hp)

number 2:

2 2 2 (hp)	2 2 2 (hp)	2 2 2 (hp)	2 2 2 (hp)	2 2 2 (hp)	2 2 2 (hp)
2 2 2 (hp)	2 2 2 (hp)	2 2 2 (hp)	2 2 2 (hp)	2 2 2 (hp)	2 2 2 (hp)
2 2 2 (hp)	2 2 2 (hp)	2 2 2 (hp)	2 2 2 (hp)	2 2 2 (hp)	2 2 2 (hp)

number 8:

8 8 8 (hp)	8 8 8 (hp)	8 8 8 (hp)	8 8 8 (hp)	8 8 8 (hp)	8 8 8 (hp)
8 8 8 (hp)	8 8 8 (hp)	8 8 8 (hp)	8 8 8 (hp)	8 8 8 (hp)	8 8 8 (hp)
8 8 8 (hp)	8 8 8 (hp)	8 8 8 (hp)	8 8 8 (hp)	8 8 8 (hp)	8 8 8 (hp)

Comprehensive Practice

Write each of the following combinations as follows:

1. Write the individual letters (PW-A-B).
2. Write the one-stroke combination of the letters (PWAB).
3. Write the home position (STPH-FPLT).
4. Repeat the exercise ten times.

☞ *practice the following, writing each combination at least ten times:*

write the individual letters	write the combination	STPH-FPLT	repeat
1. PW-A-B (pronounced B, A, final B)	PWAB	home position	10X
2. PW-AEU-B	PWAEUB	home position	10X
3. PW-E-D	PWED	home position	10X
4. PW-AOE-D	PWAOED	home position	10X
5. PW-EU-B	PWEUB	home position	10X
6. PW-EU-D	PWEUD	home position	10X
7. PW-EU-F	PWEUF	home position	10X
8. PW-EU-G	PWEUG	home position	10X
9. PW-A-G	PWAG	home postion	10X
10. KR-EU-G	KREUG	home position	10X
11. KR-AOEU-D	KRAOEUD	home position	10X
12. TKPW-A-G	TKPWAG	home position	10X
13. TKPW-AOEU-D	TKPWAOEUD	home position	10X
14. TKPW-A-B	TKPWAB	home position	10X
15. H-E-D	HED	home position	10X
16. H-AOE-D	HAOED	home position	10X
17. H-AOEU-D	HAOEUD	home position	10X
18. H-A-FD	HAFD	home position	10X
19. SKWR-A-G	SKWRAG	home position	10X
20. SKWR-AEU-D	SKWRAEUD	home position	10X
21. TP-EU-G	TPEUG	home position	10X
22. SKWR-E-D	SKWRED	home position	10X
23. PW-A-PBLG	PWAPBLG	home position	10X
24. 2 8 8 2 2 8 8 2 2 8			10X
25. 1 9 9 1 1 9 9 1 1 9			10X

When you are finished writing, take a look at your notes. Are your letters cleanly written? Did you make any errors? If you did, circle the errors in your notes with a pen. Go back and practice the letters that you made a mistake writing until you can write them perfectly.

It is most important that you learn the letters thoroughly before going on to the next lessons.

Additional Practice

Go to the:	Do the following:
Realwrite DrillBook (recommended).........	Read over and study Drill III (Lessons 5 & 6)
Realwrite NoteBook (optional)..................	Read and transcribe the notes from Exercise B, Lesson 5

UNIT 2
LESSON SIX

Warm up and Review

☞ *practice the following:*

short A
A A A (hp) A A A (hp) A A A (hp)

long A
AEU (hp) AEU (hp) AEU (hp)

initial B-
PW PW PW (hp) PW PW PW (hp)

final -B
-B -B -B (hp) -B -B -B (hp) -B -B-B (hp)

initial C-
KR KR KR (hp) KR KR KR (hp)

final -C
-SZ -SZ -SZ (hp) -SZ -SZ -SZ (hp)

initial D-
TK TK TK (hp) TK TK TK (hp)

final -D
-D -D -D (hp) -D -D -D (hp) -D -D -D (hp)

short E
E E E (hp) E E E (hp) E E E (hp)

long E
AOE AOE AOE (hp) AOE AOE AOE (hp)

initial F-
TP TP TP (hp) TP TP TP (hp)

final -F
-F -F -F (hp) -F -F -F (hp) -F -F -F (hp)

initial G-
TKPW (hp) TKPW (hp) TKPW (hp)

final -G
-G -G -G (hp) -G -G -G (hp) -G -G -G (hp)

initial H-
H H H (hp) H H H (hp) H H H (hp)

final -H
-FD -FD -FD (hp) -FD -FD -FD (hp)

short I
EU EU EU (hp) EU EU EU (hp) EU EU EU (hp)

long I
AOEU (hp) AOEU (hp) AOEU (hp)

initial J-
SKWR (hp) SKWR (hp) SKWR (hp)

final -J
-PBLG (hp) -PBLG (hp) -PBLG (hp)

number 1
1 1 1 (hp) 1 1 1 (hp) 1 1 1 (hp)

number 9
9 9 9 (hp) 9 9 9 (hp) 9 9 9 (hp) 9 9 9 (hp)

number 2
2 2 2 (hp) 2 2 2 (hp) 2 2 2 (hp)

number 8
8 8 8 (hp) 8 8 8 (hp) 8 8 8 (hp) 8 8 8 (hp)

New Letters K- and -K

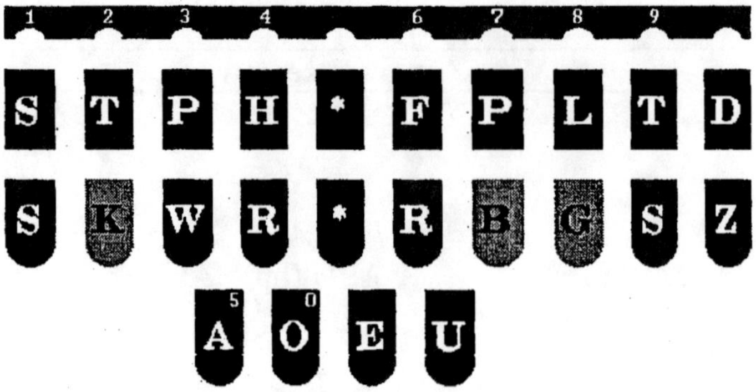

6.1 The initial side K is written by striking the K with the ring finger of the left hand.

☞ *practice the following:*

initial K-

K- K- K- (hp) K- K- K- (hp) K- K- K- (hp) K- K- K- (hp) K- K- K- (hp)
K- K- K- (hp) K- K- K- (hp) K- K- K- (hp) K- K- K- (hp) K- K- K- (hp)
K- K- K- (hp) K- K- K- (hp) K- K- K- (hp) K- K- K- (hp) K- K- K- (hp)

6.2 The final side -K is written by striking the -B and -G keys together using the middle and ring fingers of the right hand. (-K = -B + -G)

☞ *practice the following:*

final -K

-BG -BG -BG (hp) -BG -BG -BG (hp) -BG -BG -BG (hp) -BG -BG -BG (hp)
-BG -BG -BG (hp) -BG -BG -BG (hp) -BG -BG -BG (hp) -BG -BG -BG (hp)
-BG -BG -BG (hp) -BG -BG -BG (hp) -BG -BG -BG (hp) -BG -BG -BG (hp)

New Letters L- and -L

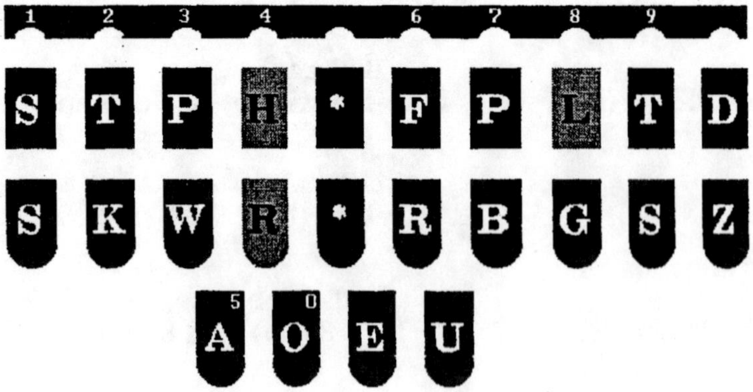

6.3 The initial side L is written by striking the H and R keys together using the index finger of the left hand. (L = H + R)

☞ *practice the following:*

initial L-

HR- HR- HR- (hp)	HR- HR- HR- (hp)	HR- HR- HR- (hp)	HR- HR- HR- (hp)
HR- HR- HR- (hp)	HR- HR- HR- (hp)	HR- HR- HR- (hp)	HR- HR- HR- (hp)
HR- HR- HR- (hp)	HR- HR- HR- (hp)	HR- HR- HR- (hp)	HR- HR- HR- (hp)

6.4 The final side -L is written by striking the home position -L key with the ring finger of t right hand.

☞ *practice the following:*

final -L

-L -L -L (hp)	-L -L -L (hp)	-L -L -L (hp)	-L -L -L (hp)	-L -L -L (hp)
-L -L -L (hp)	-L -L -L (hp)	-L -L -L (hp)	-L -L -L (hp)	-L -L -L (hp)
-L -L -L (hp)	-L -L -L (hp)	-L -L -L (hp)	-L -L -L (hp)	-L -L -L (hp)

New Letters M- and -M

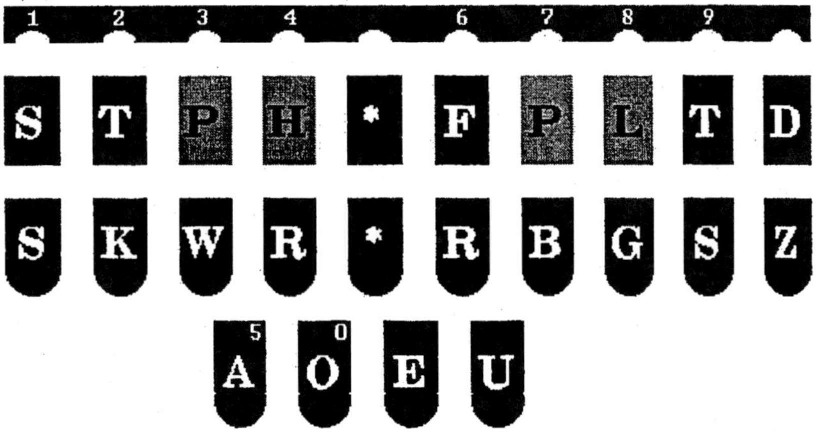

6.5 The initial side M is written by striking the home position P and H together using the mid and index fingers of the left hand. (M = P + H)

☞ *practice the following:*

initial M-

PH- PH- PH- (hp)	PH- PH- PH- (hp)	PH- PH- PH- (hp)	PH- PH- PH- (hp)
PH- PH- PH- (hp)	PH- PH- PH- (hp)	PH- PH- PH- (hp)	PH- PH- PH- (hp)
PH- PH- PH- (hp)	PH- PH- PH- (hp)	PH- PH- PH- (hp)	PH- PH- PH- (hp)

6.6 The final side -M is written by striking the home position -P and -L together using the r and middle fingers of the right hand. (-M = -P + -L)

☞ *practice the following:*

final -M

-PL -PL -PL (hp)	-PL -PL -PL (hp)	-PL -PL -PL (hp)	-PL -PL -PL (hp)
-PL -PL -PL (hp)	-PL -PL -PL (hp)	-PL -PL -PL (hp)	-PL -PL -PL (hp)
-PL -PL -PL (hp)	-PL -PL -PL (hp)	-PL -PL -PL (hp)	-PL -PL -PL (hp)

Lesson Practice

Practice the combinations until you can write them without hesitation. Learn the proper position for each letter. Hit the keys quickly and return to the home position.

☞ *practice the following:*

initial K-

K- K- K- (hp)	K- K- K- (hp)	K- K- K- (hp)	K- K- K- (hp)	K- K- K- (hp)
K- K- K- (hp)	K- K- K- (hp)	K- K- K- (hp)	K- K- K- (hp)	K- K- K- (hp)
K- K- K- (hp)	K- K- K- (hp)	K- K- K- (hp)	K- K- K- (hp)	K- K- K- (hp)

final -K

-BG -BG -BG (hp)	-BG -BG -BG (hp)	-BG -BG -BG (hp)	-BG -BG -BG (hp)
-BG -BG -BG (hp)	-BG -BG -BG (hp)	-BG -BG -BG (hp)	-BG -BG -BG (hp)
-BG -BG -BG (hp)	-BG -BG -BG (hp)	-BG -BG -BG (hp)	-BG -BG -BG (hp)

initial L-

HR- HR- HR- (hp)	HR- HR- HR- (hp)	HR- HR- HR- (hp)	HR- HR- HR- (hp)
HR- HR- HR- (hp)	HR- HR- HR- (hp)	HR- HR- HR- (hp)	HR- HR- HR- (hp)
HR- HR- HR- (hp)	HR- HR- HR- (hp)	HR- HR- HR- (hp)	HR- HR- HR- (hp)

final -L

-L -L -L (hp)	-L -L -L (hp)	-L -L -L (hp)	-L -L -L (hp)	-L -L -L (hp)
-L -L -L (hp)	-L -L -L (hp)	-L -L -L (hp)	-L -L -L (hp)	-L -L -L (hp)
-L -L -L (hp)	-L -L -L (hp)	-L -L -L (hp)	-L -L -L (hp)	-L -L -L (hp)

initial M-

PH- PH- PH- (hp)	PH- PH- PH- (hp)	PH- PH- PH- (hp)	PH- PH- PH- (hp)
PH- PH- PH- (hp)	PH- PH- PH- (hp)	PH- PH- PH- (hp)	PH- PH- PH- (hp)
PH- PH- PH- (hp)	PH- PH- PH- (hp)	PH- PH- PH- (hp)	PH- PH- PH- (hp)

final -M

-PL -PL -PL (hp)	-PL -PL -PL (hp)	-PL -PL -PL (hp)	-PL -PL -PL (hp)
-PL -PL -PL (hp)	-PL -PL -PL (hp)	-PL -PL -PL (hp)	-PL -PL -PL (hp)
-PL -PL -PL (hp)	-PL -PL -PL (hp)	-PL -PL -PL (hp)	-PL -PL -PL (hp)

Comprehensive Practice

Write each of the following combinations as follows:

1. Write the individual letters (PW-A-B).
2. Write the one-stroke combination of the letters (PWAB).
3. Write the home position (STPH-FPLT).
4. Repeat the exercise ten times.

☞ *practice the following, writing each combination at least ten times:*

write the individual letters	write the combination	STPH-FPLT	repeat
1. PW-A-PL (pronounced B, A, final M)	PWAPL	home position	10X
2. KR-AOEU	KRAOEU	home position	10X
3. TK-EU-G	TKEUG	home position	10X
4. TKPW-AOE-BG	TKPWAOEBG	home position	10X
5. H-A-G	HAG	home position	10X
6. SKWR-A-SZ	SKWRASZ	home position	10X
7. K-EU-BG	KEUBG	home position	10X
8. HR-A-F	HRAF	home position	10X
9. PH-E-G	PHEG	home postion	10X
10. 1 8 9 2 2 8 9 1 1 9 2 2 8			10X
11. HR-A-B	HRAB	home position	10X
12. H-EU-SZ	HEUSZ	home position	10X
13. PH-AEU-D	PHAEUD	home position	10X
14. TKPW-EU-F	TKPWEUF	home position	10X
15. H-A-FD	HAFD	home position	10X
16. AEU-PBLG	AEUPBLG	home position	10X
17. H-EU-BG	HEUBG	home position	10X
18. HR-E-L	HREL	home position	10X
19. SKWR-A-PL	SKWRAPL	home position	10X
20. PH-AEU-PL	PHAEUPL	home position	10X
21. HR-EU-L	HREUL	home position	10X
22. 2 8 9 1 1 9 8 2 2 9 1 8 8 2			10X
23. K-AEU-BG	KAEUBG	home position	10X
24. SKWR-A-FD	SKWRAFD	home position	10X
25. TKPW-EU-PBLG	TKPWEUPBLG	home position	10X

When you are finished writing, take a look at your paper or electronic notes. Are your letters cleanly written? Did you make any errors? Go back and practice the letters that you made a mistake writing until you can write them perfectly.

It is most important that you learn the letters and numbers thoroughly before going on to the next lessons.

Short Forms and Phrases

☞ *practice the following*:

I	(AOEU)[1]	can	K (-BG)	will	HR (-W)[2]
little	HREUL	me	PHAE	come	KPH-[3]
am	-PL	I can	AOEUBG[4]	can I	KEU
will I	HREU	I am	AOEUPL	did I	TKEU
can a	KAEU[5]	I did	AOEUD	had I	HEU
I had	AOEUFD	can he	KE	will he	HRE
he can	HAEBG	bill	PW-L		

[1] The pronoun "I" is written with a long I (AOEU); the prefix "i" is always written with a short I (EU).
[2] The final -W will be introduced in a later lesson.
[3] The short form for come KPH- (KM) is used to avoid conflict with words that begin with "com."
[4] If a phrase begins with "I" use the long I (AOEU); if a phrase ends in "I" use the short I (EU).
[5] All phrases that contain the article "a" are written with a long "a" (AEU).

Additional Practice

Go to the:	Do the following:
Realwrite DrillBook (recommended)...........	Write and practice Drill III (Lessons 5 & 6)
Realwrite NoteBook (optional).....................	Read and transcribe the notes from Exercise B, Lesson 6 and Drill III

UNIT 2
LESSON SEVEN

Warm up and Review

Strive for perfection in your warm up. Strive to write each letter with absolutely no hesitation at all. Learn the position of your fingers so that you can write the letter instantly.

☞ *practice the following:*

short A
A A A (hp) A A A (hp) A A A (hp)

long A
AEU (hp) AEU (hp) AEU (hp)

initial B-
PW PW PW (hp) PW PW PW (hp)

final -B
-B -B -B (hp) -B -B -B (hp) -B -B-B (hp)

initial C-
KR KR KR (hp) KR KR KR (hp)

final -C
-SZ -SZ -SZ (hp) -SZ -SZ -SZ (hp)

initial D-
TK TK TK (hp) TK TK TK (hp)

final -D
-D -D -D (hp) -D -D -D (hp) -D -D -D (hp)

short E
E E E (hp) E E E (hp) E E E (hp)

long E
AOE AOE AOE (hp) AOE AOE AOE (hp)

initial F-
TP TP TP (hp) TP TP TP (hp)

final -F
-F -F -F (hp) -F -F -F (hp) -F -F -F (hp)

initial G-
TKPW (hp) TKPW (hp) TKPW (hp)

final -G
-G -G -G (hp) -G -G -G (hp) -G -G -G (hp)

initial H-
H H H (hp) H H H (hp) H H H (hp)

final -H
-FD -FD -FD (hp) -FD -FD -FD (hp)

short I
EU EU EU (hp) EU EU EU (hp) EU EU EU (hp)

long I
AOEU (hp) AOEU (hp) AOEU (hp)

initial J-
SKWR (hp) SKWR (hp) SKWR (hp)

final -J
-PBLG (hp) -PBLG (hp) -PBLG (hp)

initial K-
K K K (hp) K K K (hp) K K K (hp)

final -K
-BG -BG -BG (hp) -BG -BG -BG (hp)

initial L-
HR HR HR (hp)   HR HR HR (hp))

final -L
-L -L -L (hp)   -L -L -L (hp)   -L -L -L (hp)

initial M-
PH PH PH (hp)   PH PH PH (hp))

final -M
-PL -PL -PL (hp)   -PL -PL -PL (hp)

number 1
1 1 1 (hp)   1 1 1 (hp)   1 1 1 (hp)

number 9
9 9 9 (hp)   9 9 9 (hp)   9 9 9 (hp)   9 9 9 (hp)

number 2
2 2 2 (hp)   2 2 2 (hp)   2 2 2 (hp)

number 8
8 8 8 (hp)   8 8 8 (hp)   8 8 8 (hp)   8 8 8 (hp)

New Letters N- and -N

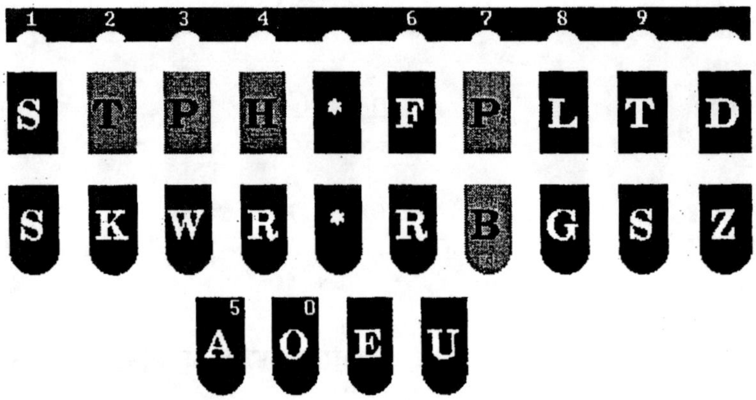

7.1 The initial side N is written by striking the T, P, and H keys together using the ring, middle, and index fingers of the left hand. (N = T + P + H)

☞ practice the following:

initial N-

TPH TPH TPH (hp)   TPH TPH TPH (hp)   TPH TPH TPH (hp)   TPH TPH TPH (hp)
TPH TPH TPH (hp)   TPH TPH TPH (hp)   TPH TPH TPH (hp)   TPH TPH TPH (hp)
TPH TPH TPH (hp)   TPH TPH TPH (hp)   TPH TPH TPH (hp)   TPH TPH TPH (hp)

7.2 The final side -N is written by striking the home position -P key together with the -B key. Strike the crack between the -P and -B using the middle finger of the right hand. (-N = -P + -B)

☞ practice the following:

final -N

-PB -PB -PB (hp)   -PB -PB -PB (hp)   -PB -PB -PB (hp)   -PB -PB -PB (hp)
-PB -PB -PB (hp)   -PB -PB -PB (hp)   -PB -PB -PB (hp)   -PB -PB -PB (hp)
-PB -PB -PB (hp)   -PB -PB -PB (hp)   -PB -PB -PB (hp)   -PB -PB -PB (hp)

New Letters O and Long O

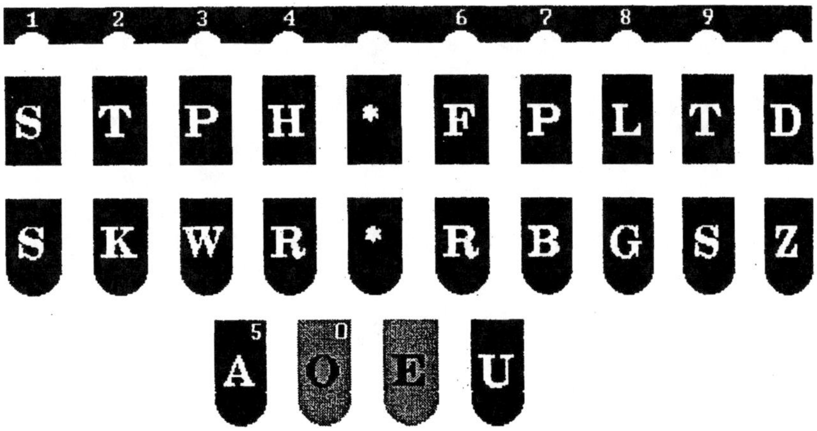

7.3 The vowel O is written with the left thumb by striking the O key.

☞ *practice the following:*

short O

O O O (hp) O O O (hp) O O O (hp) O O O (hp) O O O (hp)
O O O (hp) O O O (hp) O O O (hp) O O O (hp) O O O (hp)
O O O (hp) O O O (hp) O O O (hp) O O O (hp) O O O (hp)

The long O is an exception to the "Double-Opposite Rule" for writing long vowels that you learned earlier. The long O is formed by using the "Single-Opposite Exception." Write the long O by combining it with the vowel E only. Notice the O and the E in "Opposite Exception."

7.4 The long O is written by striking the O key and the E key together using the left and right thumbs. (Long O = O + E)

☞ *practice the following:*

long O

OE OE OE (hp) OE OE OE (hp) OE OE OE (hp) OE OE OE (hp) OE OE OE (hp)
OE OE OE (hp) OE OE OE (hp) OE OE OE (hp) OE OE OE (hp) OE OE OE (hp)
OE OE OE (hp) OE OE OE (hp) OE OE OE (hp) OE OE OE (hp) OE OE OE (hp)

New Numbers 3 and 7

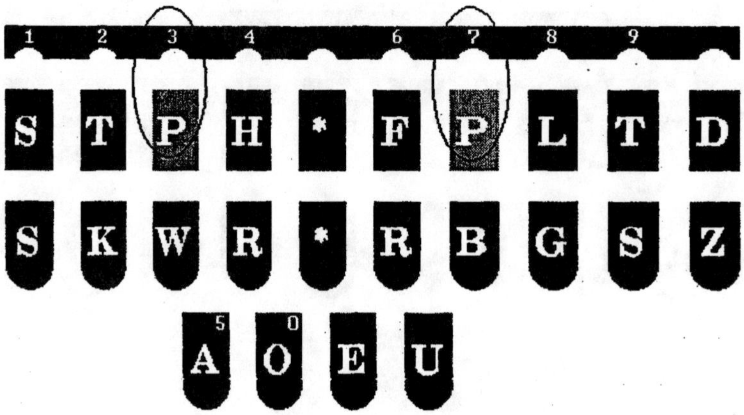

7.5 Write the number 3 with the middle finger of the left hand. Hit the crack between the home position P and the number bar, depressing both key and bar at the same time.

number 3:

3 3 3 (hp)	3 3 3 (hp)	3 3 3 (hp)	3 3 3 (hp)	3 3 3 (hp)	3 3 3 (hp)
3 3 3 (hp)	3 3 3 (hp)	3 3 3 (hp)	3 3 3 (hp)	3 3 3 (hp)	3 3 3 (hp)
3 3 3 (hp)	3 3 3 (hp)	3 3 3 (hp)	3 3 3 (hp)	3 3 3 (hp)	3 3 3 (hp)

Remember to hit the home position letter along with the number bar so that your numbers are clearly written. Hit them together, letting go to return to the home position. Use the top and flat part of your finger to depress both key and bar at the same time.

7.6 Write the number 7 with the middle finger of the right hand. Hit the crack between the home position -P and the number bar, depressing both key and bar at the same time.

number 7:

7 7 7 (hp)	7 7 7 (hp)	7 7 7 (hp)	7 7 7 (hp)	7 7 7 (hp)	7 7 7 (hp)
7 7 7 (hp)	7 7 7 (hp)	7 7 7 (hp)	7 7 7 (hp)	7 7 7 (hp)	7 7 7 (hp)
7 7 7 (hp)	7 7 7 (hp)	7 7 7 (hp)	7 7 7 (hp)	7 7 7 (hp)	7 7 7 (hp)

Lesson Practice

Even though you are keeping your eyes on the keyboard chart, try to look away from the chart after you have learned the proper position for each letter, combination, or number.

☞ *practice the following:*

initial N-

TPH TPH TPH (hp)	TPH TPH TPH (hp)	TPH TPH TPH (hp)	TPH TPH TPH (hp)
TPH TPH TPH (hp)	TPH TPH TPH (hp)	TPH TPH TPH (hp)	TPH TPH TPH (hp)
TPH TPH TPH (hp)	TPH TPH TPH (hp)	TPH TPH TPH (hp)	TPH TPH TPH (hp)

final -N

-PB -PB -PB (hp) -PB -PB -PB (hp) -PB -PB -PB (hp) -PB -PB -PB (hp)
-PB -PB -PB (hp) -PB -PB -PB (hp) -PB -PB -PB (hp) -PB -PB -PB (hp)
-PB -PB -PB (hp) -PB -PB -PB (hp) -PB -PB -PB (hp) -PB -PB -PB (hp)

short O

O O O (hp) O O O (hp) O O O (hp) O O O (hp) O O O (hp)
O O O (hp) O O O (hp) O O O (hp) O O O (hp) O O O (hp)
O O O (hp) O O O (hp) O O O (hp) O O O (hp) O O O (hp)

long O

OE OE OE (hp) OE OE OE (hp) OE OE OE (hp) OE OE OE (hp) OE OE OE (hp)
OE OE OE (hp) OE OE OE (hp) OE OE OE (hp) OE OE OE (hp) OE OE OE (hp)
OE OE OE (hp) OE OE OE (hp) OE OE OE (hp) OE OE OE (hp) OE OE OE (hp)

number 3:

3 3 3 (hp) 3 3 3 (hp) 3 3 3 (hp) 3 3 3 (hp) 3 3 3 (hp) 3 3 3 (hp)
3 3 3 (hp) 3 3 3 (hp) 3 3 3 (hp) 3 3 3 (hp) 3 3 3 (hp) 3 3 3 (hp)
3 3 3 (hp) 3 3 3 (hp) 3 3 3 (hp) 3 3 3 (hp) 3 3 3 (hp) 3 3 3 (hp)

number 7:

7 7 7 (hp) 7 7 7 (hp) 7 7 7 (hp) 7 7 7 (hp) 7 7 7 (hp) 7 7 7 (hp)
7 7 7 (hp) 7 7 7 (hp) 7 7 7 (hp) 7 7 7 (hp) 7 7 7 (hp) 7 7 7 (hp)
7 7 7 (hp) 7 7 7 (hp) 7 7 7 (hp) 7 7 7 (hp) 7 7 7 (hp) 7 7 7 (hp)

Comprehensive Practice

Write each of the following combinations as follows:

1. Write the individual letters (PW-A-B).
2. Write the one-stroke combination of the letters (PWAB).
3. Write the home position (STPH-FPLT).
4. Repeat the exercise ten times.

☞ *practice the following, writing each combination at least ten times:*

	write the individual letters	write the combination	STPH-FPLT	repeat
1.	TPH-O-PB (pronounced N-O-final N)	TPHOPB	home position	10X
2.	TPH-OE-PL	TPHOEPL	home position	10X
3.	TPH-EU-PB	TPHEUPB	home position	10X
4.	TP-A-PB	TPAPB	home position	10X
5.	TPH-A-FD	TPHAFD	home position	10X

6. PH-EU-PB	PHEUPB	home position 10X
7. PH-OE-PB	PHOEPB	home position 10X
8. HRA-PL	HRAPL	home position 10X
9. K-A-PBLG	KAPBLG	home postion 10X
10. 3 3 7 7 7 3 3 7 7 3 3 7 7		10X
11. H-OE-FD	HOEFD	home position 10X
12. TKPW-OE	TKPWOE	home position 10X
13. TP-AOE-PB	TPAOEPB	home position 10X
14. TK-AOEU-PL	TKAOEUPL	home position 10X
15. KR-AOEU-SZ	KRAOEUSZ	home position 10X
16. PW-OE-PB	PWOEPB	home position 10X
17 H-O-B	HOB	home position 10X
18. TPH-O-D	TPHOD	home position 10X
19. H-A-F	HAF	home position 10X
20. HR-A-G	HRAG	home position 10X
21. OE-FD	OEFD	home position 10X
22. 3 2 1 9 8 7 7 2 3 1 9 7 3 1		10X
23. PH-AEU-BG	PHAEUBG	home position 10X
24. SKWR-AEU-L	SKWRAEUL	home position 10X
25. TKPW-E-PB	TKPWEPB	home position 10X

When you are finished writing, take a look at your notes. Are your letters and numbers cleanly written? Did you make any errors? Go back and practice your errors until you can write every letter perfectly. It is most important that you learn the letters thoroughly before going on to the next lessons.

Additional Practice

Go to the: Do the following:

Realwrite DrillBook (recommended).......Read over and study Drill IV (Lessons 7 & 8)

Realwrite NoteBook (optional).................Read and transcribe the notes from Exercise B, Lesson 7

UNIT 2
LESSON EIGHT

Warm up and Review

Practice the following until you can write each letter, number, or combination of letters without hesitation. You are building the foundation for speed by working on your accuracy.

☞ *practice the following:*

short A
A A A (hp) A A A (hp) A A A (hp)

long A
AEU (hp) AEU (hp) AEU (hp)

initial B-
PW PW PW (hp) PW PW PW (hp)

final -B
-B -B -B (hp) -B -B -B (hp) -B -B-B (hp)

initial C-
KR KR KR (hp) KR KR KR (hp)

final -C
-SZ -SZ -SZ (hp) -SZ -SZ -SZ (hp)

initial D-
TK TK TK (hp) TK TK TK (hp)

final -D
-D -D -D (hp) -D -D -D (hp) -D -D -D (hp)

short E
E E E (hp) E E E (hp) E E E (hp)

long E
AOE AOE AOE (hp) AOE AOE AOE (hp)

initial F-
TP TP TP (hp) TP TP TP (hp)

final -F
-F -F -F (hp) -F -F -F (hp) -F -F -F (hp)

initial G-
TKPW (hp) TKPW (hp) TKPW (hp)

final -G
-G -G -G (hp) -G -G -G (hp) -G -G -G (hp)

initial H-
H H H (hp) H H H (hp) H H H (hp)

final -H
-FD -FD -FD (hp) -FD -FD -FD (hp)

short I
EU EU EU (hp) EU EU EU (hp) EU EU EU (hp)

long I
AOEU (hp) AOEU (hp) AOEU (hp)

initial J-
SKWR (hp) SKWR (hp) SKWR (hp)

final -J
-PBLG (hp) -PBLG (hp) -PBLG (hp)

initial K-
K K K (hp) K K K (hp) K K K (hp)

final -K
-BG -BG -BG (hp) -BG -BG -BG (hp)

initial L-
HR HR HR (hp)   HR HR HR (hp))

initial M-
PH PH PH (hp)   PH PH PH (hp))

initial N-
TPH TPH TPH (hp)   TPH TPH TPH (hp)

short O
O O O (hp)   O O O (hp)   O O O (hp)

number 1
1 1 1 (hp)   1 1 1 (hp)   1 1 1 (hp)

number 2
2 2 2 (hp)   2 2 2 (hp)   2 2 2 (hp)

number 3
3 3 3 (hp)   3 3 3 (hp)   3 3 3 (hp)

final -L
-L -L -L (hp)   -L -L -L (hp)   -L -L -L (hp)

final -M
-PL -PL -PL (hp)   -PL -PL -PL (hp)

final -N
-PB -PB -PB (hp)   -PB -PB -PB (hp)

long O
OE OE OE (hp)   OE OE OE (hp)

number 9
9 9 9 (hp)   9 9 9 (hp)   9 9 9 (hp)   9 9 9 (hp)

number 8
8 8 8 (hp)   8 8 8 (hp)   8 8 8 (hp)   8 8 8 (hp)

number 7
7 7 7 (hp)   7 7 7 (hp)   7 7 7 (hp)   7 7 7 (hp)

New Letters P- and -P

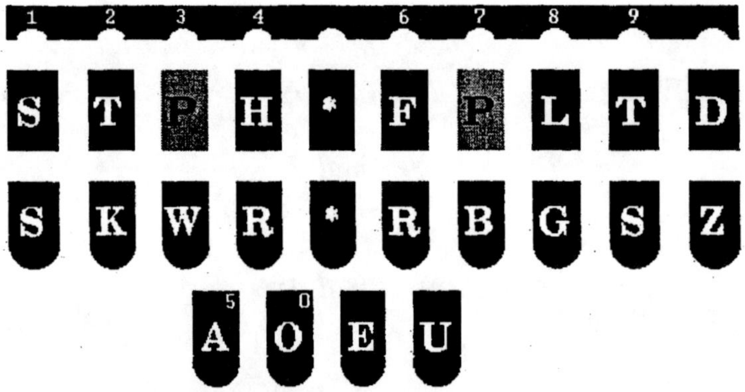

8.1 The initial side P is written by striking the home position P with the middle finger of the left hand.

☞ *practice the following:*

initial P-

P P P (hp)   P P P (hp)   P P P (hp)   P P P (hp)   P P P (hp)   P P P (hp)
P P P (hp)   P P P (hp)   P P P (hp)   P P P (hp)   P P P (hp)   P P P (hp)
P P P (hp)   P P P (hp)   P P P (hp)   P P P (hp)   P P P (hp)   P P P (hp)

8.2 The final side -P is written by striking the home position -P with the middle finger of the right hand.

☞ *practice the following:*

final -P

-P -P -P (hp) -P -P -P (hp) -P -P -P (hp) -P -P -P (hp) -P -P -P (hp)
-P -P -P (hp) -P -P -P (hp) -P -P -P (hp) -P -P -P (hp) -P -P -P (hp)
-P -P -P (hp) -P -P -P (hp) -P -P -P (hp) -P -P -P (hp) -P -P -P (hp)

New Lettters Q- and -Q

Like the letter C, the letter Q has no sound equivalent of its own. If anything, the sound of Q is a combination of the K and U sounds together. However, in Realwrite theory, there will be times when you need to designate the letter Q, therefore, you will learn an alphabetic combination to represent both the initial and final Q.

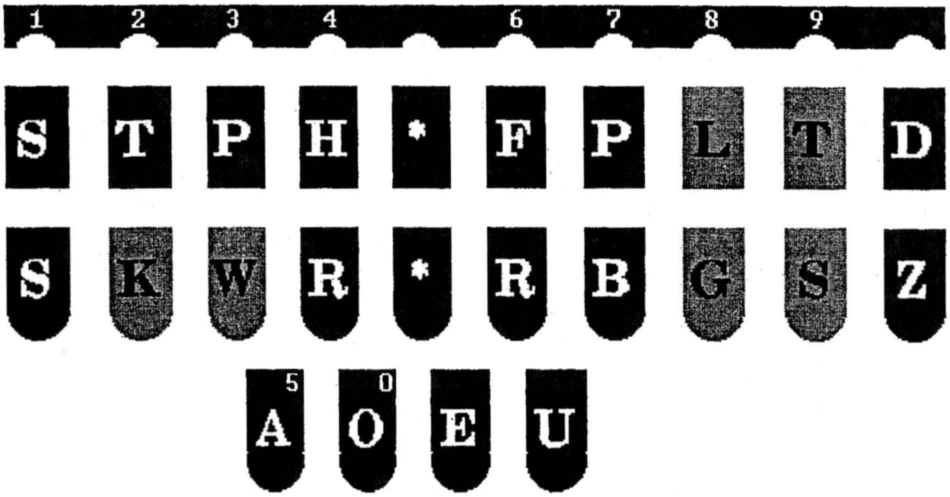

8.3 The initial side Q is written by striking the K and W keys together using the ring and middle finger of the left hand. (Q = K + W)

initial Q-

KW KW KW (hp) KW KW KW (hp) KW KW KW (hp) KW KW KW (hp)
KW KW KW (hp) KW KW KW (hp) KW KW KW (hp) KW KW KW (hp)
KW KW KW (hp) KW KW KW (hp) KW KW KW (hp) KW KW KW (hp)

8.4 The final side -Q is written by striking the –L and –G keys using the ring finger of the right hand and the -T and -S keys using the small finger of the right hand. Hit the crack between the -LG and -TS keys using the ring and small fingers of the right hand striking all four keys together. (-Q = -LG + -TS)

final -Q

-LGTS -LGTS -LGTS (hp) -LGTS -LGTS -LGTS (hp) -LGTS -LGTS -LGTS (hp)
-LGTS -LGTS -LGTS (hp) -LGTS -LGTS -LGTS (hp) -LGTS -LGTS -LGTS (hp)
-LGTS -LGTS -LGTS (hp) -LGTS -LGTS -LGTS (hp) -LGTS -LGTS -LGTS (hp)

New Letters R- and -R

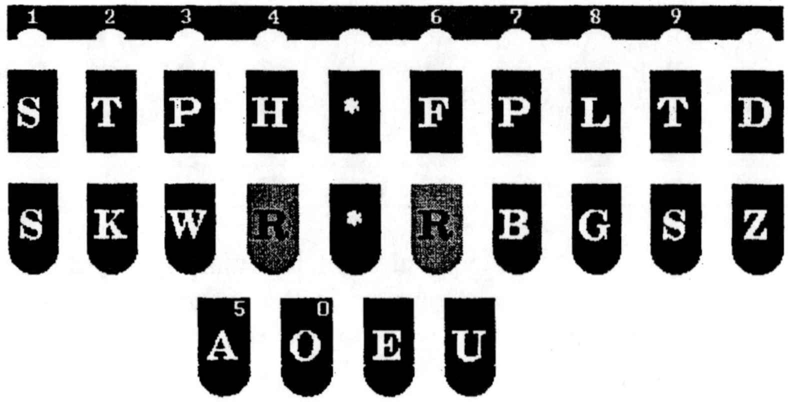

8.5 The initial side R is written by moving the index finger of the left hand from the home position H to the R key.

☞ *practice the following:*

initial R-

R R R (hp) R R R (hp) R R R (hp) R R R (hp) R R R (hp) R R R (hp)
R R R (hp) R R R (hp) R R R (hp) R R R (hp) R R R (hp) R R R (hp)
R R R (hp) R R R (hp) R R R (hp) R R R (hp) R R R (hp) R R R (hp)

8.6 The final side -R is written by moving the index finger of the right hand from the home position F to the R key.

☞ *practice the following:*

final -R

-R -R -R (hp) -R -R -R (hp) -R -R -R (hp) -R -R -R (hp) -R -R -R (hp)
-R -R -R (hp) -R -R -R (hp) -R -R -R (hp) -R -R -R (hp) -R -R -R (hp)
-R -R -R (hp) -R -R -R (hp) -R -R -R (hp) -R -R -R (hp) -R -R -R (hp)

Lesson Practice

Practice the letters and numbers until you can write them without any hesitation. Practice the letters until you can write them without looking at the chart. Do not look at your machine or the paper as you are writing.

☞ *practice the following:*

initial P-

P P P (hp) P P P (hp) P P P (hp) P P P (hp) P P P (hp) P P P (hp)
P P P (hp) P P P (hp) P P P (hp) P P P (hp) P P P (hp) P P P (hp)
P P P (hp) P P P (hp) P P P (hp) P P P (hp) P P P (hp) P P P (hp)

final -P

-P -P -P (hp)	-P -P -P (hp)	-P -P -P (hp)	-P -P -P (hp)	-P -P -P (hp)
-P -P -P (hp)	-P -P -P (hp)	-P -P -P (hp)	-P -P -P (hp)	-P -P -P (hp)
-P -P -P (hp)	-P -P -P (hp)	-P -P -P (hp)	-P -P -P (hp)	-P -P -P (hp)

initial Q-

KW KW KW (hp)	KW KW KW (hp)	KW KW KW (hp)	KW KW KW (hp)
KW KW KW (hp)	KW KW KW (hp)	KW KW KW (hp)	KW KW KW (hp)
KW KW KW (hp)	KW KW KW (hp)	KW KW KW (hp)	KW KW KW (hp)

final -Q

-LGTS -LGTS -LGTS (hp)	-LGTS -LGTS -LGTS (hp)	-LGTS -LGTS -LGTS (hp)
-LGTS -LGTS -LGTS (hp)	-LGTS -LGTS -LGTS (hp)	-LGTS -LGTS -LGTS (hp)
-LGTS -LGTS -LGTS (hp)	-LGTS -LGTS -LGTS (hp)	-LGTS -LGTS -LGTS (hp)

initial R-

R R R (hp)	R R R (hp)	R R R (hp)	R R R (hp)	R R R (hp)	R R R (hp)
R R R (hp)	R R R (hp)	R R R (hp)	R R R (hp)	R R R (hp)	R R R (hp)
R R R (hp)	R R R (hp)	R R R (hp)	R R R (hp)	R R R (hp)	R R R (hp)

final -R

-R -R -R (hp)	-R -R -R (hp)	-R -R -R (hp)	-R -R -R (hp)	-R -R -R (hp)
-R -R -R (hp)	-R -R -R (hp)	-R -R -R (hp)	-R -R -R (hp)	-R -R -R (hp)
-R -R -R (hp)	-R -R -R (hp)	-R -R -R (hp)	-R -R -R (hp)	-R -R -R (hp)

Comprehensive Practice

Write each of the following combinations as follows:

1. Write the individual letters (PW-A-B).
2. Write the one-stroke combination of the letters (PWAB).
3. Write the home position (STPH-FPLT).
4. Repeat the exercise ten times.

write the individual letters	write the combination	STPH-FPLT	repeat
1. ROEPB (pronounced R, O, final N)	ROEPB	home position	10X
2. R-O-R	ROR	home position	10X
3. KW-A-BG	KWABG	home position	10X
4. KW-OE-D	KWOED	home position	10X
5. P-AOEU-P	PAOEUP	home position	10X
6. P-EU-L	PEUL	home position	10X
7. TPH-E-D	TPHED	home position	10X
8. PH-O-R	PHOR	home position	10X
9. HR-A-P	HRAP	home postion	10X
10. 1 2 3 1 2 3 7 8 9 7 8 9			10X

11. K-A-R	KAR	home position 10X
12. SKWR-AOE-P	SKWRAOEP	home position 10X
13. H-A-FD	HAFD	home position 10X
14. TKPW-AEU-L	TKPWAEUL	home position 10X
15. TP-O-R	TPOR	home position 10X
16. PW-AOE-R	PWAOER	home position 10X
17. P-A-LGTS	PALGTS	home position 10X
18. P-E-P	PEP	home position 10X
19. P-AOE-P	PAOEP	home position 10X
20. TK-AOE-P	TKAOEP	home position 10X
21. H-E-BG	HEBG	home position 10X
22. 9 3 7 2 1 1 8 7 9 3 2 8 8 1		10X
23. R-A-LGTS	RALGTS	home position 10X
24. KR-O-SZ	KROSZ	home position 10X
25. KW-AOEU-R	KWAOEUR	home position 10X

When you are finished writing, take a look at your notes. Did you make any errors? Go back and practice the letters that you made a mistake writing until you can write them perfectly.

Short Forms and Phrases

☞ Practice the following, learning them so that you can write them without hesitation:

do	TKAO[1]	in	TPH[2]	been	PW-PB
even	AOEFPB[3]	only	OEPBL[3]	help	HEP
from	TPR-	after	AFR	under[4]	TKER
on	O[5]	into	TPHAO	many	PH-PB
could	KO	are	R-	or	R- -R
before	PW-FR			number	PWER
could I	KOEU			could he	KOE
I could	AOEUBGD			he could	HAEBGD

[1]The word "do" is always written TKAO to avoid conflicts
[2]The word "in" is always written TPH- to avoid conflict with the prefix in- written EUPB
[3]The words "even" AOEFPB and "only" OEPBL may require extra practice to write the final –FPB and final-PBL together; practice these combinations until you can write them comfortably
[4]The word "under" is written TKER to avoid conflict with the prefix under- written UPBD
[5]The word "on" is written O to avoid conflict with the prefix on- written OPB

Additional Practice

Go to the:	Do the following:
Realwrite DrillBook (recommended)..........	Write and practice Drill IV (Lessons 7 & 8)
Realwrite NoteBook (optional)....................	Read and transcribe the notes from Exercise B, Lesson 8 and Drill IV

UNIT 2 REVIEW

Lesson Review

1. Go back to each lesson and learn each new rule thoroughly.
2. Go back to each lesson and write the Lesson Practice.
3. Go back to each lesson and write the Comprehensive Practice.
4. Read back all notes and transcribe a portion of your review.

Review of Writing Rules

5.1 The vowel I is written with the right thumb by combining the letters E and U together in one stroke. (I = E + U)

5.2 The long I is written by striking the AO keys with your left thumb together with the EU key using your right thumb. (Long I = AO + EU)

5.3 The initial side J is written by striking the four keys SKWR together using the small, ring, middle, and index fingers of the left hand. (J = S + K + W + R)

5.4 The final side -J is written by striking the -PB and -LG keys together using the middle and ring fingers of the right hand. (-J = -PB + -LG)

5.5 Write the number 2 with the ring finger of the left hand. Hit the crack between the home position T and the number bar, depressing both key and bar at the same time.

5.6 Write the number 8 with the ring finger of the right hand. Hit the crack between the home position -L and the number bar, depressing both key and bar at the same time.

6.1 The initial side K is written by striking the K with the ring finger of the left hand.

6.2 The final side -K is written by striking the -B and -G keys together using the middle and ring fingers of the right hand. (-K = -B + -G)

6.3 The initial side L is written by striking the H and R keys together using the index finger of the left hand.

6.4 The final side -L is written by striking the home position -L key with the ring finger of the right hand.

6.5 The initial side M is written by striking the home position P and H together using the middle and index fingers of the left hand. (M = P + H)

6.6 The final side -M is written by striking the home position -P and -L together using the ring and middle fingers of the right hand. (-M = -P + -L)

7.1 The initial side N is written by striking the T, P, and H keys together using the ring, middle, and index fingers of the left hand. (N = T + P + H)

7.2 The final side -N is written by striking the home position -P key together with the -B key. Strike the crack between the -P and -B using the middle finger of the right hand.

7.3 The vowel O is written with the left thumb by striking the O key.

7.4 The long O is written by striking the O key and the E key together using the left and right thumbs. (Long O = O + E)

7.5 Write the number 3 with the middle finger of the left hand. Hit the crack between the home position P and the number bar, depressing both key and bar at the same time.

7.6 Write the number 7 with the middle finger of the right hand. Hit the crack between the home position -P and the number bar, depressing both key and bar at the same time.

8.1 The initial side P is written by striking the home position P with the middle finger of the left hand.

8.2 The final side -P is written by striking the -P with the middle finger of the right hand.

8.3 The initial side Q is written by striking the K and W keys together using the ring and middle finger of the left hand. (Q = K + W)

8.4 The final side -Q is written by striking the –L and –G keys using the ring finger of the right hand and the -T and -S keys using the small finger of the right hand. Hit the crack between the -LG and -TS keys using the ring and small fingers of the right hand striking all four keys together. (-Q = -LG + -TS)

8.5 The initial side R is written by moving the index finger of the left hand from the home position H to the R key.

8.6 The final side -R is written by moving the index finger of the right hand from the home position F to the R key.

Review DrillBook and NoteBook Applications

1. Review Drills III and IV from the *Realwrite DrillBook* (recommended).
2. Review Exercise B from the *Realwrite NoteBook* (optional).

UNIT EVALUATION NUMBER TWO

Unit Evaluation Number Two will cover all material from the following: *Realwrite LessonBook*, Lessons 5-8; *DrillBook*, Drills III and IV.

UNIT 3
LESSON NINE

Warm up and Review

☞ *Practice the following letters and numbers at least ten times each:*

Read the columns from left to right, then try it again, reading from top to bottom.

A	AEU	PW	-B	KR	-SZ	TK	-D	E	AOE
TP	-F	TKPW	-G	H	-FD	EU	AOEU	SKWR	-PBLG
K	-BG	HR	-L	PH	-PL	TPH	-PB	O	OE
P	-P	KW	-LGTS	R	-R	2	2	9	7
1	9	7	3	8	2	7	1	3	1
2	3	9	7	2	7	8	9	2	1
1	2	3	1	9	8	7	3	1	9

New Letters S- and -S

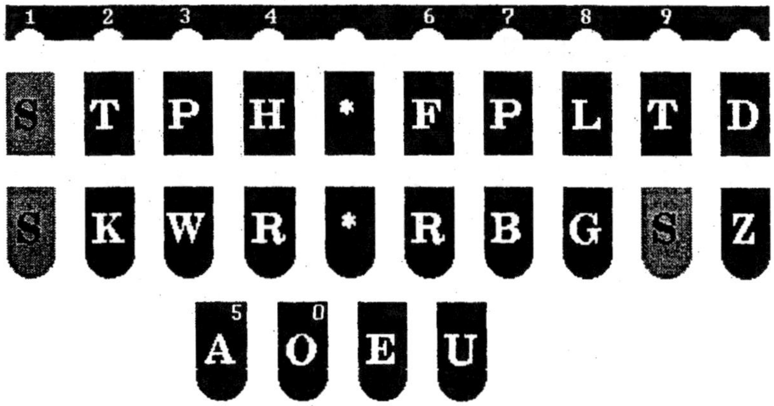

9.1 The initial side S is written by striking the home position S with the small finger of the left hand.

You may strike either the upper or lower S as both keys are connected to each other.

☞ *practice the following:*

initial S-

S S S (hp) S S S (hp) S S S (hp) S S S (hp) S S S (hp) S S S (hp)
S S S (hp) S S S (hp) S S S (hp) S S S (hp) S S S (hp) S S S (hp)
S S S (hp) S S S (hp) S S S (hp) S S S (hp) S S S (hp) S S S (hp)

9.2 The final side -S is written by striking the -S key, moving the small finger of the right hand from its home position -T down to the letter -S.

☞ <u>*practice the following:*</u>

<u>*final -S*</u>

-S -S -S (hp)　-S -S -S (hp)　-S -S -S (hp)　-S -S -S (hp)　-S -S -S (hp)
-S -S -S (hp)　-S -S -S (hp)　-S -S -S (hp)　-S -S -S (hp)　-S -S -S (hp)
-S -S -S (hp)　-S -S -S (hp)　-S -S -S (hp)　-S -S -S (hp)　-S -S -S (hp)

New Letters T- and -T

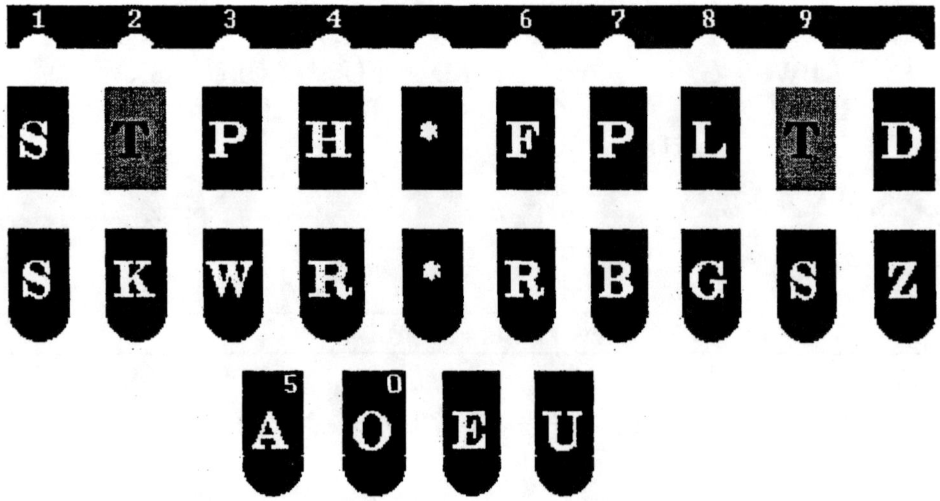

9.3 The initial side T is written by striking the home position T with the ring finger of the left hand.

☞ <u>*practice the following:*</u>

<u>*initial T-*</u>

T T T (hp)　T T T (hp)　T T T (hp)　T T T (hp)　T T T (hp)　T T T (hp)
T T T (hp)　T T T (hp)　T T T (hp)　T T T (hp)　T T T (hp)　T T T (hp)
T T T (hp)　T T T (hp)　T T T (hp)　T T T (hp)　T T T (hp)　T T T (hp)

9.4 The final side -T is written by striking the home position -T key with the small finger of the right hand.

☞ <u>*practice the following:*</u>

<u>*final -T*</u>

-T -T -T (hp)　-T -T -T (hp)　-T -T -T (hp)　-T -T -T (hp)　-T -T -T (hp)
-T -T -T (hp)　-T -T -T (hp)　-T -T -T (hp)　-T -T -T (hp)　-T -T -T (hp)
-T -T -T (hp)　-T -T -T (hp)　-T -T -T (hp)　-T -T -T (hp)　-T -T -T (hp)

New Numbers 4 and 6

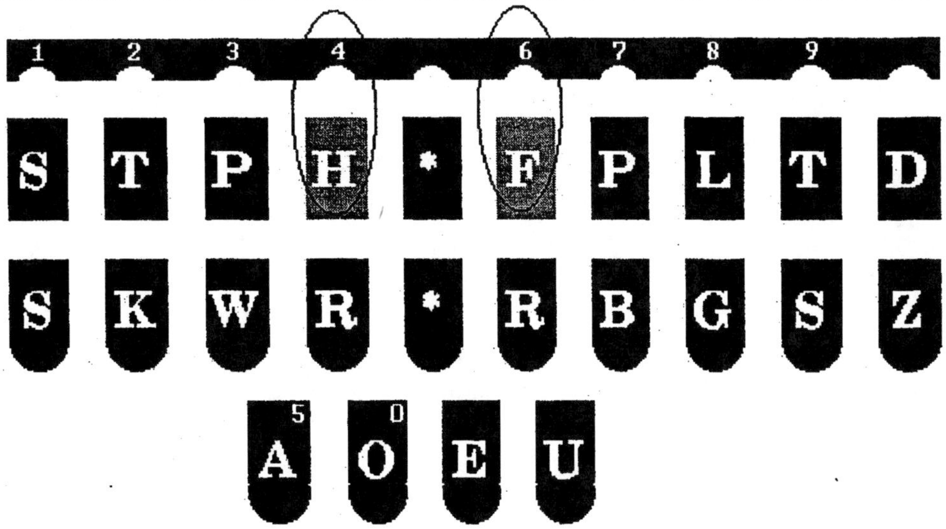

9.5 Write the number 4 with the index finger of the left hand. Hit the crack between the home position H and the number bar, depressing both key and bar at the same time.

☞ _practice the following:_

number 4:

4 4 4 (hp) 4 4 4 (hp) 4 4 4 (hp) 4 4 4 (hp) 4 4 4 (hp) 4 4 4 (hp)
4 4 4 (hp) 4 4 4 (hp) 4 4 4 (hp) 4 4 4 (hp) 4 4 4 (hp) 4 4 4 (hp)
4 4 4 (hp) 4 4 4 (hp) 4 4 4 (hp) 4 4 4 (hp) 4 4 4 (hp) 4 4 4 (hp)

Use the top, flat part of your finger to depress both key and bar at the same time. Remember to hit the numbers so that they appear clear on your paper tape. Hit the numbers and immediately return to the home position.

9.6 Write the number 6 with the index finger of the right hand. Hit the crack between the home position -F and the number bar, depressing both key and bar at the same time.

☞ _practice the following:_

number 6:

6 6 6 (hp) 6 6 6 (hp) 6 6 6 (hp) 6 6 6 (hp) 6 6 6 (hp) 6 6 6 (hp)
6 6 6 (hp) 6 6 6 (hp) 6 6 6 (hp) 6 6 6 (hp) 6 6 6 (hp) 6 6 6 (hp)
6 6 6 (hp) 6 6 6 (hp) 6 6 6 (hp) 6 6 6 (hp) 6 6 6 (hp) 6 6 6 (hp)

Lesson Practice

Learn each position thoroughly so that you do not have to hesitate.

☞ *practice the following:*

initial S-

S S S (hp)	S S S (hp)	S S S (hp)	S S S (hp)	S S S (hp)	S S S (hp)
S S S (hp)	S S S (hp)	S S S (hp)	S S S (hp)	S S S (hp)	S S S (hp)
S S S (hp)	S S S (hp)	S S S (hp)	S S S (hp)	S S S (hp)	S S S (hp)

final -S

-S -S -S (hp)	-S -S -S (hp)	-S -S -S (hp)	-S -S -S (hp)	-S -S -S (hp)
-S -S -S (hp)	-S -S -S (hp)	-S -S -S (hp)	-S -S -S (hp)	-S -S -S (hp)
-S -S -S (hp)	-S -S -S (hp)	-S -S -S (hp)	-S -S -S (hp)	-S -S -S (hp)

initial T-

T T T (hp)	T T T (hp)	T T T (hp)	T T T (hp)	T T T (hp)	T T T (hp)
T T T (hp)	T T T (hp)	T T T (hp)	T T T (hp)	T T T (hp)	T T T (hp)
T T T (hp)	T T T (hp)	T T T (hp)	T T T (hp)	T T T (hp)	T T T (hp)

final -T

-T -T -T (hp)	-T -T -T (hp)	-T -T -T (hp)	-T -T -T (hp)	-T -T -T (hp)
-T -T -T (hp)	-T -T -T (hp)	-T -T -T (hp)	-T -T -T (hp)	-T -T -T (hp)
-T -T -T (hp)	-T -T -T (hp)	-T -T -T (hp)	-T -T -T (hp)	-T -T -T (hp)

number 4:

4 4 4 (hp)	4 4 4 (hp)	4 4 4 (hp)	4 4 4 (hp)	4 4 4 (hp)	4 4 4 (hp)
4 4 4 (hp)	4 4 4 (hp)	4 4 4 (hp)	4 4 4 (hp)	4 4 4 (hp)	4 4 4 (hp)
4 4 4 (hp)	4 4 4 (hp)	4 4 4 (hp)	4 4 4 (hp)	4 4 4 (hp)	4 4 4 (hp)

number 6:

6 6 6 (hp)	6 6 6 (hp)	6 6 6 (hp)	6 6 6 (hp)	6 6 6 (hp)	6 6 6 (hp)
6 6 6 (hp)	6 6 6 (hp)	6 6 6 (hp)	6 6 6 (hp)	6 6 6 (hp)	6 6 6 (hp)
6 6 6 (hp)	6 6 6 (hp)	6 6 6 (hp)	6 6 6 (hp)	6 6 6 (hp)	6 6 6 (hp)

Comprehensive Practice

Write each of the following combinations as follows:

1. Write the individual letter combinations (T/A/B).
2. Write the one-stroke combination of letters that form the word (TAB).
3. Write the home position (STPH-FPLT).
4. Repeat the exercise at least ten times.

☞ *practice the following, writing each combination ten times:*

1. T-A-B / TAB / home position
2. S-AEU-F / SAEUF / home position
3. R-E-D / RED / home position
4. KW-E-G / KWEG / home position
5. P-O-FD / POFD / home position

6. TPH-EU-B / TPHEUB / home position
7. PH-E-D / PHED / home position
8. HR-O-G / HROG / home position
9. K-OE-P / KOEP / home position
10. 4 4 6 6 6 3 2 3 2 7 8 9

11. SKWR-A-R / SKWRAR / home position
12. H-AOEU-D / HAOEUD / home position
13. TKPW-OE / TKPWOE / home position
14. TP-AOE-L / TPAOEL / home position
15. KR-A-PL / KRAPL /home position

16. T-AOEU / TAOEU / home position
17. S-AOE-PBLG / SAOEPBLG / home position
18. R-AOEU-PL / RAOEUPL / home position
19. KW-OE-T / KWOET / home position
20. P-A-L / PAL / home position

21. TPH-E-D / TPHED / home position
22. PH-AEU-BG / PHAEUBG / home position
23. HR-E-G / HREG / home position
24. K-OE-T / KOET / home position
25. 1 2 3 4 6 7 8 9 4 1 8 9 6

26. SKWR-AOE-R / SKWRAOER / home position
27. H-OE-FD / HOEFD / home position
28. PW-O-P / PWOP / home position
29. TK-A-D / TKAD / home position
30. PW-O-B / PWOB / home position

When you are finished writing, take a look at your notes. Are your letters and numbers cleanly written? Did you make any errors? Go back and practice the letters or words where you made a mistake writing until you can write them perfectly.

It is most important that you learn the letters thoroughly before going on to the next lessons.

Additional Practice

Go to the:	Do the following:
Realwrite DrillBook (recommended)..........	Read over and study Drill V (Lessons 9 & 10)
Realwrite NoteBook (optional)..................	Read and transcribe the notes from Exercise C, Lesson 9

UNIT 3
LESSON TEN

Warm up and Review

☞ *Practice each of the following letters and numbers at least ten times each:*

Read the columns from left to right the first time, then try it again, reading from top to bottom.

A	AEU	PW	-B	KR	-SZ	TK	-D	E	AOE
TP	-F	TKPW	-G	H	-FD	EU	AOEU	SKWR	-PBLG
K	-BG	HR	-L	PH	-PL	TPH	-PB	O	OE
P	-P	KW	-LGTS	R	-R	S	-S	T	-T
1	2	3	4	6	7	8	9	7	4
3	2	1	4	7	6	7	3	2	9
8	1	3	6	4	6	9	2	3	1

New Letters U and Long U

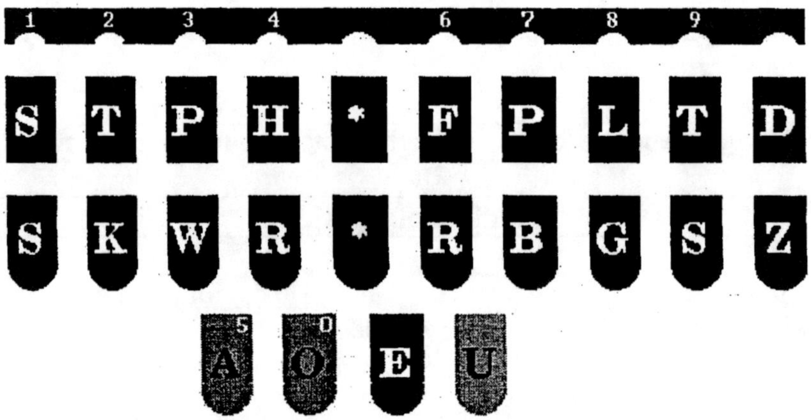

10.1 The vowel U is written using the right thumb to strike the U key.

☞ *practice the following:*

short U-

U U U (hp)	U U U (hp)	U U U (hp)	U U U (hp)	U U U (hp)
U U U (hp)	U U U (hp)	U U U (hp)	U U U (hp)	U U U (hp)
U U U (hp)	U U U (hp)	U U U (hp)	U U U (hp)	U U U (hp)

The "Double-Opposite Rule" for writing long vowels applies to the vowel U.

10. 2 The long U is written by striking the U key with your right thumb together with the AO keys using your left thumb. (Long U = AO + U)

☞ *practice the following:*

long U

AOU AOU AOU (hp) AOU AOU AOU (hp) AOU AOU AOU (hp) AOU AOU AOU (hp)
AOU AOU AOU (hp) AOU AOU AOU (hp) AOU AOU AOU (hp) AOU AOU AOU (hp)
AOU AOU AOU (hp) AOU AOU AOU (hp) AOU AOU AOU (hp) AOU AOU AOU (hp)

New Letters V- and -V

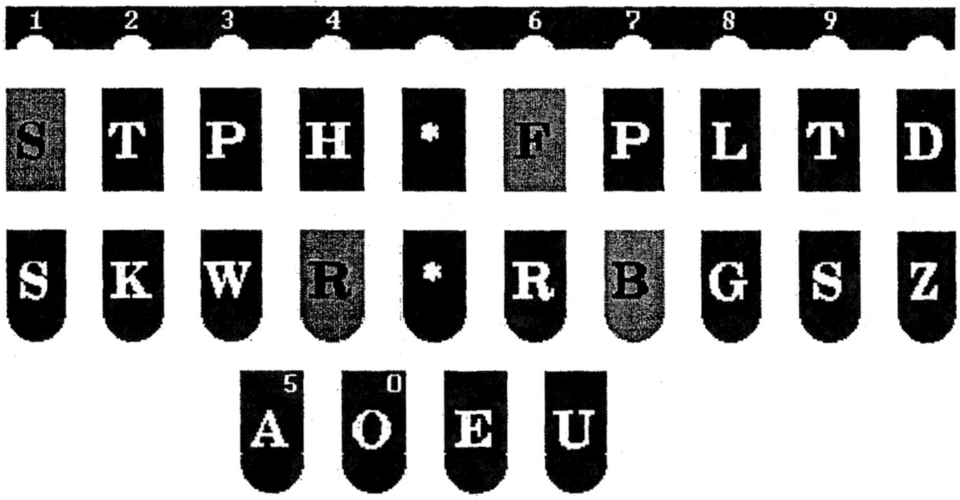

10.3 The initial side V is written by striking the S and R keys together using the small finger and the index finger of the left hand. (V = S + R)

☞ *practice the following:*

initial V-

SR- SR- SR- (hp) SR- SR- SR- (hp) SR- SR- SR- (hp) SR- SR- SR- (hp)
SR- SR- SR- (hp) SR- SR- SR- (hp) SR- SR- SR- (hp) SR- SR- SR- (hp)
SR- SR- SR- (hp) SR- SR- SR- (hp) SR- SR- SR- (hp) SR- SR- SR- (hp)

10.4 The final side -V is written by striking the -F and -B keys together using the index and middle fingers of the right hand. (-V = -F + -B)

☞ *practice the following:*

final -V

-FB -FB -FB (hp) -FB -FB -FB (hp) -FB -FB -FB (hp) -FB -FB -FB (hp)
-FB -FB -FB (hp) -FB -FB -FB (hp) -FB -FB -FB (hp) -FB -FB -FB (hp)
-FB -FB -FB (hp) -FB -FB -FB (hp) -FB -FB -FB (hp) -FB -FB -FB (hp)

New Letters W- and -W

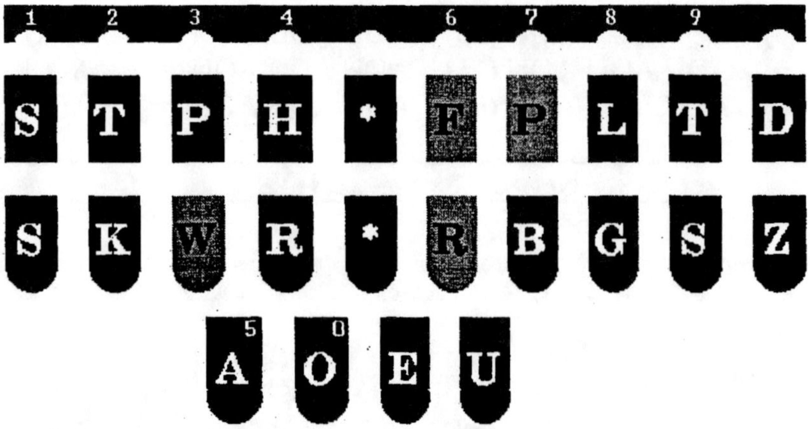

10. 5 The initial side W is written by moving the middle finger of the left hand from the home position P key to the W.

☞ *practice the following:*

initial W-

W W W (hp) W W W (hp) W W W (hp) W W W (hp)
W W W (hp) W W W (hp) W W W (hp) W W W (hp)
W W W (hp) W W W (hp) W W W (hp) W W W (hp)

10. 6 The final side -W is written by striking the -F -R and -P keys together using the index and middle fingers of the right hand. Hit the crack between the -FR keys along with the -P key. (-W = FR + P)

☞ *practice the following:*

final -W

-FRP -FRP -FRP (hp) -FRP -FRP -FRP (hp) -FRP -FRP -FRP (hp)
-FRP -FRP -FRP (hp) -FRP -FRP -FRP (hp) -FRP -FRP -FRP (hp)
-FRP -FRP -FRP (hp) -FRP -FRP -FRP (hp) -FRP -FRP -FRP (hp)

Lesson Practice

Keep your eyes on the keyboard chart until you learn the proper positioning for each new letter.

☞ *practice the following:*

short U

U U U (hp) U U U (hp) U U U (hp) U U U (hp) U U U (hp)
U U U (hp) U U U (hp) U U U (hp) U U U (hp) U U U (hp)
U U U (hp) U U U (hp) U U U (hp) U U U (hp) U U U (hp)

long U

AOU AOU AOU (hp) AOU AOU AOU (hp) AOU AOU AOU (hp) AOU AOU AOU (hp)
AOU AOU AOU (hp) AOU AOU AOU (hp) AOU AOU AOU (hp) AOU AOU AOU (hp)
AOU AOU AOU (hp) AOU AOU AOU (hp) AOU AOU AOU (hp) AOU AOU AOU (hp)

initial V-

SR- SR- SR- (hp) SR- SR- SR- (hp) SR- SR- SR- (hp) SR- SR- SR- (hp)
SR- SR- SR- (hp) SR- SR- SR- (hp) SR- SR- SR- (hp) SR- SR- SR- (hp)
SR- SR- SR- (hp) SR- SR- SR- (hp) SR- SR- SR- (hp) SR- SR- SR- (hp)

final -V

-FB -FB -FB (hp) -FB -FB -FB (hp) -FB -FB -FB (hp) -FB -FB -FB (hp)
-FB -FB -FB (hp) -FB -FB -FB (hp) -FB -FB -FB (hp) -FB -FB -FB (hp)
-FB -FB -FB (hp) -FB -FB -FB (hp) -FB -FB -FB (hp) -FB -FB -FB (hp)

initial W-

W W W (hp) W W W (hp) W W W (hp) W W W (hp)
W W W (hp) W W W (hp) W W W (hp) W W W (hp)
W W W (hp) W W W (hp) W W W (hp) W W W (hp)

final -W

-FRP -FRP -FRP (hp) -FRP -FRP -FRP (hp) -FRP -FRP -FRP (hp)
-FRP -FRP -FRP (hp) -FRP -FRP -FRP (hp) -FRP -FRP -FRP (hp)
-FRP -FRP -FRP (hp) -FRP -FRP -FRP (hp) -FRP -FRP -FRP (hp)

Comprehensive Practice

Write each of the following combinations as follows:

1. Write the individual letter combinations.
2. Write the one-stroke combination of letters.
3. Write the home position.
4. Repeat the exercise at least ten times.

For example, W-A-BG / WABG / home position, and repeat ten times.

☞ *practice the following, write each combination at least ten times:*

1. W-A-BG / WABG / home position
2. SR-OE-T / SROET / home position
3. T-AOEU-T / TAOEUT / home position
4. S-AOU / SAOU / home position
5. R-U-PB / RUPB / home position
6. TP-AOE-T / TPAOET / home position
7. TK-E-FRP / TKEFRP / home position
8. KR-E-FRP / KREFRP / home position
9. PW-U-B / PWUB / home position
10. W-O-FRP / WOFRP / home position

11. KW-OE-T / KWOET/ home position
12 P-AOE-LGTS / PAOELGTS / home position
13. TPH-U-T / TPHUT / home position
14. PH-AOE-PB / PHAOEPB / home position
15. 1 9 2 8 3 7 4 6 9 8 7 6

16. HR-U-BG / HRUBG / home position
17. K-AOU-P / KAOUP / home position
18. SKWR-E-B / SKWREB / home position
19. H-AOE-T / HAOET / home position
20. TKPW-U-PB / TKPWUPB / home position

21. KW-EU-T / KWEUT / home position
22. OE-FD / OEFD / home position
23. HR-O-FB / HROFB / home position
24. SR-A-PB / SRAPB / home position
25. 4 3 2 1 8 2 1 9 7 6 3 2

26. O-FRP / OFRP / home position
27. TKPW-A-G / TKPWAG / home position
28. S-E-T / SET / home position
29. SKWR-E-L / SKWREL / home position
30. W-A-PL / WAPL / home position

When you are finished writing, take a look at your notes. Are your letters cleanly written? Did you make any errors? Go back and practice the letters that you made a mistake writing until you can write them perfectly.

Short Forms and Phrases

☞ *practice the following:*

is	S- (-S)[1]	also	HR-S	that	THA
this	THEU	there	THR-	first	TPEURT
some	SPH-	the	-T	it	T-
they	THE	their	THEUR	take	TAE
not	TPHOT (-PB)[1]	have	SR (-FB)[1]	with	W-
were	WR-	when	WH-	where	WHR-
was	WA	very	SRE	which	WHEU
would	WO	what	WHA	write	WREU
will	HR (-FRP)	between	TWAOEPB	will not	HR-PBT
is it	ST-	is the	S-T	is that	STHA
is this	STHEU	is there	STHR-	is not	S-PB
some of	SPH-F	some are	SPH-R	that the	THAT
about the	PW-T	if the	TP-T	can the	K-T
it is	T-S	did the	TK-T	of the	-FT
will the	HR-T	in the	TPH-T	on the	OT
into the	TPHAOT	are the	R-T	from the	TPR-T
that are	THAR	can the	K-T	cannot	K-PB
they are	THER	there are	THR-R	there is	THR-S
we are	WER	we did	WAED	we have	WEFB
we had	WEFD	we can	WEBG	have you	SRAU

[1]Letters in parenthesis are final side letters that can be used in phrases.

have I	SREU	I have	AOEUFB	with you	WAU
which is	WHEUS	were you	WRAU	was he	WAE
was the	WAT	I will	AOEUFRP	they will	THEFRP
he will	HAEFRP	what is	WHAS	when is	WH-S
where the	WHR-T	when are	WH-R	where are	WHR-R
did you	TKAU[2]	will you	HRAU[2]	if you	TPAU[2]
do you	TKOU[2]	can you	KAU[2]	will you	HRAU[2]

2All phrases that end in the word "you" are written with the AU except for the phrase "do you" (TKOU).

Additional Practice

Go to the:	Do the following:
Realwrite DrillBook (recommended)............	Write and practice Drill V (Lessons 9 & 10)
Realwrite NoteBook (optional).....................	Read and transcribe the notes from Exercise C, Lesson 10 and Drill V

UNIT 3
LESSON ELEVEN

Warm up and Review

Try to write the letters without looking at any keyboard chart. Memorize the positions for each letter so that you can write without hesitation. Read the columns from left to right the first time, then try it again, reading from top to bottom.

☞ *Practice each of the following letters and numbers at least ten times each:*

A	AEU	PW	B	KR	-SZ	TK	-D	E	AOE
TP	-F	TKPW	G	H	-FD	EU	AOEU	SKWR	-PBLG
K	-BG	HR	L	PH	-PL	TPH	-PB	O	OE
P	-P	KW	LGTS	R	-R	S	-S	T	-T
U	AOU	SR	FB	W	-FRP	1	2	3	4
6	7	8	9	9	8	7	6	4	3
2	1	8	6	4	6	9	2	3	1
7	3	4	8	1	2	8	6	9	1

New Letters X- and -X

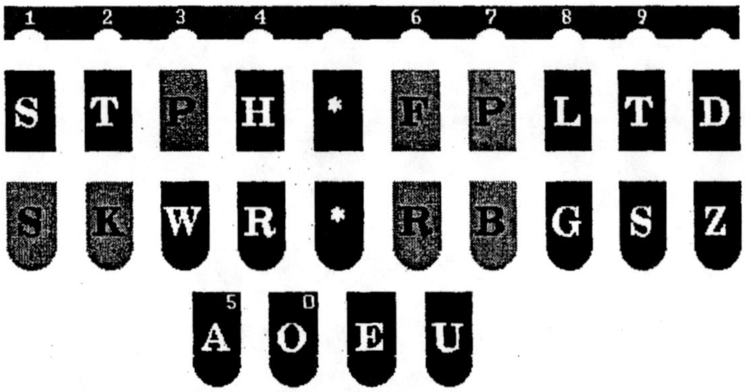

11.1 The initial side X is written by striking the S, K, and P keys together using the small, ring, and middle fingers of the left hand. (X = S + K + P)

☞ *practice the following:*

initial X-

SKP- SKP- SKP- (hp) SKP- SKP- SKP- (hp) SKP- SKP- SKP- (hp)
SKP- SKP- SKP- (hp) SKP- SKP- SKP- (hp) SKP- SKP- SKP- (hp)
SKP- SKP- SKP- (hp) SKP- SKP- SKP- (hp) SKP- SKP- SKP- (hp)

11.2 The final side -X is written by striking the -F, -R, -P, and -B keys together. Strike the crack between the -FR and -PB keys using the index and middle fingers of the right hand.
(-X = -FR + -PB)

☞ *practice the following:*

final -X

-FRPB -FRPB -FRPB (hp) -FRPB -FRPB -FRPB (hp) -FRPB -FRPB -FRPB (hp)
-FRPB -FRPB -FRPB (hp) -FRPB -FRPB -FRPB (hp) -FRPB -FRPB -FRPB (hp)
-FRPB -FRPB -FRPB (hp) -FRPB -FRPB -FRPB (hp) -FRPB -FRPB -FRPB (hp)

New Letters Y- and -Y

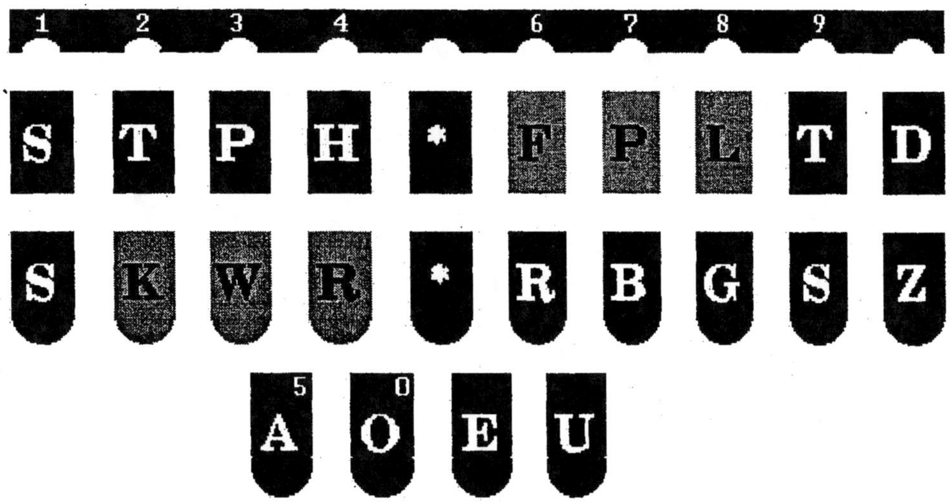

11.3 The initial side Y is written by striking the K, W, and R keys together using the ring, middle and index fingers of the left hand. (Y = K + W + R)

☞ *practice the following:*

initial Y-

KWR- KWR- KWR- (hp) KWR- KWR- KWR- (hp) KWR- KWR- KWR- (hp)
KWR- KWR- KWR- (hp) KWR- KWR- KWR- (hp) KWR- KWR- KWR- (hp)
KWR- KWR- KWR- (hp) KWR- KWR- KWR- (hp) KWR- KWR- KWR- (hp)

11.4 The final side -Y is written by striking the -F, -P, and -L keys together. Strike the keys at the same time using the index, middle, and ring fingers of the right hand. (-Y = -FPL)

☞ *practice the following:*

final -Y

-FPL -FPL -FPL (hp) -FPL -FPL -FPL (hp) -FPL -FPL -FPL (hp)
-FPL -FPL -FPL (hp) -FPL -FPL -FPL (hp) -FPL -FPL -FPL (hp)
-FPL -FPL -FPL (hp) -FPL -FPL -FPL (hp) -FPL -FPL -FPL (hp)

New Numbers 5 and 0

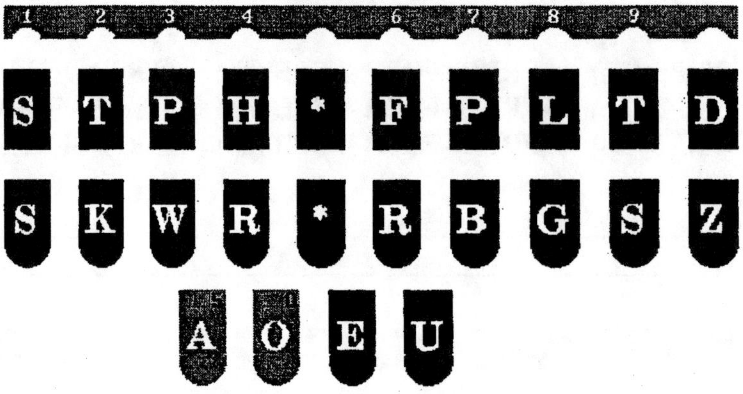

The numbers 5 and 0 are written by using the number bar along with the vowels A or O. It is important to use the number bar with the vowel O to form the zero in order for the computer to read it as a number and not a letter in realtime writing.

11.5 Write the number 5 using the left thumb to strike the vowel A key and the middle finger of the left hand reaching up to strike the number bar, both at the same time.

☞ *practice the following:*

number 5:

5 5 5 (hp)	5 5 5 (hp)	5 5 5 (hp)	5 5 5 (hp)	5 5 5 (hp)	5 5 5 (hp)
5 5 5 (hp)	5 5 5 (hp)	5 5 5 (hp)	5 5 5 (hp)	5 5 5 (hp)	5 5 5 (hp)
5 5 5 (hp)	5 5 5 (hp)	5 5 5 (hp)	5 5 5 (hp)	5 5 5 (hp)	5 5 5 (hp)

11.6 Write the number 0 using the left thumb to strike the vowel O key and the middle finger of the left hand reaching up to strike the number bar, both at the same time.

☞ *practice the following:*

number 0:

0 0 0 (hp)	0 0 0 (hp)	0 0 0 (hp)	0 0 0 (hp)	0 0 0 (hp)	0 0 0 (hp)
0 0 0 (hp)	0 0 0 (hp)	0 0 0 (hp)	0 0 0 (hp)	0 0 0 (hp)	0 0 0 (hp)
0 0 0 (hp)	0 0 0 (hp)	0 0 0 (hp)	0 0 0 (hp)	0 0 0 (hp)	0 0 0 (hp)

Writing Double-Digit Numbers in Sequence

11.7 Write a two-digit number by striking the two numbers together on the keyboard as follows. If the first number is smaller than the second number, write it in one stroke by striking the two numbers together. Write the numbers 10, 20, 30, 40, and 50 in one stroke.

For example, the number 12 is written in one stroke by striking the 1 and 2 keys together. The number 39 is written in one stroke, and so on. The numbers 10, 20, 30, 40, and 50 are all written in one stroke using the same rule. Rules for writing other numbers will be covered in the next lesson.

☞ *practice the following:*

12 13 14 15 16 17 18 19 20 23 24 25 26 27 28 29 30
34 35 36 37 38 39 40 45 46 47 48 49 50 56 57 58 59
67 68 69 78 79 89 1 2 3 4 5 6 7 8 9 0 0

Lesson Practice

☞ *practice the following*

initial X-

SKP- SKP- SKP- (hp) SKP- SKP- SKP- (hp) SKP- SKP- SKP- (hp)
SKP- SKP- SKP- (hp) SKP- SKP- SKP- (hp) SKP- SKP- SKP- (hp)
SKP- SKP- SKP- (hp) SKP- SKP- SKP- (hp) SKP- SKP- SKP- (hp)

final -X

-FRPB -FRPB -FRPB (hp) -FRPB -FRPB -FRPB (hp) -FRPB -FRPB -FRPB (hp)
-FRPB -FRPB -FRPB (hp) -FRPB -FRPB -FRPB (hp) -FRPB -FRPB -FRPB (hp)
-FRPB -FRPB -FRPB (hp) -FRPB -FRPB -FRPB (hp) -FRPB -FRPB -FRPB (hp)

initial Y-

KWR- KWR- KWR- (hp) KWR- KWR- KWR- (hp) KWR- KWR- KWR- (hp)
KWR- KWR- KWR- (hp) KWR- KWR- KWR- (hp) KWR- KWR- KWR- (hp)
KWR- KWR- KWR- (hp) KWR- KWR- KWR- (hp) KWR- KWR- KWR- (hp)

final -Y

-FPL -FPL -FPL (hp) -FPL -FPL -FPL (hp) -FPL -FPL -FPL (hp)
-FPL -FPL -FPL (hp) -FPL -FPL -FPL (hp) -FPL -FPL -FPL (hp)
-FPL -FPL -FPL (hp) -FPL -FPL -FPL (hp) -FPL -FPL -FPL (hp)

number 5:

5 5 5 (hp) 5 5 5 (hp) 5 5 5 (hp) 5 5 5 (hp) 5 5 5 (hp) 5 5 5 (hp)
5 5 5 (hp) 5 5 5 (hp) 5 5 5 (hp) 5 5 5 (hp) 5 5 5 (hp) 5 5 5 (hp)
5 5 5 (hp) 5 5 5 (hp) 5 5 5 (hp) 5 5 5 (hp) 5 5 5 (hp) 5 5 5 (hp)

number 0:

0 0 0 (hp) 0 0 0 (hp) 0 0 0 (hp) 0 0 0 (hp) 0 0 0 (hp) 0 0 0 (hp)
0 0 0 (hp) 0 0 0 (hp) 0 0 0 (hp) 0 0 0 (hp) 0 0 0 (hp) 0 0 0 (hp)
0 0 0 (hp) 0 0 0 (hp) 0 0 0 (hp) 0 0 0 (hp) 0 0 0 (hp) 0 0 0 (hp)

one-stroke numbers:

12 13 14 15 16 17 18 19 20 23 24 25 26 27 28 29 30
34 35 36 37 38 39 40 45 46 47 48 49 50 56 57 58 59
67 68 69 78 79 89 1 2 3 4 5 6 7 8 9 0 0

Comprehensive Practice

Write each of the following combinations as follows:

1. Write the individual letter combinations.
2. Write the one-stroke combination of letters.
3. Write the home position.
4. Repeat the exercise at least ten times.

For example, KWR-U-BG / YUK / home posiition, and repeat ten times.

☞ *practice the following, writing each combination at least ten times:*

1. KWR-U-BG / KWRUBG / home position
2. SKP-A-PL / SKPAPL / home position
3. W-AOEU-PB / WAOEUPB / home position
4. SR-E-T / SRET / home position
5. T-A-FRPB / TAFRPB / home position

6. S-A-FRP / SAFRP / home position
7. R-AOE-R / RAOER / home position
8. KW-AOEU-T / KWAOEUT / home position
9. P-EU-BG / PEUBG / home position
10. 12 3 45 67 89 0 3 5 7

11. TPH-E-L / TPHEL / home position
12. PH-U-PL / PHUPL / home position
13. HR-EU-BG / HREUBG / home position
14. K-OE-T / KOET / home position
15. SKWR-E-T / SKWRET / home position

16. H-U-FD / HUFD / home position
17. H-A-FD / HAFD / home position
18. TKPW-U-PB / TKPWUPB / home position
19. TP-AOEU-F / TPAOEUF /home position
20. TK-O-G / TKOG / home position

21. K-AU-S / KAUS / home position
22. PW-U-FPL / PWUFPL / home position
23. H-A-FPL / HAFPL / home position
24. TKPW-A-S / TKPWAS / home position
25. T-U-FRPB / TUFRPB / home position

26. SKP-EU-T/ SKPEUT / home position
27. S-A-FRP / SAFRP / home position
28. HR-AOU-D / HRAOUD / home position
29. TPH-OE-PB/ TPHOEPB / home position
30. 0 9 6 5 34 18 29 17

31. KWR-U-P / KWRUP / home position
32. W-EU-G / WEUG / home position
33. TP-O-FRPB / TPOFRPB / home position
34. H-EU-FB / HEUFB / home position
35. K-AOU-T / KAOUT / home position

36. KR-E-FRP / KREFRP / home position
37. PW-EU-G / PWEUG / home position
38. PW-O-FPL / PWOFPL / home position
39. 12 35 69 30 26 78 19 24 47
40. 15 39 20 58 79 17 23 46 16

When you are finished writing, take a look at your notes. Are your letters cleanly written? Did you make any errors? Go back and practice the letters that you made a mistake writing until you can write them perfectly.

Additional Practice

Go to the:	Do the following:
Realwrite DrillBook (recommended).........	Read over and study Drill VI (Lessons 11 & 12)
Realwrite NoteBook (optional)..................	Read and transcribe the notes from Exercise C, Lesson 11

UNIT 3
LESSON TWELVE

Warm up and Review

A	AEU	PW	-B	KR	-SZ	TK	D
E	AOE	TP	-F	TKPW	-G	H	-FD
EU	AOEU	SKWR	-PBLG	K	-BG	HR	-L
PH	-PL	TPH	-PB	O	OE	P	-P
KW	-LGTS	R	-R	S	-S	T	-T
U	AOU	SR	-FB	W	-FRP	SKP	-FRPB
KWR	-FPL	1	2	3	4	5	6
7	8	9	0	12	35	69	48
79	15	50	26	37	24	10	49

New Letters Z- and -Z

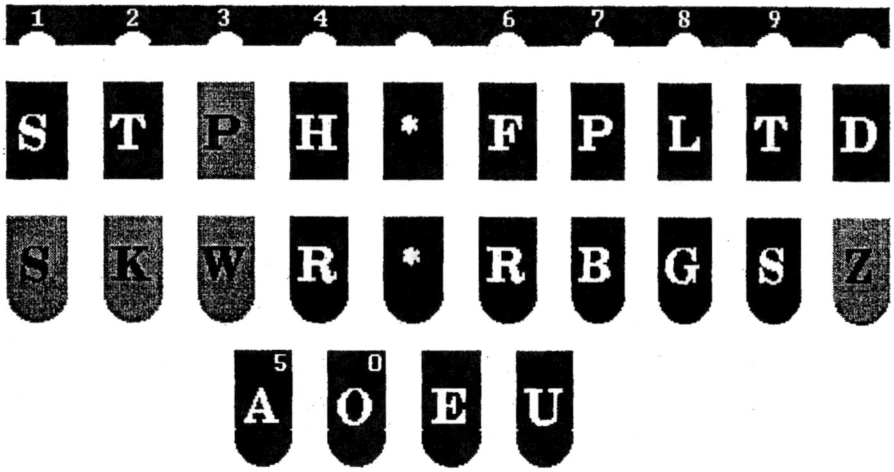

12.1 The initial side Z is written by striking the S, K, P, and W keys together using the small, middle, and ring fingers of the left hand. Strike the S and K keys along with the crack between the P and W, striking all four keys at the same time. (Z = S + K + PW)

☞ *practice the following:*

initial Z-

SKPW SKPW SKPW (hp) SKPW SKPW SKPW (hp) SKPW SKPW SKPW (hp)
SKPW SKPW SKPW (hp) SKPW SKPW SKPW (hp) SKPW SKPW SKPW (hp)
SKPW SKPW SKPW (hp) SKPW SKPW SKPW (hp) SKPW SKPW SKPW (hp)

12.2 The final side -Z is written by moving the small finger of the right hand from the home position -T to the -Z key.

☞ *practice the following:*

final -Z

-Z -Z -Z (hp)	-Z -Z -Z (hp)	-Z -Z -Z (hp)	-Z -Z -Z (hp)	-Z -Z -Z (hp)
-Z -Z -Z (hp)	-Z -Z -Z (hp)	-Z -Z -Z (hp)	-Z -Z -Z (hp)	-Z -Z -Z (hp)
-Z -Z -Z (hp)	-Z -Z -Z (hp)	-Z -Z -Z (hp)	-Z -Z -Z (hp)	-Z -Z -Z (hp)

Writing Double-Digit Numbers out of Sequence

12.3 Write any two-digit number where the first number is greater than the second number by writing the two numbers in Inverse order along with the vowel I (EU) as an indicator. The vowel I (EU) indicates that you read and transcribe the numbers in their inverse order.

This is known as the "Indicator Number Rule," where the I indicates the Inverse. For example, 19 is written in one stroke as 19. The number 91 is written in one stroke as 1 EU 9. Any two numbers that have an I (EU) before, after, or between them are transcribed or read back in their Inverse order.

This rule also holds true for numbers that end in 0 where the first digit is greater than 5. For example, the number 60 is written in one stroke as follows: 0 EU 6. The 0EU6 is read back or transcribed as 60. The I (EU) between the numbers means to read them back inversely.

☞ *practice the following:*

number	Realwrite	number	Realwrite
19	19	91	1EU9
34	34	43	34EU
59	59	95	5EU9
24	24	42	24EU
89	89	98	EU89
50	50	90	0EU9

Now try these numbers using the EU between the numbers to write them in one stroke:

81	72	95	70	42	71	95	90	76	21	43	52	93
61	32	84	74	87	83	91	60	65	51	82	41	92

12.4 To double any single-digit number to form a repeated double-digit number, write the single number along with the vowel I (EU) in the same stroke.

Repeated double-digit numbers are 11, 22, 33, 44, 55, 66, 77, 88, 99.

This is a continuation of the Indicator Number Rule; however, in this case, the vowel I indicates the command to "imitate" or repeat the single number. For example, the number 11 is written 1EU; 99 is written EU9. Any single number with the vowel EU before or after it means to read it back or transcribe it as a double number.

☞ *practice the following:*

number	Realwrite	number	Realwrite
11	1EU	44	4EU
66	EU6	99	EU9

Now try these numbers:

11 22 33 44 55 66 77 88 99 44 77 22 11 99

Number Practice (0 - 99)

You can now write any number from 0 to 99 in one stroke. Remember to use the vowel EU with numbers as an ***I****ndicator to* ***I****nverse the numbers or* ***I****mitate the number.

☞ *practice the following:*

4	6	7	91	34	92	90	13	82	99	32	93	55	31
9	4	0	81	42	72	59	48	92	61	73	41	30	69
5	1	8	12	41	29	73	44	92	58	88	77	32	96
3	2	4	11	45	41	67	94	99	23	83	44	82	75
9	1	7	32	78	87	90	32	88	37	19	55	60	89
4	6	2	33	90	30	70	0	13	45	21	78	99	50

Lesson Practice

☞ *practice the following:*

initial Z-

SKPW SKPW SKPW (hp) SKPW SKPW SKPW (hp) SKPW SKPW SKPW (hp)
SKPW SKPW SKPW (hp) SKPW SKPW SKPW (hp) SKPW SKPW SKPW (hp)
SKPW SKPW SKPW (hp) SKPW SKPW SKPW (hp) SKPW SKPW SKPW (hp)

final -Z

-Z -Z -Z (hp) -Z -Z -Z (hp) -Z -Z -Z (hp) -Z -Z -Z (hp) -Z -Z -Z (hp)
-Z -Z -Z (hp) -Z -Z -Z (hp) -Z -Z -Z (hp) -Z -Z -Z (hp) -Z -Z -Z (hp)
-Z -Z -Z (hp) -Z -Z -Z (hp) -Z -Z -Z (hp) -Z -Z -Z (hp) -Z -Z -Z (hp)

numbers

8	8	1	21	33	22	20	13	80	22	38	23	77	31
2	9	2	81	32	74	62	38	21	61	73	31	30	62
7	1	8	12	31	22	73	33	92	78	88	77	32	26

numbers

3	2	4	11	45	41	25	34	93	23	13	74	12	95
9	1	5	32	51	95	30	39	11	38	13	55	20	18
4	6	2	33	80	30	50	0	13	45	71	51	66	50

Comprehensive Practice

Write each of the following combinations as follows:

1. Write the individual letter combinations.
2. Write the one-stroke combination of letters.
3. Write the home position.
4. Repeat the exercise at least ten times.

For example, SKPW-A-G / ZAG / hp (home position), and repeat ten times.

☞ *practice the following, write each combination at least five times:*

1. SKPW-A-G / SKPWAG / hp
2. SKPW-EU-P/ SKPWEUP / hp
3. KWR-A-BG / KWRABG / hp
4. W-OE / WOE / hp
5. 49 2 93 21 66 27 75

6. TPH-U-T / TPHUT / hp
7. PH-AOEU-L / PHAOEUL / hp
8. HR-A-FRPB / HRAFRPB / hp
9. K-AOE-P/ KAOEP / hp
10. 32 58 91 29 4 5 21 49

11. TK-AOE-R / TKAOER / hp
12. SKPW-A-G / SKPWAG / hp
13. KWR-A-FRP / KWRAFRP / hp
14. H-A-FD / HAFD / hp
15. 32 18 32 74 21 33 4

16. TPH-OE / TPHOE / hp
17. S-AOEU-Z / SAOEUZ / hp
18. HR-O-FB / HROFB / hp
19. PW-A-FD / PWAFD / hp
20. 45 26 34 47 89 25 48

21. T-OE-FRP / TOEFRP / hp
22. S-AEU-PB / SAEUPB / hp
23. R-E-FRPB / REFRPB / hp
24. KW-EU-BG / KWEUBG / hp
25. 9 2 0 20 32 91 43 66 7

26. SKWR-O-B / SKWROB / hp
27. H-U-G / HUG / hp
28. TKPW-OE-T / TKPWOET / hp
29. SKWR-A-Z / SKWRAZ / hp
30. 88 21 92 0 21 30 35 52

31. K-O-FRP / KOFRP / hp
32. PW-A-PL / PWAPL / hp
33. SKWR-A-Z / SKWRAZ / hp
34. SKWR-AOEU-FB / SKWRAOEUFB /hp
35. 32 18 3 90 81 84 21 43

36. H-U-FD / HUFD / hp
37. SKPW-OE-PB / SKPWOEPB / hp
38. SKWR-A-R / SKWRAR / hp
39. K-AOE-L / KAOEL / hp
40. 51 93 22 85 97 71 32 64

Short Forms and Phrases

☞ Learn the following necessary short forms and phrases:

any	TPHEU	eye	EFPL	because	PWAUZ
done	TKOEPB	business	PWEUZ	you	KWROU (U)[1]
your	KWROUR	does	TKUZ		
could you	KAOU	did you	TKAU	will you	HRAU
about you	PWAU	that you	THAU	are you	RAU
had you	HAU	were you	WRAU	from you	TPRAU
would you	WAOU	can you	KAU	what you	WHAU
when you	WHU	with you	WAU	do you	TKOU
you had	UFD	you could	UBGD	you can	UBG
you are	UR	you have	UFB	you did	UD
you will	UFRP				
yes, sir	KWREUR	no, sir	TPHEUR		
yes, ma'am	KWREPL	no ma'am	TPHOPL		

[1]The word "you" is written KWROU; phrases are written using the vowel U.

Additional Practice

Go to the: — Do the following:

Realwrite DrillBook (recommended).............Write and practice Drill VI (Lessons 11 & 12)
Realwrite NoteBook (optional).....................Read and transcribe the notes from Exercise C, Lesson 12 and Drill VI

UNIT 3 REVIEW

Lesson Review

1. Go back to each lesson and learn each new rule thoroughly.
2. Go back to each lesson and write the Lesson Practice.
3. Go back to each lesson and write the Comprehensive Practice.
4. Read back all notes and transcribe a portion of your review.

Review of Writing Rules

9.1 The initial side S is written by striking the home position S with the small finger of the left hand.

9.2 The final side -S is written by striking the -S key, moving the small finger of the right hand from its home position -T down to the letter -S.

9.3 The initial side T is written by striking the home position T with the ring finger of the left hand.

9.4 The final side -T is written by striking the home position -T key with the small finger of the right hand.

9.5 Write the number 4 with the index finger of the left hand. Hit the crack between the home position H and the number bar, depressing both key and bar at the same time.

9.6 Write the number 6 with the index finger of the right hand. Hit the crack between the home position -F and the number bar, depressing both key and bar at the same time.

10.1 The vowel U is written using the right thumb to strike the U key.

10.2 The long U is written by striking the U key with your right thumb together with the AO keys using your left thumb. (Long U = AO + U)

10.3 The initial side V is written by striking the S and R keys together using the small finger and the index finger of the right hand. Strike both keys at the same time. (V = S + R)

10.4 The final side -V is written by striking the -F and -B keys together using the index and middle fingers of the right hand. Strike both keys at the same time. (-V = -F + -B)

10.5 The initial side W is written by moving the middle finger of the left hand from the home position P key to the W.

10.6 The final side -W is written by striking the -F, -R, and -P keys together using the index and middle fingers of the right hand. Hit the crack between the -FR keys along with the -P key. (-W = -FRP)

11.1 The initial side X is written by striking the S, K, and P keys together using the small, ring and middle fingers of the left hand. (X = S + K + P)

11.2 The final side -X is written by striking the -F, -R, -P, and -B keys together. Strike the crack between the -FR and -PB keys using the index and middle fingers of the right hand. (-X = -FR + -PB)

11.3 The initial side Y is written by striking the K, W, and R keys together using the ring, middle, and index fingers of the left hand. (Y = K + W + R)

11.4 The final side -Y is written by striking the -F, -P, and -L keys together. Strike the keys at the same time using the index, middle, and ring fingers of the right hand. (-Y = -FPL)

11.5 Write the number 5 using the left thumb to strike the vowel A key and the middle finger of the left hand reaching up to strike the number bar, both at the same time.

11.6 Write the number 0 using the left thumb to strike the vowel O key and the middle finger of the left hand reaching up to strike the number bar, both at the same time.

11.7 Write a two-digit number by striking the two numbers together on the keyboard as follows. If the first number is smaller than the second number, write it in one stroke by striking the two numbers together. Write the numbers 10, 20, 30, 40, and 50 in one stroke.

12.1 The initial side Z is written by striking the S, K, P, and W keys together using the small, middle, and ring fingers of the left hand. Strike the S and K keys along with the crack between the P and W, striking all four keys at the same time. (Z = S + K + PW)

12.2 The final side -Z is written by moving the small finger of the right hand from the home position -T to the -Z key.

12.3 Write any two-digit number where the first number is greater than the second number by writing the two numbers in Inverse order along with the vowel I (EU). The vowel I (EU) indicates that you read and transcribe the numbers in their inverse order.

12.4 To double any single-digit number to form a repeated double-digit number, write the single number along with the vowel I (EU) in the same stroke. The vowel I (EU) indicates that you imitate or double the single number.

Review DrillBook and NoteBook Applications

1. Review Drills V and VI from the *Realwrite DrillBook* (recommended).
2. Review Exercise C from the *Realwrite NoteBook* (optional).

Unit Evaluation Number Three

Unit Evaluation Number Three will cover all material from the following: *Realwrite LessonBook*, Lessons 9-12; *DrillBook*, Drills V and VI.

UNIT 4
LESSON THIRTEEN

Warm up and Review

☞ *Practice the following letters and numbers at least ten times each:*

Read the columns from left to right, then try it again, reading from top to bottom.

A	AEU	PW	-B	KR	-SZ	TK
-D	E	AOE	TP	-F	TKPW	-G
H	-FD	EU	AOEU	SKWR	-PBLG	K
-BG	HR	-L	PH	-PL	TPH	-PB
O	OE	P	-P	KW	-LGTS	R
-R	S	-S	T	-T	U	AOU
SR	-FB	W	-FRP	SKP	-FRPB	KWR
-FPL	SKPW	-Z	2	8	28	82
92	78	84	0	20	82	47
5	55	2	88	39	45	34
25	77	91	79	32	82	29

Basic Rules for Writing Words

You have already learned that you write in Realwrite what you hear in English, and you have already learned to write one-syllable words by writing the beginning consonant, vowel, and final consonant together in one stroke.

It is important to note that the beginning and ending consonant sounds may be made up of more than one consonant. For example, the word "craft" has the beginning consonants K and R together while the ending consonants are the F and T together.

These are known as multi-consonant sounds and form a very important basic concept for writing English words as they are pronounced. The keyboard is designed in such a way that we can combine consonants on the left and right side to form these multi-consonant sounds. In this lesson you will begin to learn some of these double- and triple-consonant sounds.

In addition, most common words contain more than one syllable; therefore, we need to be able to write words according to their syllabic division. In this lesson, you will also begin to learn some of these words that are more than one syllable.

Realwrite theory is different than other theories in that it is a true realtime writing system. This means that you are going to write a word using phonetics; that is, how the word sounds. You are also going to take into consideration how the word is spelled in English. This is important because this will virtually eliminate all conflicts that may have been present in other shorthand theories.

13.1 Words are written in Realwrite according to the following guidelines: consider how the word sounds, consider how the word is spelled, and apply any special rules or short forms.

Generally speaking:

13.2 Write a one-syllable word in one stroke by writing the beginning consonant sound(s), the vowel sound(s), and the final consonant sound(s) together.

Write the word according to how it sounds. In some instances, words are written the same way they are spelled in English. Some words may be shortened, and some words may require application of special principles to avoid conflicts.

13.3 Write a multi-syllabic word in as many strokes as are necessary to complete the word.

As a general rule, divide the stroking of words by writing as much of the word as possible in the first stroke, followed by a second or subsequent stroke; however, some words are more easily divided by their natural syllabic division.

Some multi-syllabic words may use shortened beginnings and endings to form a one-stroke outline. Some multi-syllabic words may use a one-stroke short form. Some multi-syllabic words may be "slurred" together for writing purposes.

Multi-Consonant Practice (ST-, -BL, -RT, -RM)

Words that contain two or more consonants together before or after a vowel are referred to as multi-consonant words. Multiple consonants are easy to write on the shorthand machine. Beginning in this lesson, you will practice multi-consonant words. Use a comma between each set of multi-consonants.

☞ *practice the following*:

ST- ST- ST- (hp)	ST- ST- ST- (hp)	ST- ST- ST- (hp)	ST- ST- ST- (hp)
ST- ST- ST- (hp)	ST- ST- ST- (hp)	ST- ST- ST- (hp)	ST- ST- ST- (hp)
ST- ST- ST- (hp)	ST- ST- ST- (hp)	ST- ST- ST- (hp)	ST- ST- ST- (hp)
-BL -BL -BL (hp)	-BL -BL -BL (hp)	-BL -BL -BL (hp)	-BL -BL -BL (hp)
-BL -BL -BL (hp)	-BL -BL -BL (hp)	-BL -BL -BL (hp)	-BL -BL -BL (hp)
-BL -BL -BL (hp)	-BL -BL -BL (hp)	-BL -BL -BL (hp)	-BL -BL -BL (hp)
-RT -RT -RT (hp)	-RT -RT -RT (hp)	-RT -RT -RT (hp)	-RT -RT -RT (hp)
-RT -RT -RT (hp)	-RT -RT -RT (hp)	-RT -RT -RT (hp)	-RT -RT -RT (hp)
-RT -RT -RT (hp)	-RT -RT -RT (hp)	-RT -RT -RT (hp)	-RT -RT -RT (hp)

-RPL -RPL -RPL (hp)	-RPL -RPL -RPL (hp)	-RPL -RPL -RPL (hp)
-RPL -RPL -RPL (hp)	-RPL -RPL -RPL (hp)	-RPL -RPL -RPL (hp)
-RPL -RPL -RPL (hp)	-RPL -RPL -RPL (hp)	-RPL -RPL -RPL (hp)

☞ *now practice the following words containing the multi-consonants*:

stick	STEUBG	stuck	STUBG	stop	STOP
stay	STAFPL	state	STAEUT	stain	STAEUPB
table	TAEUBL	double	TKOUBL	trouble	TROUBL[1]
stable	STAEUBL	bubble	PWUBL	rubble	RUBL
art	ART	start	START	part	PART
fort	TPORT	wart	WART	dart	TKART
arm	ARPL	warm	WARPL	harm	HARPL
storm	STORPL	worm	WORPL	germ	SKWRERPL

[1]Notice the word "trouble" has the multi-consonant TR- at the beginning as well as the -BL at the end

Multi-Syllabic Word Practice

You have already learned that multi-syllabic words are written in as many strokes as are necessary to complete the word. In reading these words from the textbook, the slash (/) is used to indicate the separation point between the strokes. Note the footnotes that relate to how some of the word are written.

☞ *practice the following*:

window	WIPB/TKOEFRP	driveway	TKRAOEUFB/WAEFPL[1]
Denver	TKEPB/SRER	outcome	OUT/AE/KPH-[2]
Johnson	SKWROPB/SOEPB[3]	carpet	KAR/PAET[4]
doctor	TKOK/TOR		

<u>The following footnotes are discussed in greater detail in future lessons.</u>

[1]All compound words that end in "way" use the WAEFPL in the second stroke to avoid conflicts

[2]When two single words are joined together to form one word (out and come), the vowels AE are used to form the compound word (outcome) OUT/AE/KPH- (this principal is introduced in a later lesson)

[3]All names that end in "son" use the SOEPB in the second stroke to avoid conflicts

[4]All words that end in "pet" use PAET in the second stroke to avoid conflicts

New Punctuation (Period)

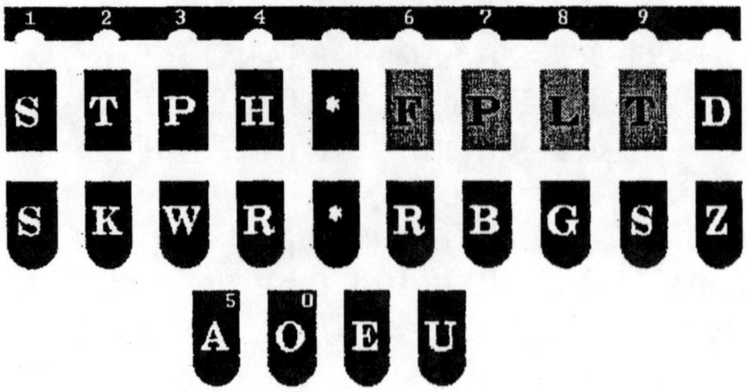

13.4 Write the symbol for the period (.) by combining the final side -F -P -L -T together in one stroke by using the four fingers of the right hand.

Short Forms and Phrases

Remember that the short forms and phrases are used to gain speed. They are used to write multi-syllabic words or phrases in one stroke. Learn them thoroughly so that you can write them without hesitation.

13.5 A short form is a quick way of writing a word. A phrase is a series of words written as one short form. All short forms and phrases have three things in common: they are easily and quickly written on the keyboard, they do not change or violate any theory rules, and they are easily recognized for quick read back and transcription.

☞ *practice the following*

ago	AOG	behalf	PWAF	being	PWAOEG
evidence	EFD	figure	TP-G	gym	TKPWEUPL
half	HAF	passenger	PAEPBG	acknowledge	ABG/TPHOPBLG[1]
apply	PHREU	behind	PWEFD	damage	TKAPBLG
gentleman	SKWRA	gentlemen	SKWRE	identify	AOEUF
Mr.	PHR-				

[1]Notice the two-stroke short form using ABG then the short form for knowledge which is TPHOPBLG.

Lesson Practice

Beginning in this lesson, you will practice writing sentences containing words and short forms you have already learned. You will also be writing some new words. In some cases, the Realwrite outline for new words will be given in parentheses. Practice these words, as well as the entire sentence, until you can write them without any hesitation.

The sentences are divided into groups of 20 words per slash (/). Note that when the slash mark is located between words then they are used for timing purposes by your instructor; however, when they are located between syllables of words, they are used to indicate more than one stroke.

☞ *practice the following:*

1. I hit my (PH-FPL) head on a table that Jill gave me. I hurt my head (HED).

2. My half sis (SEUS) and I / are in a play (PHRAFPL) about a gentleman who ate a worm.

3. The passenger in the cab was able to stop / the car only after he stuck his head out the window.

4. The damage to the car was quite (KWAOEUT) bad but / he had to fix it because he had a date.

5. A gentleman from Denver by (PW-FPL) the name of Ben Johnson / sat in the gym and broke his arm on the carpet.

6. Ben had a wart on his arm but Pat being a doctor / cut it off.

7. A car drove in the driveway. I could not identify him so I stuck my head out the window / to see.

8. I had to apply some wax to the stain on the carpet.

9. John (SKWROPB) had evidence that all / of the gentlemen had a germ.

10. The figure that I came up with was 10 not 20.

11. I will acknowledge / the storm when I see the rain.

12. My part is to start the car race at the stable and stop / it behind the fort.

13. Jill was able to see the outcome of the race.

14. Half of the gentlemen in the / home sat at the table and ate bread and soup.

15. The storm came up and then it was warm. /

Comprehensive Practice

☞ *practice the following:*

1. Practice the initial side alphabet with short vowels, writing a period after each letter.
2. Practice the final side alphabet with long vowels, writing a period after each letter.
3. Practice writing the numbers 1 to 99, writing a period after each number.
4. Practice writing a new word for each letter of the alphabet, writing a period after the word.

Additional Practice

Go to the:	Do the following:
Realwrite DrillBook (recommended).........	Read over and study Drill VII (Lessons 13 & 14)
Realwrite NoteBook (optional)..................	Read and transcribe the notes from Exercise D, Lesson 13

UNIT 4
LESSON FOURTEEN

Warm up and Review

☞ *practice the following:*

1. Practice writing the final side alphabet with the long vowels backwards, Z - A, writing a period after each letter.
2. Practice writing the numbers 99 - 1, writing a period after each number.

New Punctuation (Comma)

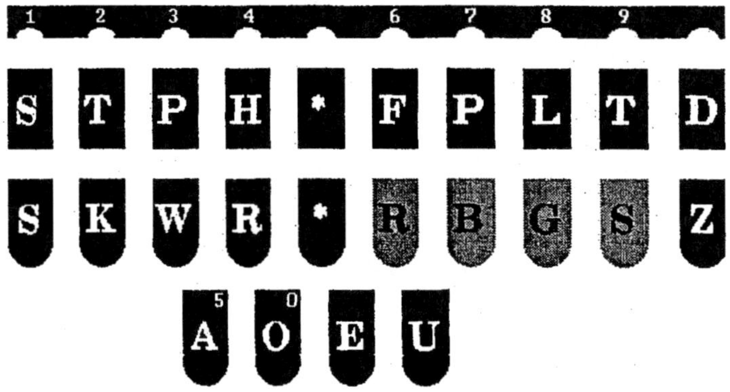

14.1 Write the symbol for the comma (,) by combining the final side -R -B -G -S together in one stroke by using the four fingers of the right hand.

Multi-Consonant Practice (SP-, -FL, -RL)

☞ *practice the following:*

SP- SP- SP- ,	SP- SP- SP- ,	SP- SP- SP- ,	SP- SP- SP- ,
SP- SP- SP- ,	SP- SP- SP- ,	SP- SP- SP- ,	SP- SP- SP- ,
SP- SP- SP- ,	SP- SP- SP- ,	SP- SP- SP- ,	SP- SP- SP- ,

-FL -FL -FL ,	-FL -FL -FL ,	-FL -FL -FL ,	-FL -FL -FL ,
-FL -FL -FL ,	-FL -FL -FL ,	-FL -FL -FL ,	-FL -FL -FL ,
-FL -FL -FL ,	-FL -FL -FL ,	-FL -FL -FL ,	-FL -FL -FL ,

-RL -RL -RL ,	-RL -RL -RL ,	-RL -RL -RL ,	-RL -RL -RL ,
-RL -RL -RL ,	-RL -RL -RL ,	-RL -RL -RL ,	-RL -RL -RL ,
-RL -RL -RL ,	-RL -RL -RL ,	-RL -RL -RL ,	-RL -RL -RL ,

☞ *now practice the following words containing the multi-consonants*:

spare	SPAEUR	spot	SPOT	speak	SPAOEBG
spend	SPEPBD	spud	SPUD	spoke	SPOEBG
raffle	RAFL	waffle	WAFL	baffle	PWAFL
duffel	TKUFL	muffle	PHUFL	ruffle	RUFL
curl	KURL	pearl	PERL	girl	TKPWEURL
whirl	WHEURL	viral	SRAOEURL	barrel	PWAEURL

Multi-Syllabic Word Practice

☞ *practice the following:*

mountain	PHOUPB/TAEUPB[1]	Newport	TPHEFRP/POERT[2]
highway	HAOEUFD/WAEFPL[3]	Cadillac	KAD/HRABG
airplane	AEUR/PHRAEPB[4]		

[1]The second stroke TAEUPB is used to conform with the spelling "tain"
[2]All compound words that end in "port" use the POERT in the second stroke to avoid conflicts
[3]All compound words that end in "way" use the WAEFPL in the second stroke to avoid conflicts
[4]All compound words that end in "plane" use the PLAEPB in the second stroke to avoid conflicts

Short Forms and Phrases

☞ *learn and practice the following short forms thoroughly*:

actual	TAOUL	almost	HR-PL	along	HR-G
aloud	HR-D	already	HR-RD	remain	R-PL
among	PHOPBG	applicable	PHREUBG	balance	PWAL[1]
basic	PWEUBG	became	PWAEUPL	become	PW-BG
detail	TKAEL[2]	emergency	PH-PBLG	enclose	KHR-

[1]Note the word "ball" is written PWAUL and the word "bawl" is written PWAFRPL
[2]In a later lesson you will learn to write the word Dale with a capital D as follows KEU-RBGS/TKAEL

Writing Words Spelled with "oo"

14.2 Write the vowels A and O together for any word that is spelled in English with a "double o" regardless of how the word is pronounced.

☞ *practice the following:*

too	TAO	pool	PAOL	door	TKAOR	moor	PHAOR
cool	KAOL	fool	TPAOL	moon	PHAOPB	poor	PAOR
book	PWAOBG	cook	KAOBG	look	HRAOBG	took	TAOBG

Writing Words with "au" Sound and Spelled with "awl" or "aw"

14.3 Write the vowels AU for any words that contain the "au" sound. If a word is spelled "alk" in English, write AUBG. If a word is spelled "all" in English, write AUL.

☞ *practice the following:*

talk	TAUBG	walk	WAUBG	stalk	STAUBG
all	AUL	stall	STAUL	tall	TAUL
hall	HAUL	mall	PHAUL	fall	TPAUL

14.4 Write AWL (AFRPL) for all words that are spelled "aul" or "awl" in English as in "haul," "maul," and "bawl."

☞ *practice the following:*

haul	HAFRPL	maul	PHAFRPL	bawl	PWAFRPL
drawl	TKRAFRPL	shawl	SHAFRPL		

14.5 Write AW (AFRP) for words that are spelled with the "aw" regardless of how the word is pronounced as in raw, law and saw.

☞ *practice the following:*

law	HRAFRP	saw	SAFRP	awe	AFRP
paw	PAFRP	raw	RAFRP	jaw	SKWRAFRP

Writing Words that Begin with Vowel in Final Stroke

In writing words that contain more than one syllable, it is important to distinguish between syllables that could be identically written at the beginning of a word and the end of a word. For example, the "er" is written at the beginning of the word "error" and at the end of the word "lesser." To make a distinction, for all words have a second stroke beginning with a vowel, a silent "y" is written in the final stroke before a vowel to "attach" the ending to the beginning of the word.

14.6 Write all multi-syllabic words that begin with a vowel in the final stroke by using the KWR- (initial Y-) before the vowel.

☞ *practice the following:*

Ozark	OEZ/KWRARBG	message	PHES/KWRAPBLG
Dennis	TKEPB/KWREUS	coffee	KOF/KWRAOE
rabbit	RAB/KWREUT		

Consider the second stroke Y- (KWR-) as a silent "attacher" and read only the vowel and consonants.

Lesson Practice

☞ *practice the following sentences until you can write them without hesitation:*

1. The spare tire will not fit the car, so I will get a cab.

2. A mountain is almost like a / big hill, but a spot in the road became as big as the mountain as we drove by.

3. I became / mad when Paul and Lee ate the pie that I already set on the table.

4. The pool door was stuck, / so I had to spend the time at home with Dale and Kim.

5. The law is the law is the / law, and among those applicable is the law that a Cadillac is a car.

6. I saw the emergency in / detail, so I can also tell you what I saw.

7. I spoke in awe as the tall girl became a / ruffle, not a muffle.

8. Kim and I took Jake and Jim to the highway in an airplane made for 4, / almost.

9. He will enclose the leaf in the duffel bag, but it is for you to see that the ball / is put in, too.

10. A girl in my school with a curl had a viral germ, but it is almost / gone.

11. Paul got sick from a waffle he ate from a barrel he won in a raffle in Newport./

Comprehensive Practice

Practice the following so that you can write the numbers quickly and accurately. Write a comma (-RBGS) after each number.

☞ *practice the following:*

28,	32,	48,	39,	10,	32,	33,	48,	21,	40,	32,	98,	10,
19,	87,	63,	50,	55,	2,	7,	29,	82,	1,	99,	28,	41,
32,	91,	0,	20,	88,	76,	67,	39,	2,	91,	32,	22,	87,
12,	21,	73,	9,	10,	15,	85,	58,	77,	92,	27,	4,	71,
44,	67,	91,	0,	3,	44,	95,	76,	90,	32,	56,	99,	22,
32,	39,	84,	92,	48,	37,	30,	55,	39,	15,	5,	7,	5,
45,	89,	9,	43,	55,	94,	84,	34,	90,	88,	32,	5,	43,
9,	3,	18,	29,	32,	53,	66,	69,	43,	90,	0,	4,	98,
44,	87,	73,	65,	31,	11,	22,	98,.	51,	40,	10,	7,	0,

Additional Practice

Go to the: Do the following:

Realwrite DrillBook (recommended)............Write and practice Drill VII (Lessons 13 & 14)
Realwrite Notebook (optional)......................Read and transcribe the notes from Exercise D, Lesson 14 and Drill VII

UNIT 4
LESSON FIFTEEN

WARM UP AND REVIEW

☞ *practice the following short forms:*

about	did	if	of	had	he
can	will	come	am	little	do
does	in	on	been	into	even
many	only	could	help	are	from
or	after	before	under	number	is
some	also	the	that	it	this
they	there	their	take	first	have
very					

New Punctuation (Question Mark)

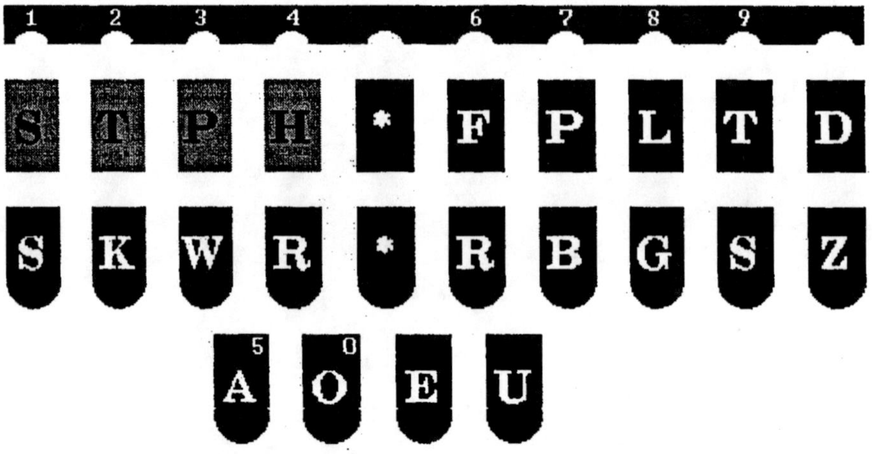

15.1 Write the symbol for the question mark (?) by combining the initial side S- T- P- H- together in one stroke by using the four fingers of the left hand.

Short Forms and Phrases

☞ *practice the following short forms:*

envelope	TPHEFL	family	TPAPL	follow	TPOL
gallon	TKPW-L	how many	HOUPL	immediate	PHAOED
important	PORPBT	item	T-PL	labor	HRAEUB
legal	HRAOEL	major	PHAEUPBLG	done	TKOEPB

Multi-Consonant Practice (SH-, -PT, -RK)

☞ *practice the following:*

SH- SH- SH- ,	SH- SH- SH-,	SH- SH- SH-,	SH- SH- SH-,
SH- SH- SH-,	SH- SH- SH-,	SH- SH- SH-,	SH- SH- SH-,
SH- SH- SH-,	SH- SH- SH-,	SH- SH- SH-,	SH- SH- SH-,

-PT -PT -PT,	-PT -PT -PT,	-PT -PT -PT,	-PT -PT -PT,
-PT -PT -PT,	-PT -PT -PT,	-PT -PT -PT,	-PT -PT -PT,
-PT -PT -PT,	-PT -PT -PT,	-PT -PT -PT,	-PT -PT -PT,

-RBG -RBG -RBG ,	-RBG -RBG -RBG,	-RBG -RBG -RBG,
-RBG -RBG -RBG,	-RBG -RBG -RBG,	-RBG -RBG -RBG,
-RBG -RBG -RBG,	-RBG -RBG -RBG,	-RBG -RBG -RBG,

☞ *now practice the following words*:

ship	SHEUP	shore	SHOR	sure	SHAOUR
show	SHOEFRP	shut	SHUT	shy	SHFPL
apt	APT	opt	OPT	kept	KEPT
dark	TKARBG	spark	SPARBG	work	WORBG
cork	KORBG	jerk	SKWRERBG	mark	PHARBG

Multi-Syllabic Word Practice

☞ *practice the following words*:

hardware	HARD/WAER[1]	message	PHES/KWRAPBLG[2]
carport	KAR/POERT[1]	airport	AEUR/POERT
Newark	TPHEFRP/KWRARBG[2]	Filmore	TPEUL/PHOER[1]

[1] Use the WAER for compound words that end in "ware," use the POERT for compound words that end in "port," and use the PHOER for compound words that end in "more."

[2] Remember the attaching silent Y- for any last stroke that begins with a vowel.

Punctuation Marks and Special Symbols (Paragraph Symbol)

You have learned three punctuation marks in Realwrite theory thus far:

-FPLT for the period (.)   -RBGS for the comma (,)   STPH- for the question mark (?)

These are the only punctuation marks that require a special designation. All other punctuation marks and symbols will follow a basic rule.

15.2 Punctuation marks and special symbols (other than the period, comma, and question mark) are formed by using the initial side to write a one- or two-letter designation together with the final side -RBGS.

The initial side letters are always letters that relate to the punctuation mark itself. For example, the colon is written K-RBGS; the semicolon is written S-RBGS and so on. You will learn these punctuation marks in later chapters.

15.3 The symbol to indicate the beginning of a new paragraph is written PA-RBGS. Write this designation once to indicate the beginning of a new paragraph.

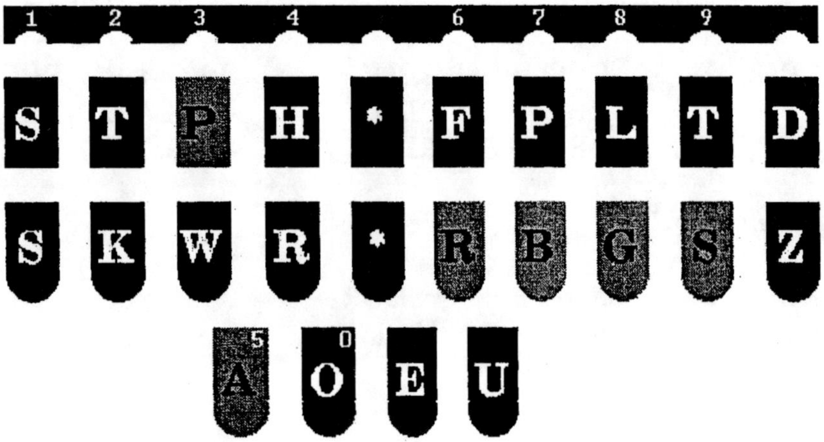

Lesson Practice

☞*Practice the following.* *(Remember to put a comma where needed, a period or question mark at the end of the sentence, and a paragraph symbol between each paragraph—even if they are not dictated.)*

I will see the family at the airport. I will be there. I am a passenger on the airplane, but / I do not have the time the plane will leave the airport. Some man said it will leave at 4, / but Ned said it was 7. If you find out, tell me.

I got a message on my hardware to / come to the Newark carport to pick up my car. Mr. Filmore said that you have an envelope for me / that will give me 1 gallon of gas. How many men are there? I will follow what you said, but / I have important legal work to do.

It was dark on the ship, so we went on shore. I am / sure that you and your wife can come to my home to see my work. My major is important to / me. I labor and I labor, but I do not seem to get too far. Do you work hard? My / family said I work too hard, but I am not about to give up. I like to work hard. /

Comprehensive Practice

Practice the Lesson Practice sections for lessons 13 - 15. When you are finished read your notes out loud, comparing them to the textbook or to the tape. Note your errors. Practice these sections again until you can write them without any errors.

Additional Practice

Go to the:	Do the following:
Realwrite DrillBook (recommended).........	Read over and study Drill VIII (Lessons 15 & 16)
Realwrite NoteBook (optional)...................	Read and transcribe the notes from Exercise D, Lesson 15

UNIT 4
LESSON SIXTEEN

Warm up and Review

☞ *practice the following phrases:*

about a	did a	if a	had a	he did	did he
he had	had he	if he	I can	can I	will I
I am	can a	did I	I did	had I	I had
had a	if a	will he	can he	could I	I could
could he	he could	is it	is the	is that	is this
is there	is not	some of	some are	that the	it is
about the	did the	if the	of the	can the	will the
in the	on the	into the	are the	from the	that are
can the	cannot	they are	there are	there is	will not

Writing Words with "ou" Sound and Spelled with "ow," "aw," or "ew"

The following set of rules apply to words that contain the "ou" sound. How the words are written depends on whether or not the they can be written in one stroke using the "ow." Learn each rule so you can write the words quickly.

16.1 Write OW (OFRP) for words that contain the "short o" sound before the "w" as in now (TPHOFRP) and pow (POFRP).

☞ *practice the following:*

now	TPHOFRP	vow	SROFRP	ow	OFRP
how	HOFRP	cow	KOFRP	bow	PWOFRP

16.2 Write OEW (OEFRP) for words that contain the "long o" sound before the "w" as in row (ROEFRP) and owe (OEFRP).

☞ *practice the following:*

tow	TOEFRP	row	ROEFRP	owe	OEFRP
low	HROEFRP	mow	PHOEFRP	sow	SOEFRP

16.3 Write OUN (OUPB) for words that end in "own" as in town (TOUPB) and drown (TKROUPB).

☞ *practice the following:*

town	TOUPB	crown	KROUPB	frown	TPROUPB
gown	TKPWOUPB	drown	TKROUPB	clown	KHROUPB

16.4 Write AW (AFRP) or EW (EFRP) for words that end in "aw" or "ew" regardless of the pronunciation as in law (HRAFRP) and few (TPEFRP).

☞ *practice the following*:

law	HRAFRP	awe	AFRP	saw	SAFRP
raw	RAFRP	jaw	SKWRAFRP	paw	PAFRP
few	TPEFRP	dew	TKEFRP	sew	SEFRP
new	TPHEFRP	pew	PEFRP	view	SREFRP

16.5 Write AUN (AUPB) for words that end in "awn" as in dawn (TKAUPB), lawn (HRAUPB), and fawn (TPAUPB).

☞ *practice the following:*

lawn	HRAUPB	dawn	TKAUPB	fawn	TPAUPB
yawn	KWRAUPB	pawn	PAUPB	drawn	TKRAUPB

Writing Words with "oi" Sound and Spelled with "oy" or "ay"

16.6 Write OY (OFPL) for words that are spelled "oy" as in toy (TOFPL) and boy (PWOFPL).

☞ *practice the following*:

boy	PWOFPL	toy	TOFPL	roy	ROFPL
joy	SKWROFPL	soy	SOFPL	coy	KOFPL

16.7 Write AY (AFPL) for words that are spelled "ay" as in say (SAFPL) and ray (RAFPL).

☞ *practice the following*:

ray	RAFPL	say	SAFPL	day	TKAFPL
bay	PWAFPL	may	PHAFPL	nay	TPHAFPL
gay	TKPWAFPL	way	WAFPL	pay	PAFPL

16.8 Write OI (OEU) for one-syllable words that are spelled with "oi" as in oil (OEUL) and toil (TOIL).

☞ *practice the following*:

toil	TOEUL	oil	OEUL	soil	SOEUL
foil	TPOEUL	coil	KOEUL	boil	PWOEUL

16.9 Write OI (OEU) for two-syllable words that have the sound of "oi" regardless of their spelling as in royal (ROEUL) and lawyer (HROEUR).

☞ *practice the following*:

lawyer HROEUR	royal ROEUL	loyal	HROEUL

Numbers in Hundreds

You have learned to write the number 0 - 99 in one stroke. Now you will write words greater than 99.

16.10 For numbers beginning with 100, write the first digit(s) in the first stroke followed by the short form H-PBD for hundred. Numbers dictated after the hundreds are written using the same rules you learned for writing 1 - 99.

For example:

100	1/H-PBD	129	1/H-PBD/29
900	9/H-PBD	992	9/H-PBD/2EU9
1600[1]	16/H-PBD	1651	16/H-PBD/15EU

[1] dictated as "sixteen hundred," not "one thousand six hundred"

For numbers containing a zero (0) between two integers, it is necessary to write the zero in a separate stroke. For example:

505	5/H-PBD/0/5	909	9/H-PBD/0/9
303	3/H-PBD/0/3	1,404	1/TH-Z/4/H-PBD/0/4

☞ *practice the following*:

473	298	500	7200	9800	332	600
550	123	999	4400	1221	777	921

Short Forms and Phrases

☞ *practice the following*:

manage	PH-G	manufacture	PH-F	maybe	PHAEUB
mechanic	PH-BG	do you	TKOU	member	PHEB
memo	PHEPL				

Multi-Consonant Practice (SM-, -FT)

☞ *practice the following*:

SPH- SPH- SPH- ,	SPH- SPH- SPH- ,	SPH- SPH- SPH- ,	SPH- SPH- SPH- ,
SPH- SPH- SPH- ,	SPH- SPH- SPH- ,	SPH- SPH- SPH- ,	SPH- SPH- SPH- ,
SPH- SPH- SPH- ,	SPH- SPH- SPH- ,	SPH- SPH- SPH- ,	SPH- SPH- SPH- ,

-FT -FT -FT ,	-FT -FT -FT ,	-FT -FT -FT ,	-FT -FT -FT ,
-FT -FT -FT ,	-FT -FT -FT ,	-FT -FT -FT ,	-FT -FT -FT ,
-FT -FT -FT ,	-FT -FT -FT ,	-FT -FT -FT ,	-FT -FT -FT ,

☞ *now practice the following words*:

small	SPHAUL	smart	SPHART	smoke	SPHOEBG
smack	SPHABG	smut	SPHUT	smile	SPHAOEUL
aft	AFT	craft	KRAFT	lift	HREUFT
raft	RAFT	rift	REUFT	soft	SOFT

Multi-Syllabic Word Practice

☞ *practice the following words*:

software	SOFT/WAER	compute	KOPL/PAOUT
Robert	ROB/KWRERT	Wilson	WEUL/SOEPB[1]
pencil	PEPBS/KWREUL[2]	briefcase	PWRAOEF/KAES[1]

[1]Use SOEPB for compound words that end in "son," use KAES for compound words that end in "case."
[2]The word pencil is an example of a word that could be written two different ways, depending upon how the word is pronounced or heard. Both ways are correct PEPB/SEUL or PEPBS/KWREUL

Lesson Practice

☞ *practice the following. Remember to put a comma where needed, a period or question mark at the end of the sentence, and a paragraph symbol between each paragraph:*

John and Joe will manage a small shop that will deal with the manufacture of software. Their shop will show / you how to compute. Now is the time to send a memo to them, and maybe you can join them. /

Do you need a pencil to write the memo? If there is a gentleman by the name of Robert Wilson / there, he will show you how to get oil from the soil.

He will also show you what to put / into your briefcase when you have to go to the shop, but he will not tell you what to do. / The art of his craft is to show you, but not tell you, so that you can do it.

Do / you smoke? If you do, can you stop? If you can stop, will you stop now? If you will, you / are smart. It is a joy not to have to smoke when I am at work.

Comprehensive Practice

Practice the Lesson Practice sections for the Lessons 13 - 16. When you are finished, read your notes out loud and compare them to the textbook or tape. Note your errors.

Additional Practice

Go to the:	Do the following:
Realwrite DrillBook (recommended)........	Write and practice Drill VIII (Lessons 15 & 16)
Realwrite NoteBook (optional).................	Read and transcribe the notes from Exercise D, Lesson 16 and Drill VIII

UNIT 4 REVIEW

Lesson Review

1. Go back to each lesson and learn each new rule thoroughly.
2. Go back to each lesson and write the Lesson Practice.
3. Go back to each lesson and write the Comprehensive Practice.
4. Read back all notes and transcribe a portion of your review.

Review of Writing Rules

13.1 Words are written in Realwrite according to the following guidelines: consider how the word is sounded, consider how the word is spelled, and apply any special rules or short forms

13.2 Write a one-syllable word in one stroke by writing the beginning consonant sound(s), the vowel sound(s), and the final consonant sound(s) together.

13.3 Write a multi-syllabic word in as many strokes as are necessary to complete the word.

13.4 Write the symbol for the period (.) by combining the final side -F -P -L -T together in one stroke by using the four fingers of the right hand.

13.5 A short form is a quick way of writing a word. A phrase is a series of words written as one short form. All short forms and phrases have three things in common: they are easily and quickly written on the keyboard, they do not change or violate any theory rules, and they are easily recognized for quick read back and transcription.

14.1 Write the symbol for the comma (,) by combining the final side -R -B -G -S together in one stroke by using the four fingers of the right hand.

14.2 Write the vowels A and O together for any word that is spelled in English with a "double o" regardless of how the word is pronounced.

14.3 Write the vowels AU for any words that contain the "au" sound. If a word is spelled "alk" in English, write AUBG. If a word is spelled "all" in English, write AUL.

14.4 Write AWL (AFRPL) for all words that are spelled "aul" or "awl" in English as in "haul," "maul," and "bawl."

14.5 Write AW (AFRP) for words that are spelled with the "aw" regardless of how the word is pronounced, as in raw, law, and saw.

14.6 Write all multi-syllabic words that begin with a vowel in the final stroke by using the KWR- (initial Y-) before the vowel.

15.1 Write the symbol for the question mark (?) by combining the initial side S- T- P- H- together in one stroke by using the four fingers of the left hand.

15.2 Punctuation marks and special symbols (other than the period, comma, and question mark) are formed by using the initial side to write a one- or two-letter designation together with the final side -RBGS.

15.3 The symbol to indicate the beginning of a new paragraph is written PA-RBGS. Write this designation once to indicate the beginning of a new paragraph.

16.1 Write OW (OFRP) for words that contain the "short o" sound before the "w" as in now (TPHOFRP) and pow (POFRP).

16.2 Write OEW (OEFRP) for words that contain the "long o" sound before the "w" as in row (ROEFRP) and owe (OEFRP).

16.3 Write OUN (OUPB) for words that end in "own" as in town (TOUPB) and drown (TKROUPB).

16.4 Write AW (AFRP) or EW (EFRP) for words that end in "aw" or "ew" regardless of the pronunciation as in law (HRAFRP) and few (TPEFRP).

16.5 Write AUN (AEPB) for words that end in "awn" as in dawn (TKAUPB), lawn (HRAUPB), and fawn (TPAUPB).

16.6 Write OY (OFPL) for words that are spelled "oy" as in toy (TOFPL) and boy (PWOFPL).

16.7 Write AY (AFPL) for words that are spelled "ay" as in say (SAFPL) and ray (RAFPL).

16.8 Write OI (OEU) for one-syllable words that are spelled with the "oi" as in oil (OEUL) and toil (TOIL).

16.9 Write OI (OEU) for two-syllable words that have the sound of "oi" regardless of their spelling as in royal (ROEUL) and lawyer (HROEUR).

16.10 For numbers beginning with 100, write the first digit(s) in the first stroke followed by the short form H-PBD for hundred. Numbers dictated after the hundreds are written using the same rules you leaned for writing 1 - 99.

Review DrillBook and NoteBook Applications

1. Review Drills VII and VIII from the *Realwrite DrillBook* (recommended).
2. Review Exercise D from the *Realwrite NoteBook* (optional).

Unit Evaluation Number Four

Unit Evaluation Number Four will cover all material from the following: *Realwrite LessonBook*, Lessons 13-16; *DrillBook*, Drills VII and VIII.

UNIT 5
LESSON SEVENTEEN

Warm up and Review

☞ *practice the following:*

489	934	122	901	400	550	623
891	90	329	812	777	921	921
123	456	789	987	654	321	912
439	232	555	193	92	55	501
582	0	290	463	339	101	376
444	89	92	9	4	84	101
23	219	91	60	30	999	506

Writing Words that Begin with Sound of "ch" or "sh"

17.1 Write words that begin with the sound of "ch" by using the initial side KH together with the remainder of the word.

☞ *practice the following:*

KH- KH- KH- , KH- KH- KH- , KH- KH- KH- , KH- KH- KH- ,
KH- KH- KH- , KH- KH- KH- , KH- KH- KH- , KH- KH- KH- ,
KH- KH- KH- , KH- KH- KH- , KH- KH- KH- , KH- KH- KH- ,

☞ *now practice the following:*

chart	KHART	chat	KHAT	chief	KHAOEF
cheat	KHAOET	cheer	KHAOER	chip	KHEUP
chime	KHAOEUPL	Chet	KHET	chin	KHEUPB

17.2 Write words that begin with the sound of "sh" by using the initial side SH together with the remainder of the word.

☞ *practice the following:*

SH- SH- SH- , SH- SH- SH- , SH- SH- SH- , SH- SH- SH- ,
SH- SH- SH- , SH- SH- SH- , SH- SH- SH- , SH- SH- SH- ,
SH- SH- SH- , SH- SH- SH- , SH- SH- SH- , SH- SH- SH- ,

☞ *now practice the following:*

sheer	SHAOER	shirt	SHEURT	shine	SHAOEUPB
ship	SHEUP	shore	SHOR	sham	SHAPL
shed	SHED	chef	SHEF		

Realtime Writing Considerations (Prefixes and Suffixes; AE Rule)

Realtime writing is taking down in shorthand what is being said, and then having it instantly transcribed on a monitor through the use of a computer. In order for the computer to recognize differences between beginnings and endings of words, it is necessary to make distinctions in writing patterns, especially between prefixes (beginning of a word) and suffixes (ending of a word). In Realwrite, there are some rules for writing the beginning and ending of words. Generally speaking:

17.3 The prefixes or beginnings of words are written with a short vowel.

For example, prevent would be written PRE/SREPBT; remit would be written RE/PHEUT; aloud would be written A/HROUD.

The rule regarding the ending of words can be divided into two different parts. You have already learned the rule regarding final strokes that begin with a vowel. For review, this rules said: **Write all multi-syllabic words that begin with a vowel in the final stroke by using the KWR- (initial Y-) before the vowel.**

For word endings that can be considered as derivatives; that is, an extention of the root word, we use a rule called the "attached ending" rule. A derivative may be the forming of the plural or past tense of a word. Or it may be the changing of the ending, for example, adding "ing" or "ly" to the root word.

17.4 Write the AE (attached ending) for all derivatives or changes in endings of root words that require a second or subsequent stroke. The AE is combined with the ending in the last stroke.

This is the general rule to follow regarding word endings. In the subsequent chapters you will learn specific rules regarding the different applications. Listed below is your first application.

Writing the Past Tense of Words

Generally, the past tense of a word is formed in English by adding a "d" or "ed" to the end of the word. In Realwrite theory, if the D can be added in the same stroke, do so. If a second or subsequent stroke is needed, write the AE (attached ending) in front of the D (AED). Some writers find it easier to consistently write the AED in the last stroke, even if it can be combined in the first stroke. This is a personal preference that you will decide as you mature in your writing ability.

However, if a one-syllable word ends in "n" you must always write the AED in the second stroke to form the past tense. This is done in order to avoid confusion with such words as "band" and "banned" or "find" and fined."

For example:

play	PHRAFPL	played	PHRAFPLD or PHRAFPL/AED
deed	TKAOED	deeded	TKAOED/AED
band	PWAPBD	banned	PWAPB/AED
find	TPAOEUPBD	fined	TPAOEUPB/AED

17.5 Write the past tense of a word by adding a -D in the same stroke when possible. If the -D cannot be added in the same stroke, use the "attached ending" rule and write AED in the second or last stroke.

☞ *practice the following*:

timed	TAOEUPLD[1]	lived	HREUFB/AED[2]	mixed	PHEUFRPBD
ruled	RAOULD	opted	OPT/AED	raided	RAEUD/AED
zapped	SKPWAPD	voted	SROET/AED	jailed	SKWRAEULD
vowed	SROFRPD	seated	SAOET/AED	razzed	RAZ/AED
stayed	STAFPLD[2]				

[1]The AED in the second stroke option will not be mentioned for all words unless it is recommended.
[2]Although the -D can be written in the same stroke, it may be easier to write the final -D in a separate stroke. Either way is correct. Both forms can be entered into your realtime dictionary.

17.6 If a one-syllable word ends in "n" do not add the -D in the same stroke; form the past tense by writing the AED in a second stroke.

☞ *practice the following:*

sinned	SEUPB/AED	fined	TPAOEUPB/AED	ruined	RAOUPB/AED

17.7 If the spelling of a word changes by forming the past tense, the new outline should reflect the new spelling.

☞ *practice the following*:

tried	TRAOEUD	died	TKAOEUD	fried	TPRAOEUD	cried	KRAOEUD

Short Forms and Phrases

☞ *practice the following until you can write them without hesitation:*

minimum	PHEUPL	most	PHO	must	PHU
month	PHOPB	monthly	PHOL	perform	PEFRPL (PEFRM)
possible	POB	public	PUBL	again	TKPWEPB
alone	HR-PB	sister	STER	used	AOUDZ

New Punctuation (Colon and Semicolon)

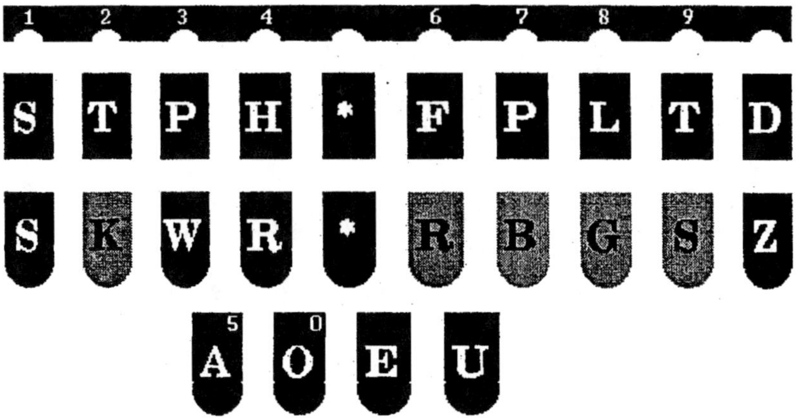

17.8 Write K-RBGS to designate the colon whenever it is dictated or as needed within dictation.

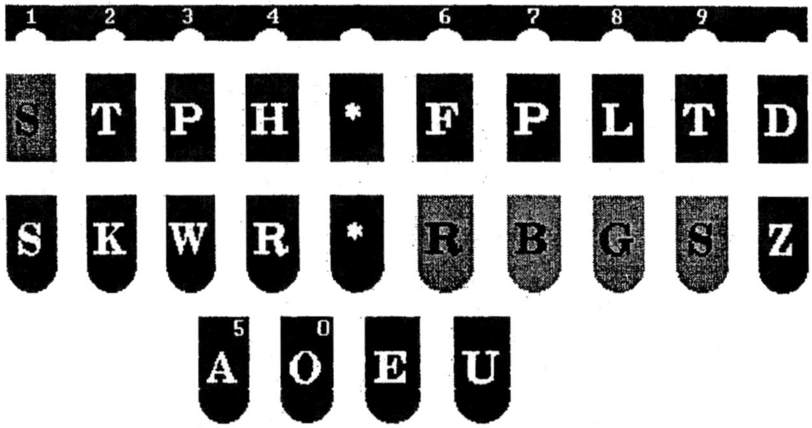

17.9 Write S-RBGS to designate the semicolon whenever it is dictated or as needed within dictation

Lesson Practice

☞ *practice the following:*

It is important to do my work again and again. Most of the work I do can be put on / a chart. The sheer (SHAOER) joy of being able to write is nice. If I perform well, then I shine. My / monthly goal (TKPWOEL) is to do the minimum; the minimum is this: I must do all that is possible to be / sure I can write.

Jan lived in a house that was near a shop that sold (SOELD) moonshine (PHAOPB/AE/SHAOEUPB). It was raided / and all of the men were jailed. They were zapped when the law came, but they vowed to never (TPHEFR) do / it again. The court ruled that they could go, but they had to pay a fine to the chief; the / fine was big. For most of the men, it was not possible to pay. Those (THOEZ) who could not pay stayed / in jail for over (SRER) a month.

When I cheer, I cheer alone. When I chat, I chat with all. I / am sure that if you opted to chat with me, you would enjoy it. Ken enjoyed (EPB/SKWROFPL/AED) the little chat we / had; Don did not. He said his shirt was too sheer for the chef to wear (WAEUR), so he was razzed / by the chief chef.

A chime told us it was time to eat; John had been seated for 1 hour / (HOUR); he cheated. Any cheat should (SHOULD) have to start again; and that is what John had to do.

Comprehensive Practice

☞ *Practice this section until you can write it without any errors. Remember to read your notes and circle your errors:*

I am sure that I hit my head on the table, because it hurt my head. Most of the pain / was due (TKAOU) to a headache (HED/KWRAEUBG). I have been alone now for 1 month; but Jane will stop by to see / if I need any food.

My sister (STER) and I are in a play about a gentleman (SKWRA) who drove a cab. / The passenger in the cab was able to stop the car only after he stuck his head out the window. / The damage to the car was quite bad, but he had to fix it alone.

A gentleman from Denver by / the name of Nick Johnson (SKWROPB/SOEPB) put in a new carpet in the gym. The public said it looked bad, so / they had to tear it all out and start again. After Mr. Johnson put it back in, he vowed not / to do any more work for a month.

Additional Practice

Go to the:	Do the following:
Realwrite DrillBook (recommended)........	Read over and study Drill IX (Lessons 17 & 18)
Realwrite NoteBook (optional)..................	Read and transcribe the notes from Exercise E, Lesson 17

UNIT 5
LESSON EIGHTEEN

Warm up and Review

☞ *practice the following:*

stick	stuck	stop	stay	state	stain	able
table	double	stable	moble	rubble	art	fort
wart	dart	arm	warm	harm	storm	worm
germ	ago	behalf	being	evidence	figure	gym
half	passenger	apply	behind	damage	identify	girl
gentlemen	gentleman	acknowledge	564	934	921	76
333	0	80	4	89	93	291
674	982	23	41	937	921	94
832	775	30	90	73	1	22

Writing the Plural of Words

18.1 The plural of a word is formed by writing the final -Z in the same stroke. If a word ends in -T, write the final -TS in the same stroke to form the plural. If a word ends in -S or -Z, write the AEZ (attached ending) in the last stroke.

The final -Z that is used to form the plural of a word is a phonetic rule and is not be confused with the "Z rule" for forming contractions that you will learn in a later lesson. Some writers prefer to use the AEZ in the last stroke to form the plural of all words; this is a personal option.

☞ *practice the following plurals of words:*

bars	PWARZ	doors	TKAORZ	coats	KOETS
seats	SAOETS	houses	HOUS/AEZ	roses	ROEZ/AEZ
girls	TKPWEURLZ	boys	PWOFPLZ	tabs	TABZ
cars	KARZ	cans	KAPBZ	pads	PADZ
passes	PAS/AEZ	kisses	KEUS/AEZ	fizzes	TPEUZ/AEZ

Numbers in Thousands

18.2 For numbers beginning with 1,000, write the first digit in the first stroke followed by the short form TH-Z for thousand. Write the hundreds digit followed by the short form H-PBD. Numbers dictated after the hundreds are written using previous number rules.

For example:

1,000	1/TH-Z	1,129	1/TH-Z/1/H-PBD/29
19,000[1]	19/TH-Z	7,992	7/TH-Z/9/H-PBD/2EU9
1,600[2]	1/TH-Z/6/H-PBD	1,651	1/TH-Z/6/H-PBD/15EU

[1] since the comma is not pronounced, the comma is not written; the comma will be translated
[2] dictated as "one thousand six hundred," not "sixteen hundred"; 1600 (sixteen hundred) would be written 16/H-PBD

It is important to note that the short form TH-Z is used only with a number. To write the words "a thousand cars," write the word thousand using the short form THOUS.

☞ *practice the following:*

34,556	36,778	94,223	55,679	12,214	12,003	5,600
58,221	92,834	9,234	1,000	2,001	91,190	9,342
45,678	92,315	34,546	72,436	55,555	64,000	1,234
45,600	23,182	34,298	99,321	79,395	50,309	5,678
87,390	78,342	21,905	8,345	81,832	9,213	92,345
6,821	21,902	32,193	44,592	2,000	15,551	4,440

Multi-Consonant Combinations (SK-, -RMZ, -BLZ, -RTS)

☞ *practice the following:*

SK- SK- SK-	SK- SK- SK-	SK- SK- SK-
SK- SK- SK-	SK- SK- SK-	SK- SK- SK-
SK- SK- SK-	SK- SK- SK-	SK- SK- SK-
-RPLZ -RPLZ -RPLZ	-RPLZ -RPLZ -RPLZ	-RPLZ -RPLZ -RPLZ
-RPLZ -RPLZ -RPLZ	-RPLZ -RPLZ -RPLZ	-RPLZ -RPLZ -RPLZ
-RPLZ -RPLZ -RPLZ	-RPLZ -RPLZ -RPLZ	-RPLZ -RPLZ -RPLZ
-BLZ -BLZ -BLZ	-BLZ -BLZ –BLZ	-BLZ -BLZ -BLZ
-BLZ -BLZ -BLZ	-BLZ -BLZ -BLZ	-BLZ -BLZ -BLZ
-BLZ -BLZ -BLZ	-BLZ -BLZ -BLZ	-BLZ -BLZ -BLZ
-RTS -RTS -RTS	-RTS -RTS -RTS	-RTS -RTS -RTS
-RTS -RTS -RTS	-RTS -RTS -RTS	-RTS -RTS -RTS
-RTS -RTS -RTS	-RTS -RTS -RTS	-RTS -RTS -RTS

☞ *now practice the following words:*

scare	SKAEUR	sky	SKFPL	skip	SKEUP
arms	ARPLZ	farms	TPARPLZ	storms	STORPLZ
tables	TAEUBLZ	bubbles	PWUBLZ	stables	STAEUBLZ
arts	ARTS	parts	PARTS	darts	TKARTS

Short Forms and Phrases

☞ *practice the following:*

begin	TKPWEUPB	began	TKPWAPB	begun	TKPW-PB
bottom	PW-PL	could not	KOPBT	did not	TK-PB
do not	TKAOPB	does not	TKUPBT	automobile	AOBL
bill	PW-L	billed	PW-LD	bills	PW-LZ
does	TKUZ	does the	TKUT		

Lesson Practice

☞ *Practice the following paragraphs until you can write them without any hesitation; make sure that you look at your notes and circle your errors:*

There were 376 cars that were there to start the race. One automobile did not have any / gas when it started; it was not able to begin. Once (WUPBS) the race began, 205 of the cars / began to skip the pit stop because the sky looked (HRAOBGD) like a storm was near (TPHAOER).

A rock (ROBG) star (STAR) was on / stage (STAEUPBLG) after the race. The name (TPHAEUPL) of the band (PWAPBD) was Roses and Kisses. They played (PHRAFPLD) loud (HROUD), but all of the / boys and girls loved their sound. Some could not hear (HAER); some did not want to hear; and some cannot hear / to this day. All of the seats were sold out; all of the doors were ajar (A/SKWRAR).

John and Jill own / (OEPB) 2 farms and 6 stables. They have 400 cows (KOFRPZ) and 300 horses (HORS/AEZ). They had 14 cans of pop / on their tables. The pop had bubbles and fizzes, but they did not have any ice. They cannot have the / pop because they have no ice (AOEUSZ). John said he would run to the store and buy some ice, but he could / not get his car started. Jill rode her bike to the store; but on the way home the bottom / of the bag fell (TPEL) out, and she spilled (SPEULD) ice all over the road.

Comprehensive Practice

☞ *Practice the following so that you can write quickly and accurately. When you are finished you're your notes out loud, comparing them to the textbook or tape. Note your errors.*

The figure for the damage to the automobile was 16,732. I did not have that / so I had to sell some of my cars. I sold my Cadillac for 24,000. I used that / to pay off my bill at the store.

Ken had a flat tire on his cab. He tried to use / (AOUZ) the spare tire, but it would not fit. He was on a mountain when he got the flat, so he / could not move (PHOFB) at all. It was an emergency; he did not want to stay because there was a storm / in the sky. Why (WH-FPL) did it have to start to rain?

By the time he got the car fixed and / got home, he was sick. The doctor told him that he had to stay in bed for 1 month; but / he could not. He got out of bed after 1 day and got a bad cold. He is now home / in bed for 6 more months (PHOPBZ), and he cannot go to work at all.

He could not pay his bills, / but they did not put him in jail. The gentleman at the store told him to pay when he can. / He was sure he could pay them monthly, but he could not. What would you do? Would you put him / in jail? Would you fire him if you were his boss? Would you hire him if he could not work? / What would / you do?

Additional Practice

Go to the: — Do the following:

Realwrite DrillBook (recommended).......Write and practice Drill IX (Lessons 17 & 18)
Realwrite NoteBook (optional).................Read and transcribe the notes from Exercise E, Lesson 18 and Drill IX

UNIT 5
LESSON NINETEEN

Warm up and Review

☞ practice the following:

spare	spend	raffle	duffel	curl	whirl
spot	spud	waffle	muffle	pearl	viral
speak	spoke	baffle	ruffle	girl	barrel
actual	aloud	among	basic	detail	almost
already	applicable	became	emergency	along	also
balance	become	enclose	too	all	law
pool	saw	door	tall	awe	Paul

Writing Words that end in "y" or "ey"

19.1 For words that end in "y" or "ey" where a second or subsequent stroke is necessary, write AEFPL (attached ending) in the final stroke.

☞ practice the following:

happy	HAP/AEFPL	sunny	SUPB/AEFPL	spicy	SPAOEUS/AEFPL
honey	HOPB/AEFPL	scary	SKAEUR/AEFPL	baby	PWAEUB/AEFPL
soapy	SOEP/AEFPL	jiffy	SKWREUF/AEFPL	marry	PHAEUR/AEFPL

Writing Words that end in "ee" or "ie"

19.2 For words that end in "ee" (double e) or "ie" write KWRAOE (silent "y") in the final stroke.

☞ practice the following:

movie PHOFB/KWRAOE   Bobbie PWOB/KWRAOE   committee KPHEUT/KWRAOE

New Punctuation (Apostrophe)

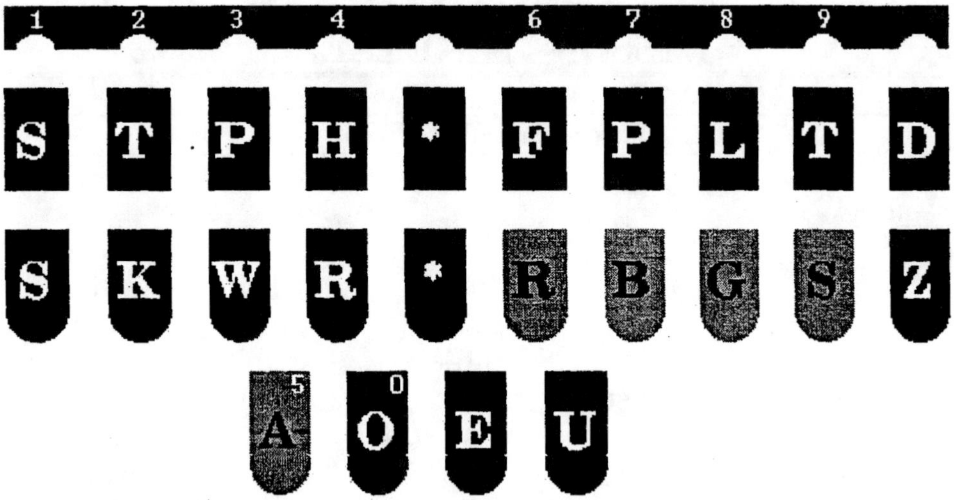

19.3 Write the A-RBGS to designate the apostrophe (') whenever it is dictated or as needed within dictation.

Writing Words that end in "ing"

19.4 The final -G is used for all words that end in "ing." When possible, write the -G in the same stroke. If the -G cannot be written in the same stroke, write the AEG (attached ending) in the last stroke.

☞ *practice the following:*

crying[1]	KRFPL/AEG	caring	KAEURG	boating	PWOET/AEG
digging	TKEUG/AEG	walking	WAUBG/AEG	talking	TAUBG/AEG
dancing	TKAPBS/AEG	moving[1]	PHOFB/AEG	dying[1]	TKFPLG
jogging	SKWROG/AEG	trying	TRFPLG	loving[1]	HROFBG

[1]For some words it is easier to write the AEG in the last stroke. Some writers use the AEG in the last stroke for all words. This is a personal preference.

19.5 If a one-syllable word ends in "n" do not add the -G in the same stroke; form the "ing" ending by writing the AEG in a second stroke.

running	RUPB/AEG	sinning	SEUPB/AEG	winning	WEUPB/AEG
dining	TKAOEUPB/AEG	spinning	SPEUPB/AEG	sunning	SUPB/AEG

Short Forms and Phrases

☞ *practice the following:*

engine	TPH-G	engineer	TPH-PBLG	enough	TPHUF
examine	SKP-PB	example	SKP-PL	finance	TP-PBS
financial	TP-PBL	general	SKWR-PB	gentle	SKWREPBL
had not	H-PB	handle	HAPBL	income	TPH-BG
carry	K-R	carrying	K-RG		

Lesson Practice

☞ *Practice the following. Practice the words and short forms presented in the lesson, as well as the words given in (parentheses):*

Little Bobbie started school (SKAOL) this morning (PHORPBG). She did not want to go to school. She could choose (KHAOZ) two of the / following (TPOLG): dancing, running, walking, jogging, talking, digging, or boating. She wanted (WAPBT/AED) to examine all of them, but she did not / have the time. She chose (KHOEZ) to follow her sister and took jogging and running.

The soapy baby sat in the / tub (TUB). She was so happy because (PWAUZ) it was sunny. She was carrying a baby doll (TKOL) that she got wet. She / began crying because the doll had not dried (TKRAOEUD). She cried (KRAOEUD) and she cried and she cried. It was scary. She / stopped (STOPD) crying after I told (TOELD) her a story (STOR/AEFPL) about a bunny (PWUPB/AEFPL) named (TPHAUEPL/AED) honey (HOPB/AEFPL).

I am moving to Pittsburgh (PITS/PWURG) in a / month. When I move, I like to set an example. I like to have enough time to handle all of / my financial worries (WOR/KWRAOEZ). My income is not great (TKPWRAEUT); I cannot handle my finances; I need help. A committee of general / financial people (PAOEPL) will help me in a jiffy. They are a caring group (TKPWRAOUP) of people.

Luke (HRAOUBG) said that he wants / (WAPBTS) to be an engineer on an engine when he grows (TKPWROEFRPZ) up. He loves (HROFBZ) engines. He will make a good engineer / because he likes trying hard.

Comprehensive Practice

☞ *practice the following*

I will see you and your family to the airport. What time did you say you will be there? I / am a passenger on the airplane, but I do not have the time the plane will leave the airport. Some / man said it would leave at 6, but Ted said it would leave at 9. If you find out, tell / me.

I got a message to come to the carport to pick up my car. Mr. Johnson said that you / have an envelope for me that will give me 5 gallons of gas for free. How many men are there? / I will follow what you said, but I have important legal work to do.

It was dark on the ship / that I was on, so we all went to the shore. I am sure that you and your wife can / come to my home to see my work. My major is important to me. I work hard; my labor is / my love. Do you work hard? Do you love your labor? My friend (TPREPBD) said I work too hard, but I / am not about to give up.

Additional Practice

Go to the:	Do the following:
Realwrite DrillBook (recommended).........	Read over and study Drill X (Lessons 19 & 20)
Realwrite Notebook (optional)..................	Read and Transcribe the notes from Exercise E, Lesson 19

UNIT 5
LESSON TWENTY

Warm up and Review

☞ *practice the following:*

ship	shore	sure	show	shut	shy	apt
opt	kept	dark	spark	work	cork	jerk
mark	envelope	family	follow	gallon	item	legal
how many	important	identify	immediate	important	labor	major

Flagged Alphabet (All Capitals)

In realtime writing for computer transcription the initial side of the alphabet is used to write the individual letters. The final side of the alphabet is used to "flag" the alphabet for the computer. There are various occasions when you will want to write the individual letters of the alphabet in different ways. Flagged alphabets are also used in "finger spelling," a technique used by captioners to spell out any word in English by writing the individual steno letters on the keyboard.

For example, there will be times when you will want all capital letters (A, B, C); or there will be times when you will want all small letters (a, b, c); and there will be times when you will want the letters "stitched" for letter-by-letter spelling (A-B-C).

All of the letter combinations on the final side of the keyboard contain the -F, which stands for "flagged" or "function." The letters used in combination with the -F indicate the particular function you want the computer to perform when transcribing. For example, to transcribe all capitals, the command -FK (function capital) will be used; to transcribe all small letters, the command -FS (function small) will be used.

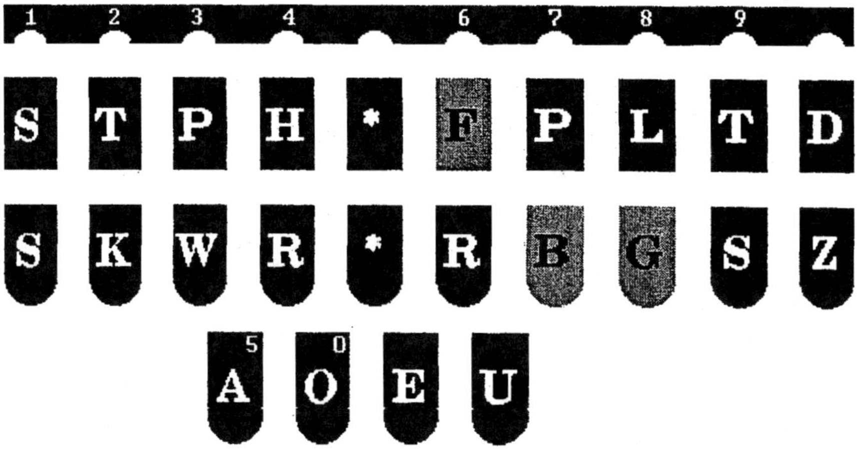

20.1 To write the alphabet in all capital letters, write the alphabetic letter on the initial side of the keyboard along with the final side -FBG (FK). Each letter requires the -FBG.

☞ *practice the following:*

alphabet	Realwrite	alphabet	Realwrite
A	A-FBG	N	TPH-FBG
B	PW-FBG	O	O-FBG
C	KR-FBG	P	P-FBG
D	TK-FBG	Q	KW-FBG
E	E-FBG	R	R-FBG
F	TP-FBG	S	S-FBG
G	TKPW-FBG	T	T-FBG
H	H-FBG	U	U-FBG
I	EU-FBG	V	SR-FBG
J	SKWR-FBG	W	W-FBG
K	K-FBG	X	SKP-FBG
L	HR-FBG	Y	KWR-FBG
M	PH-FBG	Z	SKPW-FBG

Writing Possessives of Words

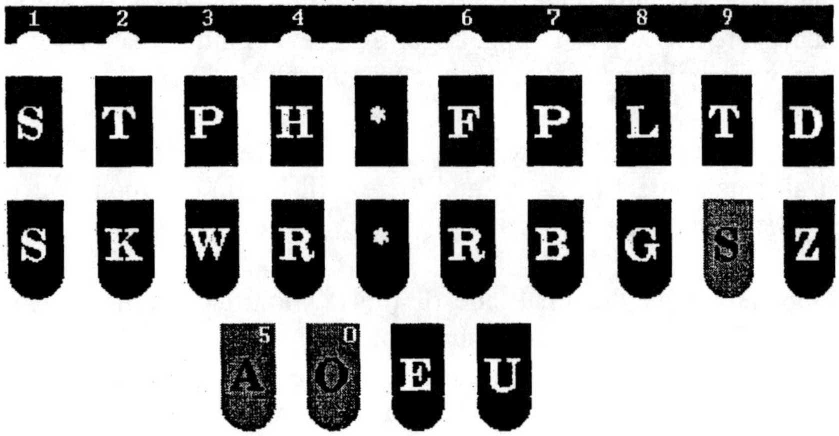

20.2 Write the AOS in the last stroke to form the 's for any word, letter, or number. Singular possessives are formed by writing AOS ('s) in the last stroke. Plural possessives are formed by writing the A-RBGS (s') in the last stroke.

For example:

the cat's house	-T/KAT/AOS/HOUS
there are 30 R's	THR-R/30/R-FBG/AOS
all the boys' hats	AUL/-T/BOFPLZ/A-RBGS/HATS

☞ *practice the following:*

cat's	KAT/AOS	Jeff's	SKWREF/AOS	Joe's	SKWROE/AOS
day's	TKAFPL/AOS	John's	SKWOPB/AOS	Ted's	TED/AOS
year's	KWRAOER/AOS	cab's	KAB/AOS	tree's	TRAOE/AOS
boys'	PWOFPLZ/A-RBGS	girls'	TKPWEURLZ/A-RBGS	men's	PHEPBZ/AOS

Short Forms and Phrases

☞ *practice the following until you can write them without hesitation:*

minute	PHEUPB	money	PHE	national	TPHAL
necessary	TPHE	neglect	TPHEG	neighbor	TPHAEUB
notify	TPH-F	object	OB	personal	PERPBL
until	TPH-L	afternoon	TPAOPB	accompany	A/K-P
argue	ARG	around	ARPBD	arrange	ARPBG

Lesson Practice

☞ *practice the following. Remember to practice the words in (parentheses) so you can write them quickly. Also learn your short forms and phrases thoroughly.*

Lee and Jeff began to argue about who (WHO) was going to pay the bill. The object of the arguing (ARG/AEG) was / not the money, but they argued (ARGD) because Lee forgot (TPOER/TKPWOT) to notify Jeff that the waitress (WAEUT/RES) had spilled coffee (KOF/KWRAOE) all over / the table. Before they paid (PAEUD) the bill, a neighbor came in and told them that a man from Dallas (TKAL/KWRAS) was / going to pay the bill for them.

It was around 12 noon (TPHAOPB) when the waitress told them that they had / to pay up or it would be necessary to call her boss. Jeff's bill was around 42; Lee's was / around 74. Before the time was up, they paid the bill and walked out the door.

On the way / out, they saw an object on the floor (TPHRAOR). They did not realize (RAOELZ) what it was until they got real close / (KHROES). It appeared (A/PAOERD) to be a personal note from Jill to Ron. They did not read the note, but picked it / up and gave it to the waitress. She notified (TPH-FD) Jill that the note was there. Jill arranged (ARPBGD) to have a / neighbor pick it up around 6.

The object of the story is: do not neglect to pay your bill. If / you do, you will be in deep trouble (TROUBL). Do you pay your bills (PW-LZ)? If not, are you sure you can buy the necessary / books (PWAOBGZ) without paying (PAFPLG)? Until you pay, the national debt (TKET) will be high (HAOEUFD).

Comprehensive Practice

☞ *Practice the following so that you can write quickly and accurately. When you are finished, take your notes and read them aloud, comparing them to the textbook. If you have any errors, circle them in your steno notes.*

John and Joe will manage a small shop that deals in the manufacture of software. Their shop will show you / how to compute (KPAOUT) numbers (PWERZ). Now is the time to send a memo to them, and maybe you can join them. / They will arrange for you to meet them at the shop.

Do you need a pen or pencil (PEPBS/KWREUL) to write / the memo? If there is a gentleman by the name of Robert Wilson there, he will show you how to get / oil from the soil. Mr. (PHR-) Wilson's (WEUL/SOEPB/AOS) home is Tampa (TAPL/PA), but he lives in Newark.

He will also show you / what to put (PUT) into your briefcase when you have (SR-) to go to the shop, but he will not tell you / what to do. He said to put about 75 pens and 45 pencils in your case so that / you will not run out. The art of his craft is to show you, but not tell you, so that / you can do it.

Do you have any figures that will not compute? Do you have any numbers that will / compute? Jeff's figures never seem to work out; while Jan's numbers always (AULZ) do. It is a joy when the figures / all come out right. Do your figures work?

Additional Practice

Go to the:	Do the following:
Realwrite DrillBook (recommended)............	Write and practice Drill X (Lessons 19 & 20)
Realwrite NoteBook (optional)....................	Read and transcribe the notes from Exercise E, Lesson 20 and Drill X.

UNIT 5 REVIEW

Lesson Review

1. Go back to each lesson and learn each new rule thoroughly.
2. Go back to each lesson and write the Lesson Practice.
3. Go back to each lesson and write the Comprehenesive Practice.
4. Read back all notes and transcribe a portion of your review.

Review of Writing Rules

17.1 Write words that begin with the sound of "ch" by using the initial side KH together with the remainder of the word.

17.2 Write words that begin with the sound of "sh" by using the initial side SH together with the remainder of the word.

17.3 The prefixes or beginnings of words are written with a short vowel.

17.4 Write the AE (attached ending) for all derivatives or changes in endings of root words that require a second or subsequent stroke. The AE is written with the ending in the last stroke.

17.5 Write the past tense of a word by adding a -D in the same stroke when possible. If the -D cannot be added in the same stroke, use the "attached ending" rule and write AED in the second or last stroke.

17.6 If a one-syllable word ends in "n" do not add the -D in the same stroke; form the past tense by writing the AED in a second stroke.

17.7 If the spelling of a word changes by forming the past tense, the new outline should reflect the new spelling.

17.8 Write K-RBGS to designate the colon whenever it is dictated or as needed within dictation.

17.9 Write S-RBGS to designate the semicolon whenever it is dictated or as needed within dictation.

18.1 The plural of a word is formed by writing the final -Z in the same stroke. If a word ends in -T, write the final -TS in the same stroke to form the plural. If a word ends in -S or -Z, write the AEZ (attached ending) in the last stroke.

18.2 For numbers beginning with 1,000, write the first digit in the first stroke followed by the short form TH-Z for thousand. Write the hundreds digit followed by the short form H-PBD. Numbers dictated after the hundreds are written using previous number rules.

19.1 For words that end in “y” or “ey” where a second or subsequent stroke is necessary, write AEFPL (attached ending) in the final stroke.

19.2 For words that end in “ee” (double e) or “ie” write KWRAOE (silent “y”) in the final stroke.

19.3 Write the A-RBGS to designate the apostrophe (') whenever it is dictated or as needed within dictation.

19.4 The final -G is used for all words that end in "ing." When possible, write the -G in the same stroke. If the -G cannot be written in the same stroke, write the AEG (attached ending) in the last stroke.

19.5 If a one-syllable word ends in "n, do not add the -G in the same stroke; form the "ing" ending by writing the AEG in a second stroke.

20.1 To write the alphabet in all capital letters, write the alphabetic letter on the initial side of the keyboard along with the final side -FBG (FK). Each letter requires the -FBG.

20.2 Write the AOS in the last stroke to form the ‘s for any word, letter,or number. Singular possessives are formed by writing AOS (‘s) in the last stroke. Plural possessives are formed by writing the A-RBGS (s’) in the last stroke.

Review DrillBook and NoteBook Applications

1. Review Drills IX and X from the *Realwrite DrillBook* (recommended).
2. Review Exercise E from the *Realwrite NoteBook* (optional).

Unit Evaluation Number Five

Unit Evaluation Number Five will cover all material from the following: *Realwrite LessonBook*, Lessons 17-20; *DrillBook*, Drills IX and X.

UNIT 6
LESSON TWENTY-ONE

Warm up and Review

☞ *practice the following:*

about a	about the	about you	are the	are you	can a
can he	can I	can the	can you	cannot	could he
could I	could you	did a	did he	did I	did the
did you	from the	from you	had a	had he	had I
had you	have I	have you	he could	he did	he had
he will	how many	I am	I can	I could	I did
I had	I have	I will			

Writing Words that Begin with "wr or "wh"

21.1 Write words that are spelled in English with "wh" by writing WH, even though the "h" is silent. Write words that are spelled in English with "wr" by writing WR, even though the "w" is silent.

For example: whet WHET wrap WRAP

☞ *practice the following:*

whale	WHAEUL	wheel	WHAOEL	while	WHAOEUL
whim	WHEUPL	whine	WHAOEUPB	whiney	WHAOEUPB/AEFPL
white	WHAOEUT	whole	WHOEL	whose	WHOES
wrap	WRAP	wreck	WREBG	writ	WREUT

Contractions using the Z-rule (Not)

A contraction is a shortened form of an English word or words. Usually it joins together or combines two syllables or words to make one shortened word. The apostrophe symbol is used as the connecting mark.

In Realwrite theory, all contractions are formed by using the final -Z to represent the contraction; but, unlike the -Z used to form the plural, the -Z used in contractions is always added to the abbreviated root word or phrase in the same stroke.

For example, the phrase cannot is written K-N; the contraction can't is written K-NZ. The -Z represents the contraction.

21.2 All contractions are written by adding the final -Z to the short form used to write the root word or phrase.

Listed below are the root phrases and contractions for the family of words that contain the word "not":

☞ *practice the following:*

phrase	Realwrite	contraction	Realwrite
are not	R-PB	aren't	R-PBZ
cannot	K-PB	can't	K-PBZ
could not	KOPBT	couldn't	KOPBZ
did not	TK-PB	didn't	TK-PBZ
does not	TKUPBT	doesn't	TKUPBZ
do not	TKAOPB	don't	TKAOPBZ
had not	H-PB	hadn't	H-PBZ
has not	SKPW-PB[1]	hasn't	SKPW-PBZ
have not	SR-PB	haven't	SR-PBZ
is not	S-PB	isn't	S-PBZ
should not	SHOUPB	shouldn't	SHOUPBZ
was not	WAEPBT	wasn't	WAEPBZ
will not	HR-PBT	won't	WOEPBZ[2]
would not	WOUPB	wouldn't	WOUPBZ
		ain't	AEUPBZ[3]

[1] short form for "has" in phrases = SKPW-
[2] modified form of root short form
[3] does not contract two words; learn as short form or exception to rule

Writing Words that Begin with a Vowel

You have already learned that it is very important that the computer be able to distinguish between the beginning of a word and the ending of a word. For that reason, you have learned to write all final stroke words that begin with a vowel by writing a "silent y," and to apply the AE rule (attached ending) for "derivatives" and words that have a "changed ending."

You have also learned that prefixes of words, regardless of their pronunciation or spelling, are always written with a short vowel. In Lesson 17, you learned that the prefixes or beginning of words are written with a short vowel.

Words that begin with a vowel must be treated in a like fashion. Listed below is a specific rule regarding words that begin with vowels:

21.3 Use a short vowel for words that begin with the single vowels "a," "e," "i," and "u." Use the long vowel OE for words that begin with the vowel "o."

For example:

amazing	A/PHAIZ/AEG	amuse	A/PHAOUZ	amass	A/PHAS
idol	EU/TKOL	icon	EU/KOPB	ideal	EU/TKAOEL
omit	OE/PHEUT	emit	E/PHEUT	usurp	U/SURP

It is important to realize that this rule cannot be violated. All prefixes that begin with a vowel are written using the short vowel, except the vowel "o." This helps to distinguish between such possible conflicts as "amass" (A/PHAS) and "a mass" (AEU PHAS) or "ideal" (EU/TKAOEL) and "I deal" (AOEU TKAOEL).

☞ *practice the following:*

abet	A/PWET	abut	A/PWUT	abuse	A/PWAOUZ
affix	A/TPEUFRPB	afraid	A/TPRAEUD	afar	A/TPAR
ajar	A/SKWRAR	alive	A/HRAOEUFB	allot	A/HROT
arise	A/RAOEUZ	appraise	A/PRAEUZ	avert	A/SRERT
astray	A/STRAFPL	attack	A/TABG	avow	A/SROFRP
idol	EU/TKOL	icon	EU/KOPB	oboe	OE/PWOE
omit	OE/PHEUT	usurp	U/SURP	unite	U/NAOEUT
utensil	U/TENS/KWREUL	oh	OEFD		

21.4 Use a long or short vowel when a word begins with a vowel that is combined with a consonant in the first stroke.

eerie	AOER/KWRAOE	umpire	UPL/PAOEUR	error	ER/KWROR
ibid	EUB/KWREUD	Europe	AOURP	err	ER

Short Forms and Phrases

☞ *practice the following:*

better	TER	circumstance	SEURBG		
company	K-P	concern	KERPB	degree	TKRAOE
describe	TKRAOEUB	determine	TKERPL	Dr.	TKR-
employ	PHROEU	employee	PHROE	employer	PHROEUR
writes	WREUZ	writing	WREUG	written	WREUPB
unity	AOUPBT	copy	KP-FPL	okay	OBG

Lesson Practice

☞ *practice the following:*

I can't appraise the writing because I don't have the copy in front (TPROPBT) of me. If I had the copy, / I could read the whole copy while you went away (A/WAFPL). Zeb was afraid to go on a boat because he / heard (HAERD) there was a big whale on the loose (HRAOS). He didn't want to tell Joan (SKWROEPB) about his fear (TPAOER), so he / put it aside (A/SAOEUD). Now, he is happy that he can look for whales in the deep sea (SAE).

Whose white rabbit / (RAB/KWREUT) came out of the hat? I haven't seen a bunny hop like that in a long time. The bunny hopped / along the road. A whole crowd of people began to clap when they saw him hop in a car. /

The / man in the car did not laugh. In fact, the man in the automobile had a wreck. He turned his / steering (STAOERG) wheel the wrong way and hit a house. He is lucky to be alive.

Aren't you sure? Can't you / see? Didn't you feel the rain? Shouldn't we wait for the man in the moon? Isn't it a nice day? / Wouldn't you want to right (RAOEUGT) a wrong? Why are you so whiney? Don't whine. Haven't you wrapped the gift yet? / I ain't going to do it.

Comprehensive Practice

☞ *practice the following. When you are finished, take your notes and read them aloud, comparing them to the textbook. If you have any errors, circle them in your steno notes. Practice this section again until you can write it without any errors.*

Isn't it important to do your work again and again? Most of the work you do can't be put on / a chart. I can't begin to tell you the sheer joy of being able to write nice. Don't abuse your / writing time. Your writing time is the most important job you will do all day long.

Janet lived in a house / that was near a shop that sold used parts. A lot of parts are sold. It is wrong to allot / a part to a box. Most parts can't be allotted, they have to be mixed. Jay said mixed parts ain't bad / for the price. Deb said mixed parts aren't bad for the price. Who was right? Jay or Deb?

Shouldn't we cheer / if we want? Couldn't we chat if we want? Wouldn't you? I had a cat once, but I vowed I / wasn't going to let it run astray. I won't let it out of the house. I hope it never runs / away. Isn't it time to eat? Don't you have to be seated by 8?

I saw Rose cheat on a / paper she wrote. She said it was her paper, but it wasn't. She got in trouble because she was wrong. / She said she was sorry. She hasn't cheated since then. Now, she helps people who are having trouble writing. /

Additional Practice

Go to the:	Do the following:
Realwrite DrillBook (recommended).........	Read over and study Drill XI (Lessons 21 & 22)
Realwrite Notebook (optional)...................	Read and transcribe the notes from Exercise F, Lesson 21

UNIT 6
LESSON TWENTY-TWO

Warm up and Review

☞ *practice the following:*

if a	if he	if the	if you	in the	into the
is it	is not	is that	is the	is there	is this
it is	no ma'am	no, sir	of the	some are	some of
that are	that the	that you	there are	there is	they are
they will	was he	was the	we are	we can	we did
we had	we have	were you	what is	which is	when are
when is	when you	where are	which is	will he	will I
will not	will you	with you	would you	yes, ma'am	yes, sir
you are	you can	you could	you did	you had	you have
you will					

Writing Words that end in "ment"

22.1 The final -PLT is used for all words that end in "ment." When possible, write the -PLT in the same stroke. If the -PLT cannot be written in the same stroke, write PHAEPBT in the last stroke.

For example:

enjoyment EPB/SKWROFPL/PHAEPBT endorsement EPB/TKORS/PHAEPBT

☞ *practice the following:*

amazement	A/PHAEUZ/PHAEPBT	basement	BAEUS/PHAEPBT
excitement	SKPAOEUT/PHAEPBT	cement	SEPLT
enjoyment	EPB/SKWROFPL/PHAEPBT	fulfillment	TPUL/TPEUL/PHAEPBT
confinement	KOPB/TPAOEUPB/PHAEPBT	harassment	HA/RAS/PHAEPBT
torment	TORPLT	lament	HRAPLT
moment	PHOEPLT	comment	KOPLT

Writing Words that end in "ght" and "gh"

22.2 Words that are spelled in English with "ght" are written with the -GT in the outline.

☞ practice the following:

right	RAOEUGT	thought	THOUGT	taught	TAUGT
brought	PWROUGT	bought	PWOUGT	caught	KAUGT
sight	SAOEUGT	tight	TAOEUGT	fight	TPAOEUGT

22.3 Write the final H (-FD) for all words that are spelled in English with "gh" and sound like "h." Write the final F for all words that are spelled in English with "gh" and sound like "f."

☞ practice the following:

high	HAOEUFD	sigh	SAOEUFD	thigh	THAOEUFD	weigh	WAEUFD
cough	KOF	tough	TUF	rough	RUF	laugh	HRAF

Large Numbers (Million, Billion, Trillion, Zillion)

22.4 For writing a large number, follow all previous rules regarding numbers. Write the number as you hear it. Use the short forms PH-L for million; -BL for billion; TR-L for trillion; SKPW-L for zillion.

Write the first digit followed by the appropriate short form. Write the second and subsequent digits followed by their appropriate short form. Use all previous rules for writing numbers 1 - 99.

For example:

32 million[1]	23EU/PH-L
55,200,000,000	5EU/-BL/2/H-PBD/PH-L
12 zillion[1]	12/SKPW-L

[1]Large numbers of a single value (1 million) are transcribed with the figure followed by the appropriate word for the numerical designation

Using the rules you have learned, you can now write any number that is dictated, large or small. For example:

500	5/H-PBD
31,476,822	13EU/PH-L/4/H-PBD/EU67/TH-Z/8/H-PB/2EU

Keep in mind that you are basically writing what you hear, numbers for numbers and short forms for number placement.

☞ practice the following:

23 billion, 231 million, 24 thousand, 345	475,425
31 million, 276 thousand, 341	87,122
16 trillion	1,435,902

Multi-Consonant Combinations (SKR-, TH-)

☞ *practice the following:*

SKR- SKR- SKR- ,	SKR- SKR- SKR- ,	SKR- SKR- SKR- ,
SKR- SKR- SKR- ,	SKR- SKR- SKR- ,	SKR- SKR- SKR- ,
SKR- SKR- SKR- ,	SKR- SKR- SKR- ,	SKR- SKR- SKR- ,
TH- TH- TH- ,	TH- TH- TH- ,	TH- TH- TH- ,
TH- TH- TH- ,	TH- TH- TH- ,	TH- TH- TH- ,
TH- TH- TH- ,	TH- TH- TH- ,	TH- TH- TH- ,

☞ *practice the following:*

scare	SKAEUR	score	SKOR	scream	SKRAOEPL
skit	SKEUT	scale	SKAEUL	scan	SKAPB
scar	SKAR	scram	SKRAPL	screw	SKREFRP
thaw	THAUFRP	theft	THEFT	theme	THAOEPL
these	THAOEZ	those	THOEZ	them	THEPL
thick	THEUBG	thin	THEUPB	then	THEPB

Short Forms and Phrases

☞ *practice the following:*

acknowledgment	ABG/TPHOPBLG/PHAEPBT	document	TKOUPLT
payment	PAEUPLT	apartment	PARPLT
appointment	POEUPLT	employment	PHROEUPLT
arrangement	ARPBG/PHAEPBT	equipment	KW-PLT
estimate	STEUPLT	investment	SREPLT
judgment	SKWRUPLT	shipment	SHEUPLT
requirement	RAOEURPLT	involvement	SROFPLT

Lesson Practice

☞ *practice the following:*

Jerry sat in amazement as he saw the 14,875 dogs chase the cat. He didn't want to scare the cat, so he called his wife to scare it away by letting (HRET/AEG) out a scream. It / didn't work (WORBG). The cat ran into the basement and stayed there until all the dogs left. The cat didn't seem / to mind (PHAOEUPBD) his / confinement until the doors were locked (HROBGD), then it tried (TRAOEUD) to get out, but couldn't.

File the document. / Use the equipment. I paid the rent on the apartment, but the payment was not due until 12. In your / estimate, what is the requirement for investment. Are you looking for employment? Those who can vote, should. Hand me one / screw and a screwdriver (SKREFRP/AE/TKRAOEUFR), and I will fix the door.

The theme of the play was a man who found / fulfillment and enjoyment in his work. Was it these or those, them or then, thick or thin? Jennifer (SKWREPB/TPER) made an / arrangement with Mr. / Wilson to cement her driveway. It was over 99,000, but it was a good job. /

Comprehensive Practice

Practice the following so that you can write the numbers quickly and accurately. When you are finished, take your notes and read them aloud, comparing them to the textbook. If you have any errors, circle them in your steno notes. Practice this section again until you can write it without any errors.

☞ *practice the following:*

Didn't you say that there were 31,945 cars at the race? Wasn't that your / judgment? Isn't that your estimate? I had an automobile in the race, but I couldn't start it because it ran / out of gas. Once the race began there was a wreck on turn 12 and most of the cars began / to stop in the pit stop. As the race started again, a storm came up in the sky and / it began to rain. It wasn't a good day at all for race fans.

Kate said that there was a rock / star on stage. She estimated that there were over 95 zillion people there. Those who were there could hear in / amazement. The / band played very well. All of the boys and girls loved to see them perform.

Didn't you / say that Ben and Betty owned a farm and stable? Didn't you say that they owned cows and horses? They / farm for the sheer enjoyment of farming. They loved to raise the pigs and ducks. Their fulfillment is growing food / on the farm.

The following numbers were called: 4, 28, 0, 86, 129, 56, / 23, 93, 424, 552, 7694, 9351, 5025, / 3492.

Additional Practice

Go to the:	Do the following:
Realwrite DrillBook (recommended).......	Write and practice Drill XI (Lessons 21 & 22)
Realwrite NoteBook (optional)................	Read and Transcribe the notes from Exercise F, Lesson 22 and Drill XI

UNIT 6
LESSON TWENTY-THREE

Warm up and Review

☞ *practice the following:*

about	accompany	actual	after
afternoon	again	ago	almost
alone	along	aloud	already
also	am	among	any
applicable	apply	are	argue
around	arrange	automobile	balance
basic	became	because	become
been	before	began	begin

Blending or "Slurring" Principle

23.1 Whenever it is possible to shorten the outline of a word without distorting it, blend the sounds by eliminating vowels or unaccented syllables and write the blended version. Care must be used to avoid confusion or misinterpretation.

This rule will be applied to various words as you continue the lessons. The first application involves words that begin with the prefix "col" or "com."

Writing Words that Begin with "col" or "com"

23.2 Write KL (KHR-) or KM (KPH-) for words that begin with "col" or "com." In some cases, the K- may be used for "com" and combined with a consonant. If it is not possible to write the word in one stroke, write KOL (KOL) or KOM (KOPH) in the first stroke.

For example:

collect KHREBGT   commit KPHEUT   combat KPWAT   compete KPAOET

☞ *practice the following:*

collect	KHREBGT	command	KPHAPBD	collide	KHRAOEUD
commit	KPHEUT	combine	KPWAOEUPB	combat	KPWAT
column	KHRUPL	commence	KPHEPBS	compete	KPAOET
commerce	KPHERS	compose	KPOEZ	compress	KPRES
complex	KPHREFRPB				

Words that end in "self" or "selves"

23.3 Write SAEFL in the second stroke for words that end in "self." Write SAEFLZ in the second stroke for words that end in "selves."

This rule applies only when the two words are connected. If "self" or "selves" are separate words, use the short forms SEFL and SEFLZ.

☞ *practice the following:*

itself	T-/SAEFL	ourselves	OUR/SAEFLZ
herself	HER/SAEFL	themselves	THEPL/SAEFLZ
himself	HEUPL/SAEFL	yourself	YOUR/SAEFL
myself	PH-FPL/SAEFL	yourselves	YOUR/SAEFLZ

Short Forms and Phrases

☞ *practice the following:*

self	SEFL	selves	SEFLZ	junior	SKWR-R
juror	SKWROR	jury	SKWRUR	injury	SKWR-FPL
instruct	STRUBGT	letter	HRER	material	TAOERL
motor	PHOER	next	TPH-FRPB	manufacture	PH-F
natural	TPHARL	open	OEP	openly	OEPL
opinion	P-PB	order	ORD	organize	ORG
comfort	K-FRT				

Lesson Practice

☞ *practice the following:*

Can't you command the boys and girls to stop arguing? I hope you don't have to give your legal opinion, / because you can't. John said he would collect all the money that the man got from the injury suit (SAOUT). He / openly bragged about the fact that he got an order from the court (KOURT).

He said he would organize a party / of 25 to compete at the next meeting. I had to instruct Joyce and Jill on what material to / use in the manufacture of drapes (TKRAEUPZ). They had an order for 2,345 natural colored (KHRORD) drapes. /

There was a wreck between a bus and a truck (TRUBG). The motor in the bus stopped, and the truck ran / into the back of the bus. No one was hurt. The manager of the bus company would not comment, but / he did say that one person did commence a lawsuit. It is a complex case. The truck struck a column / after it hit the bus, and the column fell on a crowd (KROFRPD) of people. There was only 1 injury and / that was to a cat, but the cat is commencing to feel better.

John Jones was picked to go on / the jury. He is now a juror for the case dealing with the truck and bus. He got a letter / from a lawyer (HROEUR) saying that he had to go to court. He took comfort in the fact that he got / paid for going to court.

The cow caught (KAUGT) itself on a fence. I talk to myself. All of the people / at the show paid (PAEUD) for the tickets (TEUBGTS) themselves. Jackie (SKWRABG/KWRAOE), herself, and Johnny (SKWROPB/AEFPL), himself, put on the complete (KPHRAOET) 4 course (KOURS) meal (PHAOEL). / They were proud (PROUD) of themselves. The class and I did it ourselves.

Comprehensive Practice

☞ *<u>Practice the following</u>. When you are finished, take your notes and read them aloud, comparing them to the textbook. If you have any errors, circle them in your steno notes. Practice this section again until you can write it without any errors.*

Bobbie and Jackie started school this morning. They walked to school themselves. They were so proud and happy. The / girl who taught dancing talked to them herself. The man who taught crafts showed them how to make a bow / tie himself.

A baby got all soapy because she was in the tub. She cried when she got out of / the tub. Rose and myself told her a story about a car that ran away.

There was a general opinion / among all of the people that the finances would not pay all of the bills. The bills had to be paid, / but they didn't have enough money. What were they to do? Lee said to repair motors and engines so he / organized a small repair shop. Now, he has a lot of work and he doesn't have time to order material for the / shop.

Ron is moving to Ogdon (OG/TKOPB) in a month. It has become very complex; he has an exam on the / day he moves. What would you do? He can't fail the exam because he will have to drop out of school. / He could move next month, but then he would lose (HROZ) the house. What would you do?

Additional Pratice

<u>Go to the</u>:	<u>Do the following</u>:
Realwrite DrillBook (recommended).........	Read over and study Drill XII (Lessons 23 & 24)
Realwrite Notebook (optional)..................	Read and transcribe the notes from Exercise F, Lesson 23

UNIT 6
LESSON TWENTY-FOUR

Warm up and Review

☞ *practice the following:*

begun	behalf	behind	being	between
bottom	business	can	cannot	come
could	could not	damage	detail	did not
did	do not	do	does not	does
done	emergency	enclose	engine	engineer
enough	envelope	even	evidence	examine
example	eye			

Flagged Alphabet (Lowercase Letters)

There may be times in writing for realtime that your transcript must reflect various ways of writing the alphabet. For example, you may want FBI to be transcribed in all capital letters and you may want dba (doing business as) to be transcribed in all lowercase letters.

Remember the rule you learned for writing all capital letters by using the initial side alphabetic letter and the final-side special designation (FK). The rule for writing lowercase letters is similar. In this case, you will use the FS; "F" for "flagged" and the "S" for "small" letters.

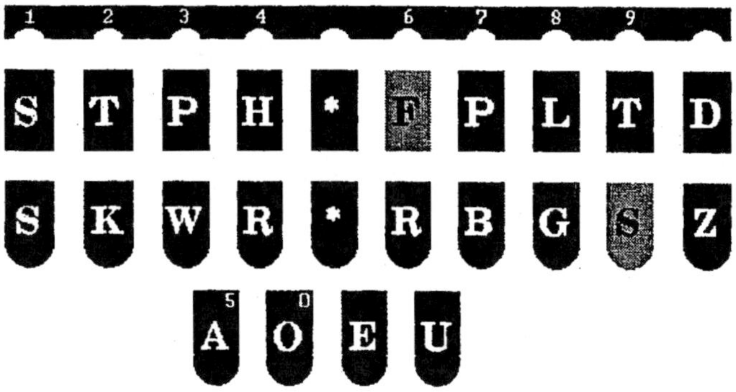

24.1 To write the alphabet in small letters, write the alphabetic letter on the initial side of the keyboard along with the final side -FS in the same stroke. Each letter requires the -FS.

A Note About Finger Spelling—Finger spelling is a technique used by captioners doing realimte (immediate translation) to spell out unfamiliar names or words or spellings that are not found in the dictionary. For example, if the name Jamez Smithe is heard, the captioner would spell out the names using the –FK for capital letters, the –FS for small letters, and the SP-RBGS to put a space between the first and last name.

☞ *practice the following:*

alphabet	Realwrite	alphabet	Realwrite	alphabet	Realwrite
a	A-FS	j	SKWR-FS	s	S-FS
b	PW-FS	k	K-FS	t	T-FS
c	KR-FS	l	HR-FS	u	U-FS
d	TK-FS	m	PH-FS	v	SR-FS
e	E-FS	n	TPH-FS	w	W-FS
f	TP-FS	o	O-FS	x	SKP-FS
g	TKPW-FS	p	P-FS	y	KWR-FS
h	H-FS	q	KW-FS	z	SKPW-FS
i	EU-FS	r	R-FS		

Writing Words that end in "shun" and "k-shun"

24.2 Write -GS for all words that end in the "shun" sound, regardless of the spelling. Combine the -GS in the last stroke of the word. Plurals are formed by writing the AEZ in the last stroke.

The "shun" words are usually words that end in "tion" or "sion." For example:

attention A/TEPBGS admission AD/PHEUGS admissions AD/PHEUGS/AEZ

☞ *practice the following:*

attention	A/TEPBGS	admission	AD/PHEUGS
compulsion	KPULGS	audition	AU/TKEUGS
mission	PHEUGS	remission	RE/PHEUGS
sensation	SEPB/SAEUGS	transmission	TRAPBS/PHEUGS
vision	SREUGS	fusion	TPAOUGS
tension	TEPBGS	invention	EUPB/SREPBGS
pension	PEPBGS	pensions	PEPBGS/AEZ
missions	PHEUGS/AEZ	auditions	AU/TKEUGS/AEZ

24.3 Write -BGS for all words that end in the "k-shun" sound, regardless of the spelling. Combine the -BGS in the last stroke of the word. Plurals are formed by writing AEZ in the last stroke.

Notice that the -BGS is not the plural of words that end in "k" or -BG. The plural form of words that end in "k" would be -BGZ. Most "k-shun" words usually end with the "ction." For example:

faction TPABGS traction TRABGS tractions TRABGS/AEZ

☞ *practice the following:*

faction	TPABGS	traction	TRABGS
transaction	TRAPBS/KWRABGS	action	ABGS
diction	TKEUBGS	fiction	TPEUBGS
section	SEBGS	fraction	TPRABGS
subtraction	SUB/TRABGS	conviction	KOPB/SREUBGS
factions	TPABGS/AEZ	actions	ABGS/AEZ
fractions	TPRABGS/AEZ	tractions	TRABGS/AEZ
convictions	KOPB/SREUBGS/AEZ	transactions	TRAPBS/ABGS/AEZ

Distinguishing Words that Begin with "shr" and "sl"

In most shorthand theories, the initial HR- represents the initial "L." This presents a problem for words that begin with "sl" (SHR) and "shr" (SHR). For that reason, most theories have a rule that makes a distinction between such words.

24.4 Write words that begin with the "sl" combination by using the SHR; write words that begin with the "shr" combination by using the SKHR.

Think of the SKHR- as an arbitrary for all words that begin with "shr."

☞ *practice the following:*

slow	SHROEFRP	slum	SHRUPL	sleep	SHRAOEP
sled	SHRED	sleek	SHRAOEBG	slug	SHRUG
shred	SKHRED	shriek	SKHRAOEBG	shrug	SKHRUG
shrine	SKHRAOEUPB	shroud	SKHROUD	shrew	SKHREFRP

Multi-Consonant Combinations (PL-)

☞ *practice the following:*

PHR- PHR- PHR- , PHR- PHR- PHR- , PHR- PHR- PHR- ,
PHR- PHR- PHR- , PHR- PHR- PHR- , PHR- PHR- PHR- ,
PHR- PHR- PHR- , PHR- PHR- PHR- , PHR- PHR- PHR- ,

☞ *practice the following:*

please	PHRAOES	pleas	PHRAOEZ	plight	PHRAOEUGT
plan	PHRAPB	plain	PHRAEUPB	plane	PHRAEPB
plum	PHRUPL	pluck	PHRUBG	plaque	PHRALGTS

Short Forms and Phrases

☞ *practice the following:*

police	PHREUS	policeman	PHRAPL	policemen	PHREPL
reply	PHRAOEU	application	PHREUBGS	condition	K-PBGS
second	SEBGD	ever	EFR	every	EFB
documentation	TKOUPLGS	down	TKOUFRP[1]		

[1]Note the distinctions between the following:
down = TKOUFRP, do you know = TKOUPB, down- (prefix) = TKOFRP

Lesson Practice

☞ *practice the following:*

The man won't call your attention to the exam. He didn't want to cause any friction between the police and / the crowd. The plan was to get the policemen to perform their mission. It caused a sensation when the document / came back without a written note.

Do you deal with subtraction? Do you ever have a fraction? If you do, / what is your conviction? John has a sleek invention that will perform any action in a fraction of a second. / Even at that speed, it is very slow. The plan is to have a reply as soon as possible.

Jan / said she would shred the application if it was not filled out right. In order to apply for the / job, he had to meet one condition. His vision had to be good, and diction had to be excellent.

Please / complete the transaction by 4 or a policeman will come to your house and get you. I cried for help, / but my pleas were not heard. Do you get plenty of sleep? If you don't, what do you do? I / release my tension by going to a movie. The movie I saw was about a slug who lived in a / slum and owned a plain sled. The star was a sleek girl who let out a shriek when she fell /out of a plane.

Comprehensive Practice

☞ Practice the following. *When you are finished, take your notes and read them aloud, comparing them to the textbook. If you have any errors, circle them in your steno notes. Practice this section again until you can write it without any errors.*

Once upon a time there was a man who had a vision. His vision was to have an invention. The / invention was a transmission that would not go slow. It was a great sensation and caught the attention of a / lot of great people.

The object of the invention was this: at a slow speed, most transmission gears work fine; / but when the speed is great, the gears begin to wear down. If the gear could work in fusion with / the main gear, then it would be better.

Zeb and Rob became policemen. They went to school to study how / to become a policeman. While at school, they wrote a personal (PERPBL) note to their friends back home. They studied very / hard and are now doing a great job.

One day at school they went to eat out. After their meal, / the waitress said that they did not have to pay because they were students. They did not want to / argue with her, so they told her they would pay the bill in 7 months.

The trouble with not paying / your bills on time is that they keep on piling up. If you realize that your bills are getting out of / control, you should try to pay a fraction at a time before you go into debt. Who wants to pay / your bills for you? I can't.

John Jones sold coffee at the market. He wanted to audition for a / part in a play, but he couldn't get off work. The trouble with working is that you have to work / from 9 to 5 and then you can't do what you want, but the good part about working is / that you get paid. You can always use the money to buy whatever you need.

If you have a compulsion / to buy a new car, you can get a good deal at a used car shop. There is a / man who will sell you a good used car at a fraction of the price. He will also fix it /for you if it doesn't run right.

Additional Practice

Go to the: — Do the following:

Realwrite DrillBook (recommended)......Write and practice Drill XII (Lessons 23 & 24)
Realwrite NoteBook (optional)................Read and transcribe the notes from Exercise F, Lessons 24 and Drill XII

UNIT 6 REVIEW

Lesson Review

1. Go back to each lesson and learn each new rule thoroughly.
2. Go back to each lesson and write the Lesson Practice.
3. Go back to each lesson and write the Comprehensive Practice.
4. Read back all notes and transcribe a portion of your review.

Review of Writing Rules

21.1 Write words that are spelled in English with "wh" by writing WH, even though the “h” is silent. Write words that are spelled in English with "wr" by writing WR, even though the “w” is silent.

21.2 All contractions are written by adding the final -Z to the short form used to write the root word or phrase.

21.3 Use a short vowel for words that begin with the single vowels “a,” “e,” “i,” and “u”. Use the long vowel OE for words that begin with the vowel “o.”

21.4 Use a long or short vowel when a word begins with a vowel that is combined with a consonant in the first stroke.

22.1 The final -PLT is used for all words that end in "ment." When possible, write the -PLT in the same stroke. If the -PLT cannot be written in the same stroke, write PHAEPBT in the last stroke.

22.2 Words that are spelled in English with "ght" are written with the -GT in the outline.

22.3 Write the final H (-FD) for all words that are spelled in English with “gh” and sound like “h.” Write the final F for all words that are spelled in English with “gh” and sound like “f.”

22.4 For writing a large number, follow all previous rules regarding numbers. Write the number as you hear it. Use the short forms PH-L for million; -BL for billion; TR-L for trillion; SKPW-L for zillion.

23.1 Whenever it is possible to shorten the outline of a word without distorting it, blend the sounds by eliminating vowels or unaccented syllables and write the blended version. Care must be used to avoid confusion or misinterpretation.

23.2 Write KL (KHR-) or KM (KPH-) for words that begin with “col” or “com.” In some cases, the K- may be used for “com” and combined with a consonant. If it is not possible to write the word in one stroke, write KOL (KOL) or KOM (KOPH) in the first stroke.

23.3 Write SAEFL in the second stroke for words that end in "self." Write SAEFLZ in the second stroke for words that end in "selves."

24.1 To write the alphabet in small letters, write the alphabetic letter on the initial side of the keyboard along with the final side -FS in the same stroke. Each letter requires the -FS.

24.2 Write -GS for all words that end in the "shun" sound, regardless of the spelling. Combine the -GS in the last stroke of the word. Plurals are formed by writing the AEZ in the last stroke.

24.3 Write -BGS for all words that end in the "k-shun" sound, regardless of the spelling. Combine the -BGS in the last stroke of the word. Plurals are formed by writing AEZ in the last stoke.

24.4 Write words that begin with the "sl" combination by using the SHR; write words that begin with the "shr" combination by using the SKHR.

Review DrillBook and NoteBook Applications

1. Review Drills XI and XII from the *Realwrite DrillBook* (recommended).
2. Review Exercise F from the *Realwrite NoteBook* (optional).

Unit Evaluation Number Six

Unit Evaluation Number Six will cover all material from the following: *Realwrite LessonBook*, Lessons 21-24; *DrillBook*, Drills XI and XII.

UNIT 7
LESSON TWENTY-FIVE

Warm up and Review

☞ *pactice the following:*

family	figure	finance	financial	first
follow	from	gallon	gentle	gentleman
gentlemen	gym	had	had not	half
handle	have	he	help	identify
identity	if	immediate	important	in
income	into	is	it	item
labor	legal	little	major	manage
manufacture	many	maybe	member	memo
minimum	minute	money	month	

Writing words that end in the Sound of "ch"

25.1 Write words that end in the sound of "ch" by using the -FP. If it is necessary to write the -FP in a separate stroke by itself, write the AEFP in the last stroke.

For example:

pitch	PEUFP	witch	WEUFP

☞ *practice the following:*

ditch	TKEUFP	pitch	PEUFP	witch	WEUFP
stitch	STEUFP	glitch	TKPWHREUFP	rich	REUFP
teach	TAOEFP	snitch	STPHEUFP	batch	PWAFP
catch	KAFP	latch	HRAFP	patch	PAFP
fetch	TPEFP	hitch	HEUFP	match	PHAFP

Writing Words that end in the Sound of "sh"

25.2 Write words that end in the sound of "sh" by using the -RB. For words that end in "ish" and require a second stroke, use the "silent y" and write KWREURB.

For example:

wish	WEURB	fish	TPEURB
dish	TKEURB	babyish	PWAEUB/KWREURB

☞ *practice the following:*

fish	TPEURB	wish	WEURB	dish	TKEURB
mash	PHARB	crash	KRARB	cash	KAERB[1]
wash	WARB	dash	TKARB	stash	STARB
lash	HRARB	sash	SARB		

boyish	PWOFPL/KWREURB
girlish	TKPWEURL/KWREURB
childish	KHAOUELD/KWREURB
babyish	PWAEUB/KWREURB

[1] carb is written KARB

Contractions using the Z-rule (Am and Are)

Remembering the Z-rule that was applied to the "not" family of contractions; the same rule applies for those contractions containing "am" and "are." The Z-rule states that all contractions are written by adding the final -Z to the short form used to write the root word or phrase.

☞ *practice the following:*

phrase	Realwrite	contraction	Realwrite
I am	AOEUPL	I'm	AOEUPLZ
they are	THER	they're	THERZ
we are	WER	we're	WERZ
you are	UR	you're	URZ

New Punctuation (Quotation Marks)

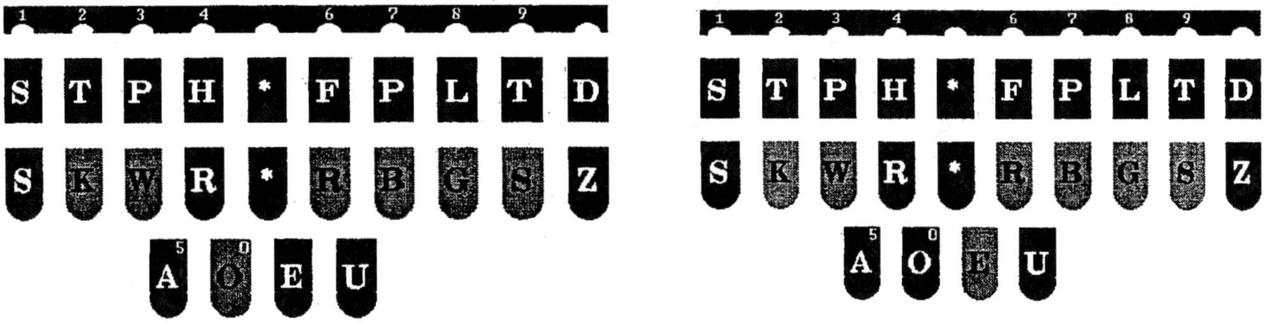

25.3 Use the KWO-RBGS for "opening" quotes. Use the KWE -RBGS for "ending" quotes.

Quotation marks come in pairs, opening and ending. The KWO signifies "quote open." The KWE means "quote end."

Words that end in the sound of "shal" or "shus"

25.4 Use the -RBL for words that end in the sound of "shal," regardless of their spelling. If a separate stroke is required, use SHAEL in the last stroke.

For example:

racial	RAEURBL	partial	PAR/SHAEL
martial	PHAR/SHAEL	facial	TPAEURBL

☞ *practice the following:*

racial	RAEURBL	spatial	SPAEURBL	facial	TPAEURBL
partial	PAR/SHAEL	martial	PHAR/SHAEL		

25.5 Use the -RBS for words that end in the sound of "shus," regardless of their spelling. If a separate stroke is required, use SHAUS in the last stroke.

For example:

delicious	TKHREURBS	fictitious	TPEUBG/TEURBS

☞ *practice the following:*

delicious	TKHREURBS	fictitious	TPEUBG/TEURBS
obnoxious	OB/TPHORBS	malicious	PHA/HREURBS
contentious	KOPB/TEPB/SHAUS	conscious	KOPB/SHAUS

Short Forms and Phrases

☞ *practice the following:*

correspond	KROPBD	credit	KRE	customer	KPHER
particular	THRAR (TLAR)	photograph	TPRAF	proceed	PROE
popular	PHRAR (PLAR)	possible	POB	prepare	PRAOEP
peculiar	KHRAR (KLAR)	principal	PRAL	principle	PR-L
probable	PRAB	probably	PRABL	problem	PREPL
always	AULZ	all right	HR-RT	onto	OPBT
machine	PH-FP	church	KH-FP	special	SP-RB
specially	SP-RBL				

Lesson Practice

☞ *practice the following:*

Probably, we better see if our credit is going to be all right before we buy a new car. The / particular car we have in mind is a "pretty red one." I'm sure that we can afford it if we / crunch our money and save. We are not rich, but we will get by if we spend less on lunch. / A stitch in time saves 9.

You're a special problem. You can't see the principal yet. Don't you have an / appointment? There was a glitch in his plan; he forgot that it is only a partial plan. He needs a / whole plan that will prepare him to do it right. It is probable that he will proceed without the plan. / If he does, we're sure that he will fall on his face.

Jeff and Jill went to church but they / have not come home yet. Could it be possible that they didn't go home? It could be possible, but not / probable. They probably stopped at the ice cream store to buy a delicious ice cream cone. You're right; that is / what they did.

They're a peculiar bunch of people; those people who take down shorthand all day long. They're / particular about what they write. They're always writing on their shorthand machine. I can tell by their facial expression that / they love their work. They love to hear a fictitious story and write it down and then read it back. /

George took a photograph of me when I was doing my work. I looked very contentious. I wish that I / could write better, but I'm doing what I can to write well. If I work harder, I will do better. /

A fish in a dish had a wish. The fish wished the dish was filled with water. I have a / customer who will pay you cash if you wash his car by noon. If you do a good job, he / will pay you double. If you are done by 9, he will probably give you an extra bonus.

She had a / girlish grin on her face. He had a boyish smile on his face. They all had a childish way about / them. Did you mash, crash, or crunch the car into the telephone pole? Abe said: "4 score and 7 years / ago."

Comprehensive Practice

☞ *Practice the following. When you are finished, take your notes and read them aloud, comparing them to the textbook. If you have any errors, circle them in your steno notes. Practice this section again until you can write it without any errors.*

Aren't you going to take a day off? Don't you feel tired? Shouldn't you relax a little bit before you / do all that work? If I were you, I wouldn't whine all the time. Whiny people never get their work / done. All they do is cry, and crying isn't going to get you very far.

Jan says "I ain't going to / do it." Jane says, "I can do it." Which one is going to do better in school? There was a man in / an automobile that had a wreck in the morning; and then, in the afternoon he had a crash. He is / lucky that he is alive.

There once was a black rabbit who had a white hat on top of its / head. I haven't seen a bunny like that in a long time. The bunny hopped along the street until it / hopped into a passing car.

Dr. Jones will employ you to affix a note to each employee who is late / for work. If the employer sees that the employee is late, he will have you pin the note on their / shirt. If they abuse their time, they will have to carry the note around all day long. The note will say what / time you did arrive.

Joan was afraid of a frog who hopped into her window. She put a pot aside / to catch the frog. The frog didn't hop in the pot, but hopped into a dish of sauce. The / front of the table was filled with loose sauce. Joan heard a scream; it was her mom; she didn't like / saucy frogs on her table.

John said he would carry the frog out the door; but when he tried to / pick up the frog, the frog zapped into a princess. Now, Joan and her mom are looking for a charming / prince in each frog they see.

Additional Practice

Go to the: Do the following:

Realwrite DrillBook (recommended)......Read over and study Drill XII (Lessons 25 & 26)
Realwrite NoteBook (optional)................Read and transcribe the notes from Exercise G, Lesson 25

UNIT 7
LESSON TWENTY-SIX

Warm up and Review

☞ *practice the following:*

monthly	most	must	necessary
neglect	neighbor	not	notify
number	object	of	on
only	or	out	passenger
perform	personal	possible	public
some	take	that	the
their	there	they	this
under	until	very	was
were	what	when	where
which	will	with	would
write	yes		

Writing Words that Begin with "in," "on," or "en"

26.1 Write EUPB- for words that begin with "in," write OPB- for words that begin with "on," write EPB- for words that begin with "en."

For example:

inmate	EUPB/PHAEUT	enjoy	EPB/SKWROFPL
onion	OPB/KWROPB	onset	OPB/SET

It is important to note the use of TPH- for the short form "in," and the O for the short form for "on." These short forms can never be used for prefixes or suffixes.

☞ *practice the following:*

inmate	EUPB/PHAEUT	insane	EUPB/SAEUPB	incur	EUPB/KUR
incorrect	EUPB/KREBGT	index	EUPB/DEFRPB	instill	EUPB/STEUL
invoke	EUPB/SROEBG	inherit	EUPB/HAEURT	infer	EUPB/TPER
ongoing	OPB/TKPWOEG	onset	OPB/SET	onion	OPB/KWROPB
enhance	EPB/HAPBS	endure	EPB/TKAOUR	enable	EPB/KWRAEUBL

Writing Words that Begin with "or" or "er"

26.2 Write OR- for words that begin with "or," write ER- for words that begin with "er."

☞ *practice the following:*

ordeal	OR/TKAOEL	orchid	OR/KEUD	orbit	OR/PWEUT
ornate	OR/TPHAEUT	organ	OR/TKPWAPB	orchard	OR/KHARD
error	ER/KWROR	ergo	ER/TKPWOE	era	ER/KWRA

Writing Dollar Amounts

26.3 All money amounts must be preceded with the special outline PHE-RBGS or TKHR-RBGS. After writing the special outline, write the numbers as you hear them, using all previous rules. Use the –SZ to indicate cents.

Note—the PHE-RBGS (money) or TKHR-RBGS (dollar) will generate the dollar sign ($) and the –SZ (cents) will generate the decimal point between the dollars and cents.

for example:

$5.89	PHE-RBGS/5/89/SZ	$16.21	TKHR-RBGS/16/12EU/SZ
$75.48	PHE-RBGS/5EU7/48/SZ	$55.00	TKHR-RBGS/5EU/0/SZ
$99	PHE-RBGS/EU9	$11.00	TKHR-RBGS/1EU/0/SZ

26.4 For large amounts of money, write the numbers as you hear them using the following short forms: TR-L for trillion; -BL for billion; PH-L for million. Write PHE-RBGS or TKHR-RBGS in the first stroke for all money amounts.

for example:

$74 million	PHE-RBGS/4EU7/PH-L	$55 billion	TKHR-RBGS/5EU/-BL
$5 trillion	PHE-RBGS/5/TR-L	$909 million	TKHR-RBGS/9/H-PBD/0/9

Note how large amounts of money are translated as $74 million not $74,000,000

26.5 Very large amounts of money are written as they are said using all previous number rules. The -DZ for dollars and/or the -SZ for cents are written in the appropriate stroke. Write PHE-RBGS or TKHR-RBGS in the first stroke for all money amounts.

for example:

$945,895,432   PHE-RBGS/9/H-PBD/45/PH-L/8/H-PBD/5EU9/TH-Z/4/H-PBD/2EU3

26.6 Use the short form TKLAR for dollar, TKLARZ for dollars, KREPBT for cent, and KREPBTS for cents when appropriate.

for example:

a million dollars	AEU/PHEUL/KWROPB/TKLARZ
one red cent	WUPB/RED/KREPBT
a hundred dollars	AEU/HUND/TKLARZ
two cents	TWO/KREPBTS

Multi-Consonant Combinations (PR-, SN-, SM-)

☞ *practice the following:*

PR- PR- PR- ,	PR- PR- PR- ,	PR- PR- PR- ,
PR- PR- PR- ,	PR- PR- PR- ,	PR- PR- PR- ,
PR- PR- PR- ,	PR- PR- PR- ,	PR- PR- PR- ,
STPH- STPH- STPH- ,	STPH- STPH- STPH- ,	STPH- STPH- STPH- ,
STPH- STPH- STPH- ,	STPH- STPH- STPH- ,	STPH- STPH- STPH- ,
STPH- STPH- STPH- ,	STPH- STPH- STPH- ,	STPH- STPH- STPH- ,
SPH- SPH- SPH- ,	SPH- SPH- SPH- ,	SPH- SPH- SPH- ,
SPH- SPH- SPH- ,	SPH- SPH- SPH- ,	SPH- SPH- SPH- ,
SPH- SPH- SPH- ,	SPH- SPH- SPH- ,	SPH- SPH- SPH- ,

☞ *practice the following:*

pray	PRAFPL	prance	PRAPBS	prairie	PRAEUR/KWRAOE
preach	PRAOEFP	precious	PRERBS	press	PRES
snag	STPHAG	snow	STPHOEFRP	snake	STPHAEUBG
snap	STPHAP	snug	STPHUG	snail	STPHAEUL
smart	SPHART	smash	SPHARB	smear	SPHAOER
smell	SPHEL	smoke	SPHOEBG	smog	SPHOG

Short Forms and Phrases

☞ *practice the following:*

practice	PRA	present	PREPBT	presence	PREPBS
previous	PR-FS	product	PROBGT	program	PRAPL
propose	PR-P	profession	PROFGS	type	TAOEUP
provide	PROEU	approximate	PRAFRPB	appropriate	PROEPT

Lesson Practice

☞ *practice the following:*

The inmate at the state jail was put away for 21 years. He committed a crime. He thought he / could get away with throwing (THROEFRPG) snow (STPHOEFRP) balls (PWAULZ) at the principal. They caught (KAUGT) him in the act. Now, his ordeal is / ongoing. He has to pay the price.

The precious little child cried when she learned that she could not have / any gum. Her mom was afraid that the gum would smear all over her face. Her dad said "no gum, / no way." Then her dad got gum on the rug. He didn't practice what he began to preach. Now, he / is sorry.

The program began at 9 sharp. In order to enable those who were late to see the whole / show, the program was started again at 10. The show was ongoing. At the onset of the show, the organ / began to play. Since the organ was out of tune, the man began to pray. He prayed while he played. /

Mr. Wilson always says: "Provide for your old age, and you will be as snug as a bug in a / rug." I propose to save $48.23 a week for life. By the time I am / 77 years old, I will / incur $988,210.34. I'm / smart because I save.

John stepped on a snail and screamed; then he stepped on a snake and ran. He / picked an orchid from the orchard and gave it to his mom as a present. There was only one snag, / there was a bee in it.

It is insane to say that there is snow on the prairie. It is / incorrect to say that the snow never melts because there was no snow to begin with. What type of program / are you doing? What an ordeal. Can you endure? Will your presence endure? Where is the index in the book? / In the beginning or at the end? What is your profession? What product do you manufacture? /

Comprehensive Practice

☞ <u>Practice the following</u>. *When you are finished, take your notes and read them aloud, comparing them to the textbook. If you have any errors, circle them in your steno notes. Practice this section again until you can write it without any errors.*

Can you appreciate the particular theme of the play? Is the theme about a girl who finds fulfillment and enjoyment / in her work? Jan didn't realize that there were so many words in the book. She made an arrangement with a / man from her home town to type the words into a little booklet for her to study. It will / be about $567.92 to have it done, but she said she was glad / that she did it.

If you file the document by 6, you will be able to use the new equipment. / She paid rent on the apartment in the amount of $339.19, but her check / bounced. Now, she is looking for employment so that she can pay off her debts. She should try to get a/ job that pays a lot of money.

Bob stood in amazement as he saw the bill from his doctor. / It was for $987,984,291.43. / He fainted when he saw the bill. Now, he is sick in bed. His mom is not letting people in / to see him because he is afraid he will not get well. He doesn't have the money to pay / so he will make payment when he can. He needs to set up an appointment with a finance man to / get an estimate.

Additional Practice

Go to the:	Do the following:
Realwrite DrillBook (recommended).......	Write and practice Drill XIII (Lessons 25 & 26)
Realwrite NoteBook (optional)................	Read and transcribe the notes from Exercise G, Lesson 26 and Drill XIII

UNIT 7
LESSON TWENTY-SEVEN

Warm up and Review

☞ *practice the following:*

about a	can a	did a	had a	have a	if a
is a	with a	that are	there are	they are	we are
what are	when are	where are	which are	you are	he can
I can	it can	that can	there can	they can	we can
what can	when can	where can	which can	you can	I could
He could	it could	that could	there could	they could	we could
what could	when could	where could	when could	you could	he did
I did	it did	that did	there did	they did	we did
what did	when did	where did	which did	you did	

Writing Final Strokes that Begin with a Vowel

As you have already learned, it is most important that you make a distinction between word endings, word beginings, and words that are written out. For example, the word "on" is written as a word by itself, as well as being used at the beginning and sometimes at the end of a word. The computer needs to know which way to transcribe the "on." For that reason, we have different ways of designating prefixes, suffixes,,and words.

The following word endings (suffixes) are a continuation of the "silent y" principle used for all final strokes that begin with a vowel.

27.1 Write all multi-syllablic words that begin with a vowel in the final stroke by using the initial "y" (KWR-) before the vowel.

Using this rule, any last stroke that begins with a vowel is written with the initial KWR. Consider the "y" as silent and read only the vowel and consonants.

☞ *practice the following:*

sewage	SEFRP/KWRAPBLG	carnage	KARPB/KWRAPBLG
passage	PAS/KWRAPBLG	lessen	HRES/KWREPB
deepen	TKAOEP/KWREPB	widen	WAOEUD/KWREPB
utensil	U/TEPBS/KWREUL	pencil	PEPBS/KWREUL
council	KOUPBS/KWREUL	lesson	HRES/KWROPB
rayon	RAFPL/KWROPB	lemon	HREPL/KWROPB
bonus	PWOEPB/KWRUS	fetus	TPAOET/KWRUS
bogus	PWOEG/KWRUS	lettuce	HRET/KWRUS

Writing Words that end in "on" or "en"

27.2 For all words that require a separate stroke for the ending "on," write the designation KWROPB. For all words that require a separate stroke for the ending "en," write the designation KWREPB.

For example:

lesson HRES/KWROPB lessen HRES/KWREPB

☞ *practice the following:*

wagon	WAG/KWROPB	cannon	KAPB/KWROPB
lemon	HREPL/KWROPB	melon	PHEL/KWROPB
lesson	HRES/KWROPB	eaten	AOET/KWREPB
liken	HRAOEUBG/KWREPB	linen	HREUPB/KWREPB
olden	OELD/KWREPB	risen	REUZ/KWREPB
waken	WAEUBG/KWREPB	tighten	TAOEUGT/KWREPB
widen	WAOEUD/KWREPB	frighten	TPRAOEUGT/KWREPB

Some words can be written with a consonant in the last stroke, thus avoiding writing the final stroke beginning with a vowel. In most cases, the syllabic division or pronunciation will dictate how the word is written.

☞ *practice the following:*

baton	PWA/TOPB	nylon	TPHFPL/HROPB	salon	SA/HROPB
arson	AR/SOPB	mason	PHA/SOPB	Jackson	SKWRABG/SOEPB

Writing Words that end in "or" or "er"

27.3 For all words that require a separate stroke for the ending "or," write the designation KWROR. For all words that require a separate stroke for the ending "er," write the designation KWRER.

For example:

lessor HRES/KWROR lesser HRES/KWRER

☞ *practice the following:*

actor	ABGT/KWROR	armor	ARPL/KWROR
error	ER/KWROR	honor	HOPB/KWROR
humor	HAOUPL/KWROR	minor	PHAOEUPB/KWROR
razor	RAEUZ/KWROR	tutor	TAOUT/KWROR
vigor	SREUG/KWROR	sector	SEKBT/KWROR

alter	ALT/KWRER	fender	TPEPBD/KWRER
buyer	PWUFPL/KWRER	anger	APBG/KWRER
dinner	TKEUPB/KWRER	diner	TKAOEUPB/KWRER
eager	AOEG/KWRER	fewer	TPEFRP/KWRER
finer	TPAOEUPB/KWRER	older	OELD/KWRER
cater	KAEUT/KWRER	caller	KAUL/KWRER
dagger	TKAG/KWRER	bigger	PWEUG/KWRER

Contractions using the Z-rule (Had/Would)

☞ *practice the following:*

I had	AOEUFD	I would	AOEUWD	I'd	AOEUDZ[1]
he had	HAEFD	he would	HAEWD	he'd	HAEDZ
she had	SHAEFD	she would	SHAEWD	she'd	SHAEDZ
they had	THEFD	they would	THEWD	they'd	THEDZ
we had	WEFD	we would	WAEWD	we'd	WAEDZ
you had	UFD	you would	UWD	you'd	UDZ

[1]In most cases, the contraction is the same for both the "had" and "would" family. The short form uses the -DZ.

New Punctuation (Parentheses)

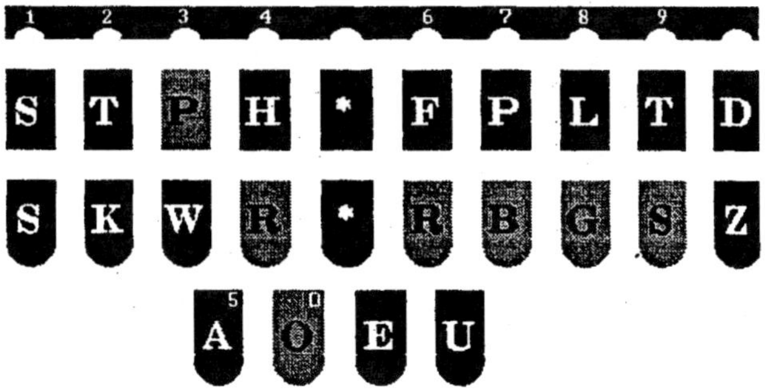

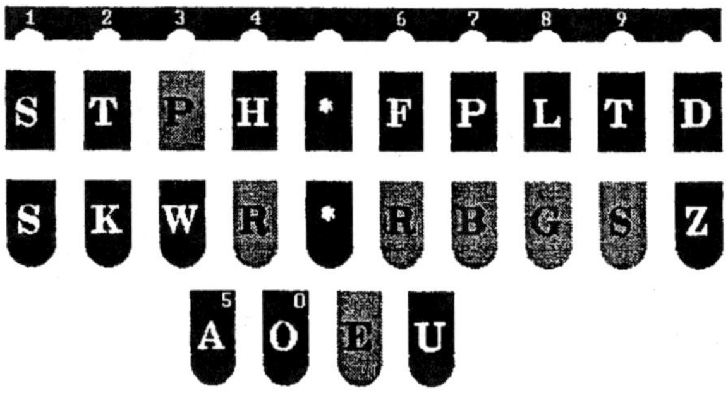

27.4 Use the PRO-RBGS for "opening" parenthesis. Use the PRE-RBGS for "ending" parenthesis.

Short Forms and Phrases

☞ *practice the following:*

occur	KUR	office	TPEUS	obtain	OBT
today	TOD	tomorrow	TOR	yesterday	KWREFPL
report	RORT	remember	RER	remind	REUPBD
return	RURPB	request	RELGTS	represent	REPT

Lesson Practice

☞ *practice the following:*

The actor in the play had a good sense of humor. He played the part of an older man who / showed his anger at dinner. I'd say he was excellent. The play started today, but they will show it again / tomorrow. I can't wait to read the report.

The report had one error in it. You'd have to search high / and low to find it. They spelled your name wrong. You'd better request that they fix it or no one / will remember you. I'd obtain an extra copy of the report and return it to the main office tomorrow by / noon.

Fewer and fewer people are able to afford to buy a new car these days. The more money they / earn, the more money they spend. I was able to obtain a good deal on a used car; it was / a station wagon.

John dressed up in a suit of armor and shot a cannon that had a melon in / it. Jill threw a baton up in the air, but it never came down. Joe tossed a lemon through a hoop / with vigor.

She'd better get a tutor to help her study if she wants to represent the school at the / exam. She cannot have one error on her exam. She is very eager to win the prize. The prize is a / brand new house. If she wins the house, she will be very happy.

Joan has a store called the "nylon / salon." She used to have a shop called the "finer diner" that sold food. She had to widen the shop to / make room for her new equipment. Now, she has one special request. She wants to remind all older people that / today is a special day for them. They can obtain a razor cut for half price.

Some say "older is / better." I say "to be a minor is finer." Jeff (who used to go to school with me) now / goes to school in Denver. He is studying (STUD/AEFPLG) to be a lawyer. He'd like to practice law.

Comprehensive Practice

☞ *Practice the following. When you are finished, take your notes and read them aloud, comparing them to the textbook. If you have any errors, circle them in your steno notes. Practice this section until you can write it without any errors.*

There was a big fight between a cow and a horse (the horse won). I can't help it, but / I talk to myself when I get excited. Did the people pay for the tickets themselves, or did they / get them free? Jan, herself, and Zeb, himself, ate a complete 4 course dinner themselves. They got sick.

The jury / could not say "yes" or "no." There was one juror who could not make up his mind. He would go / one way and then next time he would not go the same way. The court took comfort in the fact / that he was only there for one day. Now, he is gone.

Did you see the big wreck between the / train and the plane? The motor on a jet plane fell out of the sky and hit the train on / the track. The train then went off the track. No one was hurt, but the engineer couldn't stop talking about / it.

The manager of the train company tried to calm him down, but he couldn't. The manager of the jet / company would not comment on what made the motor fall off, but he did say that it was a complex / case.

Now that the collision is over (and no one is hurt), we can be proud of the way the / police took care of the case.

Additional Practice

Go to the:	Do the following:
Realwrite DrillBook (recommended).........	Read over and study Drill XIV (Lessons 27 & 28)
Realwrite Notebook (optional)...................	Read and transcribe the notes from Exercise G, Lesson 27

UNIT 7
LESSON TWENTY-EIGHT

Warm up and Review

☞ *practice the following:*

he had	I had	it had	that had	there had	they had
we had	what had	when had	where had	which had	you had
I have	that have	there have	they have	we have	what have
when have	where have	when have	will have	would have	you have
can he	could he	did he	does he	had he	if he
is he	that he	was he	what he	will he	would he
can I	could I	did I	had I	have I	if I
that I	was I	what I	will I	would I	

Flagged Alphabet (Letter-by-Letter Spelling)

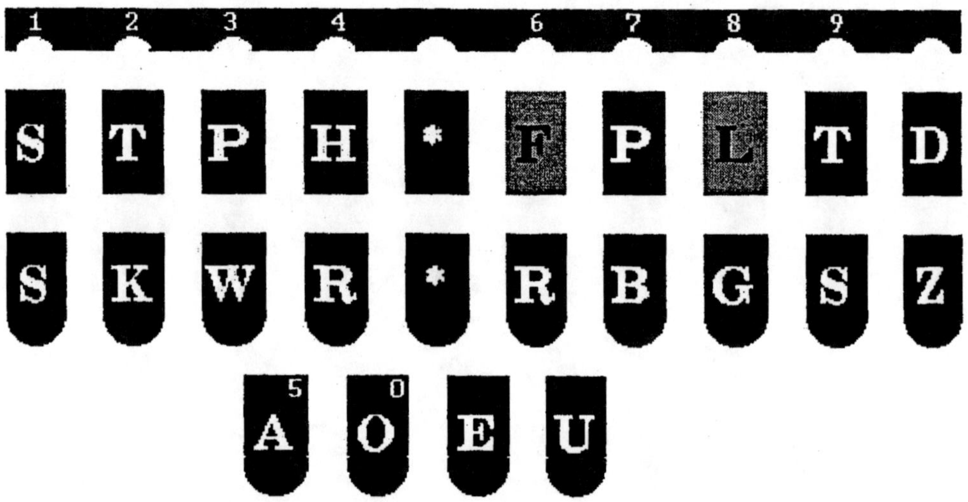

Spelling words for the record is an important part of the training of realtime writers. Very often witnesses will be asked to spell their names or to spell certain technical or medical terms. The rule for spelling words using the letter-by-letter format is similar to the other "flagged" alphabets that you have already learned.

28.1 To write the alphabet for letter-by-letter spelling, write the alphabetic letter on the initial side of the keyboard along with the final side -FL (for letter-by-letter) in the same stroke. Each letter requires the -FL.

☞ *practice the following:*

alphabet	Realwrite	alphabet	Realwrite	alphabet	Realwrite
-A-	A-FL	-J-	SKWR-FL	-S-	S-FL
-B-	PW-FL	-K-	K-FL	-T-	T-FL
-C-	KR-FL	-L-	HR-FL	-U-	U-FL
-D-	TK-FL	-M-	PH-FL	-V-	SR-FL
-E-	E-FL	-N-	TPH-FL	-W-	W-FL
-F-	TP-FL	-O-	O-FL	-X-	SKP-FL
-G-	TKPW-FL	-P-	P-FL	-Y-	KWR-FL
-H-	H-FL	-Q-	KW-FL	-Z-	SKPW-FL
-I-	EU-FL	-R-	R-FL		

New Punctuation (Hyphen)

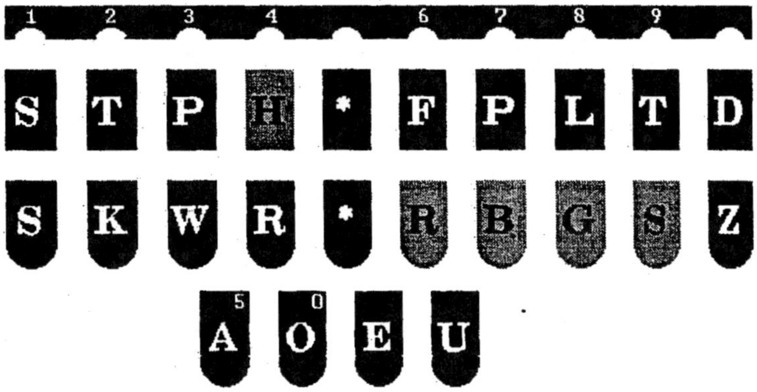

28.2 To write a hyphen, use the H-RBGS.

Word Separators and Joiners

28.3 When two words are separated, use the H-RBGS between the words.

☞ *practice the following:*

pre-natal care	PRE/H-RBGS/TPHAEUT/KWRAL/KAEUR
self-imposed tax	SEFL/H-RBGS/EUPL/POEZ/AED/TAFRPB
bi-lateral treaty	PWEU/H-RBGS/HRAT/RAL/TRAOET/AEFPL

28.4 When two words that would normally be separated form a compound word, use the designation AE between the two words to join them together to form one word.

☞ *practice the following:*

doghouse	TKOG/AE/HOUS	outlay	OUT/AE/HRAFPL
background	PWABG/AE/TKPWROUPBD	courtroom	KOURT/AE/RAOPL
bedroom	PWED/AE/RAOPL	uptown	UP/AE/TOUPB

The AE can also be combined in the first or second stroke to make a distinct way of writing the word. For example:

driveway	TKRAOEUFB/WAEFPL	stairway	STAEUR/WAEFPL

Words that Begin with "pre" or "pro"

28.5 Write PRE- for all words that begin with the prefix "pre." Write PRO- for all words that begin with the prefix "pro."

☞ *practice the following:*

prepaid	PRE/PAEUD	premier	PRE/PHAOER	prevent	PRE/SREPBT
predate	PRE/TKAEUT	predict	PRE/TKEUBGT	promote	PRO/PHOET
prorate	PRO/RAEUT	protect	PRO/TEBGT	proportion	PRO/PORGS

If a hyphen is needed between the prefix "pro" and the word, write the H-RBGS between the strokes.

For example:

pro-life	PRO/H-RBGS/LAOEUF	pro-active	PRO/H-RBGS/ABG/TEUFB

Words that Begin with "re," "be," or "de"

28.6 Write the RE- for all words that begin with the prefix "re"; write PWE- for all words that begin with the prefix "be."

☞ *practice the following:*

remit	RE/PHEUT	resume	RE/SKPWAOUPL	recall	RE/KAUL
resent	RE/SKPWEPBT	revoke	RE/SROEBG	rejoin	RE/SKWROEUPB
recant	RE/KAPBT	retire	RE/TAOEUR	revise	RE/SRAOEUZ
betray	PWE/TRAFPL	beheld	PWE/HELD	behold	PWE/HOELD

28.7 Write the TKE for all words that begin with the prefix "de," unless the "de" can be blended or "slurred" together as in words containing the dep (TKP-), dem (TKPH-) or del (TKHR-).

☞ *practice the following:*

destroy	TKE/STROFPL	defer	TKEFR	deter	TKE/TER
defame	TKE/TPAEUPL	defraud	TKE/FRAUD	degrade	TKE/TKPWRAEUD
deliver	TKHREUFR	depose	TKPOEZ	demand	TKPHAPBD
deprive	TKPRAOEUFB	depart	TKPART	delight	TKHRAOEUGT

Short Forms and Phrases

☞ *practice the following:*

worry	WOER	woman	WAPB	women	WEPB
wherever	WHREFR	whenever	WHEFR	volunteer	SRO
volume	SROUPL	visible	SREUBL	victim	SREUBGT
upon	POPB	unless	TPH-LS	unwilling	TPH-FRP
notice	TPH-TS	recent	RAOEPBT		

Lesson Practice

☞ *practice the following:*

Please remit $45.87 with your payment. A woman and a man began to demand that / we take action. I recall that the recent volume was removed (RE/PHOFBD) from the bookcase (PWAOBG/KAES). Unless you return the book as / soon as possible, we will have to revoke your license (HRAOEUS/KWRENS).

He'd destroy the paper (PAEUP/KWRER) if he could. She'd defer payment / if she could. I'd deliver the paper to the women if they wanted (WAPBT/AED) me to. Wherever I go, whenever I / see you, you are always unwilling to do what is right.

He said he was "pro-life." Upon notice of / the party, he couldn't attend (A/TEPBD). I resent having to go to jail. I made a visible mistake (PHEUS/TAE), or was it / an error? The volunteer was a victim of circumstance. When will you deliver the new car?

If I depart now, / I will demand that you resume the stand. We will prorate what you said and predate what was written. Jennifer / is a worry wart. She began to worry because it started to snow. The snow was not even visible to / the eye. I recall one day in the winter (WEUPBT/KWRER) when we had 18 feet of snow in one day. I / didn't even worry because I had my 4-wheel (4/H-RBGS/WHAOEL) drive Jeep.

The premier attraction (A/TRABGS) was a woman who could predict / tomorrow. She could not prevent a collision, but she could predict it. She even mentioned (PHEPBGS/AED) a little detail about a / fly on the wall.

What proportion of the proceeds (PRO/SAOEDZ) do you want to take with you? Why not take it / all? I can't prorate it. If you do, you will destroy all visible signs (SAOEUPBZ) of it. I demand a recount / (RE/KOUPBT). I spell relief R-E-L -I-E-F. How do you spell it? Is your name spelled J-E-N / or J-A-N?

Comprehensive Praactice

☞ *Practice the following. When you are finished, take your notes and read them aloud, comparing them to the textbook. If you have any errors, circle them in your steno notes. Practice this section again until you can write it without any errors.*

I was told that I had to complete the transaction by 8 or that 12 policemen would come to my / office to get me. I tried to cry for help, but my pleas were not heard. Please hear my pleas. /

Did you get plenty of money from the transaction? If you didn't, why not? What will you do? I have / a great deal of tension in my brain. I work too hard. I try to release my tension by reading / and seeing a movie now and then. The movie I saw was about a man and a woman who/ went on a sled ride in a snow storm. They took a trip on a sleek jet.

Shredded melon makes / good melon juice if it is squeezed (SKWAOEZ/AED) right. You have to squeeze the melon slow or you will spill the / juice. Make sure your glass is the right size. If your vision is correct, you can see for miles and / miles.

A fraction is what you will get when you deal with addition and subtraction. Which do you like better: addition (A/TKEUGS) / or subtraction (SUB/TRABGS) ? If I stand by my conviction, I will never deal with a fraction.

A policeman caught (KAUGT) my attention / when he shot his gun in the air. He said that he was trying to stop a man from robbing / a store. The man was on a mission. He wanted money, and he wanted it now. He shot the store / clerk, but she is doing fine. He ran away, but the police caught him in the alley (AL/AEFPL).

My wife has a / condition. She needs a lot of pills and drugs. I can't afford to buy them so I have to sell eggs (EGZ) / to make money. Will you buy some eggs from me? If you do, I will give you a special rate: / 9 eggs for the price of 12 or 9 eggs for $57.21. What a bargain / (PWAR/TKWPAPB).

Additional Practice

Go to the: — Do the following:

Realwrite DrillBook (recommended)........Write and practice Drill XIV (Lessons 27 & 28)
Realwrite NoteBook (optional)................Read and transcribe the notes from Exercise G, Lesson 28 and Drill XIV

UNIT 7 REVIEW

Lesson Review

1. Go back to each lesson and learn each new rule thoroughly.
2. Go back to each lesson and write the Lesson Practice.
3. Go back to each lesson and write the Comprehensive Practice.
4. Read back all notes and transcribe a portion of your review.

Review of Writing Rules

25.1 Write words that end in the sound of "ch" by using the -FP. If it is necessary to write the -FP in a separate stroke by itself, write the AEFP in the last stroke.

25.2 Write words that end in the sound of "sh" by using the -RB. For words that end in "ish" and require a second stroke, use the "silent y" and write KWREURB.

25.3 Use the KWO-RBGS for "opening" quotes. Use the KWE-RBGS for "ending" quotes.

25.4 Use the -RBL for words that end in the sound of "shal," regardless of their spelling. If a separate stroke is required, use SHAEL in the last stroke.

25.5 Use the -RBS for words that end in the sound of "shus," regardless of the spelling. If a separate stroke is required, use SHAUS in the last stroke.

26.1 Write EUPB- for words that begin with "in," write OPB- for words that begin with "on," write EPB- for words that begin with "en."

26.2 Write OR- for words that begin with "or," write ER- for words that begin with "er."

26.3 All money amounts must be preceded with the special outline PHE-RBGS or TKHR-RBGS. After writing the special outline, write the numbers as you hear them, using all previous rules. Use the –SZ to indiate cents.

26.4 For large amounts of money, write the numbers as you hear them using the following short forms: TR-L for trillion; -BL for billion; PH-L for million. Write PHE-RBGS or TKHR-RBGS in the first stroke for all money amounts.

26.5 Very large amounts of money are written as they are said using all previous number rules. The -DZ for dollars and/or the -SZ for cents are written in the appropriate stroke. Write PHE-RBGS or TKHR-RBGS in the first stroke for all money amounts.

26.6 Use the short form TKLAR for dollar, TKLARZ for dollars, KREPBT for cent, and KREPBTS for cents when appropriate.

27.1 Write all multi-syllabic words that begin with a vowel in the final stroke by using the initial Y- (KWR-) before the vowel.

27.2 For all words that require a separate stroke for the ending "on," write the designation KWROPB. For all words that require a separate stroke for the ending "en," write the designation KWREPB.

27.3 For all words that require a separate stroke for the ending "or," write the designation KWROR. For all words that require a separate stroke for the ending "er," write the designation KWRER.

27.4 Use the PRO-RBGS for "opening" parenthesis. Use the PRE-RBGS for "ending" parenthesis.

28.1 To write the alphabet for letter-by-letter spelling, write the alphabetic letter on the initial side of the keyboard along with the final side -FL (for letter-by-letter) in the same stroke. Each letter requires the -FL.

28.2 To write a hyphen, use the H-RBGS.

28.3 When two words are separated, use the H-RBGS between the words.

28.4 When two words that would normally be separated form a compound word, use the designation AE between the two words to join them together to form one word.

28.5 Write PRE- for all words that begin with the prefix "pre." Write PRO- for all words that begin with the prefix "pro."

28.6 Write the RE- for all words that begin with the prefix "re"; write PWE- for all words that begin with the prefix "be."

28.7 Write the TKE for all words that begin with the prefix "de," unless the "de" can be blended or "slurred" together as in words containing the dep (TKP-), dem (TKPH-), or del (TKHR-).

Review DrillBook and NoteBook Applications

1. Review Drills XIII and XIV from the *Realwrite DrillBook* (recommended).
2. Review Exercise G from the *Realwrite NoteBook* (optional).

Unit Evaluation Number Seven

Unit Evaluation Number Seven will cover all material from the following: *Realwrite LessonBook*, Lessons 25-28; *DrillBook*, Drills XIII and XIV.

UNIT 8
LESSON TWENTY-NINE

Warm up and Review

☞ *practice the following:*

he is	it is	that is	there is	this is	what is
when is	where is	which is	is the	on the	or the
that the	under the	was the	what the	when the	where the
which the	will the	with the	would the	is there	is this
are you	can you	could you	did you	do you	from you
had you	have you	if you	that you	were you	what you
where you	will you	with you	would you	he will	I will
it will	that will	there will	they will	this will	we will
what will	when will	where will	which will	you will	

Writing Words that end in "ly," "le," or "el"

29.1 For all words that end with the "ly" ending, write the -L in the same stroke. If it is necessary to write the -L in a separate stroke, write the HRAEFPL (LAEY) in the last stroke.

☞ *practice the following:*

surely	SHAOURL	rarely	RAEURL
lonely	HROEPBL	dearly	TKAOERL
sadly	SAD/HRAEFPL	safely	SAEUFL
fairly	TPAEURL	barely	PWAEURL
badly	PWAD/HRAEFPL	lately	HRAEUT/HRAEFPL
timely	TAOEUPL/HRAEFPL	scarcely	SKAEURS/HRAEFPL
wisely	WAOEUZ/HRAEFPL	likely	HRAOEUBG/HRAEFPL
hardly	HARD/HRAEFPL	correctly	KREBGT/HRAEFPL

29.2 If the first syllable of the word ends in the consonant "l," write the AEFPL in the final stroke.

☞ *practice the following:*

daily	TKAEUL/AEFPL	early	ERL/AEFPL	jelly	SKWREL/AEFPL
rally	RAL/AEFPL	holly	HOL/AEFPL	silly	SEUL/AEFPL

29.3 For all words that end with the "le" or "el" combine the -L in the same stroke if possible. If a second stroke is necessary, write the AEL (le) or KWRAEL (el) in the last stroke.

☞ *practice the following:*

trouble	TROUBL	double	TKOUBL	bubble	PWUBL
apple	AP/AEL	maple	PHAEUP/AEL	angle	APBG/AEL
waffle	WAFL	hassle	HAS/AEL	tassel	TAS/KWRAEL[1]
muffle	PHUFL	duffel	TKUFL	truffle	TRUFL

[1]Words that end in "el" are written with the KWRAEL ending, however, your dictionary can be programmed to define TAS/AEL for tassel.

29.4 In writing the AEL in the second stroke of words that end in "le," it may be necessary to begin the second stroke with a leftover consonant.

☞ *practice the following:*

ample	APL/PAEL	sample	SAPL/PAEL	trample	TRAPL/PAEL

Writing Words that end in "fer" or "ver"

29.5 For all words that end in "fer" or "ver," write the -FR in the same stroke. If it is necessary to write the "fer" or "ver" in a separate stroke, use FER or SRER.

☞ *practice the following:*

offer	OFR	over	OEFR	cover	KOFR
never	TPHEFR	sliver	SHREUFR	silver	SEUL/SRER
wafer	WAFR[1]	waiver	WAEUFR	waver	WAEFR
safer	SAFR[1]	saver	SAEUFR[2]	suffer	SUFR

[1]Where a conflict occurs between words that end in "fer" and "ver" use the short vowel for the "soft" consonant "fer" words; use the long vowel for the "hard" consonant "ver" words.

[2]while "saver" (one who saves something) is not found in the dictionary, it is a common "slang" word. Note the outline for savor is SAFB/KWROR.and savior SAFB/KWRAOR)

Contractions using Z-Rule (Have)

The following phrases and their contractions are a continuation of the Z-rule.

☞ *practice the following:*

phrase	Realwrite	contraction	Realwrite
I have	AOEUFB	I've	AOEUFZ[1]
they have	THEFB	they've	THEFZ
we have	WEFB	we've	WEFZ
you have	UFB	you've	UFZ

[1] drop the B from the V and add the Z

New Punctuation (Exclamation Point, Slash)

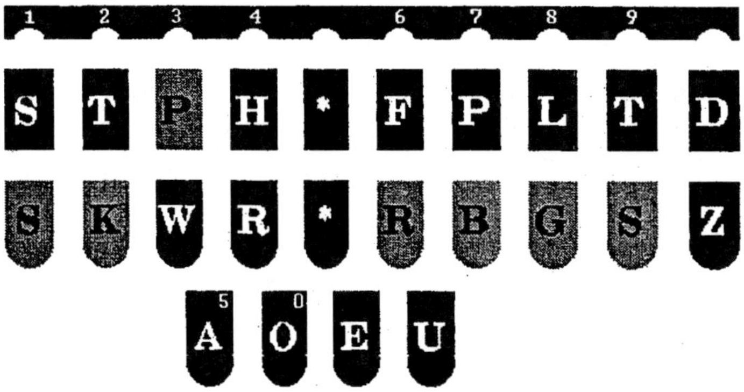

29.6 Write the SKP-RBGS to designate the exclamation point as needed in dictation.

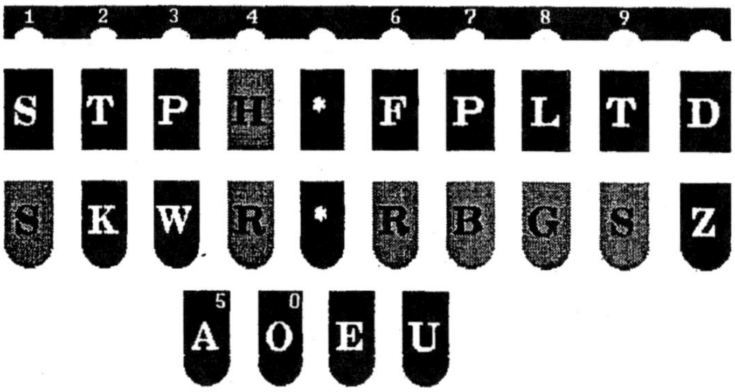

29.7 Write the SL-RBGS to designate the slash mark whenever it is needed in dictation.

Short Forms and Phrases

☞ *practice the following:*

ability	ABLT	above	PWOFB	accept	SEP
ask	SK-	basis	PWEUS	certain	SERPB
certificate	SERT	department	TKEPT	difference	TPREPBS
different	TPREPBT	dozen	TKOZ	easy	AOES
really	R-L	truly	T-Y		

Lesson Practice

☞ *practice the following:*

Surely, you must be kidding. How can I offer you a silver coin when all I have is gold? Will / you take a hundred dollar bill? I've given you the choice; I won't ask you again. I can't keep going / over and over the same request. Please tell me your opinion.

Now, you are in deep trouble. In fact, you / are in double trouble. You took the wrong sample of apple juice and mixed it with maple syrup (SEUR/KWRUP). Now, we've / got to get a waiver for the mess you made. It will require a certificate from the department of juice / and syrup, and that is not easy to obtain.

Lately, I've felt different about how I practice. Now, I spend / 3 hours a night practicing my outlines. I'm becoming a real whiz at shorthand. In fact, rarely do I / miss an outline. I'm so good that I can safely write every word I hear in a fraction of / a minute. My teacher says I'm great!

The difference between good writers (WREURZ) and bad writers is scarcely noted / in how they look sitting at the machine. What really counts is how they read back and how they translate (TRAPBS/HRAEUT) /their work. You never can judge good writers by how they look; and you can never judge a / book by its cover.

Rex is a saver of whatever he can save. He saves mice, dice, rice, and jelly. / His mom tries to clean up his room daily, but she can't. There is too much stuff. His room needs / cleaning, badly. I am certain that he could clean it in a timely fashion (FAGS) if he had a dozen friends / to help him. It would be easy with a dozen friends.

Ray looked sadly at the work he had to / do. He did not have the ability to get it all done in 8 hours. He couldn't accept the fact / that he needed help. He would not ask for help. He could not go over all of the material in such (SUFP) / a short period (PAOERD) of time. He failed the exam, and now he is truly sorry. He is likely to pass / the exam the next time, because now he has wisely put aside enough time to study.

You've been quiet (KWET) / for some time now. We've come to help you. Even though (THOUFD) it is early, we did bring you some bread / and jelly to get you through (THROUFD) the day. Don't ask for any more, they've eaten (AOET/KWREPB) it all up. I've no more / to offer you.

Comprehensive Practice

☞ *practice the following:*

The child was very childish for his age. The boy was very boyish, and the girl was very girlish. Joe / mashed a lemon, Jill smashed a Cadillac, and Jen crunched a carrot (KAEURT).

I wish the fish in the dish would / dance. If the fish in the dish did a little jig, I would be rich. I have about 400 customers / who will pay a lot of cash to see a fish dance in a dish. If the fish did a two-step, / I'd take a photograph and sell it for a great deal of money.

The man in the store will probably / sell you a used shorthand machine for $400. I would look for one that you could hook up to your / computer (KPAOUT/KWRER). A computer will set you back about a thousand bucks (PWUBGZ), but it will help you do your work / quicker (KWEUBG/KWRER) than lightning (HRAOEUGT/TPHAEG). You might even be able to do your work better.

Men and women who write on shorthand / machines are a peculiar group (TKPWROUP) of people. They practice day and night. They pound (POUPBD) away on their machine like a crazy (KRAEUZ/AEFPL) / bunch of boys and girls. But when they are all done (TKOEPB), they make about a million dollars a year!

Let / me tell you a fictitious (TPEUBG/TEURBS) story about a goat who lived in a hut. The goat loved to eat trash / cans. Every time the goat saw a trash can, he would get a funny facial expression. This particular goat would / only eat trash cans that were painted (PAEUPBT/AED) white. Why, I don't have a clue. He must have thought they looked like ice / cream. He thought they were delicious because he ate a big trash can in 2 minutes (PHEUPBZ) flat.

When you go to / church, make sure you pray. It is possible or is it probable? Probably, it is more possible than it is / probable. The problem is, I forgot which one it is. I have a special appointment with my teacher to find out / what it is. There is only one glitch; I can't remember what time the appointment is, 7 or 8. My / plan is to go at 7; and if she is not there, I will practice until 8. I need to prepare / for the appointment.

My credit rating (RAEUT/AEG) is excellent (SKPHREPBT). I can get whatever I want on credit. I bought a cat, / a hat, a bat, a car, a house, a shirt, 9 pairs of shoes (SHAOUZ), a dog leash (HRAOESH), and a new / shorthand machine all on credit. Now, all I have to do is pay the bills. My monthly bill is / $4,898.28. The ad (AD) said: "easy credit." It didn't say anything about / "easy payments." I only have 25 cents (KREPBTS) to my name. I'm in trouble!

Additional Practice

Go to the:	Do the following:
Realwrite DrillBook (recommended).......	Read over and study Drill XV (Lessons 29 & 30)
Realwrite NoteBook (optional)................	Read and transcribe the notes from Excerise H, Lesson 29

UNIT 8
LESSON THIRTY

Warm up and Review

1. Practice the alphabet (A - Z) using the -FBG ending for all caps.
2. Practice the alphabet (A - Z) using the -FS ending for all small letters.
3. Practice the alphabet (A - Z) using the -FL ending for letter-by-letter spelling.

Writing Words that Begin wtih "ext," "ex," or "x-"

30.1 Write the ST- for words that begin with "ext."

☞ *practice the following:*

extra	STRA	extend	STEPBD	extent	STEPBT
external	STERPBL	extinction	STEUPBGS	extension	STEPBGS
extol[1]	STOL	extreme	STRAOEPL[2]	exterior	STAOER/KWRAOR

[1]stole = STOEL [2]stream = STRAEPL

30.2 Write the SKP- for words that begin with "ex" followed by any vowel or consonant except "ext."

The SKP- is used for all words that begin with "exc," "exh," "exp," "exch," and "ex" followed by a vowel. If it is possible to write the consonant that follows the "ex," do so. If it is not possible, ignore the consonant and write as much of the word as you can in the same stroke.

☞ *practice the following:*

exile	SKPAOEUL	expel	SKPEL	excise	SKPAOEUZ
excellent	SKPHREPBT	exhale	SKPHAEUL	exact	SKPABGT
excuse	SKPAOUS	excuse	SKPAOUZ	exam	SKPAPL
express	SKPRES	excite	SKPAOEUT	excess	SKPES
exercise	SKPER/SAOEUZ	exit	SKPEUT	explore	SKPHROR
excellence	SKPHREPBS	exhort	SKPHORT	export	SKPORT
expedite	SKPE/TKAOEUT	exude	SKPAOUD	excrete	SKPRAOET
expend	SKPEPBD	exhume	SKPAOUPL	execute	SKPAOUT

30.3 Write EX (E-FRPB) in the first stroke for words that begin with the prefix "ex-" where the hyphen (-) is required between prefix and word.

The EFRPB is dictionary-defined as ex- and will be transcribed with the hyphen.

☞ *practice the following:*

ex-spouse	EFRPB/SPOUS	ex-partner	EFRPB/PART/TPHER
ex-	EFRPB	ex-employee	EFRPB/PHROE

Writing Dates and Clock Time

30.4 For all dates that are dictated without any dividing marks between the numbers, automatically write the slash (SL-RBGS) between the month, day, and year. The hyphen (H-RBGS) may also be used.

For example:

10/21/94	10/SL-RBGS/1EU2/SL-RBGS/4EU9
3/1/75	3/SL-RBGS/1/SL-RBGS/5EU7
12-27-92	12/H-RBGS/27/H-RBGS/2EU9

30.5 For clock time, write the hour figure with the K- or -BG in the same stroke to indicate the colon after the hour, then write the minute figure as dictated.

☞ *practice the following:*

1:05	1BG/50EU	2:10	2BG/10	3:15	3BG/15	4:20	4BG/20
5:25	5BG/25	6:30	K6/30	7:35	K7/35	8:40	K8/40
9:45	K9/45	10:50	10BG/50	11:55	1EUBG/5EU	12:59	12BG/59

30.6 For clock time, use A-PL for a.m. and P-PL for p.m. in the last stroke. Use AOBG in the last stroke for the word "o'clock" when dictated.

☞ *practice the following:*

10:22 a.m.	10BG/2EU/APL	4:30 p.m.	4BG/30/P-PL
9:30 p.m.	K9/30/P-PL	11:54 a.m.	1EUBG/45EU/A-PL
1:00 o'clock	1BG/AOBG	12:00 o'clock	12-BG/AOBG
7:00 o'clock	K7/AOBG	12 noon	12/TPHAOPB

Multi-Consonant Combinations (TW-, TR-)

☞ *practice the following:*

TW- TW- TW-, TW- TW- TW-, TW- TW- TW-,
TW- TW- TW-, TW- TW- TW-, TW- TW- TW-,
TW- TW- TW-, TW- TW- TW-, TW- TW- TW-,

TR- TR- TR- ,	TR- TR- TR- ,	TR- TR- TR- ,
TR- TR- TR- ,	TR- TR- TR- ,	TR- TR- TR- ,
TR- TR- TR- ,	TR- TR- TR- ,	TR- TR- TR- ,

☞ *practice the following:*

two	TWO	twin	TWEUPB	twilight	TWEU/HRAOEUGT
twirl	TWEURL	tweed	TWAOED	twice	TWAOEUS
trench	TREPB/AEFP	trap	TRAP	trip	TREUP
train	TRAEUPB	trolley	TROL/AEFPL	trumpet	TRUPL/PET

Short Forms and Phrases

☞ *practice the following:*

x-ray	SKPRAFPL	excel	SKP-L	notice	TPH-TS
develop	TKEFL	difficult	TKEUFT	effect	EFBGT
effort	EFRT	familiar	TPHRAR	finish	TP-RB
accident	STK-PBT	husband	HUZ		

Lesson Practice

☞ *practice the following:*

Do you have the exact size that I need for the drapes? If you don't, will you get them for / me? I need them by 7:00 o'clock because I plan on putting them in my new apartment. My friend, Rob, / is coming over to help me study for my exam. We are working extra hard because we want to ace (AEUS) / the exam. We plan on studying from 9:30 p.m. until around 11:15 p.m. I want to stop at / 11:30 p.m. because I have to call my mom and dad.

If you finish before I do, will you / please excuse me. My excuse is this: I had two extra chores to do before noon. I didn't get them / done; now, I have to stay and finish them. I will make an extra effort to be done by 1:00 o'clock. /

My husband and I went on a skiing (SKAOEG) trip to Aspen (AS/PEPB). We went to the top of the mountain and / skied (SKAOED) down hill. It was excellent. We even got to go on a train and a trolley. What a great / trip. We plan on going twice again in the summer (SUPL/KWRER) of 1998 and in the winter, 19 / 99.

Peg began to twirl the baton but she fell in a trench, or was it a ditch? Really, / it was a ditch covered with snow. Are you familiar with where the accident took place? There was a notice / there to watch your step. Now, Peg has to have an x-ray done on her leg. She made an appointment / to go to the doctor at 10:54 a.m. sharp. If she can't make it, she has no / excuse. The doctor will ask her to exhale and inhale twice.

To perform with excellence requires a great deal of skill and practice. Does your / practice excite you like it should? Practice is like exercise; you have to get into the habit (HABT) of doing / it day in and day out. I have a friend by the name of Jay who has a twin by / the name of Joy. Jay and Joy get up in the morning and start to practice at 7:15 a.m. They / don't stop until twilight. They are excellent at what they do.

Tommy (TOPL/AEFPL) used to play the trumpet in the school / band. He would express himself in how he played. He played quite (KWAOEUT) well until one day he ate (AEUT) a lemon right before / he was to play the trumpet before the queen. He played badly. Now, he plays the drum for the chief (KHAOEF). /

Fran had a brown tweed suit he wore on a date with Deb who wore a tan tweed dress. They / looked like a pair of tweedy (TWAOED/AEFPL) pies (PAOEUZ).

What would be the effect if you had a gallon of sauce before / you swam in the sea? I'll bet you'd begin to develop pains in your side by the time you swam / a mile and a half. I wouldn't touch the stuff before I swam. I might enjoy some after the race, but / I'd want to finish first, first.

Comprehensive Practice

☞ practice the following:

It would surely be insane for you to go out in this snowstorm without your boots and mittens (PHEUT/KWREPBZ) on. If you / don't own a hat, I'll give you mine. I have a tweed hat. What type of hat do you like / to wear? You can't endure in the cold unless you dress right.

My dad is a professional (PROFL) snake charmer (KHARPL/KWRER). He makes / the snakes dance when he plays his trumpet. You should see how they twirl and twirl to the sound / of the trumpet. One time my dad stopped playing the trumpet, and the snakes fell to the ground. My mom / screamed so loud, they ran away. We found them in the apple orchard.

I have to have $56.90 / by 7:22 p.m., or I will have to pay an extra $5.98. The reason I need all the / money is because I bet a man that a horse named "speedy" would win the race. Speedy ran slowly. / Now, I have to pay quickly (KWEUBG/HRAEFPL) or they will harm me. I don't want to be harmed. Will you lend / me the money? I'll pay you back by 8 o'clock tomorrow afternoon. If I don't pay, I'll give you my / gold watch and my silver ring.

The name of the program is: "How to save lives by living a safe / life." It will begin at 5:34 p.m. sharp. If you can come to the program, do so. If you / can't, you'll have to give the principal an excuse. He would not even excuse his own son from coming to / the show. Good luck!

The preacher (PRAOEFP/KWRER) at the church talked about how to pray when you play. He said that / praying is a lot like playing. The more you play, the more you like it; and the more you pray, the / better you feel. There's only one snag. I can never remember to pray except when I need help, but I can / always remember to play.

Two girls at the show played the organ and the flute (TPHRAOUT). They were really bad. In / fact, they were so bad, the cat who lived in the basement packed his bags and ran away. Now the / precious little cat is gone, and no one has any clue (KHRAOU) where it is. I heard it went to a / home for unwanted (UPB/WAPBT/AED) cats. Now the cat is happy (it doesn't have to hear the organ and flute any / more).

Additional Practice

Go to the: Do the following:

Realwrite DrillBook (recommended).........Write and practice Drill XV (Lessons 29 & 30)
Realwrite NoteBook (optional)...................Read and transcribe the notes from Exercise H, Lesson 30 and Drill XV

UNIT 8
LESSON THIRTY-ONE

Warm up and Review

☞ *practice the following:*

$56.56	$567.89	$5,690.12	$98,890.45	$9,934,245.21
$87.23	$871.21	$8,218.23	$45,987.12	$2,912,321.11
$ 5.19	$123.45	$5,872.94	$73,215.99	$3,776,290.55
7:22 a.m.	9:17 p.m.	4:44 p.m.	5:30 a.m.	9:19 a.m.
12:01 a.m.	12:02 p.m.	5:55 a.m.	11:07 p.m.	1:12 a.m.
7:00 o'clock	9:00 o'clock	12:00 o'clock	3:00 o'clock	4:00 o'clock
4-12-75	8-12-94	12-31-94	5-27-72	6-4-70

Writing Words that end in "ty" OR "ity"

31.1 Write the -T in the same stroke for words that end in "ty" or "ity." If the -T cannot be written in the first stroke, combine the -T in a second or subsequent stroke or write the TAEFPL in the last stroke.

☞ *practice the following:*

safety	SAEUFT	clarity	KHRAEURT
charity	KHAEURT	majority	PHAPBLGT
rarity	RAEURT	minority	PHAOEU/TPHORT
tranquility	TRAPB/KWEULT	humility	HAOU/PHEULT
density	TKEPBS/TAEFPL	humidity	HAOUPLD/TAEFPL
brevity	PWREFT[1]	sensitivity	SEPBS/TEUFT
booty	PWAOT/AEFPL[2]	longevity	HROPB/SKWREFT

[1] For words that end in "vty" or "vity" use the -FT.

[2] For words that end in t, write the t in the first stroke and the AEFPL in last stroke.

Writing Words that end in "rv" or "rf"

31.2 For all words that end with an "rv" or "rf" write the -FRB in the same stroke.

☞ *practice the following:*

nerve	TPHEFRB	serve	SEFRB	swerve	SWEFRB
surf	SUFRB	turf	TUFRB	dwarf	TKWAFRB
curve	KUFRB	starve	STAFRB	carve	KAFRB
scarf	SKAFRB	wharf	WHAFRB	Marv	PHAFRB

Contractions using the Z-rule (Will)

☞ *practice the following:*

phrase	Realwrite	contraction	Realwrite
I will	AOEUFRP	I'll	AOEUFRPZ
it will	T-FRP	it'll	T-FRPZ
he will	HAEFRP	he'll	HAEFRPZ
she will	SHAEFRP	she'll	SHAEFRPZ
they will	THEFRP	they'll	THEFRPZ
we will	WEFRP	we'll	WEFRPZ
you will	UFRP	you'll	UFRPZ

New Punctuation (Dash, Back Slash)

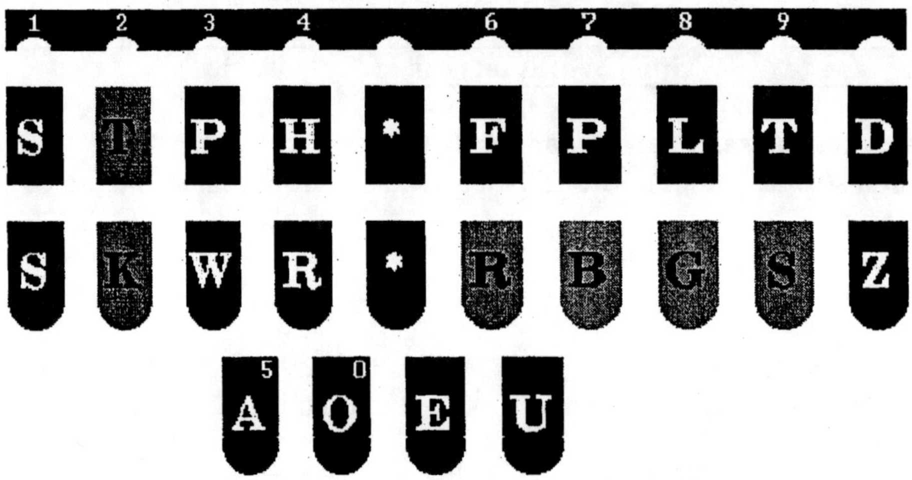

31.3 Write the D-RBGS whenever the dash (--) is needed within dictation.

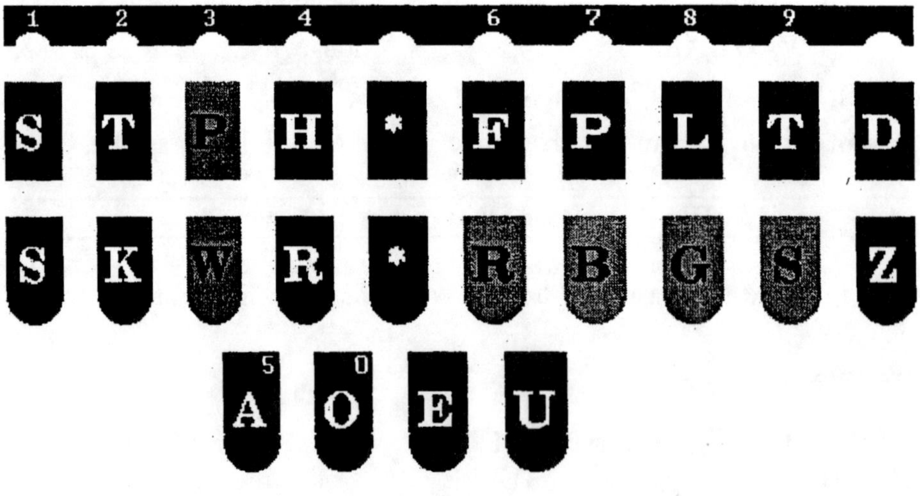

31.4 Write the PW-RBGS whenever the back slash (\ ) is needed within dictation.

Short Forms and Phrases

☞ *practice the following:*

service	S-FB	wonderful	WOFL	whatever	WHAFR
usual	AOURB	unusual	TPHAOURB	sudden	SUD
usually	AOURBL	unusually	TPHAOURBL	suggest	SUG
technical	T-FP	support	SUPT	sufficient	SUF
supervise	SPR-FB				

Lesson Practice

☞ *practice the following:*

Whatever you had to say is wonderful, except that you tend to get a little bit too technical with / your words. May I suggest that you can reach more people by using words that are not unusual. Usually, this / will do the trick; but it might be a good thought to keep in mind that you may have to define (TKE/TPAOEUPB) / words that are used unusually.

He had the nerve to tell me that we could not go out to dinner / because he didn't have enough money to pay for surf and turf. After that, I told him that I would / starve and never go out to a dinner with him. He said he was sorry and took me to an / unusual steak (STAEUBG) house that sold the most delicious prime rib. I had a salad, (SAL/KWRAD) and he had beef. Now, I'm / hungry (HUPBG/RAEFPL).

The technical support offered by the school was excellent. All you had to do was pick up the phone (TPOEPB) / and dial (TKAOEUL) H-E-L-P. I tried (TRAOEUD) it once, but I got the wrong number. I got Joe's (SKWROE/AOS) Pizza / (PAOE/SKPWA) by mistake. I ordered (ORD/AED) a big pizza while I was waiting (WAEUT/AEG). It was sufficient enough for me and my 28 / friends. We had a party (PART/AEFPL).

I appreciate your taking the time to carve my pumpkin (PUPL/KEUPB) yesterday. Today I put it on / the ledge with a candle (KAPBD/AEL) in it. It looked so pretty (PRET/AEFPL). I appreciate it.

John said that he'd supervise the / majority of the people who come to the office. He has great sensitivity for those in need of charity. He'll / speak with clarity and brevity. They'll appreciate what he says, I'm sure. We'll have a good time.

I suggest you / come about 9 o'clock to the service. If you come after 10:22, you may not be able to get / in. The majority of people arrive (A/RAOEUFB) by 7:14 p.m., but some have the nerve to come at about / 6:22 a.m.

We'll feel great tranquillity (TRAPB/KWEULT) if we help a charity. The one I'll support takes care of stray / cats and dogs. I suggest you find one you like, one that is not too unusual. Whatever one you / choose, they'll appreciate what you do.

If you swerve around this curve, you'll miss that deer (TKAOER) in the road (-RD). But / if you don't swerve, you'll have a crash for sure. And I'd hate to see you smash your new automobile / after you paid cash for it. Didn't you say you gave the man $17,459.24 for the car? / That is a lot of money to lose just because you won't swerve around this curve.

She'll split the booty / with her friend, Ben. It is a rarity that they'll not fight over the money--they always fight--even / over a scarf. Support your local shorthand machine writer. They need all the support they can get. /

Comprehensive Practice

☞ *practice the following:*

Peg says, "Practice while you can or you won't be able to later." Her words are wise. Pete says: "I / don't have to practice, I can get by." His words are not very smart. We'll see how they do / on the exam. The exam is tomorrow. Peg is studying hard. Pete is not. I bet Peg gets a higher (HAOEUFD/KWRER) mark / than Pete. Peg got a grade of 100; Pete got a 52.

Bob and Carol (KAEURL) and Liz all had a store / that they owned. They sold great food at a nice price. I bought an apple for a buck and a dozen / eggs for a dime. I wanted some grape juice, but they were all out of it. I had to settle (SET/AEL) / for grapefruit (TKPWRAEUP/AE/TPRAOUT).

I have a tutor who will help you study for your exam. She is great with subtraction and addition. / She can do marvels (PHAFRLZ) with fractions. She even can handle (HAPBL) problems that have numbers in the millions and billions. What / a whiz!

John dressed up in a new tux to go to a dance with Jill. John took her a flower (TPHROFRP/KWRER), but it wilted (WEULT/AED) / on the way to the dinner. Jill got mad and left the dinner alone. She walked halfway home until a / cab picked her up. The cab took her home, but it cost her $25.96. Now, she says that / she is going to send a bill to John to get her money back.

A station wagon zoomed (SKPWAOPLD) right by / me when I was walking my dog in the park. It splashed (SPHRARBD) mud on my new suit. Now, I have to / get it cleaned; and it will put me back about $20. What would you do? I'll call the cab / company and complain.

I have a few coins I can spend. Will you take me to the store so I can / buy some penny candy? I love gum drops. I can get a pound and a half of gum drops for / a few cents. I only have two cents. I wonder (WOPBD/KWRER) how many I'll get for that. I'll request that he / put them in a bag so that I can share them with my friends. Would you like a gum drop? /

The police made a report. There was one error in the report. They said the time of the crime was / 9. They'd better check their clocks; it was only 7 to 9. I'll get an extra copy of the report / and return it to the main office today or tomorrow. The report was made yesterday, but we didn't get a copy / of it until noon.

Do you have a good sense of humor? I hope so because I forgot to tell / you that you need to go 500 words a minute by the end of the month. What an excellent way / to gain speed. Practice at 500, and then you are only expected to reach 50 words a minute. What do you / say?

Additional Practice

Go to the:	Do the following:
Realwrite DrillBook (recommended)..........	Read over and study Drill XVI (Lessons 31 & 32)
Realwrite NoteBook (optional)....................	Read and transcribe the notes from Exercise H, Lesson 31

UNIT 8
LESSON THIRTY-TWO

Warm up and Review

☞ *practice the following:*

correspond	credit	customer	particular	peculiar	victim
photograph	popular	possible	prepare	principal	upon
principle	probable	probably	problem	proceed	unless
always	all right	until	practice	present	unwilling
presence	previous	product	program	propose	machine
profession	type	provide	approximate	appropriate	wherever
occur	office	obtain	today	tomorrow	whenever
yesterday	report	remember	remind	return	volunteer
request	represent	worry	woman	women	volume

Flagged Alphabet (Letters with a Period)

In realtime writing, you will be asked to write initials in a person's name or for an organization. You may want the initials to be transcribed along with a period.

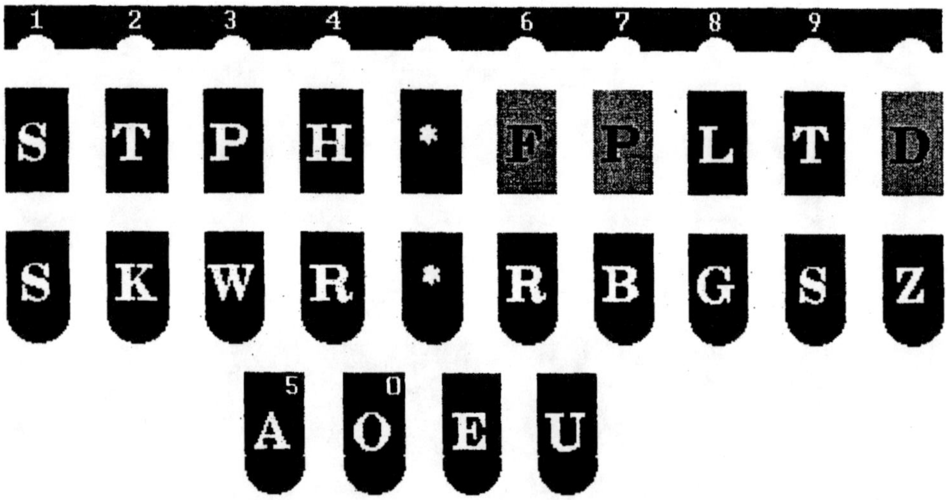

32.1 To write the alphabet in all capital letters with a period after each letter, write the alphabetic letter on the initial side of the keyboard along with the final side -FPD in the same stroke.

☞ *practice the following:*

alphabet	Realwrite	alphabet	Realwrite	alphabet	Realwrite
A.	A-FPD	J.	SKWR-FPD	S.	S-FPD
B.	PW-FPD	K.	K-FPD	T.	T-FPD
C.	KR-FPD	L.	HR-FPD	U.	U-FPD
D.	TK-FPD	M.	PH-FPD	V.	SR-FPD
E.	E-FPD	N.	TPH-FPD	W.	W-FPD
F.	TP-FPD	O.	O-FPD	X.	SKP-FPD
G.	TKPW-FPD	P.	P-FPD	Y.	KWR-FPD
H.	H-FPD	Q.	KW-FPD	Z.	SKPW-FPD
I.	EU-FPD	R.	R-FPD		

Writing Words that Begin with "kn"

In realtime writing, a distinction is made between words that sound alike but are spelled dfferently. For example, we want to write the word "not" one way and the word "knot" another way.

32.2 For all words that begin with the "kn," regardless of the pronunciation, use the STP- to distinguish between words that begin with "n."

☞ *practice the following:*

knew	STPEFRP	new	TPHEFRP	knee	STPAOE
knot	STPOT	not	TPHOT	kneel	STPAOEL
knight	STPAOEUGT	night	TPHAOEUGT	knife	STPAOEUF
knead	STPAOED	need	TPHAOED	knock	STPOBG
know	STPOEFRP	knob	STPOB	known	STPOEPB
knit	STPEUT	knuckle	STPUBG/AEL	knapsack	STPAP/SAEBG

Multi-Consonant Combinations (SPR-, STR-)

☞ *practice the following:*

SPR- SPR- SPR- , SPR- SPR- SPR- , SPR- SPR- SPR- ,
SPR- SPR- SPR- , SPR- SPR- SPR- , SPR- SPR- SPR- ,
SPR- SPR- SPR- , SPR- SPR- SPR- , SPR- SPR- SPR- ,

STR- STR- STR- , STR- STR- STR- , STR- STR- STR- ,
STR- STR- STR- , STR- STR- STR- , STR- STR- STR- ,
STR- STR- STR- , STR- STR- STR- , STR- STR- STR- ,

☞ *practice the following:*

spree	SPRAOE	spray	SPRAFPL	sprite	SPRAOEUT
sprig	SPREUG	sprint	SPREUPBT	spirit	SPEURT
spurt	SPURT	strut	STRUT	strike	STRAOEUBG
stroll	STROEL	strip	STREUP	stripe	STRAOEUP

Short Forms and Phrases

☞ *practice the following:*

incident	STKEUPBT	accomplish	PHREURB	daughter	TKAUR
account	K-PBT	data	TKAT	suppose	SPOEZ
deduct	TK-BGT				

Lesson Practice

☞ *practice the following:*

I knew that the incident was going to happen because my daughter told me. She knew because a friend / told her. Her friend knew because the police told him. The police had known all the time because I told / them. Now, we all know.

My mom knit me a pretty purple (PURPL) sweater (SWET/KWRER) about a month ago. It had one / brown stripe down the front of it, and two green stripes down the back. I'm proud to wear it because / my mom made it, even though one sleeve is bigger, and there is no neck.

I needed / a job so I took one in a store that makes bread (PWRED). I knead the dough (TKOEFD) at night, and then / I use a knife to cut the dough. I then spray a pan with oil and put the dough in / the pan and throw it in the oven (OFB/KWREPB). It is difficult to know when to take the bread out, so / I have a clock I watch. I'm supposed (SPOEZ/AED) to bake it for 20 minutes, but I usually let it cook / for about 25. Then I take it out and wrap it up and put it in a case to.sell. / Do you want to buy some fresh bread?

Michael (PHAOEUBG/KWREL) and Michelle (PHEURB/KWREL) collected a great deal of data for their account / of the accident. They went from door to door collecting the data. They had a very difficult time finding people / at home, but they knew what to do and where to go.

Jess used to spurt the sprint in less / than 1 minute. He hurt his knee yesterday. Now, he has to strut with a crutch (KRUFP). He can't bend his knee; / he can't even kneel. The doctor told him to stay off his knee for 6 months. That is a / very difficult thing for Jess to accomplish. He loves to spurt the sprint; now, he can't even stroll the strip. / But he has not lost his spirit. He says he will be ready to spurt again in no time at / all.

A knight in shining (SHAOEUPBG) armor rode (ROED) in on a white horse. The bright knight only worked at night--what / a sight! One night the knight began to knock on my door. I didn't know who it was, so I / didn't go to the door. He went away and rode off into the twilight (TWEU/HRAOEUGT).

If you have an extra savings / account, they will deduct your payments every week. You do not have to worry about it. I had an account / like that, but the people who deducted the money went on strike, and I didn't make the payment on time. / My son and daughter got a lawyer for me, and they helped me settle the account.

Ron got a new knapsack / as a gift. He used to take it with him wherever he went. He loved it because he could fill / it with all his books and papers (PAEUP/KWRERZ) when he left home for the day. By the time he got to / the office, he was all set.

Comprehensive Practice

☞ practice the following:

Do you happen to know what proportion of the tax is going for the proceeds? I know that the man / who looked at the account said that he could not prorate it any more. If you were to / do a recount of all of the visible data that you had, I'm sure you would find that an error / was made.

Her name was Jenny, and she spelled it J-E-N-N-Y. She was the premier attraction / in the show. She used to stand on one hand and recite a poem (POEPL) about a frog and a dog. / I don't even need to mention how much the people laughed when she would perform. When she had to depart, / the people demanded that she stay. She decided to resume her career as a one-hand-stand actor. Now, she / is happy.

Did you know that there was a party at my house yesterday? I'm sorry that you couldn't attend, / but I resent your coming over today and demanding that I give you some of the cake that I baked. / If you want cake, you'll have to bake it yourself. I won't volunteer to bake it for you unless you / give me 4 weeks notice, then I will even deliver it for you if you want.

I'd like to see / you defer payment on the account for 12 months. If you did that, I could afford to buy the new / carpet for the hallway (HAUL/WAEFPL). How do you feel about a red carpet with a bright green stripe? Where you go, you'll / be able to see it and whatever you spill on it will never show.

If we decide that we like / the rug, we'll have to make payment of $987.25 by tomorrow afternoon. If we / want to, we can have it delivered in time for your new chair and table to arrive. Let me know / if you want the rug or not.

Additional Practice

Go to the:	Do the following:
Realwrite DrillBook (recommended).......	Write and practice Drill XVI (Lessons 31 & 32)
Realwrite NoteBook (optional).................	Read and transcribe the notes from Exercise H, Lesson 32, Drill XVI

UNIT 8 REVIEW

Lesson Review

1. Go back to each lesson and learn each new rule thoroughly.
2. Go back to each lesson and write the Lesson Practice.
3. Go back to each lesson and write the Comprehensive Practice.
4. Read back all notes and transcribe a portion of your review.

Review of Writing Rules

29.1 For all words that end with the "ly" ending, write the -L in the same stroke. If it is necessary to write the -L in a separate stroke, write the HRAEFPL (LAEY) in the last stroke.

29.2 If the first syllable of the word ends in the consonant "l," write the AEFPL in the final stroke.

29.3 For all words that end with the "le" or "el" combine the -L in the same stroke if possible. If a second stroke is necessary, write the AEL (le) or KWRAEL (el) in the last stroke.

29.4 In writing the AEL in the second stroke of words that end in "le," it may be necessary to begin the second stroke with a leftover consonant.

29.5 For all words that end in "fer" or "ver," write the -FR in the same stroke. If it is necessary to write the "fer" or "ver" in a separate stroke, use FER or SRER.

29.6 Write the SKP-RBGS to designate the exclamation point as needed in dictation.

29.7 Write the SL-RBGS to designate the slash mark whenever it is needed in dictation.

30.1 Write the ST- for words that begin with "ext."

30.2 Write the SKP- for words that begin with "ex" followed by any vowel or consonant except "ext."

30.3 Write EX (E-FRPB) in the first stroke for words that begin with the prefix "ex-" where the hyphen (-) is required between prefix and word.

30.4 For all dates that are dictated without any dividing marks between the numbers, automatically write the slash (SL-RBGS) between the month, day, and year. The hyphen (H-RBGS) may also be used.

30.5 For clock time, write the hour figure with the K- or -BG in the same stroke to indicate the colon after the hour, then write the minute figure as dictated.

30.6 For clock time, use A-PL for a.m. and P-PL for p.m. in the last stroke. Use AOBG in the last stroke for the word "o'clock" when dictated.

31.1 Write the -T in the same stroke for words that end in "ty" or "ity." If the -T cannot be written in the first stroke, combine the -T in a second or subsequent stroke or write the TAEFPL in the last stroke.

31.2 For all words that end with an "rv" or "rf" write the -FRB in the same stroke.

31.3 Write the D-RBGS whenever the dash (--) is needed within dictation.

31.4 Write the PW-RBGS whenever the back slash (\ ) is needed within dictation.

32.1 To write the alphabet in all capital letters with a period after each letter, write the alphabetic letter on the initial side of the keyboard along with the final side -FPD in the same stroke.

32.2 For all words that begin with the "kn," regardless of the pronunciation, use the STP- to distinguish between words that begin with "n."

Review DrillBook and Notebook Applications

1. Review Drills XV and XVI from the *Realwrite DrillBook* (recommended).
2. Review Exercise H from the *Realwrite NoteBook* (optional).

Unit Evaluation Number Eight

Unit Evaluation Number Eight will cover all material from the following: *Realwrite LessonBook*, Lessons 29-32; *DrillBook*, Drills XV and XVI.

UNIT 9
LESSON THIRTY-THREE

Warm up and Review

☞ *practice the following:*

I'm	we're	they're	you're	I'd	she'd	we'd
he'd	they'd	you'd	I've	we've	they've	I'll
you've	he'll	they'll	you'll	she'll	we'll	it'll
aren't	couldn't	doesn't	hadn't	haven't	shouldn't	won't
ain't	can't	didn't	don't	hasn't	wasn't	isn't
wouldn't	itself	herself	himself	myself	ourselves	
yourself	themselves	yourselves				

Writing Words that end in Sound of "able" or "ible"

33.1 For all words that end with the sound of "able" or "ible," write the -BL in the same stroke or combined in a second stroke. If a separate stroke is necessary, write KWRABL (able) or KWREUBL (ible) in the last stroke.

☞ *practice the following:*

durable	TKAOURBL	adorable	A/TKORBL
liable	HRAOEUBL	deplorable	TKE/PHRORBL
commendable	KPHEPBD/KWRABL	regrettable	RE/TKPWRET/KWRABL
assessable	A/SES/KWRABL	comfortable	K-FRT/KWRABL
dependable	TKPEPBD/KWRABL	notable	TPHOET/KWRABL
remarkable	RE/PHARBG/KWRABL	workable	WORBG/KWRABL
sensible	SEPBS/KWREUBL	accessible	ABG/SES/KWREUBL
compatible	KPAT/KWREUBL		

Writing Words that end in Sound of "ability" or "ibility"

33.2 For all words that end with the sound of "ability" or "ibility," write the -BLT in the same stroke or combined i a second stroke. If a separate stroke is necessary, write KWRABLT (ability) or KWREUBLT (ibility) in the last stroke.

☞ *practice the following*

durability	TKAOURBLT	mobility	PHOEBLT
dependability	TKPEPBD/KWRABLT	irritability	EURT/KWRABLT
sensibility	SEPBS/KWREUBLT	compatibility	KPAT/KWREUBLT
accessibility	ABG/SES/KWREUBLT		

Contractions using the Z-rule (Is)

☞ *practice the following:*

phrase	Realwrite	contraction	Realwrite
how is	HOFRPS	how's	HOFRPZ
it is	T-S	it's[1]	T-Z
that is	THAS	that's	THAZ
there is	THRS	there's	THRZ
what is	WHAS	what's	WHAZ
where is	WHRS	where's	WHRZ
who is	WHOS	who's[2]	WHOZ

[1] note the following distinctions: it is (T-S), it's (T-Z), its (EUTS)
[2] note the following distinctions: who is (WHOS), who's (WHOZ), whose (WHOES)

New Punctuation (Decimal Point, Point)

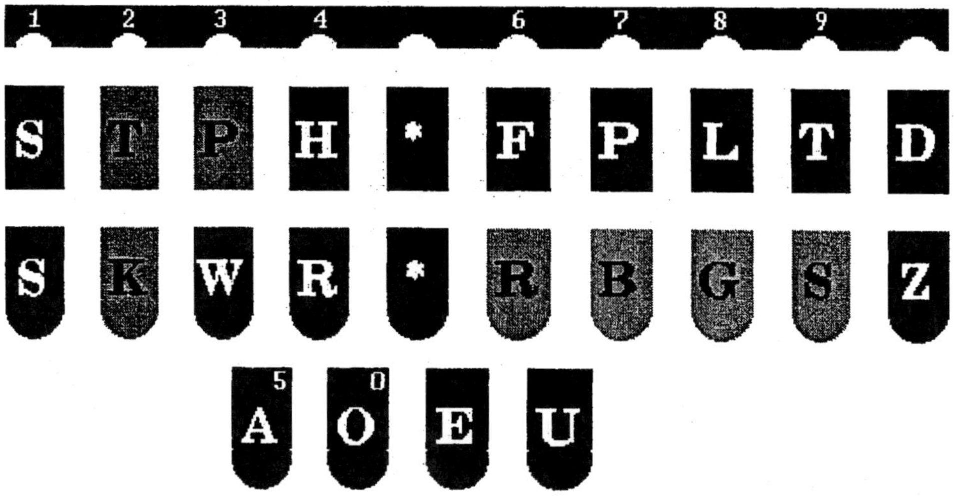

33.3 Write the DP-RBGS to designate the decimal point whenever it is dictated.

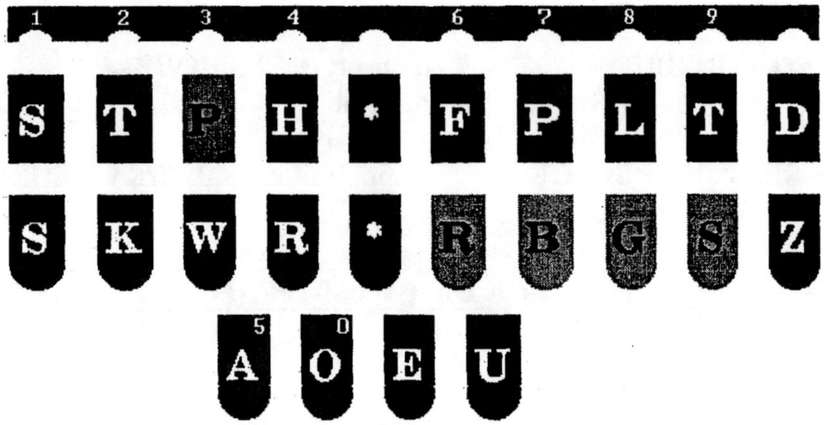

33.4 Write the POEU-RBGS to designate the word point whenever it is dictated.

For example

dictated as	written as	transcribed as
"ten point one two"	10/POEU-RBGS/12	10.12
"forty-five, decimal point, zero six"	45/DP-RBGS/0/6	45.06
"fifty-two, point O nine"[1]	2EU5/POEU-RBGS/0/9	52.09

[1]Even though a person may say the letter "O," the number zero (0) is transcribed.

Writing the Days of the Week

There are a number of items that we can "group" together and follow one specific rule. Among these items are the days of the week, the months of the year, states, and so on.

33.5 Write the days of the week using a two- or three-letter designation on the initial side, combined with the -FPLT on the final side.

☞ *practice the following:*

Monday	PHO-FPLT	Tuesday	TU-FPLT	Wednesday	WE-FPLT
Thursday	THU-FPLT	Friday	TPREU-FPLT	Saturday	SA-FPLT
Sunday	SU-FPLT				

Short Forms and Phrases

☞ *practice the following:*

America	PHERBG	American	PHERPB	against	TKPWEBS
hospital	HOPT	hotel	HOELT	motel	PHOELT
human	HAOUPL	article	ARL	avenue	AFB
amount	APLT	advance	SRAPBS	auto	AUT
especial	SPERB	especially	SPERBL		

Lesson Praactice

☞ *practice the following:*

I can't remember if the party is on Monday, Tuesday, or Wednesday. John says it's on Monday, but I say it's / on Wednesday. I'll have to ask Mary when I see her at the hospital. She is a nurse at Memorial / Hospital. She used to work at the American Hotel, but she went to school to learn about nursing. She is a / good nurse.

I know that it would be very sensible if you put aside an amount of money each week / to save for the new auto that you want. If you give them an advance, they will save it for / you. That's what I would do, but it's up to you. How's your credit? Can you get a loan? Will / you feel comfortable making payments of $124.89 a month?

My old car is / no longer dependable. It is regrettable that I have to get rid of it. It has been a comfortable car. / I saw an adorable little red sports car / that I loved, but it'll be about $23,893.78 / to buy it. If I could write an article on how compatible computers / are with space travel, I could make enough money to put down. Will you look at my article? It is / a great story.

On Saturday of this week, we will make all doorways (TKAOR/WAEFPLZ) accessible for the handicap. We will widen / the doors, and we will make sure that every door is on the same level as the sidewalk. There will / be no more steps. The work that you are doing is commendable, but please make sure that what you do / is durable. There's one more thing I want to say: you are a great human being.

My dad, Sam, owned / a motel by the seaside. My mom, Sue, sold seashells by the seashore (SAE/AE/SHOR). They made a lot of money, but / the amount of money they put aside was very little. Sue and Sam no longer sell seashells (SAE/AE/SHELZ) by the seashore; / but they do they buy burnt burgers by the bag full.

What's going on? Who's been doing your work for / you? Where's the man who was supposed to bring the new equipment? Were you born in America? Are you an / American? Did you stay in a hotel or a motel? Did you drive down the street and across the avenue / or across the street and down the avenue? Is today Saturday or Sunday? Is tomorrow Friday or Thursday? I have / an appointment on Wednesday.

Please tell me if you want an appointment on Monday, Tuesday, Wednesday, Thursday, or Friday. We / are only open for half a day on Saturday from 10:00 a.m. until 4 p.m. We are closed / on Sunday. Please tell me when you want your appointment, and I'll see what I can do.

How's this for / a great number: 456.231? Or how about this one: 223.891? / My favorite number is 7777.77. It is very special to me, especially / since I was born on 7-7-77 at 7:07 in the morning.

Comprehensive Practice

☞ *practice the following:*

Why have you been so quiet? Don't you know that we've come to help you study? We even brought you / some bread and jelly in case you get hungry. The only problem is, we only have enough for 2 people, / so don't throw a party, please. We've no more to offer.

There is no way in the world that Sandy / and Ray could get all their work done by 8 o'clock. They had way too little time. They looked sadly / at the pile of homework. Ray began to cry, Sandy began to sigh (SAOEUFD). Do you think they'd accept help? They / could go over all of the material and study hard for the exam. I bet they could do it if they / tried. It would truly be wise they started now.

Did you know that the gas station is having a sale / on gas? You can now buy 2 gallons of gas for the price of 1 gallon. That's a saving / double the regular (REG) price. The regular price is $1.49 a gallon; now, it is $1.09. / The name of the gas station is the Gas Saver. If you get there by noon, you'll get a free / balloon (PWHRAOPB). I went back 12 different times; and now, I have a dozen balloons. I have 6 red ones, 3 / green ones, 1 black ones, and 1 white one. I'm proud of my balloon collection.

The difference between addition and / subtraction is how you look at the problem. How you get the solution (SHRAOUGS) is different each way. Make sure you know / what you're doing before you begin the problem or you'll end up with a fraction. Most fractions are difficult to / handle, unless you know what you're doing. My friend, Zeb, is a whiz at subtraction; but he can't do addition. / My friend, Deb, is great at addition; but she doesn't even know how to begin subtraction. They make a fine / pair.

Can you pass the highway in safety? I'll wait here until you make it across the street safely. Lately, / there's been a lot of traffic (TRAFBG) on the road, especially big trucks. Watch your step.

I have the following juices / on special: apple juice, grape juice, orange juice, and maple juice. You may ask me how I got juice from / a maple, and I'll tell you my secret (SE/KRET): I add water to the syrup! Please don't tell my boss, or / he'll fire me for sure. Which one would you prefer? Apple, grape, orange or maple?

I have only one request: / can you turn silver into gold? If you can, you will make a lot of money. I knew a man / who could take a silver coin and make it into gold. He paid $45.00 for the silver coin and / then sold the gold coin for $357.24. He makes (PHAEUBGZ) a lot of money; / now, he is very, very rich. I tried it once, but my silver coin turned into tin. Now, I am / very, very poor.

Additional Practice

Go to the:	Do the following:
Realwrite DrillBook (recommended).........	Read over and study Drill XVII (Lessons 33 & 34)
Realwrite NoteBook (optional)..................	Read and transcribe the notes from Exercise I, Lesson 33

UNIT 9
LESSON THIRTY-FOUR

Warm up and Review

☞ *practice the following:*

particular	peculiar	photograph	popular	possible
practice	prepare	presence	present	previous
principal	principle	probable	probably	problem
proceed	product	profession	program	propose
provide	whatever	whenever	whereever	ability
above	accept	accident	accomplish	account
all right	always	approximate	appropriate	ask

Writing Words that Begin with "enter" and "inter"

34.1 Write the EPBT for words that begin with the prefix "enter." Write the EUPBT for words that begin with the prefix "inter."

☞ *practice the following:*

entertain	EPBT/TAEUPB	enterprise	EPBT/PRAOEUZ
intersection	EUPBT/SEBGS	intercede	EUPBT/SAOED
interface	EUPBT/TPAEUS	interpose	EUPBT/POEZ
interrupt	EUPBT/RUPT	intersession	EUPBT/SEGS
Internet	EUPBT/TPHET	interact	EUPBT/KWRABGT

Writing Words that Begin with "des" or "dis"

34.2 Write the STK- ("d" and "s" reversed) for words that begin with the prefix "des" or "dis." Combine the STK with a vowel in the first stroke if necessary. If it is necesary to write the "des" or "dis" in a separate stroke, write the TKES or TKEUS.

☞ *practice the following:*

despair	STKPAEUR	descent	STKEPBT
design	STKAOEUPB	desire	STKAOEUR
disparity	STKPAEURT	dispel	STKPEL
disprove	STKPROFB	disable	STKAEUBL
disallow	STKA/LOFRP	disservice	TKEUS/S-FB
disease	STKAOEZ	disenchant	STKEPB/KHAPBT
discourage	TKEUS/KAOURPBLG	disclaimer	TKEUS/KHRAEUPL/KWRER

In some cases, the pronunciation of the word may dictate that the prefix "des" or "dis" be divided in such a way that the consonant be placed in the second stroke.

☞ *practice the following:*

dissent	TKEU/SEPBT	decent	TKE/SEPBT

Writing Fractions in Words or Figures

Fractions are written two different ways, depending upon whether or not you want them transcribed as words or figures.

34.3 Write fractions phonetically as you hear them when they are to be transcribed as words.

dictated as:	written as:	transcribed as:
one half[1]	WUPB/HAF	one-half
two thirds	TWO/THEURDZ	two-thirds
three thirds	THRAOE/THEURDZ	three-thirds

[1]The phonetic system of writing numbers will be presented in future lessons.

☞ *practice the following:*

one-half	WUPB/HAF	two-thirds	TWO/THEURDZ
three-thirds	THRAOE/THEURDZ	one-third	WUPB/THEURD

34.4 Write fractions that are to be transcribed using numbers by combining the numerator with the initial R- or final -R in the first stroke. Write the denominator for the second stroke.

Numbers, or combinations of numbers, using the 1 - 5 and 0 use the final -R. Numbers, or combinations of numbers using the 6 - 9 use the initial R

dictated as:	written as:	transcribed as:
one half	1R/2	1/2
two thirds	2R/3	2/3
one sixteenth	1R/16	1/16
four fifths	4R/5	4/5
eight tenths	R8/10	8/10

☞ *practice the following:*

1/2	1R/2	2/3	2R/3	3/4	3R/4
4/7	4R/7	9/13	R9/13	11/16	1EUR/16
7/9	R7/9	10/32	10R/23EU	6/17	R6/17

Note 1: Large fractions can be written with the slash (/) SHR-RBGS separating the numerator from the denominator. For example 28/100 can be written 28/SHR-RBGS/1/H-PBD.

Note 2: When a fractions needs to be separated from a whole number as 1 1/2 it is necessary to generate a space between them. This is done by using the SP-RBGS for the space. For example. 1 1/2 would be written 1/SP-RBGS/1R/2.

Short Forms

☞ *practice the following:*

disclose	STKHROEZ	destroy	STKROFPL
discuss	STKUS	distribute	STKREUBT
discussion	STKUGS	discount	STKOUPBT
distribution	STKREUBGS	distinguish	STKWEURB
disagree	STKRAOE	disassociate	STKA/SOERBT

Lesson Praactice

☞ *practice the following:*

I got a great discount at the store; I got 1/3 off for every 2 things I bought. Also, / for every new thing you buy, you get a punch on your supersaver ticket. I have 5 punches so the / next time I buy something, I'll get it free. Isn't that great? I figure my total savings is about 1/5 of / every dollar.

The discussion about the new enterprise was about how much money it would take to start up. We / had to fill out a disclaimer before we could begin asking for a loan. The disparity between what we had / and what we wanted to borrow (PWO/ROEFRP) was so much that they had to disallow our loan. However, when I disclosed / the fact that I had $21,390,210.32 in / my savings account, the loan for $45,000 was approved; and there was no more discussion.

I'll have / to disassociate myself from the service. Did you send in the new design yet? Don't despair. I'll meet you at / the intersection of Main Street and Maple Lane.

Wanda (WAPB/TKA) knew that she had to interrupt the speaker in order / to make the announcement (A/TPHOUPBS/PHAEPLT). She walked on the stage and whispered WHEUS/PERD) in the gentleman's ear: "There's a fire in the back / storage (STORPBLG) room." The fire didn't destroy the whole building (BEULD/AEG), but it did damage (TKAPBLG) the rear portion.

I'll interpose a thought / here: Can computers interface with human beings? True, we have been able to entertain ourselves with computer games, but / what about the discussion referring (REFRG) to quantum (KWAPBT/KWRUPL) applications (PHREUBGS/AEZ)?

Jeff knew that in order to disclose the whole incident, he / would have to do a disservice to his friends. He didn't know what to do. Should he tell what happened, / or should he make up a story? He didn't despair; he told them exactly what happened, but then he explained / that it was not their fault. He said that a huge U.F.O landed in his back yard, and / a little green man took the money. What do you think? Is that really what happened?

Comprehensive Practice

☞ *practice the following:*

Do you want to go deep sea diving with me? We can be at the seashore by noon and / get our equipment ready by 1 o'clock. If we hurry, we can catch the ship that leaves shore at 1:10 / p.m. I have plenty of extra air if you need it; I just got some. Let me know / by 10 o'clock so I can call my friends Jill and Jake. They said they wanted to come along if / we go.

Do you know if tweed is in style (STAOEUL) or not this time of year? I have 10 tweed / suits and 14 tweed hats that I'd like to wear, but I don't want to be out of style. I / also have 22 tweed ties. Do you think tweed will ever be in style again? I surely hope so.

My / daughter, Michelle, wanted to play the drums in the school band. I told her that if she wanted / to play well, she'd have to practice every night after school. She said she would--and she did--for / about 2 weeks. Then she wanted to play the trumpet. I told her she could if she wanted to / practice day and night. She said she'd do it--and she did--for about 2 days. Now she wants to / know if she can play the flute. What do you think I should tell her?

I'll take 3 lemons, 4 / melons, 5 apples, and a bunch of carrots (KAEURTS) and mix them all together to make a special potion (POEGS). How's that / for a treat that will give you extra pick up and go.

Excellence is acquired by hard work and practice. / No matter (PHAT/KWRER) what you do in this life, you need to practice hard, not hardly practice. Even a baby who / is learning to walk needs to practice day after day to perfect his or her walking. Talking also requires practice. / So does dancing and skiing. I knew a man who used to practice counting (KOUPBT/AEG) money so that he would be / ready when he became rich.

Would you prefer to fall in a ditch or a trench? It really doesn't / make any difference, does it? I hope you don't sprain your arm. If you fall, try to fall lightly so that / you don't get hurt. Don't fall on your hand, please. We don't want you to hurt your hand or break / it. If you do, get an x-ray immediately (PHAOED/HRAEFPL).

I thought I heard every excuse that was possible under / the sun, but this one was new to me. My daughter told me she missed the train because she thought / she had tickets for the plane. She went to the airport, not the train station. When she found out her / error, she had to catch the bus. She was 8 hours late for her appointment.

Will you please begin / to finish your work. If you can't finish by 9:00 p.m., put it in the box marked with / the letter X (SKP-FBG). Please make sure that you spell my name correctly KREBGT/HRAEFPL). It is spelled Z-A-L-A-N- / S-K-Y. Most people spell it Z-E-L-E-N-S-K-I, but I don't. My dad says our way / of spelling it is correct. It is said exactly the way it is spelled.

My friends are all coming over / to my apartment tonight for a party. We are celebrating (SEL/PWRAEUT/AEG) the fact that I passed (PAS/AED) my speed take at 225 / words a minute. I feel great and so do all my friends. Now, I can use my skill to get / a job and work as a court reporter. I can't wait to get my very first check. I'm so happy, / I could cry; I don't know why.

Additional Practice

Go to the:	Do the following:
Realwrite DrillBook (recommended)..........	Write and practice Drill XVII (Lessons 33 & 34)
Realwrite NoteBook (optional)..................	Read and transcribe the notes from Exercise I, Lesson 34, Drill XVII

UNIT 9
LESSON THIRTY-FIVE

Warm up and Review

☞ *practice the following:*

Practice writng the numbers 1-1000 as quickly as you can, putting a comma between each number.

Writing Words that end in the Sounds of "ng," "nk," or "nj"

Words that end in "ng," "nk," and "nj," are written very quickly and easily when the basic principle is understood. This principle states that the words are written as they sound "ng," "nk," and "nj." However, since we can't write the "nk" and "nj" together, we use the "F" key in place the "n." Therfore "nk" is written -FK; "nj" is written -FJ.

35.1 For all words that end in the sound of "ng" write the -PBG (-NG) in the same stroke.

☞ *practice the following:*

sang	SAPBG	bang	PWAPBG	rang	RAPBG
thing	THEUPBG	sing	SEUPBG	ding	TKEUPBG
wrong	WROPBG	ring	REUPBG	wing	WEUPBG

35.2 For all words that end in the sound of "nk" write the -FBG (-FK) in the same stroke.

☞ *practice the following:*

sank	SAFBG	bank	PWAFBG	rank	RAFBG
think	THEUFBG	sink	SEUFBG	tank	TAFBG
thank	THAFBG	wink	WEUFBG	drink	TKREUFBG

35.3 For all words that end in the sound of "nj" write the -FPBLG (-FJ) in the same stroke.

☞ *practice the following:*

tinge	TEUFPBLG	range	RAFPBLG	twinge	TWEUFPBLG
binge	PWEUFPBLG	singe	SEUFPBLG	fringe	TPREUFPBLG

New Punctuation (Initial Caps, All Caps)

In dictating names of places or things that require a capital letter (Memorial Hospital), or in dictating a proper name that is in direct conflict with a word (Ray or ray), a special designation is used at the beginning of the word to be capped. This designation is KEU-RBGS (initial caps). If an entire word is to be capalized, the designation KA-RBGS (all caps) is used.

Note that words that are preceded by the special symbols KEU-RBGS or KA-RBGS have to be defined in your personal dictionary. The symbols are used for distinction purposes and must be defined for each use.

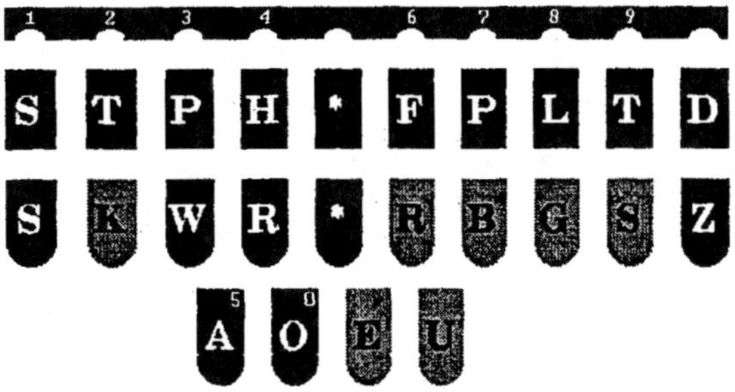

35.4 To designate an "initial cap" for a person, place, or thing, use the designation KEU-RBGS before the word.

☞ *practice the following:*

Ray	KEU-RBGS/RAFPL	Joy	KEU-RBGS/SKWROFPL
Mark	KEU-RBGS/PHARBG	Frank	KEU-RBGS/TPRAFBG
Matt	KEU-RBGS/PHAT	Pat	KEU-RBGS/PAT

Note: Each entry must be defined in your personal dictionary.

35.5 To designate "all caps" for a word, use the designation KA-RBGS before the word. Each separate word requires a separate designation.

☞ *practice the following:*

OUT	KA-RBGS/OUT	NOW	KA-RBGS/TPHOFRP
STOP	KA-RBGS/STOP	YIELD	KA-RBGS/KWRAOELD

Note: Each entry must be defined in your personal dictionary.

Short Forms and Phrases

☞ *practice the following:*

advertise	TEUZ	advice	SREUS	advise	SREUZ
affect	AFBGT	confer	KER	connect	KEBGT
connection	KEBGS	conference	KERPBS	consider	KR-
considerable	KR-B	considerably	KR-BL	considerate	KR-T
orange	ORPBG				

Lesson Practice

☞ *practice the following:*

Ray sang a sad song about a cowboy and a cowgirl who rode away into the twilight at sunset. / The cowgirl's name was Joy. They wouldn't take any advice so they had to pay the bank all the money / they had. Now, they no longer have a range to roam on. They no longer sing "home, home on the / range." Now, they sing, "home, home on the desert" (TKE/SKPWERT).

I'll advertise in the paper that I have an orange Ford / for sale. I'll mention (PHEPBGS) the fact that the buyer can save a considerable amount of money if they buy my / car. I'll mark down the price one-half. The car only has 234,901 / miles on it!

Mark will be frank about the advice he'll give you. Mark says: "Do what is right." Frank / says: "Mark my / words, you'll rank number one if you do what I say." He said to ring the bell at 10:31 / sharp. If you don't, you'll be in considerable trouble, and that will affect your next performance (PEFRPL/KWRAPBS).

Matt will confer / with Bill on how to go about making the connection from the sink to the tank. He'll need to consider / every possible angle so that the thing will work. I think if he marked out on a map which / way the pipes are supposed to go, he'll be all right. He thinks that he can put pipes wherever / he wants to. I'll bet if he does that, he'll mess up badly. I'd advise him to call a plumber / (PHRUPL/KWRER) NOW!

Consider this: 1/3 of all people who put their money in a bank never spend that money for 4 years. / Think of that. If you put away $54.23 every payday, or 1/10 of your paycheck, you'd / be able to save about $54,009.23 in a little less than 5 years. Isn't that smart?

Please / do not mix up these words: sang and sank, bang and bank, rang and rank, thing and think, / or sing or sink. Also, make sure you can write these words with very few problems: tinge, range, binge, / singe, and fringe.

Comprehensive Practice

☞ *practice the following:*

My friends, Sam, Nick, and Alex (AL/KWREFRPB) all found a box buried (BUR/KWRAOED) in my back yard. When they opened the / box, it contained silver and gold coins. They split the booty so that Sam got 1/3, Nick got 1/3, and / Alex got 1/3. I told them that I should get some, because they found it in my yard. / They gave me the empty (EPLT/AEFPL) box. I sold the box for $435.82 and kept the money for myself. /

Mr. Johnson had an accident in his automobile. He was supposed to go straight, but he took a curve to / the left. He ended up going over a bank and landing in a pond. Luckily (HRUBG/HRAEFPL), he wasn't hurt, but his car / was. It cost me $5,790.21 to have it fixed. He had to have a new headlight, a new / right front door, two new tires, and a new grill and fender. He said the accident was caused because a / bumble bee flew in his window and stung him on the nose (NOEZ).

My mom and dad gave to the local charity / to promote brevity and clarity in speech. The name of the charity is FREE Speech. You'll hear a free speech / every time you attend a meeting. Each member (PHEB) is supposed to give a speech every month. My mom spoke about "how / to fix a flat tire in 2 minutes." My dad spoke about fixing a computer problem when it comes up. /

My friend, Ned, was in the service. He served for 12 years in the Air Force. He flew a jet / plane. Now that he is out of the service, he flies for American Airlines. He makes about 52 flights a year. / He also makes about $320,000 a year. He's rich, but he works hard for his money.

If you / call the man who is supposed to supervise the majority of the cats, he'll be there in 10 minutes. / If you ask him to treat the cats with a little sensitivity, he will. If you ask him which ones / belong in a minority, cats or dogs, he'll tell you. He'll appreciate any comments you have about the cats.

I / got a thank you note from my roommate at school. I sent her a get well card and a gift / because she was ill. She had the flu (TPHRU), and she had it bad. She had to stay in bed for / 10 days straight and couldn't eat food. She's better now, but she's weak (WAEBG). I sent her a dozen roses. I / hope she gets better by the time school starts.

The book I got was too technical (T-FP) for me. I couldn't / even read the first page. I took it back and asked for one that was easier (AOES/KWRAER) to read. The book they / gave me was called, "The Cat in the Hat." It was much better. I liked it so much that / I ordered a copy for my boss. It was only $14.95 because it was on sale.

It takes a great deal / of nerve to be able to walk downtown after midnight. I would never walk alone. I'd take 2 friends / with me. If I go out at night, I call my friends, and they come running over. The three of / us went to a move yesterday. It didn't get over until 1 o'clock in the morning. By the time / we got home, it was 1:32 a.m.

What a wonderful invention (EUPB/SREPBGS) the shorthand machine is, except for one / thing. I don't like the fact that half of the alphabet (AL/TPA/PWET) is missing. I don't like adding two or three / letters to make one letter, but I'm getting used to it now. I can even read the S K W R / as the letter J, and the T P H as the letter N. I don't think I like the / L G T S as the final (TPAOEUPBL) Q.

Additional Practice

Go to the:	Do the following:
Realwrite DrillBook (recommended).......	Read over and study Drill XVIII (Lessons 35 & 36)
Realwrite NoteBook (optional).................	Read and transcribe the notes from Exercise I, Lesson 35

UNIT 9
LESSON THIRTY-SIX

Warm up and Review

☞ *practice writing the following fractions using numbers and the R-rule:*

1/2	2/3	3/4	5/6	7/8	9/10	11/12
12/15	9/20	44/100	2 2/3	9 9/19	8 3/4	4 1/2
28 1/2	9 2/3	1 1/3	2 2/3	3 3/4	4 5/6	9 1/2
6 7/8	7 8/9	8 9/10	10 11/12	11 12/13	12 13/14	1 1/3
13 14/15	14 15/16	15 16/17	16 17/18	17 18/19	18 19/20	6 3/4

Flagged Alphabet (Parentheses Surrouding)

Continuing the different ways of "flagging" the alphabet, there will be times when you will want to represent the alphabet with parentheses surrounding the individual letters. For example, when referring to paragraph (A) and (B); or parts (C) and (D).

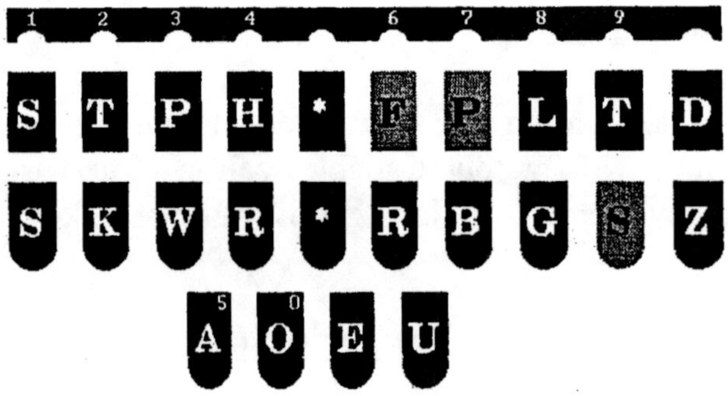

36.1 To write the alphabet so that it appears with a parenthesis before and after each individual letter. Write the alphabetic letter on the initial side of the keyboard along with the final side -FPS (parentheses surround) in the same stroke.

☞ *practice the following:*

alphabet	Realwrite	alphabet	Realwrite	alphabet	Realwrite
(A)	A-FPS	(J)	SKWR-FPS	(S)	S-FPS
(B)	PW-FPS	(K)	K-FPS	(T)	T-FPS
(C)	KR-FPS	(L)	HR-FPS	(U)	U-FPS
(D)	TK-FPS	(M)	PH-FPS	(V)	SR-FPS
(E)	E-FPS	(N)	TPH-FPS	(W)	W-FPS
(F)	TP-FPS	(O)	O-FPS	(X)	SKP-FPS
(G)	TKPW-FPS	(P)	P-FPS	(Y)	KWR-FPS
(H)	H-FPS	(Q)	KW-FPS	(Z)	SKPW-FPS
(I)	EU-FPS	(R)	R-FPS		

Writing Words that Begin with "fore" or "un"

36.2 Write the TPOER at the beginning of words that start with the prefix "fore" or "for."

☞ *practice the following:*

forbid	TPOER/PWEUD	forgot	TPOER/TKPWOT
forget	TPOER/TKPWET	forgive	TPOER/TKPWEUFB
forgave	TPOER/TKPWAEUFB	forgiven	TPOER/TKPWEUFPB
forego	TPOER/TKPWOE	format	TPOER/PHAT
foreword	TPOER/WORD	foretell	TPOER/TEL

36.3 Write the UPB at the beginning of words that start with the prefix "un." If a hyphen is needed to separate the words, write the H-RBGS between the two words.

☞ *practice the following:*

uncover	UPB/KOFR	unable	UPB/KWRAEUBL
unnecessary	UPB/TPHE	unclear	UPB/KHRAOER
undesirable	UPB/STKAOEURBL	unpack	UPB/PABG
un-cola	UPB/H-RBGS/KOE/HRA	unforgetable	UPB/TPOER/TKPWET/KWRABL

Writing Words that Begin with "div" or "dev"

36.4 Write the TKW- (DW) for words that begin with the"div" or "dev" prefix. If the TKW- cannot be written in the same stroke, write the TKEUFB ("div") or TKEFB ("dev") in the first stroke, followed by the completed outline.

☞ *practice the following:*

divorce	TKWORS	divide	TKWAOEUD	division	TKWEUGS
devise	TKWAOEUZ	devote	TKWOET	devotion	TKWOEGS
device	TKWAOEUS	diverse	TKWERS	divine	TKWAOEUPB
devour	TKWOUR	deviate	TKWAEUT	deviation	TKWAEUGS

Short Forms and Phrases

☞ *practice the following:*

inch	TPH-FP	include	KHRAU	incorporate	TPHORPT
incorporated	TPHORPD	increase	TPHRAOES	indicate	KAET
beyond	KWROPBD	capital	KAL	authority	THORT
continue	T-PB				

Lesson Practice

☞ *practice the following:*

The divorce is now final. They had to divide up all they owned. The division was very, very hard. They / had to devise a plan where they would each get one half of what they owned. They had to include / the car, the house, the couch, the chairs, the cat, the computer, the table, the television (TEL/SREUGS), and their marble collection. / They could not deviate from the plan.

I had a mouse in the house that would devour my food. / Yesterday, I set a trap for the mouse with cheese and crackers. Today, I found a note from the mouse / asking for wine. The mouse thinks (THEUFBGZ) I run a diner.

My dad used to say: "Give them an inch, and they'll / take a mile." My mom used to say: "Give them a mile, and they'll ask for more." I like to / incorporate their sayings into my own little thought. I say, " Don't give them an inch or a mile, but give / them a smile."

Ronald (ROPB/KWRALD) started his own store about 33 years ago with only $5.92 to his name. / His store is now incorporated into one of the largest burger makers in the world. He makes burgers by the / billion. Maybe you've heard of his store before, it's called Burger World.

The paragraph (PAEUR/TKPWRAF) began with the letter (P), but the / next one was marked with the letter (R). I don't know what happened to the (Q). Have / you seen a loose (Q)?

Beyond all doubt (TKOUT), the woman spoke with great authority. She spoke about a diverse / devotion to work and how to increase the amount of time you devote to work by two thirds. She did / indicate that it would be very difficult to continue without a proper plan. In fact, she said to include / a certificate with your application. I've almost begun the process (PRO/SES), but I need your help.

Comprehensive Practice

☞ *practice the following:*

If you put aside $5.00 a day for 15 days, you'll have enough money to buy a new knapsack. / If you put aside an additional 50 cents a day, you can have the extra special, super-duper knapsack that / comes with a hidden pocket and your choice of 15 different colors. I got the good one because my / dad paid for it. I got a red one with a pink stripe. I keep my secret (SE/KRET) notes in it.

My mom opened a / savings account at the American Bank and got a free can opener. She gave the can opener to my dad / so he could open cans of dog food to feed our dog, Steno (STEPB/KWROE).

If you deduct the interest, you are / going to get in your savings account and keep that in a special account, you'll see how quickly it / accumulates (A/KAOUPL/HRAEUTZ).

Do you bowl (PWOEFRPL)? I do. I had 10 strikes in a row, and my score was 300. I got / a prize. I got a new bowling ball (PWAUL) and a smart case to carry it in. I liked it, except / I didn't like the color. It had green swirls in it with a red stripe going one way and / brown stripes on the side. It was really ugly (UG/HRAEFPL). I tried to trade it in for a new one, / but the man at the store laughed at me. I tried to give it to my niece (TPHAOES), but she cried. I cut / it in half and made bookends out of it.

Mr. Knight was a policeman. He worked the night beat (PWAOET). He caught / a robber (ROB/KWRER) who broke into the bank and stole $52,901.32. The money was marked, so he was / easy to catch. He got a reward for catching the thief. He got a set of bookends made out of / a bowling ball that was cut in half. He's very, very proud of his new bookends.

Can you spell spurt? (SPURT)? I spell it S-P-U-R-T. Can you spell sprint? I spell it S-P-R-I-N-T. / How about strut? I spell it S-T-R-O-T, but I think it's supposed to be spelled / S-T-R-U-T. Do you know? Let me know when you find out. Maybe you can look it / up.

I have one strip of grass that grows and grows and grows. I mow (PHOEFRP) it every day, even twice a / day at times, but it keeps on growing. I even tried collecting the grass after I mow it, but that / doesn't help. I don't mind, but right now the grass is 2 feet tall, and I mowed it 5 minutes / ago. The grass is not green, but brown. I think it's hay (HAFPL), but Rob thinks its straw. What do you / think it is?

Do you have the correct technical data to distribute the fractions over the life of the loan? / If you don't, you better get it correct, or all of your fractions will be off. I'll give you the / correct data. It is this: 42, 8790, 11, 32, 124, 901, and 8. Make sure you copy them / correctly.

Michael, Michelle, Ray, Sam, Jill, Mark, Denny, Tom, Bob, Sue, Jen, Jill, Jack, and Jim are all coming to my / party. Can you come, too? It starts at 9:00 o'clock. Bring a dish to pass and a case of soda (SOED/KWRA). / You don't have to bring a gift, but if you do, I'd appreciate a new 4-wheel drive Jeep. I'm / not picky, but I'd like it in red.

Can you bake bread in an oven? I can. I used a /new microwave (PHAOEUBG/ROE/WAEFB) recipe (RES/PAOE) that only takes 5 minutes. I baked some yesterday, and it looked like fresh soup (SOUP). I thought / I did it right, but I didn't. I told my daughter it was bread soup, and she loved it. She / added some beans and rice and ate it all up.

Can you knit? I knew you could. Will you knit / me a nice hat? I need it before winter sets in. If I could have one that covers my ears, / I'd appreciate it. Also, If I could have a blue (PWHRAOU) one to match my yellow (KWRE/HROEFRP) coat, that would be great! / Could I have it by tomorrow?

If you saw the incident, tell the policeman. If you saw the accident, / tell the policeman. If you didn't see it, then tell him that. He needs to know all of the people / who saw it and all of the people who didn't see it. Tell him what you saw or what you / didn't see, and tell him now. Tell him what you know.

Additional Practice

Go to the: Do the following:

Realwrite DrillBook (recommended)......Write and practice Drill XVIII (Lessons 35 & 36)

Realwrite NoteBook (optional)...............Read and transcribe the notes from Exercise I, Lesson 36 and Drill XVIII

UNIT 9 REVIEW

LESSON REVIEW

1. Go back to each lesson and learn each new rule thoroughly.
2. Go back to each lesson and write the Lesson Practice.
3. Go back to each lesson and write the Comprehensive Practice.
4. Read back all notes and transcribe a portion of your review.

Review of Writing Rules

33.1 For all words that end with the sound of "able" or "ible," write the -BL in the same stroke or combined in a second stroke. If a separate stroke is necessary, write KWRABL (able) or KWREUBL (ible) in the last stroke.

33.2 For all words that end with the sound of "ability" or "ibility," write the -BLT in the same stroke or combined i a second stroke. If a separate stroke is necessary, write KWRABLT (ability) or KWREUBLT (ibility) in the last stroke.

33.3 Write the DP-RBGS to designate the decimal point whenever it is dictated.

33.4 Write the POEU-RBGS to designate the word point whenever it is dictated.

33.5 Write the days of the week using a two- or three-letter designation on the initial side, combined with the -FPLT on the final side.

34.1 Write the EPBT for words that begin with the prefix "enter." Write the EUPBT for words that begin with the prefix "inter."

34.2 Write the STK- ("d" and "s" reversed) for words that begin with the prefix "des" or "dis." Combine the STK with a vowel in the first stroke if necessary. If it is necesary to write the "des" or "dis" in a separate stroke, write the TKES or TKEUS.

34.3 Write fractions phonetically as you hear them when they are to be transcribed as words.

34.4 Write fractions that are to be transcribed using numbers by combining the numerator with the initial R- or final -R in the first stroke. Write the denominator for the second stroke.

35.1 For all words that end in the sound of "ng" write the -PBG (-NG) in the same stroke.

35.2 For all words that end in the sound of "nk" write the -FBG (-FK) in the same stroke.

35.3 For all words that end in the sound of "nj" write the -FPBLG (-FJ) in the same stroke.

35.4 To designate an "initial cap" for a person, place or thing, use the designation KEU-RBGS before the word.

35.5 To designate "all caps" for a word, use the designation KA-RBGS before the word. Each separate word requires a separate designation.

36.1 To write the alphabet so that it appears with a parenthesis before and after each individual letter, write the alphabetic letter on the initial side of the keyboard along with the final side -FPS (parentheses surround) in the same stroke.

36.2 Write the TPOER at the beginning of words that start with the prefix "fore" or "for."

36.3 Write the UPB at the beginning of words that start with the prefix "un." If a hyphen is needed to separate the words, write the H-RBGS between the two words.

36.4 Write the TKW- (DW) for words that begin with the "div" or "dev" prefix. If the TKW- cannot be written in the same stroke, write the TKEUFB ("div") or TKEFB ("dev") in the first stroke, followed by the completed outline.

Review DrillBook and NoteBook Applications

1. Review Drills XVII and XVIII from the *Realwrite DrillBook* (recommended).
2. Review Exercise I from the *Realwrite NoteBook* (optional).

Unit Evaluation Number Nine

Unit Evaluation Number Nine will cover all material from the following: *Realwrite LessonBook*, Lessons 33-36; *DrillBook*, Drills XVII and XVIII.

UNIT 10
LESSON THIRTY-SEVEN

Warm up and Review

☞ *practice the following:*

$45.92	$334.21	$8231.02	4:29 a.m.	8 o'clock	5 1/3	4-21-94
$21.67	$211.91	$9112.29	6:14 p.m.	9 o'clock	2 1/2	1-1-95
$ 7.21	$999.18	$8214.59	7:15 p.m.	12 o'clock	12 3/4	12-15-82
$95.68	$387.77	$1132.41	2:17 a.m.	1 o'clock	4 1/8	5/12/72
$66.87	$871.90	$3491.55	1:45 a.m.	5 o'clock	3 1/4	7/9/50

Flagged Alphabet (Hyphens Before or After)

There may be instances where you will want to transcribe the letters of the alphabet with a hyphen before or after the letter. For example, Defendant's Exhibit 1-A, apartment 4-C, or Exhibit F-2.

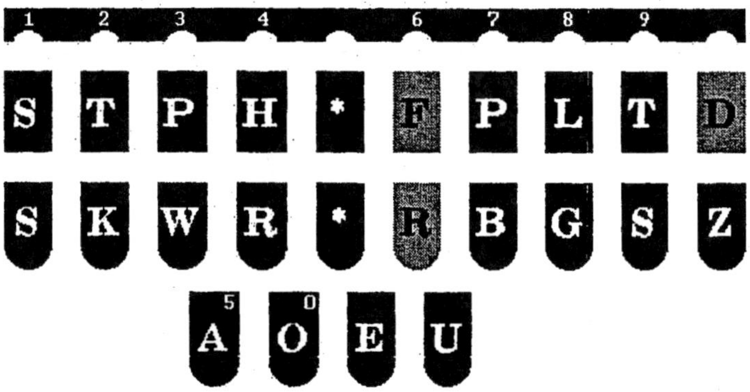

37.1 To write the alphabet so that the hyphen appears at the right of each letter, write the alphabetic letter on the initial side of the keyboard along with the final side -FRD. (Flagged Right Dash) in the same stroke.

☞ *practice the following:*

alphabet	Realwrite	alphabet	Realwrite	alphabet	Realwrite
A-	A-FRD	J-	SKWR-FRD	S-	S-FRD
B-	PW-FRD	K-	K-FRD	T-	T-FRD
C-	KR-FRD	L-	HR-FRD	U-	U-FRD
D-	TK-FRD	M-	PH-FRD	V-	SR-FRD
E-	E-FRD	N-	TPH-FRD	W-	W-FRD
F-	TP-FRD	O-	O-FRD	X-	SKP-FRD
G-	TKPW-FRD	P-	P-FRD	Y-	KWR-FRD
H-	H-FRD	Q-	KW-FRD	Z-	SKPW-FRD
I-	EU-FRD	R-	R-FRD		

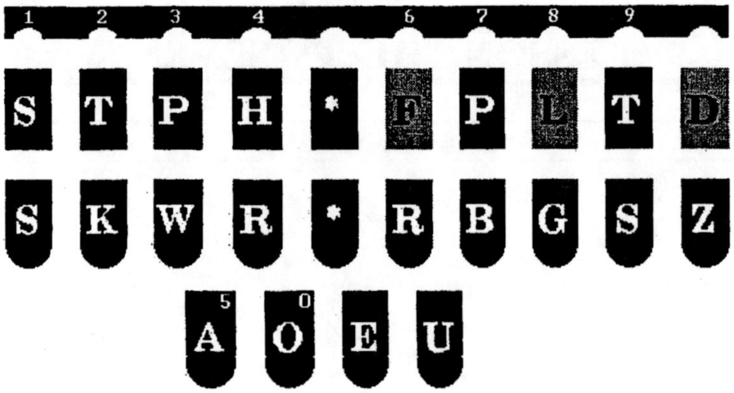

37.2 To write the alphabet so that the hyphen appears at the left of each letter, write the alphabetic letter on the initial side of the keyboard along with the final side -FLD (Flagged Left Dash) in the same stroke.

☞ *practice the following:*

alphabet	Realwrite	alphabet	Realwrite	alphabet	Realwrite
-A	A-FLD	-J	SKWR-FLD	-S	S-FLD
-B	PW-FLD	-K	K-FLD	-T	T-FLD-
-C	KR-FLD	-L	HR-FLD	-U	U-FLD
-D	TK-FLD	-M	PH-FLD	-V	SR-FLD
-E	E-FLD	-N	TPH-FLD	-W	W-FLD
-F	TP-FLD	-O	O-FLD	-X	SKP-FLD
-G	TKPW-FLD	-P	P-FLD	-Y	KWR-FLD
-H	H-FLD	-Q	KW-FLD	-Z	SKPW-FLD
-I	EU-FLD	-R	R-FLD		

Writing Words that end in the Sound of "th"

37.3 For words that end in "th" write the -TD in the same stroke. If it is necessary to write the -TD in a separate stroke, write the attached ending AETD in the last stroke.

Keep in mind that the -TD is very easily written with a conscientious "shift-to-the-right-one-position" on the final side. This should be done quickly and smoothly, immediately returning to the home position.

☞ *practice the following:*

bath	PWATD	faith	TPAEUTD	mouth	PHOUTD
cloth	KHROTD	youth	KWRAOUTD	teeth	TAOETD
breathe	PWRAOETD	breath	PWRETD	tooth	TAOTD
truth	TRAOUTD	death	TKETD	sooth	SAOTD
smother	SPHOTD/KWRER	clothe	KHROETD	moth	PHOTD
leather	HRETD/KWRER	feather	TPETD/KWRER	filth	TPEUL/AETD

Writing Words that end in "ther"

☞ practice the following:

other	OTD	another	TPHOTD	either	ETD
mother	PHOETD	father	TPATD	brother	PWROTD
further	TPRUTD	farther	TPRATD	bother	PWOTD
neither	TPHETD	gather	TKPWATD	rather	RATD
together	TOTD				

Writing Roman Numerals

37.4 To designate a Roman numeral, write the special designation RO-RBGS, followed by the regular number using the number bar.

Regular numbers are written using all previous rules that you have learned. All Roman numerals will hav to be defined in your personal dictionary in order for them to translate.

☞ practice the following:

I	RO-RBGS/1	XI	RO-RBGS/1EU
II	RO-RBGS/2	XV	RO-RBGS/15
III	RO-RBGS/3	XX	RO-RBGS/20
IV	RO-RBGS/4	L	RO-RBGS/50
V	RO-RBGS/5	LX	RO-RBGS/60
VI	RO-RBGS/6	C	RO-RBGS/1/H-PBD
IX	RO-RBGS/9	D	RO-RBGS/5/H-PBD
X	RO-RBGS/10	M	RO-RBGS/1/TH-Z

Short Forms and Phrases

☞ practice the following:

although	HR-TD	health	HETD	earth	R-TD
method	PH-TD	wealth	WETD	birth	PWR-TD
weather	W-TD	forth	TPR-TD	depth	TKP-TD
whether	WH-TD	breadth	BRAETD	width	WEUTD
length	HRAETD				

Lesson Practice

☞ practice the following:

It takes a great deal of faith to be able to hear a word and then write it without looking / at the keyboard on your shorthand machine. Either you can do it, or you can't. I knew a man who / could write at about 300 words a minute, but he had to practice. His father and mother were both court / reporters. He now works for a court and is very, very happy.

If the weather is nice, my brother and / sister and I are all going to go shopping for a gift for our mother and father. Jill wants to / buy them a new bath tub. John wants to surprise them with a new car. I want to get them a / leather recliner (RE/KHRAOEUPB/KWRER) so they can relax at night. I think we'll just give them a gift certificate and let them / choose what they want. What do you think?

Neither you nor I can go to the show at 9:00 o'clock / because we don't have a ride. My friend, Ben said he would take us, but he has to be / home by 9:15. My other friend, Jen, said she could take us, but she couldn't leave until 9:30. / I could probably ask my father if I could take his car, but he usually needs it because he is on / call at the office. Will you give us a ride? We'll pay you $23.52.

The further I go, the / farther I get behind. Or is it the farther I go, the further I get behind? Do you know which / one it is? Either, neither, or both? I have another thought; I'll change it to say: "The more I get behind, / the more behind I get."

My mother works in an office where they clean teeth. I went in to have / my teeth cleaned and wound up with a tooth pulled (PULD). My mouth was sore for about 5 hours afterwards (AFR/WARDZ). It / hurt so bad, I couldn't breathe; I had trouble catching my breath. I'd rather go to school than go back to / that office again.

There is great truth in the old saying that a moth gathers no moss. I think I / have that wrong. I think it's a rolling stone that gathers no moss and a moth eats cloth.

I have / a store called the "Leather Feather." I sell leather feathers. Would you like to buy any? I have a special / every Tuesday. You can buy two leather feathers at 1/2 the price. That's a savings of over $3.00. I / usually sell the feathers by the dozen. I'd be willing to sell you a dozen leather feathers for $45.92 / if you don't tell other people. If the word got out that I was selling them so cheap, I'd have / to almost give them away. I won't even sell them that cheap to my mother, my father, or my brother. /

Although I know that there is a method to your madness, I still don't know what to think about your / actions. Would you rather have good health or great wealth? Some say that birth leads to death; others say death leads / to birth. What do you think? Some say the earth is round; some say it is flat. What do you / say? Some say youth is only for the young; some say experience is only for the mature (PHA/TAOUR). What do you / say?

Please pass the ketchup (KET/KHUP) and mustard (PHUS/TARD). Never mind, don't bother, I'd rather have the relish (RE/HREUFB), pickles (PEUBG/AELZ), and onions (OPB/YOPBZ). Do you / have any bread?

Comprehensive Practice

☞ *practice the following:*

The winning number in the lotto (HROT/KWROE) was 41-4-23-14-7-22; the supplemental (SUP/HRAPLT/KWRAL) number was 6. I have / an appointment for Wednesday at 7:30 a.m. I can't make it. Can I change it to Thursday at 8 o'clock? / If not, I'll have to cancel (KAPB/SEL) it and make it for a different day.

I am an American, but I / was born in France. I came to America when I was 4 years old. My mother and father brought me / over on a boat. We all came over together, although my health was bad and we were poor. Now, / we are (WER) healthy and wealthy.

A sudden snowstorm came up and stranded us on the highway. Luckily, there was a / motel near by. We spent the night in the lobby drinking coffee and trying to keep warm. The storm lasted / for two more nights. By the time it ended, we had 6 feet of snow.

I want to make sure / that every man, woman, and child will have accessibility to the new courthouse. If it is not accessible, it is not / acceptable. Are you and your friend compatible? Are you and your friend dependable? I've only one regrettable thought; there's never / enough time to do all I want to do in one day; I need an extra 8 hours.

My sneakers / are comfortable. They're Nikes (THPAOEU/KAOEZ). I wear (WAER) them so much, I have a hole in the bottom. I'm going to buy / a new pair (PAEUR) as soon as I get some money. They're kind of expensive (SKPEPB/SEUFB). On sale, they're $234.58. / My dad wanted to know if they were made from gold or silver. He doesn't think it's very sensible to / pay that much for sneakers, but I conned (KOPBD) him into buying them for me. I told him that at / $234.58, he'd only be paying about a penny and a half a day to make me happy.

Additional Practice

Go to the:	Do the following:
Realwrite DrillBook (recommended).......	Read over and study Drill XIX (Lessons 37 & 38
Realwrite NoteBook (optional)................	Read and transcribe the notes from Exercise J, Lesson 37

UNIT 10
LESSON THIRTY-EIGHT

WARM UP AND REVIEW

☞ *practice the following:*

1. Practice the letters of the alphabet in all capitals (X-FBG).
2. Practice the letters of the alphabet in all small letter (X-FS).
3. Practice the letters of the alphabet in letter by letter spelling (X-FL).
4. Practice the letters of the alphabet with a period after each letter (X-FPD).

Writing Words that end in "st," "sk," or "sm"

38.1 For words that end in "sk" and "sm," write the -SZ in the same stroke.

Keep in mind that the -SZ is very easily written with a "shift-to-the-right-one-position" on the final side. This should be done quickly and smoothly, immediately returning to the home position.

☞ *practice the following:*

mask	PHASZ	cask	KASZ	task	TASZ
flask	TPHRASZ	bask	PWASZ	dusk	TKUSZ
musk	PHUSZ	tusk	TUSZ	desk	TKESZ
risk	REUSZ	whisk	WHEUSZ	disc	TKEUSZ
prism	PREUSZ	chasm	KHASZ	spasm	SPASZ
schism	SKHEUSZ	sarcasm	SAR/KASZ		

38.2 For words that end in "st" write the -SZ in the same stroke; however, for one-syllable words that contain the vowel "a" use the AE within the same stroke.

☞ *practice the following:*

cost	KOSZ	lost	HROSZ	frost	TPROSZ
quest	KWESZ	trust	TRUSZ	exist	SKPEUSZ
mist	PHEUSZ	rust	RUSZ	midst	PHEUD/AESZ
mast	PHAESZ	cast	KAESZ	last	HRAESZ
fast	TPAESZ	past	PAESZ	blast	PWHRAESZ

38.3 For words that end in "ism" and "ist" and require a separate stroke, use the SKPWEUPL for "ism" and the KWREUSZ for "ist."

☞ *practice the following:*

truest	TRAOUSZ	truism	TRAOU/SKPWEUPL
dualist	TKAOUL/KWREUSZ	dualism	TKAOUL/SKPWEUPL
perfectionist	P-FBGS/KWREUSZ	perfectionism	P-FBGS/SKPWEUPL
realist	RAEL/KWREUSZ	realism	RAEL/SKPWEUPL

Each time the -SZ is used, it is used for a distinct purpose and, therefore, cannot be confused. When used with a number, it means cents; when used as a short form, it is translated as that short form and nothing else; and when used as one of the "sk" "sm" or "st" endings, it is not in conflict with any other word pattern.

Frequent Phrases (Any, Every)

The following are phrases used as pronouns or adverbs. If the transcription calls for two separate words, write the words out phonetically as in the words "any body" (TPHEU/PWOD/AEFPL).

☞ *practice the following:*

pronouns:

anybody	TPHEUB	anyone	TPHEUPB	anything	TPHEUPBG
everybody	KWR-B	everyone	KWR-PB	everything	KWR-PBG

adverbs:

anyhow	TPHEUFD	anymore	TPHEUPL	anyway	TPHEUFPL
anyplace	TPHEUPS	anywhere	TPHEUFRP		
everyplace	KWR-PS	everywhere	KWR-FRP	everyday	KWR-D

Short Forms and Phrases

☞ *practice the following:*

satisfy	S-F	satisfaction	S-FBGS	satisfactory	S-FR
satisfying	S-FG	secretary	SEBG	season	SAEPB
signature	STPHAOUR	sister	STER	disk	STKEUK
dust	TKUS				

Lesson Practice

☞ *practice the following:*

Anybody who wants to go to the movie will have to pay the full price today. Yesterday, it cost you / $2.50 to get in; today it will cost you $5.00. When was the last time anyone got in / the movie for less than $5.00? Everybody I know pays at least $7.50. You'd better get there before / the show starts, or you'll have to wait in the lobby until intermission (EUPBT/PHEUGS).

I don't need your sarcasm; I need your / trust. I'm on a quest for truth and justice (SKWRUSZ/KWREUS). Do you know where I can find them? I'll search high and / low.

The weather has turned cold, and now, there is a frost on the grass. At dusk there is a mist / in the air that exists (SKPEUSZ/AEZ) for at least (HRAOESZ) 6 hours.

I put a new disk into the drive, but it / still didn't work. I even formatted the disk; it still didn't work. This is the last time I buy a disk / at a discount store. I got 25 disks for $1.35. I usually pay $1.25 for one / disk. I'll have to get some better disks tomorrow.

Has anyone seen the new desk I bought for my secretary? I / suppose it's satisfactory, but I'd prefer a bigger one. There isn't enough room for her computer keyboard, her disk drive, / her laser (HRAEUZ/KWRER) printer, her monitor (PHOPB/TOR), and her purse (PURS). I think if I got her another desk to put next to this / desk, she might have enough room. What do you think?

My secretary asked me to put my signature on a paper. / I told her I'd do it after I looked at it. After I examined the document, I decided not to sign / it. If I had signed it, I would have given away my cat. I can't give up my cat; she / gives me too much satisfaction. I love my hamster (HAPLS/TER), too. They both play with a prism I have hanging in / the window. They love to bat it across the room.

This is the season for colds due to flu / (TPHRU). My sister had a fever, my brother had a headache, my mother had a sore throat, and my father had / pains in his head. I felt fine until I came home and found them all sick. Now I don't feel / so good. I think I'll make myself some chicken soup and go to bed. That will be very, very satisfying. /

Anybody want to dance with me? Anyone want to run with me? I dance at dawn and run at dusk. I / dance slow, but I run fast. We'll have a blast, trust me.

Dualism is a truism. The particular task that you have / to do will entail (EPB/TAEUL) a great deal of risk. Are you ready to undergo that risk? If not, tell me / now. If you prefer, I'll call Stan to do the job. He doesn't mind. Everyone knows that Stan is the man / to get the job done fast. But if you want to do it, do it now!

I had a muscle / (MUS/AEL) spasm. I went to the doctor. He sent me to the hospital. I got a shot in my arm. Now, / I'm all right.

Comprehensive Practice

☞ *practice the following:*

Have you ever heard of such a thing? Little green men from Mars? Jeff said that when he looked out / his window to see what all the noise was, he saw a flying saucer with flashing green and red lights / on it. A little green man talked to him, but he would not disclose his mission. He wanted to know / where Jeff's leader was. Jeff took him to his boss at Hot Dog Land.

Never, ever interpose a thought when / I'm thinking, please. I don't think that often; and when I do, I need complete quiet! Yesterday I had a / thought, but today it is gone. Maybe tomorrow I'll have one. If you have to interrupt me, wait until I've / completed my thought.

I went into the service station and asked for a headlight for my car. He gave me a new / battery (PWAT/RAEFPL) instead. I didn't mind until he told me that I needed the battery to make the headlight work. He / said I'd have to pay $14.58 for the light and $5.98 for the battery. I told him what I / thought and walked out the door. There was no more discussion. I ended up going to a car garage (TKPWRAPBLG) and / getting it fixed for $10.87. I got a discount because I bought my car there.

I didn't know that / I had to have a disclaimer (TKEUS/KHRAEUPL/KWRER) filed with my certificate. Why didn't you tell me? Now, I have to get a / lawyer and have him type it up. It'll probably be about $567.90 to have it done. I / wish you'd told me before. My friend, Tom, is a lawyer, and he would have done it for free. / He is in France now.

I will not discuss the account with you until you bring me the right paper. / This is the wrong one. I need the one that shows the distribution of profits (PROFTS) for the entire year, not / just the month. You should be able to distinguish between the two reports. I hope that they have not / been destroyed in the fire that you had. If they have been destroyed, we'll have to call the main office / in the morning to get a copy.

Additional Practice

Go to the:	Do the following:
Realwrite DrillBook (recommended)........	Write and practice Drill XIX (Lessons 37 & 38)
Realwrite NoteBook (optional).................	Read and transcribe the notes from Exercise J, Lesson 38 and Drill XIX

UNIT 10
LESSON THIRTY-NINE

Warm up and Review

☞ *practice the following:*

I'll	you've	we're	it'll	can't	won't
wouldn't	you're	it's	what's	how's	I'm
didn't	you'll	they're	ain't	isn't	who's
I'd	he'd	she'll	we'd	they'd	I've
they've	we've	he's	she's	we'd	they'll
that'll	couldn't	she'd	aren't	it's	that's

Writing Words that are out of Sequence

There are certain words that are considered "out of sequence" according to the arrangement of the machine shorthand keyboard. Therefore, it is necessary to take the consonants that cannot be completed in the first stroke and write them in a separate stroke. These final-stroked consonants must be written with the AE (attached ending).

These words can roughly be divided into words that end with the "mp," "lk," "lm," "nch," and "rch."

39.1 Final consonants that cannot be written in the same stroke as the root word are written in a separate stroke along with the AE (attached ending).

☞ *practice the following:*

-mp words:

jump	SKWRUPL/AEP	pump	PUPL/AEP	champ	KHAPL/AEP
skimp	SKEUPL/AEP	stamp	STAPL/AEP	swamp	SWAPL/AEP

-lk words:

milk	PHEUL/AEBG	silk	SEUL/AEBG	folk	TPOEL/AEBG
talk[1]	TAUBG	walk	WAUBG	chalk	KHAUBG

-lm words:

film	TPEUL/AEPL	realm	REL/AEPL	whelm	WHEL/AEPL
calm[1]	KAUPL	palm	PAUPL	psalm	SAUPL

[1]Words containing the diphthong "au" before "lk" and "lm" are written using AU

-nch words:

lunch	HRUPB/AEFP	bunch	PWUPB/AEFP	branch	PWRAPB/AEFP
bench	PWEPB/AEFP	crunch	KRUPB/AEFP	ranch	RAPB/AEFP
pinch	PEUPB/AEFP	punch	PUPB/AEFP	brunch	PWRUPB/AEFP

-rch words:

birch	PWEUR/AEFP	arch	AR/AEFP	lurch	HRUR/AEFP
march	PHAR/AEFP	scorch	SKOR/AEFP	starch	STAR/AEFP
torch	TOR/AEFP	smirch	SPHEUR/AEFP	porch	POR/AEFP

Frequent Phrases (No, Some)

The following are phrases used as pronouns or adverbs. If the transcription calls for two separate words, write the words out phonetically as in the words "some day" (SPH/TKAFPL)

☞ *practice the following:*

pronouns:

nobody	TPHOEB	no one	TPH-PB	nothing	TPHOPBG
somebody	SPH-B	someone	SPH-PB	something	SPH-PBG

adverbs:

no how	TPHOEFD	no way	TPHOEFPL	nowhere	TPHOEFRP
somehow	SPH-FD	some way	SPH-FPL	somewhere	SPH-FRP
someday	SPH-D	someplace	SPH-PS	somewhat	SWA-
sometime	SPH-T	sometimes	SPH-TS		

Writing the Months of the Year

Remembering the "group designation" -FPLT that was used for the days of the week, the months of the year can be written using the same designation.

39.2 Write the months of the year using a two- or three-letter designation on the initial side, combined with the -FPLT on the final side.

☞ *practice the following:*

January	SKWRA-FPLT	July	SKWRU-FPLT
February	TPE-FPLT	August	AU-FPLT
March	PHA-FPLT	September	SE-FPLT
April	A-FPLT	October	O-FPLT
May	PHAEU-FPLT	November	TPHO-FPLT
June	SKWRAOU-FPLT	December	TKE-FPLT

Writing Prefixes and Suffixes that may be Separate Words

As you have already learned, it is sometimes necessary to distinguish a word beginning from a separate word or a word ending.

39.3 For words that begin with prefixes that could be considered separate words, write them according to the following chart:

English	*prefix-*	*word/short form*
down	**TKOFRP**	**TKOUFRP**
enter	**EPBT**	**TPHER**
fore[1]	**TPOER**	**TP-R**
over	**OEFR**	**SRER**
post	**POESZ**	**POES**
self	**SEF**	**SEFL**
super	**SAOUP**	**SPER**
under	**UPBD**	**TKER**
up	**UP/AE**	**UP**
out	**OUT/AE**	**OUT**
in	**EUPB**	**TPH-**

[1]Note the difference between "fore" as a prefix TPOER; "fore" as a word TP-R; "fore" as an ending suffix FAOR; "for" as a word TPOR, and "four" as a number TPOUR.

39.4 For words that end with suffixes that could be considered separate words or the beginning of another word, write them according to the following chart:

word ending	*suffix*	*word/short form*
-shal	**SHAEL**	**(shall) SHAL**
-ment	**PHAEPBT**	**(meant) PHEPBT**
-less	**HRAES**	**(less) HRES**
-ful (full)	**TPAUL**	**(full) TPUL**
-let (lette)	**HRAET**	**(let) HRET**
-for (fore)	**TPAOR**	**(for) TPOR**
-nette	**TPHAET**	**(net) TPHET**
-over	**AE/OEFR**	**SRER**
-up	**AE/UP**	**UP**
-out	**AE/OUT**	**OUT**
-under	**AE/UPBD**	**TKER**

Short Forms and Phrases

☞ *practice the following:*

search	SEFP	answer	SWER	individual	SREUD
correspondence	KREPBS	maximum	PH-FRPB	Mr.	PHR-
Mrs.	PHR-S	Ms.	PH-Z	Miss	PH-S
person	PERPB	personal	PERPBL		

Lesson Practice

☞ *practice the following:*

Mr. and Mrs. Smith (SPHEUTD) own a grocery (TKPWROES/RAEFPL) store. Every Monday they have a special on milk and bread. On Tuesday / you can buy soda pop and chips at half price. On Wednesday hot dogs and hamburgers (HAPL/PWURG/KWRERZ) are on sale. Thursday / is the day that you can get steak (STAEBG) and beef for $2.49 a pound. Friday is fish day; and / on the weekend, you can buy chicken (KHEUBG/KWREPB) and turkey (TURBG/AEFPL) for 99 cents a pound.

Nobody knows the trouble I've seen. / No one knows what I'm going through. Nothing you say or do will help me, except a fresh jar of peanut / (PAOE/TPHUT) butter (PWUT/KWRER) and a box of crackers (KRABG/KWRERZ).

Ms. Jones, my steno teacher, says that she loves teaching; she teaches because she / likes to see her students (STU/TKEPBTS) learn. She treats each individual pupil (PU/PEUL) the same. She writes steno on the chalkboard (KHAUBG/AE/BORD) / with great speed. She writes steno on the machine even faster.

I know all there is to know about / the incident. This is all I know: somebody, somewhere, sometime, did something to someone, someplace, somehow. I also know that / nobody, nohow, noway, nowhere, is willing to say anything about nothing to no one. Please don't tell the police where you / got all this important data.

I'm in a lurch. I put starch on a silk blouse that I was going / to iron (AOEURPB), but I let it set too long and it began to scorch. The blouse was white; now, it / is white with a brown stain. I told my mother I didn't do it; I told her a mouse in the / house did it.

This is my goal for the new year: by the end of January, I hope to be / at 80 words a minute. By the end of February, 100; March, 120; April, 140; / and May, 140 words a minute. Then, in the summer I plan on reaching 160 words / a minute in June, 180 words a minute in July, and 200 words a minute in August. / When I come back to school in September, I'll be at 220 words a minute; in October, 240 / words a minute; in November, 260 words a minute; and in December, 280 words a minute. What do you think of my goals?

Is it Miss or Mrs. or Ms. Sullivan (SUL/SRAPB)? What is your / answer? Where were you on the night of January 22, 1992? Your answer is that you were / at church? How about the night of November 17, 1983? Where were you then, / Miss Sullivan?

What is / the maximum speed you can go on this street? Does anyone know the answer? Do you have a stamp for / my letter that I'm sending to my sister who has a friend of a friend who knows you?

In my / search for true happiness, (HAP/TPHAES) I found it in a correspondence course on cooking. I can do lunch for 12 and / brunch for 24. I'm a whiz in the kitchen (KEUFP/KWREPB). You should see the smoke fly when I get / out my mixer. I can crack a dozen eggs with one hand tied behind my back. My specialty (SPERBLT) is toasted tuna / (TU/TPHA) shells stuffed with jelly. I don't like to brag, but I'm the best. Would you like to see me boil / some water (WAUT/KWRER)?

Is it true that you were born on July 4, 1975? If not, when were you / born? What is your birthday (PWR-TD/TKAEFPL)? Mine is November 31, 1960! Do you believe (PWHRAOEFB) me?

I have a personal / request. The next time I have to go get gas, will you come along and pump the gas for me. / I hate to admit it, but I don't know how. The last time I pumped gas, I got it all / over my brand new sneakers (STPHAOEBG/KWRERZ). The person in the store told me never to come back. He said it was / nothing personal, but that I just could not pump gas. Please come with me so I can get gas for my car. /

Comprehensive Practice

☞ *practice the following:*

I used to know a reporter that used to write the words sang and sank the same way. Now / that we have a special way of writing these words, we can distinguish (TKWEURB) between the two. This rule / also applies for bang and bank, rang and rank, and thing and think. Isn't that great!

If you were / to spend 1/3 of every hour that you practice your shorthand by reading back what you take down, you would / be so much further ahead. In addition, spend another 15 minutes of every hour working for speed and the rest / of the time working for accuracy (ABG/RA/SAEFPL).

Pete made a film about a tank that sank in the pond. Nobody could / find the tank. Somehow, it appeared (A/PAOERD) in the water out of nowhere. Somebody was in it. I think it was / another man with a mask. He looked spooky. I think it must have been a horror (HOR/AOR) film. I wasn't scared, / much!

Frank serves lunch at noon. Mark serves brunch from 10:00 a.m. until 1:00 p.m. Pat serves supper (SUP/KWRER) from 4:00 / p.m. until 7:00 p.m. Does anyone know what time dinner is?

I like to spend January, February and March in / Aspen (AS/PEPB); April, May, and June in Paris (PAR/KWREUS); July, August, and September in Rome (KEU-RBGS/ROEPL); October and November in London (HROPB/TKOPB); and December / at home with my family.

Will you please advertise that I have a computer for sale. It is a 486 / SX with a 130 megabyte (PHEG/PWFPLT) hard drive, a CD ROM, a VGA monitor (PHOPB/TOR); and a / laser printer. It really is super. I'm only asking $1,290. I'll also throw in DOS / (TKOS) 7.0 and WordPerfect 7.0. It comes with Windows already installed. Want to buy it?

If you'll / sing me a song, I'll play you a tune. When a bell rings, does it go ding or dong? What's / the difference between a ring and a ding? How high can you jump? I can jump 6 feet straight up / in the air. In fact, I'm a chimp, I mean a champ, when it comes to jumping (SKWRUPL/PAEG).

Additional Practice

Go to the:	Do the following:
Realwrite DrillBook (recommended)......	Read over and study Drill XX (Lessons 39 & 40)
Realwrite NoteBook (optional)................	Read and transcribe the notes from Exercise J, Lesson 39

UNIT 10
LESSON FORTY

Warm up and Review

☞ *practice the following:*

1:23 a.m.	3:24 a.m.	4:56 a.m.	7:23 a.m.
9:30 p.m.	5:21 p.m.	8:01 p.m.	10:36 p.m.
12:45 a.m.	11:30 a.m.	9:17 a.m.	6:01 a.m.
2:22 p.m.	6:49 p.m.	7:45 p.m.	11:11 p.m.
1 o'clock	2 o'clock	3 o'clock	4 o'clock
5 o'clock	6 o'clock	7 o'clock	8 o'clock
9 o'clock	10 o'clock	11 o'clock	12 o'clock

Word Divisions and Word Endings

Listed below are some rules regarding word division and word endings. Some of these rules supplement rules that have already been presented. Learn them thoroughly and practice applying them to new words.

40.1 If possible, write multi-syllabic words, one syllable at a time with word endings combined in the same stroke.

For example:

swimming SWEUPLG walked WAUBGD

Some writers prefer to write all derivatives of words with a second stroke, choosing not combine the ending in the same stroke.

40.2 If you cannot write a multi-syllabic word in one stroke, write as much of a word as you can in the first stroke, followed by a second and subsequent stroke to complete the outline, combining the word ending in the last stroke if possible.

For example:

dancing TKAPBS/AEG endearment EPB/TKAOERPLT

40.3 Where the last stroke of a mutli-syllabic word may be confused with the first stroke of the next word, use the AE rule (or an adaptation of the rule) in the last stroke.

For example:

marshal PHAR/SHAEL endorsement EPB/TKORS/PHAEPBT

40.4 Derivatives of words should be written in the same stroke or combined in a second or subsequent stroke. If a separate stroke is required, write the AE before the derived ending.

For example:

meeting PHAOET/AEG	houses HOUS/AEZ

Some writers prefer to write all derivatives of words with a second stroke, choosing not combine the ending in the same stroke.

40.5 Some endings or suffixes require the AE to be written between ending consonants.

For examaple:

heavenly HEFPB/HRAEFPL	dictionary TKEUBG/RAEFPL

40.6 If a final stroke begins with a vowel, write the KWR- before the vowel.

For example:

dresser TKRES/KWRER	minor PHAOEUPB/KWROR

40.7 If a word ends in a single vowel, precede the vowel with the KWR, unless the vowel can be written with a consonant.

For example:

beta	PWET/KWRA	soda	SOED/KWRA
hobo	HOE/PWOE	mini	PHEUPB/KWRAOE
maxi	PHAFRPB/KWRAOE	semi	SEPL/KWRAOEU

40.8 For words that end in "ier," write KWRAER in the last stroke.

For example:

heavier HEFB/KWRAER	busier PWEUZ/KWRAER

40.9 For words that end in "iest," write KWRAESZ in the last stroke.

For example:

heaviest HEFB/KWRAESZ	busiest	PWEUZ/KWRAESZ

40.10 For words that end in "ior," write the KWRAOR in the last stoke.

For example:

savior SAEUFB/KWRAOR	senior SAOEPB/KWRAOR

40.11 For words that end in "ous," write KWROUS, regardless of the pronunciation.

For example:

righteous	RAOEUGT/KWROUS	virtuous	SRERT/KWROUS
jealous	SKWREL/KWROUS		

40.12 For words that end in "ure," write KWRUR in the last stroke.

For example:

denture TKEPBT/KWRUR	leisure HRAOEZ/KWRUR
seizure SAOEZ/KWRUR	closure KHROEZ/KWRUR
mature PHAT/KWRUR	venture SREPBT/KWRUR

40.13 For words that end in "ize," write KWRAOEUZ in the last stroke, unless the last stroke can be combined with a consonant.

For example:

materialize TAOERL/KWRAOEUZ	finalize TPAOEUPBL/KWRAOEUZ
baptize PWAP/TAOEUZ	hypnotize HEUP/TPHO/TAOEUZ

40.14 For words that end in "tiv," write TEUFB.

For example:

sensitive SEPBS/TEUFB	narrative TPHAEUR/TEUFB

40.15 For words that end in "tivity," write TEUFT.

For example:

sensitivity SEPBS/TEUFT	nativity TPHA/TEUFT

40.16 For words that end in "tively," write TEUFL.

For example:

sensitively SEPBS/TEUFL	relatively REL/TEUFL

40.17 For words that end in "istic," write STEUSZ.

For example:

materialistic TAOERL/STEUSZ	realistic RAOEL/STEUSZ

40.18 For words that end in "istically," write SKHRAEFPL.

For example:

materialistically TAOERL/SKHRAEFPL	realistically RAOEL/SKHRAEFPL

40.19 for words that end in "ically," write KHRAEFPL.

For example:

theoretically THE/RET/KHRAEFPL	categorically KAT/TKPWOR/KHRAEFPL

40.20 For words that end in "lessly," write SHRAEFPL.

For example:

helplessly HEP/SHRAEFPL faithlessly FAITD/SHRAEFPL

40.21 for words that end in "fully," write TPHRAEFPL.

For example:

helpfully HEP/TPHRAEFPL faithfully FAITD/TPHRAEFPL

40.22 For words that end in "ingly," write TKPWHRAEFPL.

For example:

knowingly STPOEFRP/TKPWHRAEFPL lovingly HROFB/TKPWHRAEFPL

40.23 For words that end in "zation," write SKPWAEUGS.

For example:

sterilization STAEURL/SKPWAEUGS hospitalization HOPT/SKPWAEUGS

40.24 For words that end in "ology," write KWROLG.

For example:

biology PWEU/KWROLG physiology TPEUZ/KWROLG

☞ *practice the following:*

beta	PWET/KWRA	coca	KOEL/KWRA
cola	KOEL/KWRA	coma	KOEPH/KWRA
comma	KOPL/KWRA	soda	SOED/KWRA
papa	PA/PA	mama	PHA/PHA
visa	SRAOEZ/KWRA	semi	SEPL/KWRAOEU
anti	APBT/KWRAOEU	taxi	TAFRPB/KWRAOE
khaki	KABG/KWRAOE	mini	PHEUPB/KWRAOE
maxi	PHAFRPB/KWRAOE	pepsi	PEPS/KWRAOE
echo	EBG/KWROE	hero	HAOER/KWROE
limo	HREUPL/KWROE	taco	TABG/KWROE
typo	TAOEUP/KWROE	steno	STEPB/KWROE
cafe	KAF/KWRAEU	acne	ABG/TPHAOE
acme	ABG/PHAOE	coffee	KOF/KWRAOE
toffee	TOF/KWRAOE	movie	PHOFB/KWRAOE
heavier	HEFB/KWAER	busier	PWEUZ/KWAER
happier	HAP/KWAER	crazier	KRAEUZ/KWAER
heaviest	HEFB/KWAESZ	busiest	PWEUZ/KWAESZ

savior	SAEUFB/KWAOR	junior	SKWRAOUPB/KWAOR
superior	SAOUP/KWAOR	interior	EUPBT/KWRAOR
radio	RAEUD/KWROE	stereo	STAEUR/KWROE
righteous	RAOEUGT/KWROUS	virtuous	SREURT/KWROUS
jealous	SKWREL/KWROUS	impetuous	EUPL/PET/KWROUS
mature	PHAT/KWRUR	adventure	AD/SREPBT/KWRUR
denture	TKEPBT/KWRUR	closure	KHROEZ/KWRUR
leisure	HRAOEZ/KWRUR	seizure	SAOEZ/KWRUR
materialize	TAOERL/KWRAOEUZ	baptize	PWAP/TAOEUZ
scrutinize	SKRAOUT/TPHAOEUZ	hypnotize	HEUP/TPHO/TAOEUZ
sensitive	SEPBS/TEUFB	negative	TPHEG/TEUFB
sensitivity	SEPBS/TEUFT	negativity	TPHEG/TEUFT
sensitively	SEPBS/TEUFL	negatively	TPHEG/TEUFL
realistic	RAOEL/STEUSZ	futuristic	TPAOUR/STEUSZ
realistically	RAOEL/SKHRAEFPL	futuristically	TPAOUR/SKHRAEFPL
fanatically	TPAPBT/KHRAEFPL	theoretically	THE/RET/KHRAEFPL
helplessly	HEP/SHRAEFPL	shamelessly	SHAEUPL/SHRAEFPL
effortlessly	EFRT/SHRAEFPL	spinelessly	SPAOEUPB/SHRAEFPL
helpfully	HEP/TPHRAEFPL	shamefully	SHAEUPL/TPHRAEFPL
gratefully	TKPWRAEUT/TPHRAEFPL	thankfully	THAFBG/TPHRAEFPL
lovingly	HROFB/TKPWHRAEFPL	accordingly	A/KORD/TKPWHRAEFPL
sterilization	STAEURL/SKPWAEUGS	hospitalization	HOPT/SKPWAEUGS
zoology	SKPWAO/KWROLG	biology	PWEU/KWROLG
outbid	OUT/AE/PWEUD	blackout	PWABG/AE/OUT
outspoken	OUT/AE/SPOEBG/KWREPB	workout	WORBG/AE/OUT
upbeat	UP/AE/PWAOET	checkup	KHEBG/AE/UP
upstage	UP/AE/STAEUPBLG	lockup	HROBG/AE/UP
overpay	OEFR/PAFPL	hangover	HANG/AE/OEFR
overplan	OEFR/PHRAPB	crossover	KROS/AE/OEFR
underage	UPBD/AEUPBLG	underdog	UPBD/TKOG

Lesson Practice

☞ practice the following:

For most of us, the thing that is foremost on our minds is doing what is right. The sign had / big bold letters that said, "Enter, prize." I am going to start a new enterprise (EPBT/PRAOEUZ). Is it up or down, / time to get up or down? The judge says that we will have some downtime during the Christmas (KHREUS/MAES) / vacation (SRAEUBGS).

I'm going to the superdome (SAOUP/TKOEPL) to see the superbowl (SAOUP/PWOEFRPL). The building had a really super dome on top. Please don't / cook the turkey so that it is overdone. As you are hurrying through those papers, don't forget to go over done / ones. If you would like, I can ask the postman to deliver your package (PABG/KWRAPBLG) by noon. There is a man who / stands guard at the post, he is called a post man. I'm going under; cut here. Don't undercut your / losses.

I have a booklet that explains how to make Coca Cola. I tried it, but I ended up with cocoa / (KOE/KOE). I think there was a typo in the booklet. Is there a stairway in your new house? Are you happier / now that you're all moved in? Who's happiest? You or your cat? Who's craziest? Who's busiest? I know I'm busier / and crazier now than I was last month.

I'll have one cup of coffee, one taco, one Pepsi, one / hero sandwich (SAPBD/WEUFP), and one Alka Seltzer (AL/KA/SELT/SKPWER). I hope that's not indicative of what I have for lunch every day.

Don't / get jealous, but Miss Pearson is having surf and turf. She put it on her visa. She came to the / cafeteria (KAF/TAOER/KWRA) in a limo. I had to take a taxi.

Did you say you put a coma or a comma after / the verb? Was he in a semi-coma? Mama and Papa run a small cafe next to the movie house. / They have a specialty called a mini-taco and a maxi-taco. The mini-taco is $1.10; the maxi-taco / is $10.01. They will give Taco Bell a run for their money.

Watch your posture. Be ambitious about your / future. You are superior. Who is your savior? I have a very, very sensitive tooth. The dentist (TKEPBT/KWREUSZ) decided to sensitize / the tooth and then he pulled it! My only comment was "ouch"!

How would you characterize the material? Can you materialize / the character? I will be able to help you on the following dates: January 22, February 15, March 20, / April 1, and May 30. I will be gone during the months of June, July and August. We can meet / again on September 4, October 12, November 15, and December 3. Please let me know which dates you can make / and which ones you can't.

Comprehensive Practice

I doubt very much if what she said is the truth. In fact, I find it hard to believe. / She said she had a ticket to the superbowl game next week. Everyone knows that the superbowl isn't played until / January. She said she is going to the superdome. Everybody knows that the superbowl is being played in Denver this year. She / did indicate that she may be wrong. I think she's right, she's wrong!

Make sure you can read back every paragraph / that you take down word for word. If you can't read it back quickly, write it again and again / until you write it without any errors and then read it back as quickly as you can. This is the secret / (SE/KRET) of gaining speed. Also, make sure that you do section (A), (B), (C), (D), (E), and (F) every night for / homework.

If I had $45.92, I'd go McDonald's (PHABG/TKOPBLD/AOS) and buy 38 cheeseburgers, 24 / orders of fries, 8 milkshakes, and 25 cokes. I'd bring them all home to my friends and have a / party. That's what I'd do if I had $45.92. Maybe I'll take up a collection / to see if I can raise enough money to go. Will you donate any money? I already have the 92 / cents; now, all I need is the $45.00. How much will you give?

I can't remember whether / I'm supposed to go to the play with my mother or father or my brother or sister. I know one / of them asked me about a month ago, and I said, "Yes." Now, all I have to do is remember / which one asked me. I think it was my brother, Ted; but it could have been my sister, Jill. I / don't think it was my mother because she is working tonight; and I doubt if it was my father, he / doesn't like to go to things like that. He'd rather take me to a football game or a baseball game. / Come to think of it, that's where I'm supposed to go tonight. I wish I could remember where I'm going / and who is taking me.

There's a big limo in front of our house. It's red and has a white / stripe down the middle (PHEUD/AEL). It had a big sign on the side of it that said: "Acme Taxi Service." I / don't remember calling a cab, but I may have. I'll go out and ask the man who called him.

I'm / happier today than I was yesterday, but I'm also busier. I'm sadder today than I was yesterday, but I'm also / crazier. This is the busiest time of year to go shopping. I couldn't even get near the store. I think / I'll go home and come back tomorrow when they're not so busy.

My teacher gave me back my paper and / circled (SEUR/KAELD) a large typo. I thought I had done superior work, but I didn't. Maybe I'm overly sensitive, but / I didn't appreciate the grade I got. I got a 99; I thought I deserved (STKEFRB/AED at least (HRAOESZ) a grade of / 100. What do you think?

Please make these appointments NOW: Mr. and Mrs. Robert Jones for 9:22 / a.m. on Monday, November 22, 1994; Miss Susan Smith for 10:14 a.m. on Tuesday, / October 13, 1995; Ms. Betty Frank for 12:00 noon on Wednesday, June 15, 1995; Mr. Ted / Johnson for 1:14 p.m. on Thursday, February 26, 1996; and Fred Hopkins for 8:30 / a.m. on Friday, April 13, 1997. Please do not make any appointments (POEUPLTS) for Saturday or Sunday. Remember / that we are on vacation for the months of August and September.

Additional Practice

Go to the: Do the following:

Realwrite DrillBook (recommended)......Write and practice Drill XX (Lessons 39 & 40)

Realwrite NoteBook (optional)................Read and transcribe the notes from Exercise J, Lessons 40 and Drill XX

UNIT 10 REVIEW

Lesson Review

1. Go back to each lesson and learn each new rule thoroughly.
2. Go back to each lesson and write the Lesson Practice
3. Go back to each lesson and write the Comprehensive Practice.
4. Read back all notes and transcribe a portion of your review.

Review of Writing Rules

37.1 To write the alphabet so that the hyphen appears at the right of each letter, write the alphabetic letter on the initial side of the keyboard along with the final side -FRD (Flagged Right Dash) in the same stroke.

37.2 To write the alphabet so that the hyphen appears at the left of each letter, write the alphabetic letter on the initial side of the keyboard along with the final side -FLD (Flagged Left Dash) in the same stroke.

37.3 For words that end in "th" write the -TD in the same stroke. If it is necessary to write the -TD in a separate stroke, write the attached ending AETD in the last stroke.

37.4 To designate a Roman numeral, write the special designation RO-RBGS, followed by the regular number using the number bar.

38.1 For words that end in " "sk" and "sm," write the -SZ in the same stroke.

38.2 For words that end in "st," write the -SZ in the same stroke; however, for one-syllable words that contain the vowel "a" use the AE within the same stroke.

38.3 For words that end in "ism" and "ist" and require a separate stroke, use the SKPWEUPL for "ism" and the KWREUSZ for "ist."

39.1 Final consonants that cannot be written in the same stroke as the root word are written in a separate stroke along with the AE (attached ending).

39.2 Write the months of the year using a two- or three-letter designation on the initial side, combined with the -FPLT on the final side.

39.3 For words that begin with prefixes that could be considered separate words, write them according to the following chart:

English	*prefix-*	*word/shortform*
down	TKOFRP	TKOUFRP
enter	EPBT	TPHER
fore	TPOER	TP-R
over	OEFR	SRER
post	POESZ	POES
self	SEF	SEFL
super	SAOUP	SPER
under	UPBD	TKER
up	UP/AE	UP
out	OUT/AE	OUT
in	EUPB	TPH-

39.4 For words that end with suffixes that could be considered separate words or the beginning of another word, write them according to the following chart:

word ending	*suffix*	*word*/short form
-shal	SHAEL	(shall) SHAL
-ment	PHAEPBT	(meant) PHEPBT
-less	HRAES	(less) HRES
-ful (full)	TPAUL	(full) TPUL
-let (lette)	HRAET	(let) HRET
-for (fore)	TPAOR	(for) TPOR
-nette	TPHAET	(net) TPHET
-over	AE/OEFR	SRER
-out	AE/OUT	OUT
-under	AE/UPBD	TKER

40.1 If possible, write multi-syllabic words one syllable at a time with word endings combined in the same stroke.

40.2 If you cannot write a multi-syllabic word in one stroke, write as much of a word as you can in the first stroke, followed by a second and subsequent stroke to complete the outline, combining the word ending in the last stroke if possible.

40.3 Where the last stroke of a mutli-syllabic word may be confused with the first stroke of the next word, use the AE rule (or an adaption of the rule) in the last stroke.

40.4 Derivatives of words should be written in the same stroke or combined in a second or subsequent stroke. If a separate stroke is required, write the AE before the derived ending.

40.5 Some endings or suffixes require the AE to be written between ending consonants.

40.6 If a final stroke begins with a vowel, write the KWR- before the vowel.

40.7 If a word ends in a single vowel, precede the vowel with the KWR, unless the vowel can be written with a consonant.

40.8 For words that end in "ier," write KWRAER in the last stroke.

40.9 For words that end in "iest," write KWRAESZ in the last stroke.

40.10 For words that end in "ior," write the KWRAOR in the last stoke.

40.11 or words that end in "ous," write KWROUS, regardless of the pronunciation.

40.12 For words that end in "ure," write KWRUR in the last stroke.

40.13 For words that end in "ize," write KWRAOEUZ in the last stroke, unless the last stroke can be combined with a consonant.

40.14 For words that end in "tiv," write TEUFB.

40.15 For words that end in "tivity," write TEUFT.

40.16 For words that end in "tively," write TEUFL.

40.17 For words that end in "istic," write STEUSZ.

40.18 For words that end in "istically," write SKHRAEFPL.

40.19 For words that end in "ically," write KHRAEFPL.

40.20 For words that end in "lessly," write SHRAEFPL.

40.21 For words that end in "fully," write TPHRAEFPL.

40.22 For words that end in "ingly," write TKPWHRAEFPL.

40.23 For words that end in "zation," write SKPWAEUGS.

40.24 For words that end in "ology," write KWROLG.

Review DrillBook and NoteBook Applications

1. Review Drills XIV and XV from the *Realwrite DrillBook* (recommended).
2. Review Exercise J from the *Realwrite NoteBook* (optional).

Unit Evaluation Number Ten

Unit Evaluation Number Ten will cover all material from the following: *Realwrite LessonBook*, Lessons 37-40; *DrillBook*, Drills XIX and XX.

UNIT 11
LESSON FORTY-ONE

Beginning in this lesson the shorthand outline are given to you in their English equivalent. For example, you will be told to write the word "now" as NOW, not TPHOFRP; the word "you" is given to you as YOU, not KWROU. In other words, you are transposing in your own mind the combinations of keyboard letters used to represent a shorthand letter (TPH = N, -FRP = -W, KWR = Y). Having the letters appear in their English form will help to solidify your foundation of basic theory, and it will improve your read-back and transcription skills.

You will also be given the opportunity to review all of the theory at the beginning of each of the remaining lessons. Use this opportunity to thoroughly learn the basic theory. You must have a good theory foundation before you will be able to gain any speed. A good theory foundation means that you do not hesitate in writing any word, phrase, short form, number, date, punctuation mark, and so on.

The Lesson and Comprehensive Practice section will concentrate on two-voice material. The skill of taking multi-voice dictation will be helpful in all aspects of court and realtime reporting. Continue to use your *DrillBook* and *LessonBook* that accompany the remaining lessons.

Review of Punctuation Marks and Symbols

punctuation mark	Realwrite combination
period .	-FPLT
comma ,	-RBGS
question mark ?	STPH-
new paragraph	PA-RBGS
colon :	K -RBGS
semicolon ;	S -RBGS
apostrophe '	A -RBGS
open quote "	KWO-RBGS
end quote "	KWE-RBGS
open parenthesis (	PRO-RBGS
end parenthesis)	PRE -RBGS
exclamation point !	X-RBGS
slash /	SL-RBGS
back slash \	B-RBGS
hyphen -	H-RBGS
dash --	D-RBGS
decimal point .	DP-RBGS
point .	POI-RBGS
initial caps	KI-RBGS
Roman numerals	RO-RBGS

New Miscellaneous Punctuation

Listed below are some punctuation marks that may come up in dictation. Since you will be realtime verbatim writers, it is important for you to be able to write all symbols and have them transcribed.

punctuation mark	Realwrite combination
asterisk (star) *	ST-RBGS
ampersand (and) &	AEU-RBGS
at sign @	T-RBGS
pound sign #	PO-RBGS
number sign #	NU-RBGS
dollar sign $	DL-RBGS
percent sign %	PE-RBGS
caret ^	KR-RBGS
plus sign +	PL-RBGS
equal sign =	E-RBGS
minus sign -	MI-RBGS
tilde ~	TI-RBGS
open bracket [	BRO-RBGS
end bracket]	BRE-RBGS
greater than >	GR-RBGS
lesser than <	LE-RBGS
underscore _	U-RBGS

Phonetic Numbers (Part I)

The following short forms are used for writing numbers phonetically (without using the number bar). The phonetic numbers you learn in this lesson will be used in the following lessons to form compound numbers that are written phonetically.

☞ *practice the following:*

one	WUPB	eleven	LEV	ten	TEN
two	TWO	twelve	TWEFL	twenty	TWEY
three	THRAOE	thirteen	THAOEN	thirty	THIY
four	FOUR	fourteen	FRAOEN	forty	TPROY
five	FAOIV	fifteen	FAOEN	fifty	TPIY
six	SIX	sixteen	XAOEN	sixty	SIY
seven	SEV	seventeen	VAOEN	seventy	SEY
eight	AIGT	eighteen	AOEN	eighty	AIY
nine	NAOIN	nineteen	NAOEN	ninety	NAOIY

Short Forms

☞ *practice the following:*

total	TOELT	tonight	TONT	testimony	TEM
specific	SPEFK	standard	STARD	zero	ZROE
respect	R-S	result	RULT	ready	R-D
really	R-L	reason	RAOEN	reasonably	RAOEBL
recognize	ROZ	regular	REG	recommend	ROM
require	RAOIR				
yes	YES	yes, sir	YIR	yes ma'am	YEPL
no	NOE	no, sir	NIR	no, ma'am	NOPL

Salutations

Learn the following short forms for use in writing the salutation of a letters:

Dear Sir	D-S	Dear Mr.	DMR-
Dear Ms.	DM-Z	Dear Miss	DM-S
Dear Mrs.	DMR-S	Dear Madam	D-M
Ladies and Gentlemen	LAJ	Gentlemen	JE
Gentlemen and Ladies	JAL	To Whom it may concern	TWERN

Question and Answer

One of the most important things that separates an electronic tape recorder from a human verbatim writer is the fact that the realtime writer has the capacity to designate different speakers. Where the tape recorder cannot tell you which person is speaking and will often "blur" voices together; the court and realtime reporter use special designations to signify different speakers or to represent a question (Q) or an
answer (A).

The symbols used to designate different speakers and question and answer (Q & A) material are used not only in court and legal proceedings, but are also used in any situation where two or more people are talking. Beginning in this lesson, you will learn the special symbols used by court and realtime reporters to designate a question and an answer.

41.1 The designation used to indicate a QUESTION is the entire left-hand bank of keys, using the four fingers of the left hand: STKPWHR. Depress the eight keys all at the same time, returning immediately to the home position.

After writing the symbol for the question, the verbatim reporter then takes down what is said, adding punctuation within the question (commas, semicolons, periods, colons, etc.); however, the question never ends with a question mark. The computer is programmed to end a question with a question mark automatically. As soon as the question is finished you should immediately strike the symbol for the answer.

41.2 The designation used to indicate an ANSWER is the entire right-hand bank of keys, using the four fingers of the right hand: FRPBLGTS. Depress the eight keys all at the same time, returning immediately to the home position.

After writing the symbol for the answer, continue writing what is said, adding punctuation. The answer does not end with a period because the computer will automatically add the period when it is translated. As soon as the answer is finished, you should immediately strike the symbol for the question.

☞ *practice the following symbols using the STKPWHR for the Q and the FRPBLGTS for the A:*

Q Q Q Q Q A A A A A	A A A A A Q Q Q Q Q	Q Q Q Q Q A A A A A	A A A A A Q Q Q Q Q
Q A Q A Q A Q A Q A	A Q A Q A Q A Q A Q	Q A Q A Q A Q A Q A	A Q A Q A Q A Q A Q

☞ *now practice the following dictation:*

Q Please tell the court what your name is?
A My name is Maggie Jetson.
Q And is it Miss or Mrs. Jetson? /
A It is Ms. Jetson, please.
Q And where do you live right now, Ms. Jetson?
A I am living with my brother / right now, and we live at 222 Main Street.
Q And how old are you right now?
A Well, yesterday was / my birthday, so I am 32 right now.
Q Is it your wish to give testimony today regarding this case / or do you wish to wait until some other time?
A No, sir. I want to get it over with.
Q Will / you please speak up so we can all hear you?
A Yes, sir.
Q Now, do you recognize the man sitting at / the table with the other lawyer. Do you see him, first of all?
A Yes, sir; I do see him. He / is the man who attacked me on the night of July 4.
Q I did not ask you that. I merely asked you / if you recognized him?
A Yes, sir, I do.
Q And what is his name, do you know?
A Yes, sir. His name / is George Jetson.
Q Are you related to him?
A Yes, sir, he is my other brother.
Q I see. Will you be / a little more specific in your answer. How many brothers do you have?
A Well, I have 8 brothers and 5 / sisters.

Q So that would be \ how many children, total?
A Well, including myself, that would be 14 children that my mother and father had.
Q With respect to / the attack, did your brother have reason to attack you?
A I don't think so. He said that I took / his dog away from him. I will swear that I had nothing to do with his dog missing.
Q What is / his dog's name, do you know?
A Yes, his dog was named Zero.
Q I'm sorry, but you'll have to answer that question / again, was it really named Zero?
A Yes, sir.
Q That was the dog's regular name?
A Yes, sir, it was.
Q Now, tonight / we are going to start to get into the case involving this missing dog. Can you recommend to the Court / what happened to the dog at all? Are you ready to tell the court what happened?
A I'll tell you / the truth and that's all I can tell you. I don't know what happened to Zero that night. / The last time I saw Zero he was in the back yard with another dog.
Q Now, are you asking us / to believe that you had nothing to do with the missing dog?
A That is right, sir. I do not / know nothing about nothing. If I knew anything I'd tell you, but I'm telling, I don't.
Q Do you know the / name of the other dog that Zero was with the last time you saw him?
A Yes, the other dog's name / was Venus.

Additional Practice

Go to the:	Do the following:
Realwrite DrillBook (recommended)........	Read over and study Drill XXI (Lessons 41 & 42)
Realwrite NoteBook (optional)	Read and trasncribe the notes from Exercise K, Lesson 41

UNIT 11
LESSON FORTY-TWO

Review the "Flagged" Alphabet

to write the alphabet in:	write each letter in combination with:
all captial letters A B C	-FK
all small letters a b c	-FS
letter-by-letter spelling A-B-C	-FL
all capital letters with period A. B. C.	-FPD
surrounded by parentheses (A) (B) (C)	-FPS
hyphen at right A- B- C-	-FRD
hyphen at left -A -B -C	-FLD

Phonetic Numbers (Part II)

Using the short forms from Part I of Phonetic Numbers, you can now write one through sixty.

☞ *practice the following:*

twenty-one	TWEY/WUN	forty-one	FROY/WUN
twenty-two	TWEY/TWO	forty-two	FROY/TWO
twenty-three	TWEY/THRAOE	forty-three	FROY/THRAOE
twenty-four	TWEY/FOUR	forty-four	FROY/FOUR
twenty-five	TWEY/FAOIV	forty-five	FROY/FAOIV
twenty-six	TWEY/SIX	forty-six	FROY/SIX
twenty-seven	TWEY/SEV	forty-seven	FROY/SEV
twenty-eight	TWEY/AIGT	forty-eight	FROY/AIGT
twenty-nine	TWEY/NAOIN	forty-nine	FROY/NAOIN
thirty-one	THIY/WUN	fifty-one	FIY/WUN
thirty-two	THIY/TWO	fifty-two	FIY/TWO
thirty-three	THIY/THRAOE	fifty-three	FIY/THRAOE
thirty-four	THIY/FOUR	fifty-four	FIY/FOUR
thirty-five	THIY/FAOIV	fifty-five	FIY/FAOIV
thirty-six	THIY/SIX	fifty-six	FIY/SIX
thirty-seven	THIY/SEV	fifty-seven	FIY/SEV
thirty-eight	THIY/AIGT	fifty-eight	FIY/AIGT
thirty-nine	THIY/NAOIN	fifty-nine	FIY/NAOIN

SHORT FORMS AND PHRASES

☞ *practice the following:*

agency	AGS	agent	AGT	careful	KAIF
carried	K-RD	federal	TPRAL	carefully	KAIFL
guilty	G-Y	issue	IRB	listen	LIFN
future	FAOUR	picture	TAOUR	local	LOEL
purpose	PURP	question	KWE	positive	POZ
possibly	POBL	U. S.	UZ	United States	NAITS

Realtime Writing Principles

Beginning in this chapter, you will learn what realtime writing is and why it has been important to take into consideration the different writing patterns you used for Realwrite outlines. You have already applied some of the realtime writing rules.

Realtime writing is the ability to take down what is being said word-for-word in such a way that what you write can instantly be translated by a computer using a dictionary of words. Upon translation, the computer will then generate an immediate transcript on the computer monitor. This transcript is available for viewing, editing, and eventual hard-copy printing.

There are three things necessary to perform realtime writing successfully. These are:

1. A shorthand machine that is connected to a computer or has the capacity to store data on disk or microchip for later downloading into a computer.
2. A computer system with screen, keyboard, disk drive, and enough memory to handle the particular task you are performing.
3. Appropriate translation software, including a dictionary.

In addition, you will need a good, conflict-free machine shorthand theory that will enable you to write words for immediate translation and transcription. And, of course, you need to master that theory. In the remaining lessons you will learn more about realtime writing.

Question and Answer Practice

☞ *practice the following:*

Q Please state your name and your address for the record, sir.
A My name is John Smith and I live at / 41 West Street in this city.
Q And how long have you lived at that address, sir?
A Well, to tell / you the truth, I just moved there about two weeks ago. Before that time, I lived over on East Avenue.
Q And / how long did you live on East Avenue?
A About a year and a half, maybe two years.

Q Now, are you / employed?
A Yes, sir, I am.
Q And where are you employed right now?
A Right now I work for an agency that / deals with taking pictures for visa applications for people who are leaving or entering the United States. I have been / working undercover now for the F.B.I. I am what is called a special agent.
Q I see. Now, / can you please tell us what your title is?
A Yes. I am a federal agent with the U.S. Department / of Labor. I am stationed with the local office.
Q Are you here to talk to us about possibly telling us / who is in this picture that we are looking at now?
A Yes, sir. I can tell you because I took / the picture.
Q And who is it, please, sir?
A The gentleman in the picture is a man by the name of / Ted Rogers. He is wanted in 50 states for passing drugs and other crimes.
Q Are you positive?
A Yes, sir, I / am positive.
Q You say he is guilty of selling drugs, is that what you said?
A No, sir. I said he was / guilty of passing drugs.
Q Please listen to the question carefully and give us your answer again. What is it / that this man is charged with?
A Well, to tell you the truth, he has been charged with selling drugs. Now, / that's what the purpose of bringing him into court was. He carried drugs into the United States from another / country.
Q So, tell us now, and be careful please, was he carrying drugs, passing drugs, or selling drugs?
A Well, our / special agent in charge of the case told me to be very careful about how I answer that question.
Q Well, / how do you answer it?
A I would if I could, but I can't.
Q And why can't you answer that question, / sir?
A Well, because I really don't know what he was charged with. That is an issue that is not under / my control. My only purpose in being a part of this case was to take a picture and then / to tell you what was in the picture. I had nothing to do with the case after that. I really / can't help you.
Q Mr. Smith, I would appreciate it if in the future you would confine your answer solely to / the question I ask you.
A Yes, sir, I'll certainly try to if I can.

Additional Practice

Go to the: Do the following:
Realwrite DrillBook (recommended).......Write and practice Drill XXI (Lessons 41-42)
Realwrite NoteBook (optional)................Read and transcribe the notes from Exercise K, Lesson 42 and Drill XXI

UNIT 11
LESSON FORTY-THREE

Review Rules for Writing Numbers and Figures

To write a number this way:	Use the principle:	For example:
A single digit	Write one number at atime	2
A two-digit number where first number is smaller than second	Combine the two numbers in one stroke	23
A two digit number where first number is larger than second	Write two numbers in inverse order with EU beore, between, or after the numbers	2EU9
A two-digit number containing 1 – 5 and 0	Combine two numbers in one stroke	10
A two-digit number containing 6 – 9 and 0	Inverse two numbers and use EU	0EU7
To double any single-digit number	Write single number with EU before or after	EU8
Numbers beginning with 100	Write H-ND for hundred followed by numbers using rules above	6/H-ND/2EU
Large numbers	Same rules as above using M-L for million, -BL for billion, TR-L for trillion, and Z-L for zillion	2EU8/-BL/9/M-L/4/TH-Z/1/H-ND/2EU5
Dollars and cents	Precede all money amounts with ME-RBGS or DL-RBGS use –SZ for cents in same or separate stroke	ME-RBGS/EU9/78/-SZ
Large amounts of money	Same rules as above, using TR-L for trillion, -BL for billion, M-L for million	DL-RBGS/4EU2/-BL
Dates when dictated without a division mark	Number for month, day, year, separated by SL-RBGS or H-RBGS	4/SL-RBGS/2/SL-RBGS/79
Hours with minutes	Write hour figure with K- or –K in ame stroke followed by minute figure	K-9/30
a.m. or p.m.	Wirte A-M or P-M in separate stroke	K-9/30/A-M
O'clock	Write AOK in last stroke	7/AOK
Fractions written phonetically	Write number phonetically separated by slash (SL-RBGS	THRAOE/SL-RBGS/FEUTDZ
Fractions written figuratively	Write numerator with R- or –R in sme stroke followed by figure for denominator; separate whole number from fraction with space (SP-RBGS); large fractions can be separated with a slash (SL-RBGS)	4R/5 1/SP-RBGS/1R/2 29/SL-RBGS/100
Roman numerals	Write RO-RBGS followed by number	RO-RBGS/5

Phonetic Numbers (Part III)

Continuing to use the rules for writing phonetic numbers, 61 - 99 can be written as follows:

☞ *practice the following:*

sixty-one	SIY/WUN	eighty-one	AIY/WUN
sixty-two	SIY/TWO	eighty-two	AIY/TWO
sixty-three	SIY/THRAOE	eighty-three	AIY/THRAOE
sixty-four	SIY/FOUR	eighty-four	AIY/FOUR
sixty-five	SIY/FAOIV	eighty-five	AIY/FAOIV
sixty-six	SIY/SIX	eighty-six	AIY/SIX
sixty-seven	SIY/SEV	eighty-seven	AIY/SEV
sixty-eight	SIY/AIGT	eighty-eight	AIY/AIGT
sixty-nine	SIY/NAOIN	eighty-nine	AIY/NAOIN
seventy-one	SEY/WUN	ninety-one	NAOIY/WUN
seventy-two	SEY/TWO	ninety-two	NAOIY/TWO
seventy-three	SEY/THRAOE	ninety-three	NAOIY/THRAOE
seventy-four	SEY/FOUR	ninety-four	NAOIY/FOUR
seventy-five	SEY/FAOIV	ninety-five	NAOIY/FAOIV
seventy-six	SEY/SIX	ninety-six.	NAOIY/SIX
seventy-seven	SEY/SEV	ninety-seven	NAOIY/SEV
seventy-eight	SEY/AIGT	ninety-eight	NAOIY/AIGT
seventy-nine	SEY/NAOIN	ninety-nine	NAOIY/NAOIN

Short Forms and Phrases

☞ *practice the following:*

position	ZIGS	physical	F-L	okay	OK
official	FEUSHL	record	RORD	refund	REFN
purchase	PR-CH	proper	PROR	national	NAL
negligence	NEGS	negligent	NEGT	contain	TAIN
happen	HAP	happening	HAPG	interest	TR-
contact	KAKT	contract	KRAKT		

Complimentary Closings

Learn the following shortforms for use in writing the complimentary closing of letters:

sincerely	S-Y	sincerely yours	S-YZ	yours sincerely	KWR-S
respectfully	R-Y	respectfully yours	R-YZ	yours resepectfully	KWR-R
cordially	K-Y	cordially yours	K-YZ	yours cordially	KWR-K
truly	T-Y	truly yours	T-YZ	yours truly	KWR-T
very sincerely	V-S	very respectfully	V-R	very cordially	V-BG
very truly	V-RT	very truly yours	VE/T-YZ		

Question and Answer Practice

☞ *practice the following:*

Q Now, would you be so kind as to tell us your full name so that the court reporter at my / left can get it into the record?
A Yes. I would be happy to. My full name is Georgia Jones.
Q And, / Miss Jones, would you also tell us where it is that you live?
A Yes. I am currently living at the / Sunshine Motel.
Q And what position do you hold at the Sunshine Motel?
A I am the maid in charge of all / of the rooms at the motel.
Q And how many maids are employed at the motel, do you know?
A Yes. I / have 16 people under me. I am in charge of 16 other maids.
Q Okay. Now, tell me this, what / is your official title at the motel? Do you have an official title?
A Yes, sir, I do. I am the / head maid, that is my official title.
Q Okay. Now, do you remember the happening of this accident that we are / talking about today? Let me begin by asking you this question. What date did the accident happen on? /
A Well, as far as I can remember, I think it was February 22, 1991.
Q And tell us what happened, / if you will.
A Well, I was asked by another maid if she could take about an hour off so that / she could go and make a purchase. I thought it would be all right so I told her to go ahead. / Then she asked me if she could use my automobile.
Q And what did you say?
A I told her she could, but / I told her to be very, very careful. I just bought the car a week ago.
Q What kind of a / car was it, please?
A It was a brand new Cadillac.
Q And what happened after that?

A Well, the next thing / I knew, I got a phone call from the police. They told me that my car had been involved / in a hit and run accident. They said that my car made contact with an elderly man on the corner / of Main and Maple. They asked me to come down to the police station.

Q And did you go / to the police station?

A Yes, sir. After I let my anger settle a little. I went to the police / station.

Q What did they tell you?

A They told me that I had been negligent in letting someone else use / my car. I told them that I was not guilty of negligence, but, rather, it was the other maid who / was the proper one who should be charged.

Q Was this a car that you had leased or what?

A Yes. / I leased it from national car rental. I had a contract with them that said that if I ever let / anyone else use my car, they would not be responsible for any damage, they had no interest in the case / at all. I tried to get a refund from them, but they wouldn't give me nothing.

Additional Practice

Go to the:	Do the following:
Realwrite DrillBook (recommended)......	Read over and study Drill XXII (Lessons 43 & 43)
Realwrite NoteBook (optional)................	Read and transcribe the notes from Exercise K, Lesson 43

UNIT 11
LESSON FORTY-FOUR

Review Rules for Writing Endings of Words

To write a word this way:	Use the principle:	For example:
Past tense "ed"	Write –D in same stroke or AED in separate stroke except for words ending in "n" or in conflict	DANS/AED, TAUKD
Plural "s" or "es"	-Z in same stroke or AEZ in separate stroke, use-S for words that end in –T	KATS, HOUS/AES ROEZ/AEZ
"y" or "ey"	-Y in same stroke or AEY in separate stroke	SK-Y, SHAOIN/AEY
"ee" or "ie"	YAOE in final stroke	MOV/YAOE
"ing"	-G in same stroke or AEG in separate stroke, except for words ending in "n" or in conflict	WAUK/AEG, SWIMG
Possessive or 's	AOS	BOB/AOS
Plural possessives s'	A-RBGS in last stroke	TKPWEURLZ/A-RBGS
"ment"	-MT in lst stroke or MAENT in separate stroke	SKPAOERMT, KON/FAOIN/ MAENT
"self" or "selves"	SAEFL or SAEFLZ in last stroke	HER/SAEFL
All "shun" endings	-GS in same stroke or AEGS in separate stroke	STAIGS
All "k-shun" endings	-BGS in same stroke or AEBGS in separate stroke	FRABGS
"ch"	-FP in ame stroke or AEFP in separate stroke	DICH, FREN/AECH
"sh"	-RB in same stroke or AERB in separate stroke	WISH, FRESH
All "shal" endings	-RBL in same stroke or SHAEL in separate stroke	SPASHL, MAR/SHAEL
All "shus" endings	-RBS in same stroke or SHAUS in separate stroke	KAUSHS, PRE/TEN/SHAUS
"on" and "en"	YON or YEN in separate stroke	LES/YON, LES/YEN
"or" or "er"	YOR or YER in separate stroke	KURS/YOR, KAOEP/YER
"ly"	-L in same stroke or LAEY in separate stroke	PAOURL, LOV/LAEY
"y" fo rwords ending in "l"	-L in first stroke, AEY in separate stroke	DOL/AEY, JOL/AEY
"le" or "el"	-L in same stroke or combine in separate stroke with consonant, AEL for "le" and YAEL for "el"	TROUBL, AM/PAEL, HAS/AEL, TAS/YAEL
"fer" and "ver"	-FR in same stroke or FER or VER in separate stroke	OFR, SIL/VER
"ty" and "ity"	-T in same stroke or TAEY in separate stroke	PAOURT, HAOUMD/TAEY
"rv" and "rf"	-FRB in same stroke	KUFRB, SKAFRB
"able" and "ible"	-BL in same stroke or YABL or YIBL in separate stroke	DAOURBL, DPEND/YABL, SENS/YIBL
"ng"	-NG in same stroke	RANG
"nk"	-FK in same stroke	RAFK
"nj"	-NJ in same stroke	RAFJ
"th"	-TD in same stroke or AETD in last stroke	BROTD
"st" "sk" "sm"	-SZ in same stroke or AESZ in last stroke	BURSZ, THIRSZ, PRISZ
One syllable "ast" words	AESZ within same stroke	FAESZ
Second stroke for "ist" and "ism"	YISZ fr "ist" and ZIM for "ism"	RAEL/YISZ, RAEL/ZIM
Consonants out of sequence	Root word followed by AE and consonant	RAM/AEP, MIL/AEK
Second stroke double vowel	Last stroke YAER, YAESZ, YAOR	BIZ/YAER, BIZ/YAESZ
"ure"	Combine AOUR with consonant or YUR in last stroke	RAPT/YUR
"ous"	Combine OUS within consonant or YOUS in last stroke	JEL/YOUS

"ize"	Combine with consonant or YAOIZ in last stroke	VAOIT/LAOIZ
"tize"	TAOIZ in last stroke	BAP/TAOIZ
"tiv"	TIV in separate stroke	RE/SEP/TIV
"tivity"	TIFT in separate stroke	RE/SEP/TIFT
"tively"	TIFL in separate stroke	RE/SEP/TIFL
"istic"	STISZ in separate stroke	AL/TRAOU/STISZ
"isticlly"	SKLAEY in separate stroke	RAEL/SKLAEY
"ically"	KLAEY in separate stroke	HY/PO/THET/KLAEY
"lessly"	SLAEY in separate stroke	NAOED/SLAEY
"fully"	FLAEY in separate stroke	RE/GRET/FLAEY
"ingly"	GLAEY in separate stroke	KNOW/GLAEY
"zation"	ZAIGS in separate stroke	RAEL/ZAIGS
Single vowel ending	Y- before vowel	KOEL/YA, GUR/YU
"ness"	NAES in separate stroke	KAOIND/NAES
"less"	LAES in separate stroke	KAIR/LAES
"ful" "full"	FAUL in separate stroke	GRAIT/FAUL
"let" "lette"	LAET in separate stroke	LAOEF/LAET
"for" "fore"	FAOR in separate stroke or –F in same stroke	HAOERT/FAOR, THR-F
"ology"	YOLG in separate stroke	RAID/YOLG
"nette"	NAET in separate stroke	BAS/NAET

Phonetic Numbers (Part IV)

For phonetic numbers from 100 and above, use the following short forms:

HUND for hundred and write all numbers phonetically
THOUS for thousand and write all numbers phonetically
MLON (PHRON) for million and write all numbers phonetically
BLOPB for billion and write all numbers phonetically
TROPB for trillion and write all numbers phonetically
ZOPB for zillion and write all numbers phonetically

☞ *practice the following:*

one hundred twenty-two	WUN/HUND/TWEY/TWO
two hundred fifty-four	TWO/HUND/TPEUY/FOUR
six hundred seventy-eight	SIX/HUND/SEY/AEUGT
nine hundred forty	NAOIN/HUND/FROY
four thousand three hundred	FOUR/THOUS/THRAOE/HUND
nine thousand eight hundred	NAOIN/THOUS/AEUGT/HUND

Short Forms and Phrases

☞ practice the following:

invest	VEFT	invoice	VOEU	involve	VOFL
magazine	MAZ	matter	M-T	members	MEBZ
remove	R-V	remain	R-M	president	PREZ
recent	RAOENT	receipt	RAOET	receive	RAOEV
organization	ORGS	situate	SWAIT	situation	SWAIGS

Question and Answer Practice

☞ practice the following:

Q Now, I will ask you please to state your name and your address for the record, please.
A Yes, sir. My / name is Karl Rey. That's spelled R-E-Y, and I live at 422 4th Street.
Q Do you / live here in this city?
A Yes, sir; I do.
Q And how long have you lived on 4th Street, Mr. Rey? /
A Well, I have lived on 4th Street about 50 years now. I actually grew up on 4th Street and have / lived all my life in the same general area.
Q I see. Now, what is it that you do for a / living?
A Right now I am president of an organization that deals with putting out a magazine on how to invest / money in stocks and bonds.
Q And what is the name of your organization and your magazine?
A My organization is Invest / Smart and the name of the magazine is Invest Now.
Q And you say you are the president of Invest Smart?
A Yes, sir; / I am.
Q And how many members are on the board of directors of your organization?
A Well, I would say there are 5 / of us now. We had to remove one member last week because of a situation that involved another matter. / I'd rather not go into that right now if I don't have to.
Q That's all right. But we need / to know all of the facts pertaining to your organization in order to limit our scope of direction here today. / Can you tell us if the removal of that member of your board involved the receipt of stolen money?
A Yes, sir. / He did receive money from an unknown source.
Q How long did he remain on your board after it was discovered / that he had received this money?
A About ten months, as far as I know.
Q Was there something about an invoice / that was not correct?
A Yes, sir; that is how they found out about it.
Q What was the date that they / first learned about this matter; do you know?
A Yes. I believe it was January 22, 1991, that the police / first received word that something was wrong. Now, later on in March was the date that they actually began investigating. /

Q And when did the arrest take place?
A About ten months later, late October or early November.
Q And were you / present when the arrest was made?
A No, sir; I was not. I was out of town on a business meeting / that day.
Q Now, let's turn our attention to another matter, Mr. Rey. Is it true that the man who was / arrested for this crime is really your brother. Isn't that true?
A No, sir, it is not. He is my half / -brother.

Realtime Writing Principles

Realtime writing is not only meant for the court or legal environment, although it has proven very useful in that capacity. Realtime writing is used in any setting where the instantaneous word is needed. Of particular interest is the use of realtime writing for the hearing impaired. This specialized form of realtime writing is often referred to as "closed captioning." Closed captioning is used in classrooms, meetings, and for television programs.

The modern-day verbatim specialist, using the most advanced form of technology available, has proven to be the best possible method of capturing the spoken word for instant translation.

Today's realtime writer uses a skill that no man-made machine has ever been able to duplicate. This "skill" is the capacity to THINK. The professional court reporter of today is unsurpassed in achieving an instant and accurate transcript that is error-free. But, of course, key to all this is the necessity of a good shorthand theory.

You are on the verge of joining one of the most intriguing professions in the world. It is important that you learn your theory and learn it well. If you have not done so already, go back and review the Realwrite theory until you know it thoroughly. It is vital to your future career that you write accurately and without hesitation now.

Additional Practice

Go to the: Do the following:
Realwrite DrillBook (recommended).......Write and practice Drill XXII (Lessons 43 &44)
Realwrite NoteBook (optional)................Read and transcribe the notes from Exercise K, Lesson 44 and Drill XXII

UNIT 11 REVIEW

Lesson Review

1. Go back to each lesson and learn each new rule thoroughly.
2. Go back to each lesson and write the Lesson Practice.
3. Go back to each lesson and write the Comprehensive Practice.
4. Read back all notes and transcribe a portion of your review.

Review of Writing Rules

1. Go back to the "Review Rules" section for each Lesson 41 to 44. Make sure that you have mastered all of the material presented in these lessons. If you need to, refer back to the original lesson where the theory was taught.

2. Practice all of the phonetic numbers until you can write them without any hesitation.

3. Practice the salutations and complimentary closings so that you can write them smoothly.

4. Read over the realtime writing principles so that you understand why it is important to write accurately and smoothly.

5. Practice all of the short forms you have learned so far.

6. Practice the Question and Answer material for each lesson, keeping in mind the new rules you have learned for proper designations.

41.1 The designation used to indicate a QUESTION is the entire left-hand bank of keys, using the four fingers of the left hand: STKPWHR. Depress the eight keys all at the same time, returning immediately to the home position.

41.2 The designation used to indicate an ANSWER is the entire right-hand bank of keys, using the four fingers of the right hand: FRPBLGTS. Depress the eight keys all at the same time, returning immediately to the home position.

Review DrillBook and NoteBook Applications

1. Review Drills XXI and XXII from the *Realwrite DrillBook* (recommended).
2. Review Exercise K from the *Realwrite NoteBook* (optional).

Unit Evaluation Number Eleven

Unit Evaluation Number Eleven will cover all material from the following: *Realwrite LessonBook*, Lessons 41-44; *DrillBook*, Drills XXI and XXII.

UNIT 12
LESSON FORTY-FIVE

Review of Z-rule for Writing Contractions

contraction	Realwrite	contraction	Realwrite
aren't	R-NZ	hasn't	Z-NZ
can't	K-NZ	haven't	SR-NZ
couldn't	KONZ	isn't	S-NZ
didn't	TK-NZ	shouldn't	SHOUNZ
doesn't	TKUNZ	wasn't	WANZ
don't	TKAONZ	won't	WOENZ
hadn't	H-NZ	wouldn't	WOUNZ
I'm	AOIMZ	ain't	AINZ
they're	THERZ	we're	WERZ
you're	URZ	I'd	AOIDZ
he'd	HAEDZ	she'd	SHAEDZ
they'd	THEDZ	we'd	WAEDZ
you'd	UDZ	I've	AOIFZ
they've	THEFZ	we've	WEFZ
you've	UFZ	I'll	AOIWZ
it'll	T-WZ	he'll	HAEWZ
she'll	SHAEWZ	they'll	THEWZ
we'll	WEWZ	you'll	UWZ
how's	HOWZ	it's	T-Z
that's	THAZ	there's	THRZ
what's	WHAZ	where's	WHRZ
who's	WHOZ		

Numeric Ordinals (1-50)

Numeric ordinals are written by writing the number in figures using all preceding rules, followed by the appropriate attached-ending ordinal in the last stroke as follows:

or ordinals that end in	use the attached ending
"st"	AESZ
"nd"	AEND
"rd"	AERD
"th"	AETD

☞ practice the following:

1st	1/AESZ	26th	26/AETD
2nd	2/AEND	27th	27/AETD
3rd	3/AERD	28th	28/AETD
4th	4/AETD	29th	29/AETD
5th	5/AETD	30th	30/AETD
6th	6/AETD	31st	13EU/AESZ
7th	7/AETD	32nd	23EU/AEPBD
8th	8/AETD	33rd	3EU/AERD
9th	9/AETD	34th	34/AETD
10th	10/AETD	35th	35/AETD
11th	1EU/AETD	36th	36/AETD
12th	12/AETD	37th	37/AETD
13th	13/AETD	38th	38/AETD
14th	14/AETD	39th	39/AETD
15th	15/AETD	40th	40/AETD
16th	16/AETD	41st	14EU/AESZ
17th	17/AETD	42nd	24EU/AEND
18th	18/AETD	43rd	34EU/AERD
19th	19/AETD	44th	4EU/AETD
20th	20/AETD	45th	45/AETD
21st	12EU/AESZ	46th	46/AETD
22nd	2EU/AEND	47th	47/AETD
23rd	23/AERD	48th	48/AETD
24th	24/AETD	49th	49/AETD
25th	25/AETD	50th	50/AETD

Short Forms and Phrases

☞ practice the following:

subject	SUJ	success	SES	superintendent	SAOUPT
research	R-CH	testify	TEF	respond	SPOND
observe	ZEFRB	operate	PRAIT	representation	REPGS
qualify	KWAUF	regard	RARD	occasion	KAIGS
perhaps	PRAPS	city	STI	children	KHIRPB
control	KROEL	contribute	KRIBT	comfort	K-FRT

Compass Points

North	NORT	northeast	NAOESZ	northwest	NOESZ
South	SOUTD	southeast	SAOESZ	southwest	SWESZ
East	AOESZ	West	WESZ		

Realtime Conflict Elmination (Long A)

The basic premise behind realtime writing is the use of one distinct outline for one word, even when two or more words may sound alike. If two words sound the same, and are written the same way, then a "conflict" may occur when transcribing. In Realwrite theory, there are basic conflict elimination rules that enable you to write each word in a consistently distinct pattern. Beginning in this lesson, you will learn these rules.

45.1 In eliminating a conflict between two words that contain the "long a" sound, use the AE for words that contain both the "a" and the "e" in the English spelling. Use the AEU (long a) for all other words.

For example:

maid MAID   made MAED

45.2 In eliminating a conflict between two words that contain the "long a" sound, use the AE for words that do not contain the "a" and "i" in their English spelling.

For example:

faint FAINT   feint FAENT

45.3 If a conflict cannot be eliminated between two words that contain the "long a" sound by applying all previous rules, write the word in two strokes.

For example:

vail VAIL   vale VAEL   veil VAEU/AEL

45.4 In eliminating a conflict between two words that contain an "a" and "e" in their English spelling, use the AE for the words that have the "ae" in order. Use the "long a" (AEU) for words that have the "e" before the "a."

For example:

break BRAIK   brake BRAEK

☞ practice the following words that sound the same, but are written differently:

long a AEU		*AE*		*other words*	
aid	AEUD	aide[1]	YAEUD	ade	YAED
AIDS	AEUDZ				
air	AEUR			heir	HEUR
bail	BAIL	bale	BAEL		
bear	BAIR	bare	BAER		
break	BRAIK	brake	BRAEK		
fair	FAIR	fare	FAER		
faint	FAINT	feint	FAEPBT		
great	GRAEUT	grate	GRAET		
hair	HAIR			hare[2]	HAR
maid	MAID	made	MAED		
mail	MAEUL	male	MAEL		
rain	RAIN	rein	RAEN	reign	RAEU/AEN
vail	VAIL	vale	VAEL	veil	VAEU/AEL
wait	WAIT			weight	WAIGT
waive	WAIV	wave	WAEV		
wear	WAEUR	ware	WAER		

[1]Certain one-syllable words that begin with a vowel are written with the initial Y (KWR-).
[2]HAER is the word "hear."

Question and Answer Practice

☞ *practice the following:*

Q Mrs. Jones, would you be so kind as to tell the court your age?
A Yes, sir; I am 42 years old. /
Q And how many children do you have?
A My husband and I have four children. We have three boys and a / girl.
Q Thank you, Mrs. Jones. Now, you have agreed to come here today to testify regarding the subject matter / of an altercation that came up between yourself and the superintendent of schools; is that not so?
A Yes, sir.
Q And when / did this altercation take place?
A Well, it was last year; it must have been around this same time of year. / I think it was in June because my children were studying for their final exams.
Q Perhaps you can tell us / what happened?
A Yes, sir. I am employed by the city as a crossguard. I help the children get across the / street where the traffic gets heavy. Well, the traffic control device was out of order so I

took it upon / myself to go to the middle of the road and stop traffic so that the children could get across.

Q Go / ahead, can you tell us what else happened?

A Yes. The superintendent came out and asked me how I qualify to / direct traffic. I told him that it was an emergency and that the children had to get to school. Well, / he started to respond by saying that I had no right to do it; that I did not qualify; that / I didn't observe proper safety rules; that I could contribute to an accident; and that I was fired.

Q Please go / on.

A The next thing I know, he was out in the middle of the street directing traffic; and there / is an accident.

Q Now, our research indicates that you told the superintendent that you quit; that you had no success / in talking to the superintendent; that he made no representation about firing you; but, rather, that you left the children / in the care and comfort of another person; and when all this occurred, he came out and took things in his /own hands.

A That's not true, sir.

Q Perhaps you can respond to the question, then, and tell us your version of what happened./

A Like I told you. He came out and told me I was all through. He's the one who fired me; / I didn't leave until he told me to.

Q Do you know of anyone who saw this happen?

A Yes, the children. / They'll tell you what really happened that day.

Q Very well. We'll have the children testify in just a moment. / Right now I want to know if you saw the accident happen?

A No, I did not. I just heard a screech, / and then I heard a crash, and I looked and a car and truck had collided in the intersection. /

Additional Practice

Go to the:	Do the following:
Realwrite DrillBook (recommended).......	Read over and study Drill XXIII (Lessons 45 & 46)
Realwrite NoteBook (optional)................	Read and transcribe the notes from Exercise L, Lesson 45

UNIT 12
LESSON FORTY-SIX

Review Days of Week and Months of Year

Monday	MO-FPLT	January	JA-FPLT	July	JU-FPLT
Tuesday	TU-FPLT	February	FE-FPLT	August	AU-FPLT
Wednesday	WE-FPLT	March	MA-FPLT	September	SE-FPLT
Thursday	THU-FPLT	April	A-FPLT	October	O-FPLT
Friday	FREU-FPLT	May	MAI-FPLT	November	NO-FPLT
Saturday	SA-FPLT	June	JAOU-FPLT	December	DE-FPLT
Sunday	SU-FPLT				

Numeric Ordinals (51-100)

☞ *practice the following:*

51st	15EU/AESZ	76th	EU67/AETD
52nd	25EU/AEND	77th	EU7/AETD
53rd	35EU/AERD	78th	78/AETD
54th	45EU/AETD	79th	79/AETD
55th	5EU/AETD	80th	0EU8/AETD
56th	56/AETD	81st	1EU8/AESZ
57th	57/AETD	82nd	2EU8/AEND
58th	58/AETD	83rd	3EU8/AERD
59th	59/AETD	84th	4EU8/AETD
60th	0EU6/AETD	85th	5EU8/AETD
61st	1EU6/AESZ	86th	EU68/AETD
62nd	2EU6/AEND	87th	EU78/AETD
63rd	3EU6/AERD	88th	EU8/AETD
64th	4EU6/AETD	89th	89/AETD
65th	5EU6/AETD	90th	0EU9/AETD
66th	EU6/AETD	91st	1EU9/AESZ
67th	67/AETD	92nd	2EU9/AEND
68th	68/AETD	93rd	3EU9/AERD
69th	69/AETD	94th	4EU9/AETD
70th	0EU7/AETD	95th	5EU9/AETD

71st	1EU7/AESZ	96th	EU69/AETD
72nd	2EU7/AEND	97th	EU79/AETD
73rd	3EU7/AERD	98th	EU89/AETD
74th	4EU7/AETD	99th	EU9/AETD
75th	5EU7/AETD	100th	1/H-PBD/AETD

Short Forms and Phrases

☞ *practice the following:*

communicate	K-MT	classify	KL-F
communication	K-MGS	character	KAIRK
convenience	VAOENS	understand	SDAND
convenient	VAOENT	understood	SDAOD

Realtime Conflict Elimination (Long E)

46.1 In eliminating a conflict between words that contain the "long e" sound, use the AE for all words that contain both vowels "a" and "e" regardless of their order. Use the "long e" for all other words, including words that contain the "double e."

For example:

here	HAOER	hear	HAER
beet	BAOET	beat	BAET

46.2 If a conflict cannot be eliminated between two words that contain the "long e" sound by applying all previous rules, write the word in two strokes.

For example:

meet MAOET   meat MAET   mete MAOE/AET

☞ practice the following words that sound the same, but are written differently:

long e AOE		*AE*		*exceptions to rule*	
beet	BAOET	beat	BAET		
discreet	SDRAOET	discrete	SDRAET		
meet	MAOET	meat	MAET	mete	MAOE/AET
see	SAOE	sea	SAE		
seed	SAOED			cede	KRAOED[1]
seen	SAOEN			scene	SKAOEN
steel	STAOEL	steal	STAEL		
sweet	SWAOET	suite	SWAET		
wee	WAOE			we	WE
week	WAOEK	weak	WAEK		

[1] creed is written KRAED

Question anad Answer Practice

☞ *practice the following:*

Q Would you state your name for the record?
A My name is Arnold J. Smythe.
Q And how do you spell your name, / Mr. Smythe?
A S-M-Y-T-H-E.
Q And where do you live?
A 9 Crescent Park.
Q And what is your job? What / do you do for a living, sir?
A I am a general contractor; I do construction work, and I build / things.
Q What type of things do you build?
A I build houses and small buildings, but I usually just do small / jobs for people who need to have things done around the house.
Q I see. So are we to understand that you / will hire yourself out as a carpenter to do work around people's houses?
A Yes, sir.
Q What type of work / would this be?
A Well, it would be anything from fixing a door or a window to adding on an addition / or a garage to an existing house.
Q I see. Now, tell us this, did you have any communication at all, / did you communicate in any way with a Mr. Donald Roberts regarding the possible construction of a doghouse for / him and his family?
A Yes, sir; I did.
Q And when did that communication first take place?
A Last year.
Q When last / year?
A About the middle of April.
Q Tell us about that communication, if you would, please, sir?
A All right. It / was my understanding that I would build a doghouse at my convenience for their pet dog.
Q Who was it who started / the communication? How did the original deal start?
A My wife answered a telephone call from Mr. Roberts.
Q I see. So your / wife is a central character in this complaint?
A Well, I don't know what you mean. My wife took the order; / I complied; I built the doghouse.
Q And what was it that your wife understood was to be done by / your construction company?
A If it was convenient, we were to construct a doghouse on their property.
Q And what was the / size of this doghouse, sir?
A Well, that's where the conflict comes in. My wife says that he did request / a doghouse that was 1500 square feet of living space. Now, he says that he wanted only 15 square feet. /
Q Tell me this, sir, did you build the doghouse?

A Yes, sir; we did.
Q And how much did it cost to / have the doghouse built?
A About $11,000 complete.
Q And Mr. Roberts refuses to pay the bill?
A Yes, sir.
Q Why does / he refuse to pay the bill?
A Because he says he only ordered a doghouse that was 15 square feet, not 1500 / square feet.
Q I see. Do you have any proof at all that he requested a doghouse be built that was / 1500 square feet?
A Yes, sir, I do.
Q What proof do you have, sir?

Additional Practice

Go to the: — Do the following:

Realwrite DrillBook (Recommended)......Write and practice Drill XXIII (Lessons 45 & 46)
Realwrite NoteBook (optional).................Read and transcribe the notes from Exercise L, Lesson 46 and Drill XXIII

UNIT 12
LESSON FORTY-SEVEN

Review Word Beginnings

To write a word this way:	Use the principle:	For example:
Sound of "ch"	Write KH- at beginning of word	KHART
Sound of "sh"	Write Sh- at beginning of word	SHORT
Prefix with a consonant/vowel	Write short vowel within prefix	PRE/VENT
Words spelled with "wh"	Write WH- at beginning of word	WHAOIT
Words spelled with "wr"	Write WR- at beginning of word	WRAP
Words beginning with prefix "a"	Write short vowel A in first stroke	A/MAS
"col" or "com"	Eliminate vowel and write KL- or KM- combined with rest of word	KLEKT, KMAND
Words spelled with "shr"	Write SKHR- at beginning of word	SKHRAOEK
"pre" "pro" and "pra"	Write PRE, PRO or PRA at beginning of word	PRO/PORGS
"re" "be" and "de"	Write RE, BE, or DE unless the "de" can be combined as in DP for "dep" or DM for "dem" or DL for "del"	RE/MIT, BE/TRAY, DMAND
"ex"	Write X- combined with remainder of word, leaving out consonants that cannot be written; use ST for "ext" words	XIBT, STIFKT
"ex-" or "x"	Write EX in first stroke, followed by remainder of word in last stroke	EX/SPOUS, EX/PREZ
"kn"	Write STP- at beginning of word	STPOK
"enter" and "inter"	Write ENT or INT in first stroke	ENT/TAIN, INT/VEW
"des" and "dis"	Write SD- in first stroke combined with remainder of outline; if necessary write SDA in first stroke or write DES or DIS	SDAOID, DIS/S-V
"fore" "for" "un"	Write FOER or UN (H-RBGS) if necessary	FOER/GOT
"div" "dev"	Write DW- combined with remainder of word or DIV or DEV if necessary	DWAOID, DWIGS
Prefix "down"	Write DOW in first stroke	DOW/TOUN
Prefix "super"	Write SAOUP in first stroke	SAOUP/MAN
Prefix "over"	Write OEFR in first stroke	OEFR/DOEN
Prefix "post"	Write POESZ in first stroke	POESZ/MAN
Prefix "under"	Write UND in first stroke	UND/KUT
Prefix "out"	Write OUT/AE	OUT/AE/BID
Prefix "up"	Write UP/AE	UP/AE/BAOET

Phonetic Ordinals (Part I)

☞ *practice the following:*

first	FEURT	eleventh	LETD	tenth	TETD
second	SEKD	twelfth	TWETD	twentieth	TWEY/AETD
third	THIRD	thirteenth	THAOETD	thirtieth	THEUY/AETD
fourth	FOTD	fourteenth	FRAOETD	fortieth	TPROY/AETD
fifth	FEUTD	fifteenth	FAOETD	fiftieth	TPEUY/AETD
sixth	SEUTD	sixteenth	XAOETD	sixtieth	SEUY/AETD
seventh	SETD	seventeenth.	VAOETD	seventieth	SEY/AETD
eighth	AEUTD	eighteenth	AOETD	eightieth	AEUY/AETD
ninth	NAOITD	nineteenth	NAOETD	ninetieth	NAOEUY/AETD

Using the above phonetic ordinals, you can now combine them to write other numbers as follows:

twenty-first	TWEY/FIRT	forty-first	FROY/FIRT
twenty-second	TWEY/SEKD	forty-second	FROY/SEKD
twenty-third	TWEY/THIRD	forty-third	FROY/THIRD
twenty-fourth	TWEY/FOTD	forty-fourth	FROY/FOTD
twenty-fifth	TWEY/FITD	forty-fifth	FROY/FITD
twenty-sixth	TWEY/SITD	forty-sixth	FROY/SITD
twenty-seventh	TWEY/SETD	forty-seventh	FROY/SETD
twenty-eighth	TWEY/AITD	forty-eighth	FROY/AITD
twenty-ninth	TWEY/NAOITD	forty-ninth	FROY/NAOITD
thirty-first	THIY/FIRT	fifty-first	FIY/FIRT
thirty-second	THIY/SEKD	fifty-second	FIY/SEKD
thirty-third	THIY/THIRD	fifty-third	FIY/THIRD
thirty-fourth	THIY/FOTD	fifty-fourth	FIY/FOTD
thirty-fifth	THIY/FITD	fifty-fifth	FIY/FITD
thirty-sixth	THIY/SITD	fifty-sixth	FIY/SITD
thirty-seventh	THIY/SETD	fifty-seventh	FIY/SETD
thirty-eighth	THIY/AITD	fifty-eighth	FIY/AITD
thirty-ninth	THIY/NAOITD	fifty-ninth	FIY/NAOITD

Short Forms and Phrases

☞ *practice the following:*

emphasis	EPLS	emphasize	EMZ	enable	NAIBL
enclosure	KLAOUR	enter	NER	equal	KWL-
indict	TKAOIT	generally	J-NL	industry	STREU
inform	N-FRM	initial	NISHL		

Realtime Conflict Elimination (Long I and Long O)

47.1 In eliminating a conflict between words that contain the "long i" sound, use the AOEU for all words and make the distinction by writing as close to the English spelling as possible.

For example:

lite HRAOEUT light HRAOEUGT

☞ *practice the following:*

long I (AOEU)		*English spelling*		*exceptions to the rule*	
bite	BAOIT	byte	B-YT		
		buy	BUY	bye	BEY
		by	B-Y		
				bi-	BI
die	TKAOI	dye	TK-Y		
lite	HRAOIT	light	HRAOIGT		
mite	MAOIT	might	MAOIGT		
nite	NAOIT	night	NAOIGT	knight	STPAOEUGT
rime	RAOIM			rhyme	R-Y/AEM
rite	RAOIT	right	RAOIGT	riot	RAOI/YOT
sign	SAOIN			sine	SAOI/AEN
site	SAOIT	sight	SAOIGT	cite	KRAOIT
time	TAOIM			thyme	T-Y/AEM

47.2 In eliminating a conflict between two words that contain the "long o" sound, use the OE (long o) for the word that ends in the silent vowel "e" in the English spelling. Use the O (short o) for all other words in conflict.

For example:

lode LOED load LOD

47.3 In eliminating other conflicts involving the long O, use the proper English spelling along with other applicable rules.

For example:

toe TOE   tow TOW

☞ *practice the following:*

long O (OE)		*short O (O)*		*exception to rule*	
bolder	BOELD/KWRER			boulder	BOULD/KWRER
doe	DOE			dough	DOUFD
groan	GROEN			grown	GROUN
lode	LOED	load	LOD		
lone	LOEN	loan	LON		
moan	MOEN			mown	MOUN
pole	POEL	poll	POL		
roam	ROEM			Rome	KI-RBGS/ROEM
rode	ROED			road	-RD
role	ROEL	roll	ROL		
sole	SOEL			soul	SOUL
shone	SHOEN			shown	SHOUN
throne	THROEN			thrown	THROUN

Question and Answer Practice

☞ *practice the following:*

Q Now, would you be so kind as to put into the record your name, sir?
A Yes. My name is James Bond. /
Q Please tell us what you do for a living, Mr. Bond.
A I am a janitor for a local industry here / in the city.
Q I see. And would you please inform us as to the name of this industry?
A Yes. It is / Tri-State Manufacturing Company.
Q Tell us, is that also referred to by the initials TSM?
A Yes, sir.
Q Now, / to begin our questioning this afternoon, I would like to go into the matter of what your duties were at / TSM?
A Well, just general cleanup, you know. I would sweep up in the plant and make sure / everything was in order.
Q Generally speaking, just cleaning up?
A Yes, sir.
Q Do you happen to remember the date of this / incident, June 4, 1990?
A Yes, sir.
Q Do you happen to remember what time you did enter the plant that / day?
A Yes, sir. It was around 8 o'clock that morning.
Q And did someone inform you of the accident, or how did you / find out about it?
A My boss, Mr. Powers, came over and told me that someone had put a bomb in an enclosure / right next to the main plant. He told me that the bomb was set to go off at 9:05 a.m. / and that they were evacuating the employees right away.

Q And what else did he say, anything else?
A Well, / he did emphasize that it was necessary to remove our cars from the parking lot in order to enable the / fire department to get in.
Q I see. And what was your initial response to this information?
A I was shocked. I didn't know / what to do. I really never had any other experience in my life that would be equal to this. I was / really scared.
I didn't know what to do.
Q And what did you do after you were told / all this? Where did you go?
A Well, I went into the bathroom and just stayed there.
Q How long did you / remain in the bathroom?
A I don't know, maybe ten or fifteen minutes.
Q Is it true that you really went back / to your home and told a friend that you had planted a bomb at work and that you were waiting for the / whole thing to blow up?
A No, sir. I never did that, and I never said that. Why would I indict / myself in such a manner?
Q Is it not true that you planted the bomb yourself because you hated your work / and you had a fight with your boss?
A No, sir.
Q And is it not true that you were seeking revenge / because your boss had informed you the day before that he was not happy with your work and that / you were going to be fired?

Short Forms for States

47.4 All states and territories of the United States are written using the standard two-letter abbreviation. Each state is a two stroke short form, writing one letter at a time on the initial side along with the -FPLT on the final side.

☞ *practice the following:*

Alabama	A-FPLT/L-FPLT	Montana	PH-FPLT/T-FPLT
Alaska	A-FPLT/K-FPLT	Nebraska	TPH-FPLT/E-FPLT
Arizona	A-FPLT/SKPW-FPLT	Nevada	TPH-FPLT/SR-FPLT
Arkansas	A-FPLT/R-FPLT	New Hampshire	TPH-FPLT/H-FPLT
California	KR-FPLT/A-FPLT	New Jersey	TPH-FPLT/SKWR-FPLT
Colorado	KR-FPLT/O-FPLT	New Mexico	TPH-FPLT/PH-FPLT
Connecticut	KR-FPLT/T-FPLT	New York	TPH-FPLT/KWR-FPLT
Delaware	TK-FPLT/E-FPLT	North Carolina	TPH-FPLT/KR-FPLT
Florida	TP-FPLT/HR-FPLT	North Dakota	TPH-FPLT/TK-FPLT
Georgia	TKPW-FPLT/A-FPLT	Ohio	O-FPLT/H-FPLT

Hawaii	H-FPLT/EU-FPLT	Oklahoma	O-FPLT/K-FPLT
Idaho	EU-FPLT/TK-FPLT	Oregon	O-FPLT/R-FPLT
Illinois	EU-FPLT/HR-FPLT	Pennsylvania	P-FPLT/A-FPLT
Indiana	EU-FPLT/TPH-FPLT	Rhode Island	R-FPLT/EU-FPLT
Iowa	EU-FPLT/A-FPLT	South Carolina	S-FPLT/KR-FPLT
Kansas	K-FPLT/S-FPLT	South Dakota	S-FPLT/TK-FPLT
Kentucky	K-FPLT/KWR-FPLT	Tennessee	T-FPLT/TPH-FPLT
Louisiana	HR-FPLT/A-FPLT	Texas	T-FPLT/SKP-FPLT
Maine	PH-FPLT/E-FPLT	Utah	U-FPLT/T-FPLT
Maryland	PH-FPLT/TK-FPLT	Vermont	SR-FPLT/T-FPLT
Massachusetts	PH-FPLT/A-FPLT	Virginia	SR-FPLT/A-FPLT
Michigan	PH-FPLT/EU-FPLT	Washington	W-FPLT/A-FPLT
Minnesota	PH-FPLT/TPH-FPLT	West Virginia	W-FPLT/SR-FPLT
Mississippi	PH-FPLT/S-FPLT	Wisconsin	W-FPLT/EU-FPLT
Missouri	PH-FPLT/O-FPLT	Wyoming	W-FPLT/KWR-FPLT

Canal Zone	KR-FPLT/SKPW-FPLT
District of Columbia	TK-FPLT/KR-FPLT
Guam	TKPW-FPLT/U-FPLT
Puerto Rico	P-FPLT/R-FPLT
Virgin Islands	SR-FPLT/EU-FPLT

Additional Practice

Go to the: Do the following:

Realwrite DrillBook (recommended)......Read over and study Drill XXIV (Lessons 47 & 48)

Realwrite NoteBook (optional)................Read and transcribe the notes from Exercise L, Lesson 47

UNIT 12
LESSON FORTY-EIGHT

Review of Major Writing Rules

Words are written in Realwrite according to the following guidelines:

1. Consider how the word is sounded; consider how the word is spelled; apply any special rules or short form.

2. Write a one-syllable word in one stroke. Write the word according to sound. In some instances, words are written according to how they are spelled in English. Some words may be abbreviated, and some words may have special applications.

3. Write a multi-syllabic word in as many strokes as are necessary. In some cases, follow syllabic division. In some cases, write as much of the word as possible in first stroke, followed by second and subsequent strokes.

4. A short form is a shortened form of writing a word. A phrase is a series of words written as a short form.

5. Write the AO for words spelled with a "double o" (BAOK, TAOK).

6. Write the AU together for words that contain the "au" sound (TAUK); write the AFRP for words spelled with the "aw" (LAW).

7. Write the OU for words that contain the "ou" sound (BOUNS); write the OFRP for words spelled with the "ow" (KOW, TOEW); write OUPB for words spelled "own" (TOUN, FROUN).

8. Write AFRP and EFRP for words spelled with "aw" or "ew" (RAW, KHEW).

9. Write the OEU for words that contain the sound of "oi" (TOIL, SOIL); write OFPL for words spelled with the "oy" (TOY, BOY).

10. If the spelling of a word changes from its original root word either by adding a past tense or a plural; change the outline to reflect the spelling (TR-Y, TRAOEUD).

11. Whenever it is possible to shorten the outline of a word without distorting it, "blend" or "slur" the word by eliminating vowels or unaccented syllables and write the "compacted" version (DLAY, KMENT).

12. When two words are used that would normally be separated and you wish to have them joined together or connected in the translation, use the designation AE between the two words to connect them (OUT/AE/LAY, BAOK/AE/KAEUS).

13. When two words are used that would normally be separated and you wish to hyphenate the words in the translation, use the H-RBGS (hyphen) between the words (FIRT/H-RBGS/KLAS).

14. If possible, write multi-syllable words one syllable at a time with word endings combined in the same stroke (RAIRT); if this is not possible, write as much of the word as possible in the first stroke, combining the ending in the last stroke if possible (EN/DAOERMT).

15. Use the AE rule in the last stroke for derivatives of words (DANS/AED).

16. Combine a word ending in the same stroke as the root word or in last stroke (SWIMG).

17. Where possible, if a word ending requires a separate stroke, begin the word ending with a consonant (DIBGS/RAEY), unless it is a derivative (DAIT/AED).

18. Use the "silent y" for any last stroke that begins with a vowel (SWIM/YER).

19. Last strokes beginning with a single or double vowel are generally written with the KWR- (HEV/YAER, STAIR/YOE, KOEL/YA).

Phonetic Ordinals (Part II)

☞ *practice the following:*

sixty-first	SIY/FIRT	eighty-first	AIY/FIRT
sixty-second	SIY/SEKD	eighty-second	AIY/SEKD
sixty-third	SIY/THIRD	eighty-third	AIY/THIRD
sixty-fourth	SIY/FOTD	eighty-fourth	AIY/FOTD
sixty-fifth	SIY/FITD	eighty-fifth	AIY/FITD
sixty-sixth	SIY/SITD	eighty-sixth	AIY/SITD
sixty-seventh	SIY/SETD	eighty-seventh	AIY/SETD
sixty-eighth	SIY/AITD	eighty-eighth	AIY/AITD
sixty-ninth	SIY/NAOITD	eighty-ninth	AIY/NAOITD
seventy-first	SEY/FIRT	ninety-first	NAOIY/FIRT
seventy-second	SEY/SEKD	ninety-second	NAOIY/SEKD
seventy-third	SEY/THIRD	ninety-third	NAOIY/THIRD
seventy-fourth	SEY/FOTD	ninety-fourth	NAOIY/FOTD
seventy-fifth	SEY/FITD	ninety-fifth	NAOIY/FITD

seventy-sixth	SEY/SITD	ninety-sixth	NAOIY/SITD
seventy-seventh	SEY/SETD	ninety-seventh	NAOIY/SETD
seventy-eighth	SEY/AITD	ninety-eighth	NAOIY/AITD
seventy-ninth	SEY/NAOITD	ninety-ninth	NAOIY/NAOITD

For phonetic ordinals from 100 and above, use the following rules:

HUTD	for hundredth and write all ordinals phonetically
THOUTD	for thousandth and write all ordinals phonetically
MITD	for millionth and write all ordinals phonetically
BITD	for billionth and write all ordinals phonetically
TRITD	for trillionth and write all ordinals phonetically
ZITD	for zillionth and write all ordinals phonetically

Short Forms and Phrases

☞ *practice the following:*

inquire	KWIR	inquiry	KWIR/AEY	insure	NAOUR
outside	OUD	inside	NAOID	recommendation	ROMGS
idea	DA	area	RA	acre	AK
into	NAO	unto	UNT	onto	ONT

very many VEM	too many TAOM	so many SOEM	how many HOUM
very much VECH	too much TAOCH	so much SOECH	how much HOUCH

Realtime Conflict Elimination (Vowel U, Miscellaneous)

48.1 In eliminating a conflict between two words that contain the "u" sound, write the word as close to the English spelling as possible.

For example:

flue	FLAOU	flew	FLEW	flu	FLU

☞ *practice the following:*

long U (AOU)		*English spelling*		*others*	
blue	BLAOU	blew	BLEFRP	bleu	BLU
flue	FLAOU	flew	FLEW	flu	FLU
revue	RE/VAOU	review	RE/VEW		
sue	SAOU	sew	SEW	Sue	KEU-RBGS/SAOU

48.2 In eliminating conflicts with words that begin with the "s," write the S for words that begin with "s" in the English spelling, write SK for words that begin with "sc"; and write KR for words that begin with "c" in the English spelling.

for example:

sent	SENT	scent	SKEPBT	cent	KRENT

☞ *practice the following:*

"s" words		*"sc" words*		*"c" words*		other words	
seed	SAOED			cede	CAOED		
seen	SAOEN	scene	SKAOEN				
sent	SENT	scent	SKEPBT	cent	KRENT		
site	SAOEUT			cite	KRAOIT	sight	SAOIGT

48.3 In eliminating conflicts with words that begin with "ex" and "ext," write the SKP for words that begin with "ex" and write the ST for words that begin with "ext."

for example:

expend XEPBD	extend STEPBD

☞ *practice the following:*

ex" words	*"ext" words*
expend XEND	extend STEND
export XORT	extort STORT

48.4 Some one-stroke words that begin with a vowel in the English will use an intitial Y- (KWR-) to eliminate a conflict.

for example:

isle	AOEUL	aisle	YAOEUL

☞ *practice the following:*

aisle	YAOIL	aide	YAEUD	ade	YAED

48.5 In eliminating conflicts with words that end in a double consonant in the English spelling, use the vowels AU for the word containing the double consonant.

for example:

put	PUT	putt	PAUT

☞ *practice the following:*

ad	AD	add	AUD
but	BUT	butt	BAUT
put	PUT	putt	PAUT

Question and Answer Practice

☞ *practice the following:*

Q Now, the purpose of our gathering here today in my office is to conduct an inquiry into the matter of / whether you were permitted to insure people or not. So let me begin by asking you your name / and the name of your company or business.

A My name is Joseph O' Hern, and I am an agent with Allstate / Insurance Company.

Q Thank you, Mr. O' Hern. I would like to inquire a little bit into how you first became employed by / Allstate. Can you tell me how you got into the insurance business?

A Sure. I answered an ad in the paper, / and I filled out an application.

Q Did you go to an interview, or how were you hired?

A Well, I / filled out the application; and then they called me in. They asked me what area I would like to / cover. We really didn't get too much into my background or anything at that point.

Q Did you ask for a recommendation / from anyone before you were hired?

A No, sir.

Q Did they ask about any outside employment?

A No, sir.

Q Did they / inquire into your schooling at all?

A No, sir.

Q Did you have to take a test or anything?

A No, sir.

Q Do / you mean to sit there and tell us that you were just hired on the spot without any checking / of your applications or any recommendation from anyone?

A Yes, sir. They said they needed the people, and they hired me / right on the spot.

Q Did they tell you that you could open your own office and begin to sell insurance? /

A Yes, sir. That was my understanding.

Q Where did you get the idea that you could do that?

A Well, from what / they said to me. They said that I could get into the business if I paid them a small fee.

Q I see. / And how much was that fee?

A Well, they said that since I was more or less on the inside, I / only had to pay $5,000 to begin with. I also had to give them a portion of what I made each / week.

Q And what was that portion?

A I had to give them 1/3 of what I made.

Q What about the / size of your area? What area did you cover?

A I had the whole city and a portion of the outskirts. /

Q Now, did you, in fact, insure a house for a man by the name of Ted Jenson?

A Yes, sir.

Q And / do you know the size of this particular house?

A I believe it was about 3,000 square feet, and it also included / an acre of land with a pond and a barn located on it.

Q And what was the cost of the insurance / coverage?

A I charged him $672 a year.

Q And how much of that did you keep for yourself?

A I kept / the whole amount because I felt as though I earned it.

Q Now, tell me this, was there a fire at / the home of Mr. Jenson?

A Yes, sir. It is my understanding that the whole place burned down.

Q And do you know / for a fact that Mr. Jenson tried to cash in on his insurance / coverage and that Allstate refused to pay him / anything, saying that he did not have any coverage at all?

A That is my understanding, yes, sir.

Additional Practice

Go to the:	Do the following:
Realwrite DrillBook (recommended)........	Write and practice Drill XXIV (Lessons 47 & 48)
Realwrite NoteBook (optional).................	Read and transcribe the notes from Exercise L, Lesson 48 and Drill XXIV

UNIT 12 REVIEW

Lesson Review

1. Practice all numeric and phonetic ordinals until you can write them without any hesitation.
2. Practice the short forms for directions and states so you can write them smoothly.
3. Read over the realtime writing principles so that you understand why it is important to write accurately and smoothly.
4. Practice all of the short forms you have learned so far.

Review of Writing Rules

45.1 In eliminating a conflict between two words that contain the "long a" sound, use the AE for words that contain both the "a" and the "e" in the English spelling. Use the AEU (long a) for all other words.

45.2 In eliminating a conflict between two words that contain the "long a" sound, use the AE for words that do not contain the "a" and "i" in their English spelling.

45.3 If a conflict cannot be eliminated between two words that contain the "long a" sound by applying all previous rules, write the word in two strokes.

45.4 In eliminating a conflict between two words that contain an "a" and "e" in their English spelling, use the AE for the words that have the "ae" in order. Use the long a (AEU) for words that have the "e" before the "a."

46.1 In eliminating a conflict between words that contain the "long e" sound, use the AE for all words that contain both vowels "a" and "e" regardless of their order. Use the "long e" for all other words, including words that contain the "double e."

46.2 If a conflict cannot be eliminated between two words that contain the "long e" sound by applying all previous rules, write the word in two strokes.

47.1 In eliminating a conflict between words that contain the "long i" sound, use the AOEU for all words and make the distinction by writing as close to the English spelling as you can.

47.2 In eliminating a conflict between two words that contain the "long o" sound, use the OE (long o) for the word that ends in the silent vowel "e" in the English spelling. Use the O (short o) for all other words in conflict.

47.3 In eliminating other conflicts involving the long O, use the proper English spelling along with other applicable rules.

47.4 All states and territories of the United States are written using the standard two-letter abbreviation. Each state is a two stroke short form, writing one letter at a time on the initial side along with the -FPLT on the final side.

48.1 In eliminating a conflict between two words that contain the "u" sound, write the word as close to the English spelling as possible.

48.2 In eliminating conflicts with words that begin with the "s," write the S for words that begin with "s" in the English spelling, write SK for words that begin with "sc"; and write KR for words that begin with "c" in the English spelling.

48.3 In eliminating conflicts with words that begin with "ex" and "ext," write the SKP for words that begin with "ex" and write the ST for words that begin with "ext."

48.4 Some one stroke words that begin with a vowel in the English will use an initial Y- (KWR-) to eliminate a conflict.

48.5 In eliminating conflicts with words that end in a double consonant in the English spelling, use the vowels AU for the word containing the double consonant.

Review DrillBook and NoteBook Applications

1. Review Drills XXIII and XXIV from the *Realwrite DrillBook* (recommended).
2. Review Exercise L from the *Realwrite NoteBook.* (ptional).

Unit Evaluation Number Twelve

Unit Evaluation Number Twelve will cover all material from the following: *Realwrite LessonBook*, Lessons 45-48; *DrillBook*, Drills XXIII and XXIV.

A

American PHERPB [33]
among PHOPBG [14]
amount APLT [33]
& *ampersand* (and) AEU-RBGS [41]
ample APL/PAEL [29]
angle APBG/AEL [29]
another TPHOTD [37]
answer SWER [39]
anti APBT/KWRAOEU [40]
any TPHEU [12]
anybody TPHEUB [38]
anyhow TPHEUFD [38]
anymore TPHEUPL [38]
anyone TPHEUPB [38]
anyplace TPHEUPS [38]
anything TPHEUPBG [38]
anyway TPHEUFPL [38]
anywhere TPHEUFRP [38]
apartment PARPLT [22]
' *apostrophe* A -RBGS [19]
apple AP/AEL [29]
applicable PHREUBG [14]
application PHREUBGS [24]
apply PHREU [13]
appointment POEUPLT [22]
appraise A/PRAEUZ [21]
appropriate PROEPT [26]
approximate PRAFRPB [26]
April A-FPLT [39]
apt APT [15]
arch AR/AEFP [39]
are not R-PB [21]
are R- [8]
are the R-T [10]
are you RAU [12]
area RA [48]
aren't R-PBZ [21]
argue ARG [20]
arise A/RAOEUZ [21]
Arizona A-FPLT /SKPW-FPLT [47]
Arkansas A-FPLT /R-FPLT [47]
armor ARPL/KWROR [27]
arms ARPLZ [18]
around ARPBD [20]
arrange ARPBG [20]
arrangement ARPBG/PHAEPBT [22]
arson AR/SOPB [27]
article ARL [33]
arts ARTS [18]
ask SK- [29]
assessable A/SES/KWABL [33]
associate SOERBT [34]
* *asterisk* (star) ST-RBGS [41]
astray A/STRAFPL [21]
@ *at sign* T-RBGS [41]
attack A/TABG [21]
attention A/TEPBGS [24]
audition AU/TKEUGS [24]
auditions AU/TKEUGS/AEZ [24]
August AU-FPLT [39]
authority THORT [36]
auto AUT [33]
automobile AOBL [18]
avenue AFB [33]
avert A/SRERT [21]
avow A/SROFRP [21]
awe AFRP [14]

B

B PW-FBG [20]
-B- PW-FL [28]
-B PW-FLD [37]
B- PW-FRD [37]
b PW-FS [24]
B. PW-FPD [32]
(B) PW-FPS [36]
baby PWAEUB/AEFPL [19]
babyish PWAEUB/KWREURB [25]
\ *back slash* B-RBGS [31]
background PWABG/AE/TKPWROUPBD [28]
badly PWAD/HRAEFPL [29]
bail BAIL [45]
balance PWAL [14]
bale BAEL [45]
bang PWAPBG [35]
bank PWAFBG [35]

butt BAUT [48]
buy BUY [47]
buyer PWUFPL/KWRER [27]
by B-Y [47]
bye BEY [47]
byte B-YT [47]

C

C KR-FBG [20]
-C- KR-FL [28]
-C KR-FLD [37]
C- KR-FRD [37]
c KR-FS [24]
C. KR-FPD [32]
(C) KR-FPS [36]
cab's KAB/AOS [20]
Cadillac KAD/HRABG [14]
cafe KAF/KWRAEU [40]
California KR-FPLT /A-FPLT [47]
caller KAUL/KWRER
calm KAUPL [39]
can a KAEU [6]
can he KE [6]
can I KEU [6]
can K (-BG) [6]
can the K-T [10]
can you KAU [12]
Canal Zone KR-FPLT /SKPW-FPLT [47]
cannon KAPB/KWROPB [27]
cannot K-PB [10]
cans KAPBZ [18]
can't K-PBZ [21]
capital KAL [36]
carb KARB [25]
careful KAIF [42]
carefully KAIFL [42]
^ *caret* KR-RBGS
caring KAEURG [19]
carnage KARPB/KWRAPBLG [27]
carport KAR/POERT [15]
carried K-RD [42]
carry K-R [19]
carrying K-RG [19]
cars KARZ [18]
carve KAFRB [31]
cash KAERB [25]
cask KASZ [38]
cast KAESZ [38]
cat's KAT/AOS [20]
catch KAFP [25]
cater KAEUT/KWRER [27]
caught KAUGT [22]
cede KRAOED [46]
cement SEPLT [22]
cent CEPBT [48]
certain SERPB [29]
certificate SERT [29]
chalk KHAUBG [39]
champ KHAPL/AEP [39]
character KAIRK [46]
charity KHAEURT [31]
chart KHART [17]
chasm KHASZ [38]
chat KHAT [17]
cheat KHAOET [17]
cheer KHAOER [17]
chef SHEF [17]
Chet KHET [17]
chief KHAOEF [17]
childish KHAOUELD/KWREURB [25]
children KHIRPB [45]
chime KHAOEUPL [17]
chin KHEUPB [17]
chip KHEUP [17]
church KH-FP [25]
circumstance SEURBG [21]
cite KRAOIT [47]
city STI [45]
clarity KHRAEURT [31]
classify KL-F [46]
closure KHROEZ/KWRUR [40]
cloth KHROTD [37]
clothe KHROETD [37]
clown KHROUPB [16]
coats KOETS [18]
coca KOEBG/KWRA [40]
coffee KOF/KWRAOE [14]

coil KOEUL [16]
cola KOEHR/KWRA [40]
collect KHREBGT [23]
collide KHRAOEUD [23]
: *colon* K -RBGS [17]
Colorado KR-FPLT /O-FPLT [47]
column KHRUPL [23]
coma KOEPH/KWRA [40]
combat KPWAT [23]
combine KPWAOEUPB [23]
come KPH- [6]
comfort K-FRT [23]
comfortable K-FRT/KWRABL [33]
, *comma* -RBGS [14]
comma KOPH/KWRA [40]
command KPHAPBD [23]
commence KPHEPBS [23]
commendable KPHEPBD/KWRABL [33]
comment KOPLT [22]
commerce KPHERS [23]
commit KPHEUT [23]
committee KPHEUT/KWRAOE [19]
communicate K-MT [46]
communication K-MGS [46]
company K-P [21]
compatibility KPAT/KWREUBLT [33]
compatible KPAT/KWREUBL [33]
compete KPAOET [23]
complex KPHREFRPB [23]
compose KPOEZ [23]
compress KPRES [23]
compulsion KPULGS [24]
compute KOPL/PAOUT [16]
concern KERPB [21]
condition K-PBGS [24]
confer KER [35]
conference KERPBS [35]
confinement KOPB/TPAOEUPB/PHAEPBT [22]
connect KEBGT [35]
Connecticut KR-FPLT /T-FPLT [47]
connection KEBGS [35]
conscious KOPB/SHAUS [25]
consider KR- [35]
considerable KR-B [35]
considerably KR-BL [35]
considerate KR-T [35]
contact KAKT [43]
contain TAIN [43]
contentious KOPB/TEPB/SHAUS [25]
continue T-PB [36]
contract KRAKT [43]
contribute KRIBT [45]
control KROEL [45]
convenience VAOENS [46]
convenient VAOENT [46]
conviction KOPB/SREUBGS [24]
convictions KOPB/SREUBGS/AEZ [24]
cook KAOBG [14]
cool KAOL [14]
copy KP-FPL [21]
cordially K-Y [43]
cordially yours K-YZ [43]
cork KORBG
correspond KROPBD [25]
correspondence KROPBS [39]
cost KOSZ [38]
cough KAUF [22]
could he KOE [8]
could I KOEU [8]
could KO [8]
could not KOPBT [18]
could you KAOU [12]
couldn't KOPBZ [21]
council KOUPBS/KWREUL [27]
cover KOFR [29]
cow KOFRP [16]
coy KOFPL [16]
craft KRAFT [16]
crash KRARB [25]
crazier KRAEUZ/KWRAER [40]
credit KRE [25]
creed KRAED [46]
cried KRAOEUD [17]
crown KROUPB [16]
crunch KRUPB/AEFP [39]

E

East AOESZ [45]
easy AOES [29]
eaten AOET/KWREPB [27]
echo EBG/KWROE [40]
eerie AOER/KWRAOE [21]
effect EFBGT [30]
effort EFRT [30]
effortlessly EFRT/SHRAEFPL [40]
eight AIGT [41]
eighteen AOEN [41]
eighteenth AOETD [47]
eighth AEUTD [47]
eightieth AEUY/AETD [47]
eighty AIY [41]
eighty-eight AIY/AIGT [43]
eighty-eighth AIY/AITD [48]
eighty-fifth AIY/FITD [48]
eighty-first AIY/FIRT [48]
eighty-five AIY/FAOIV [43]
eighty-four AIY/FOUR [43]
eighty-fourth AIY/FOTD [48]
eighty-nine AIY/NAOIN [43]
eighty-ninth AIY/NAOITD [48]
eighty-one AIY/WUN [43]
eighty-second AIY/SEKD [48]
eighty-seven AIY/SEV [43]
eighty-seventh AIY/SETD [48]
eighty-six AIY/SIX [43]
eighty-sixth AIY/SITD [48]
eighty-third AIY/THIRD [48]
eighty-three AIY/THRAOE [43]
eighty-two AIY/TWO [43]
either ETD [37]
eleven LEV [41]
eleventh LETD [47]
emergency PH-PBLG [14]
emphasis EPLS [47]
emphsize EMZ [47]
employ PHROEU [21]
employee PHROE [21]
employer PHROEUR [21]
employment PHROEUPLT [22]
enable NAIBL [47]
enclose KHR- [14]
enclosure KLAOUR [47]
] *end bracket* BRE-RBGS [41]
) *end parenthesis* PRE -RBGS [27]
"*end quote* KWE-RBGS [25]
endure EPB/TKAOUR [26]
engine TPH-G [19]
engineer TPH-PBLG [19]
enhance EPB/HAPBS [26]
enjoyment EPB/SKWROFPL/PHAEPBT [22]
enough TPHUF [19]
enter NER [47]
enterprise EPBT/PRAOEUZ [34]
entertain EPBT/TAEUPB [34]
envelope TPHEFL [15]
equal KWL- [47]
= *equal sign* E-RBGS [41]
equipment KW-PLT [22]
era ER/KWRA [26]
ergo ER/TKPWOE [26]
err ER [21]
error ER/KWROR [21]
especial SPERB [33]
especially SPERBL [33]
estimate STEUPLT [22]
Europe AOURP [21]
even AOEFPB [8]
ever EFR [24]
every EFB [24]
everybody KWR-B [38]
everyday KWR-D [38]
everyone KWR-PB [38]
everyplace KWR-PS [38]
everything KWR-PBG [38]
everywhere KWR-FRP [38]
evidence EFD [13]
ex- EFRPB [30]
exact SKPABGT [30]
exam SKPAPL [30]
examine SKP-PB [19]
example SKP-PL [19]
excell SKP-L [30]
excellence SKPHREPBS [30]

excellent SKPHREPBT [30]
excess SKPES [30]
excise SKPAOEUZ [30]
excite SKPAOEUT [30]
excitement SKPAOEUT/PHAEPBT [22]
! *exclamation point* X-RBGS [29]
excrete SKPROAET [30]
excuse SKPAOUS [30]
excuse SKPAOUZ [30]
execute SKPAOUT [30]
ex-employee EFRPB/PHROE [30]
exercise SKPER/SAOEUZ [30]
exhale SKPHAEUL [30]
exhort SKPHORT [30]
exhume SKPAOUPL [30]
exile SKPAOEUL [30]
exist SKPEUSZ [38]
exit SKPEUT [30]
ex-partner EFRPB/PART/TPHER [30]
expedite SKPE/TKAOEUT [30]
expel SKPEL [30]
expend SKPEPBD [30]
explore SKPHROR [30]
export SKPORT [30]
express SKPRES [30]
ex-spouse EFRPB/SPOUS [30]
extend STEPBD [30]
extension STEPBGS [30]
extent STEPBT [30]
exterior STAOER/KWRAOR [30]
external STERPBL [30]
extinction STEUPBGS [30]
extol STOL [30]
extort STORT [48]
extra STRA [30]
extreme STRAOEPL [30]
exude SKPAOUD [30]
eye EFPL [12]

F

F TP-FBG [20]
-F- TP-FL [28]
-F TP-FLD [37]
F- TP-FRD [37]
f TP-FS [24]
F. TP-FPD [32]
(F) TP-FPS [36]
facial TPAEURBL [25]
faction TPABGS [24]
factions TPABGS/AEZ [24]
faint FAINT [45]
fair FAIR [45]
fairly TPAEURL [29]
faith TPAEUTD [37]
fall TPAUL [14]
familiar TPHRAR [30]
family TPAPL [15]
fanatically TPAPBT/KHRAEFPL [40]
fare FAER [45]
farms TPARPLZ [18]
farther TPRATD [37]
fast TPAESZ [38]
father TPATD [37]
fawn TPAEPB [16]
feather TPETD/KWRER [37]
February TPE-FPLT [39]
federal TPRAL [42]
feint FAEPBT [45]
fetch TPEFP [25]
fetus TPAOET/KWRUS [27]
few TPEFRP [16]
fewer TPEFRP/KWRER [27]
fiction TPEUBGS [24]
fictitious TPEUBG/TEURBS [25]
fifteen FAOEN [41]
fifteenth FAOETD [47]
fifth FEUTD [47]
fiftieth TPEUY/AETD [47]
fifty TPIY [41]
fifty-eight FIY/AIGT [42]
fifty-eighth FIY/AITD [47]
fifty-fifth FIY/FITD [47]
fifty-first FIY/FIRT [47]
fifty-five FIY/FAOIV [42]
fifty-four FIY/FOUR [42]
fifty-fourth FIY/FOTD [47]
fifty-nine FIY/NAOIN [42]

fifty-ninth FIY/NAOITD [47]
fifty-one FIY/WUN [42]
fifty-second FIY/SEKD [47]
fifty-seven FIY/SEV [42]
fifty-seventh FIY/SETD [47]
fifty-six FIY/SIX [42]
fifty-sixth FIY/SITD [47]
fifty-third FIY/THIRD [47]
fifty-three FIY/THRAOE [42]
fifty-two FIY/TWO [42]
fight TPAOEUGT [22]
figure TP-G [13]
film TPEUL/AEPL [39]
Filmore TPEUL/PHOR [15]
filth TPEUL/AETD [37]
finance TP-PBS [19]
financial TP-PBL [19]
fined TPAOEUPB/AED [17]
finer TPAOEUPB/KWRER [27]
finish TP-RB [30]
first TPEURT [10]
fish TPEURB [25]
five FAOIV [41]
fizzes TPEUZ [18]
flask TPHRASZ [38]
flew FLEW [48]
Florida TP-FPLT /HR-FPLT [47]
flu FLU [48]
flue FLAOU [48]
foil TPOEUL [16]
folk TPOEL/AEBG [39]
follow TPOL [15]
fool TPAOL [14]
forbid TPOER/PWEUD [36]
forego TPOER/TKPWOE [36]
foretell TPOER/TEL [36]
foreword TPOER/WORD [36]
forgave TPOER/TKPWAEUFB [36]
forget TPOER/TKPWET [36]
forgive TPOER/TKPWEUFB [36]
forgiven TPOER/TKPWEUFPB [36]
forgot TPOER/TKPWOT [36]
format TPOER/PHAT [36]
forth TPR-TD [37]
fortieth TPROY/AETD [47]
forty TPROY [41]
forty-eight FROY/AIGT [42]
forty-eighth FROY/AITD [47]
forty-fifth FROY/FITD [47]
forty-first FROY/FIRT [47]
forty-five FROY/FAOIV [42]
forty-four FROY/FOUR [42]
forty-fourth FROY/FOTD [47]
forty-nine FROY/NAOIN [42]
forty-ninth FROY/NAOITD [47]
forty-one FROY/WUN [42]
forty-second FROY/SEKD [47]
forty-seven FROY/SEV [42]
forty-seventh FROY/SETD [47]
forty-six FROY/SIX [42]
forty-sixth FROY/SITD [47]
forty-third FROY/THIRD [47]
forty-three FROY/THRAOE [42]
forty-two FROY/TWO [42]
four FOUR [41]
fourteen FRAOEN [41]
fourteenth FRAOETD [47]
fourth FOTD [47]
fraction TPRABGS [24]
fractions TPRABGS/AEZ [24]
Friday TPREU-FPLT [33]
fried FRAOEUD [17]
frighten TPRAOEUGT/KWREPB [27]
fringe TPREUFPBLG [35]
from the TPR-T [10]
from TPR- [8]
from you TPRAU [12]
frost TPROSZ [38]
fulfillment TPUL/TPEUL/PHAEPBT [22]
further TPRUTD [37]
fusion TPAOUGS [24]
future FAOUR [42]
futuristic TPAOUR/STEUSZ [40]
futuristically TPAOUR/SKHRAEFPL [40]

G

G TKPW-FBG [20]

-G- TKPW-FL [28]
-G TKPW-FLD [37]
G- TKPW-FRD [37]
g TKPW-FS [24]
G. TKPW-FPD [32]
(G) TKPW-FPS [36]
gallon TKPW-L [15]
gather TKPWATD [37]
gay TKPWAFPL [16]
general SKWR-PB [19]
generally J-NL [47]
gentle SKWREPBL [19]
gentleman SKWRA [13]
Gentlemen and Ladies JAL [41]
Gentlemen JE-FPLT [41]
gentlemen SKWRE [13]
Georgia TKPW-FPLT /A-FPLT [47]
girlish TKPWEURL/KWREURB [25]
girls TKPWEURLZ [18]
girls' TKPWEURLZ/A-RBGS [20]
glitch TKPWHREUFP [25]
gown TKPWOUPB [16]
grate GRAET [45]
gratefully TKPWRAEUT/TPHRAEFPL [40]
great GRAEUT [45]
> *greater than* GR-RBGS [41]
groan GROEN [47]
grown GROUN [47]
Guam TKPW-FPLT /U-FPLT [47]
guilty G-Y [42]
gym TKPWEUPL [13]

H

H H-FBG [20]
-H- H-FL [28]
-H H-FLD [37]
H- H-FRD [37]
h H-FS [24]
H. H-FPD [32]
(H) H-FPS [36]
had a HAEU [4]
had H- (-FD) [4]
had he HE [4]
had I HEU [6]
had not H-PB [19]
had you HAU [12]
hadn't H-PBZ [21]
hair HAIR [45]
half HAF [13]
hall HAUL [14]
handle HAPBL [19]
happen HAP [43]
happening HAPG [43]
happier HAP/KWAER [40]
happy HAP/AEFPL [19]
harassment HA/RAS/PHAEPBT [22]
hardly HARD/HRAEFPL [29]
hardware HARD/WAER [15]
hare HAR [45]
has not SKPW-PB [21]
hasn't SKPW-PBZ [21]
hassle HAS/AEL [29]
haul HAFRPL [14]
have I SREU [[10]
have not SR-PB [21]
have SR (-FB) [10]
have you SRAU [10]
haven't SR-PBZ [21]
Hawaii H-FPLT /EU-FPLT [47]
he can HAEBG [6]
he could HAEBGD [8]
he did HAED [4]
he had HAEFD [4]
he HAE (E) [4]
he will HAEFRP [10]
he would HAEWD [27]
health HETD [37]
hear HAER [45]
heavier HEFB/KWAER [40]
heaviest HEFB/KWAESZ [40]
he'd HAEDZ [27]
heir HEUR [45]
he'll HAEFRPZ [31]
help HEP [8]
helpfully HEP/TPHRAEFPL [40]
helplessly HEP/SHRAEFPL [40]
hero HAOER/KWROE [40]

J

K

kneel STPAOEL [32]
knew STPEFRP [32]
knife STPAOEUF [32]
knight STPAOEUGT [32]
knit STPEUT [32]
knob STPOB [32]
knock STPOBG [32]
knot STPOT [32]
know STPOEFRP [32]
known STPHOEPB [32]
knuckle STPUBG/AEL [32]

L

L HR-FBG [20]
-L- HR-FL [28]
-L HR-FLD [37]
L- HR-FRD [37]
l HR-FS [24]
L. HR-FPD [32]
(L) HR-FPS [36]
labor HRAEUB [15]
Ladies and Gentlemen LAJ [41]
lament HRAPLT [22]
lash HRARB [25]
last HRAESZ [38]
latch HRAFP [25]
lately HRAEUT/HRAEFPL [29]
laugh HRAF [22]
law HRAFRP [14]
lawn HRAEPB [16]
lawyer HROEUR [16]
leather HRETD/KWRER [37]
legal HRAOEL [15]
leisure HRAOEZ/KWRUR [40]
lemon HREPL/KWROPB [27]
length HRAETD [37]
lessen HRES/KWREPB [27]
< *lesser than* LE-RBGS [41]
lesson HRES/KWROPB [27]
letter HRER [23]
liable HRAOEUBL [33]
lift HREUFT [16]
light HRAOIGT [47]
likely HRAOEUBG/HRAEFPL [29]
liken HRAOEUBG/KWREPB [27]
limo HREUPH/KWROE [40]
linen HREUPB/KWREPB [27]
listen LIFN [42]
lite HRAOIT [47]
little HREUL [6]
lived HREUFB/AED [17]
load LOD [47]
loan LON [47]
local LOEL [42]
lode LOED [47]
lone LOEN [47]
lonely HROEPBL [29]
longevity HROPBG/SKWREFT [31]
look HRAOBG [14]
lost HROSZ [38]
Louisiana HR-FPLT /A-FPLT [47]
loving HROFBG [19]
lovingly HROFB/TKPWHRAEFPL [40]
low HROEFRP [16]
loyal HROEUL [16]
lunch HRUPB/AEFP [39]
lurch HRUR/AEFP [39]

M

M PH-FBG [20]
-M- PH-FL [28]
-M PH-FLD [37]
M- PH-FRD [37]
m PH-FS [24]
M. PH-FPD [32]
(M) PH-FPS [36]
machine PH-FP [25]
made MAED [45]
magazine MAZ [44]
maid MAID [45]
mail MAEUL [45]
Maine PH-FPLT /E-FPLT [47]
major PHAEUPBLG [15]
majority PHAPBLGT [31]
male MAEL [45]
malicious PHA/HREURBS [25]
mall PHAUL [14]
mama PHA/PHA [40]

manage PH-G [16]
manager PH-R [23]
manufacture PH-F [16]
many PH-PB [8]
maple PHAEUP/AEL [29]
March PHA-FPLT [39]
march PHAR/AEFP [39]
mark PHARBG [15]
marry PHAEUR/AEFPL [19]
martial PHAR/SHAEL [25]
Marv PHAFRB [31]
Maryland PH-FPLT /TK-FPLT [47]
mash PHARB [25]
mask PHASZ [38]
mason PHA/SOPB [27]
Massachusetts PH-FPLT /A-FPLT [47]
mast PHAESZ [38]
match PHAFP [25]
materalize TAOERL/KWRAOEUZ [40]
material TAOERL [23]
matter M-T [44]
mature PHAT/KWRUR [40]
maul PHAFRPL [14]
maxi PHAFRPB/KWRAOE [40]
maximum PH-FRPB [39]
May PHAEU-FPLT [39]
may PHAFPL [16]
maybe PHAEUB [16]
me PHAE [6]
meat MAET [46]
mechanic PH-BG [16]
meet MAOET [46]
melon PHEL/KWROPB [27]
member PHEB [16]
members MEBZ [44]
memo PHEPL [16]
mens' PHEPBZ/A-RBGS [20]
message PHES/KWRAPBLG [14]
mete MAOE/AET [46]
method PH-TD [37]
Michigan PH-FPLT /EU-FPLT [47]
midst PHEUD/AESZ [38]
might MAOIGT [47]
milk PHEUL/AEBG [39]
mini PHEUPB/KWRAOE [40]
minimum PHEUPL [17]
Minnesota PH-FPLT /TPH-FPLT [47]
minor PHAOEUPB/KWROR [27]
minority PHAOEU/TPHORT [31]
- minus sign MI-RBGS [41]
minute PHEUPB [20]
Miss PH-S [39]
mission PHEUGS [24]
missions PHEUGS/AEZ [24]
Mississippi PH-FPLT /S-FPLT [47]
Missouri PH-FPLT /O-FPLT [47]
mist PHEUSZ [38]
mite MAOIT [47]
mixed PHEUFRPBD [17]
moan MOEN [47]
mobility PHOEBLT [33]
moment PHOEPLT [22]
Monday PHO-FPLT [33]
money PHE [20]
Montana PH-FPLT /T-FPLT [47] [47]
month PHOPB [17]
monthly PHOL [17]
moon PHAOPB [14]
moor PHAOR [14]
most PHO [17]
motel PHOELT [33]
moth PHOTD [37]
mother PHOETD [37]
motor PHOER [23]
mountain PHOUPB/TAEUPB [14]
mouth PHOUTD [37]
movie PHOFB/KWRAOE [19]
moving PHOFB/AEG [19]
mow PHOEFRP [16]
mown MOUN [47]
Mr. PHR- [13]
Mrs. PHR-S [39]
Ms. PH-Z [39]
muffle PHUFL [29]
musk PHUSZ [38]
must PHU [17]

myself PH-FPL/SAEFL [23]

N

N TPH-FBG [20]
-N- TPH-FL [28]
-N TPH-FLD [37]
N- TPH-FRD [37]
n TPH-FS [24]
N. TPH-FPD [32]
(N) TPH-FPS [36]
national TPHAL [20]
natural TPHARL [23]
nay TPHAFPL [16]
Nebraska TPH-FPLT /E-FPLT [47]
necessary TPHE [20]
need TPHAOED [32]
negative TPHEG/TEUFB [40]
negatively TPHEG/TEUFL [40]
negativity TPHEG/TEUFT [40]
neglect TPHEG [20]
negligence NEGS [43]
negligent NEGT [43]
neighbor TPHAEUB [20]
neither TPHETD [37]
nerve TPHEFRB [31]
Nevada TPH-FPLT /SR-FPLT [47]
never TPHEFR [29]
New Hampshire TPH-FPLT /H-FPLT [47]
New Jersey TPH-FPLT /SKWR-FPLT [47]
New Mexico TPH-FPLT /PH-FPLT [47]
new paragraph PA-RBGS [15]
new TPHEFRP [16]
New York TPH-FPLT /KWR-FPLT [47]
Newark TPHEFRP/KWRARBG [14]
Newport TPHEFRP/PORT [14]
next TPH-FRPB [23]
night TPHAOEUGT [32]
nine NAOIN [41]
nineteen NAOEN [41]
nineteenth NAOETD [47]
ninetieth NAOEUY/AETD [47]
ninety NAOIY [41]
ninety-eight NAOIY/AIGT [43]
ninety-eighth NAOIY/AITD [48]
ninety-fifth NAOIY/FITD [48]
ninety-first NAOIY/FIRT [48]
ninety-five NAOIY/FAOIV [43]
ninety-four NAOIY/FOUR [43]
ninety-fourth NAOIY/FOTD [48]
ninety-nine NAOIY/NAOIN [43]
ninety-ninth NAOIY/NAOITD [48]
ninety-one NAOIY/WUN [43]
ninety-second NAOIY/SEKD [48]
ninety-seven NAOIY/SEV [43]
ninety-seventh NAOIY/SETD [48]
ninety-six NAOIY/SIX [43]
ninety-sixth NAOIY/SITD [48]
ninety-third NAOIY/THIRD [48]
ninety-three NAOIY/THRAOE [43]
ninety-two NAOIY/TWO [43]
ninth NAOITD [47]
nite NAOIT [47]
no how TPHOEFD [39]
no one TPH-PB [39]
no TPHOE [41]
no way TPHOEFPL [39]
no, ma'am TPHOEPL [12]
no, sir TPHEUR [12]
nobody TPHOEB [39]
North Carolina TPH-FPLT /KR-FPLT [47]
North Dakota TPH-FPLT /TK-FPLT [47]
North NORT [45]
northeast NAOESZ [45]
northwest NOESZ [45]
not TPHOT (-PB) [10]
notable TPHOEP/KWRABL [33]
nothing TPHOPBG [39]
notice TPH-TS [28]
notify TPH-F [20]
November TPHO-FPLT [39]
now TPHOFRP [16]
nowhere TPHOEFRP [39]
number PWER [8]
number sign NU-RBGS [41]
nylon TPHFPL/HROPB [27]

O

O O-FBG [20]

P

peculiar KHRAR (KLAR) [25]
pencil PEPBS/KWREUL [16]
Pennsylvania P-FPLT /A-FPLT [47]
pension PEPBGS [24]
pensions PEPBGS/AEZ [24]
Pepsi PEPS/KWRAOE [40]
% percent sign PE-RBGS [41]
perfectionism P-FBGT/SKPWEUPL [38]
perfectionist P-FBGT/KWREUSZ [38]
perform PEFRPL [17]
perhaps PRAPS [45]
. period -FPLT [13]
person PERPB [39]
personal PERPBL [20]
pew PEFRP [16]
photograph TPRAF [25]
physical F-L [43]
picture TAOUR [42]
pinch PEUPB/AEFP [39]
pitch PEUFP [25]
plain PHRAEUPB [24]
plan PHRAPB [24]
plane PHRAEPB [24]
plaque PHRALGTS [24]
pleas PHRAOEZ [24]
please PHRAOES [24]
plight PHRAOEUGT [24]
pluck PHRUBG [24]
plum PHRUPL [24]
+ plus sign PL-RBGS [41]
. point POI-RBGS [33]
pole POEL [47]
police PHREUS [24]
policeman PHRAPL [24]
policemen PHREPL [24]
poll POL [47]
pool PAOL [14]
poor PAOR [14]
popular PHRAR (PLAR) [25]
porch POR/AEFP [39]
position ZIGS [43]
positive POZ [42]
possible POB [17]
possibly POBL [42]
 # pound sign PO-RBGS [41]
practice PRA [26]
prairie PRAEUR/AOE [26]
prance PRAPBS [26]
pray PRAFPL [26]
preach PRAOEFP [26]
precious PRERBS [26]
predate PRE/TKAEUT [28]
predict PRE/TKEUBGT [28]
premier PRE/PHAOER [28]
prepaid PRE/PAEUD [28]
prepare PRAOEP [25]
presence PREPBS [26]
present PREPBT [26]
president PREZ [44]
press PRES [26]
prevent PRE/SREPBT [28]
previous PR-FS [26]
principal PRAL [25]
principle PR-L [25]
prism PREUSZ [38]
probable PRAB [25]
probably PRABL [25]
problem PREPL [25]
proceed PROE [25]
product PROBGT [26]
profession PROFGS [26]
program PRAPL [26]
pro-life PRO/H-RBGS/LAOEUF [28]
promote PRO/PHOET [28]
proper PROR [43]
proportion PRO/PORGS [28]
propose PR-P [26]
prorate PRO/RAEUT [28]
protect PRO/TEBGT [28]
provide PROEU [26]
psalm SAUPL [39]
public PUBL [17]
Puerto Rico P-FPLT /R-FPLT [47]
pump PUPL/AEP [39]
punch PUPB/AEFP [39]
purchase PR-CH [43]

purpose PURP [42]
put PUT [48]
putt PAUT [48]

Q

Q KW-FBG [20]
-Q- KW-FL [28]
-Q KW-FLD [37]
Q- KW-FRD [37]
q KW-FS [24]
Q. KW-FPD [32]
(Q) KW-FPS [36]
qualify KWAUF [45]
quest KWESZ [38]
question KWE [42]
? *question mark* STPH- [15]

R

R R-FBG [20]
-R- R-FL [28]
-R R-FLD [37]
R- R-FRD [37]
r R-FS [24]
R. R-FPD [32]
(R) R-FPS [36]
rabbit RAB/KWREUT [14]
racial RAEURBL [25]
radio RAEUD/KWROE [40]
raft RAFT [16]
raided RAEUD/AED [17]
rain RAIN [45]
rally RAL/AEFPL [29]
ranch RAPB/AEFP [39]
rang RAPBG [35]
range RAFPBLG [35]
rank RAFBG [35]
rarely RAEURL [29]
rarity RAEURT [31]
rather RATD [37]
raw RAFRP [14]
ray RAFPL [16]
rayon RAFPL/KWROPB [27]
razor RAEUZ/KWROR [27]
razzed RAZ/AED [17]
ready R-D [41]
realism RAOEL/SKPWEUPL [38]
realist RAOEL/KWREUSZ [38]
realistic RAOEL/STEUSZ [40]
realistically RAOEL/SKHRAEY [40]
realize RAOEL/KWRAOEUZ [14]
really R-L [29]
realm REL/AEPL [39]
reason RAOEN [41]
reasonably RAOEBL [41]
recall RE/KAUL [28]
recant RE/KAPBT [28]
receipt RAOET [44]
receive RAOEV [44]
recent RAOENT [28]
recognize ROZ [41]
recommend ROM [41]
recommendation ROMGS [48]
record RORD [43]
refund REFN [43]
regard RARD [45]
regrettable RE/TKPWRET/KWRABL [33]
regular REG [41]
reign RAEU/AEN [45]
rein RAEN [45]
rejoin RE/SKWROEUPB [28]
remain R-M [14]
remarkable RE/PHARBG/KWRABL [33]
remember RER [27]
remind REUPBD [27]
remission RE/PHEUGS [24]
remit RE/PHEUT [28]
remove R-V [44]
reply PHRAOEU [24]
report RORT [27]
represent REPT [27]
representation REPGS [45]
request RELGTS [27]
require RAOIR [41]
requirement RAOEURPLT [22]
research R-CH [45]
resent RE/SKPWEPBT [28]
respect R-S [41]
respectfully R-Y [43]

respectfully yours R-YZ [43]
respond SPOND [45]
result RULT [41]
resume RE/SKPWAOUPL [28]
return RURPB [27]
review RE/VEW [48]
revoke RE/SROEBG [28]
revue RE/VAOU [48]
Rhode Island R-FPLT /EU-FPLT [47]
rhyme R-Y/AEM [47]
rich REUFP [25]
rift REUFT [16]
right RAOEUGT [22]
righteous RAOEUGT/KWROUS [40]
rime RAOIM [47]
ring REUPG [35]
risen REUZ/KWREPB [27]
risk REUSZ [38]
rite RAOIT [47]
road -RD [47]
roam ROEM [47]
Robert ROB/KWRERT [14]
rode ROED [47]
role ROEL [47]
roll ROL [47]
Roman numerals RO-RBGS [37]
Rome KA-RBGS/ROEM [47]
roses ROEZ/AEZ [18]
rough RUF [22]
row ROEFRP
roy ROFPL [16]
royal ROEUL [16]
ruined RAOUPB/AED [17]
ruled RAOULD [17]
running RUPB/AEG [19]

S

S S-FBG [20]
-S- S-FL [28]
-S S-FLD [37]
S- S-FRD [37]
s S-FS [24]
S. S-FPD [32]
(S) S-FPS [36]
sadly SAD/HRAEFPL [29]
safely SAEUFL [29]
safer SAFR [29]
safety SAEUT [31]
salon SA/HROPB [27]
sample SAPL/PAEL [29]
sang SAPBG [35]
sank SAFBG [35]
sarcasm SAR/KASZ [38]
sash SARB [25]
satisfaction S-FBGS [38]
satisfactory S-FR [38]
satisfy S-F [38]
satisfying S-FG [38]
Saturday SA-FPLT [33]
saver SAEUFR [29]
savior SAEUFB/KWAOR [40]
saw SAFRP [14]
say SAFPL [16]
scale SKAEUL [22]
scan SKAPB [22]
scar SKAR [22]
scarcely SKAEURS/HRAEFPL [29]
scare SKAEUR [18]
scarf SKAFRB [31]
scarry SKAEUR/AEFPL [19]
scene SKAOEN [46]
scent SKENT [48]
schism SKHEUSZ [38]
scorch SKOR/AEFP [39]
score SKOR [22]
scram SKRAPL [22]
scream SKRAOEPL [22]
screw SKREFRP [22]
scrutinize SKRAOUT/TPHAOEUZ [40]
sea SAE [46]
search SEFP [39]
season SAEPB [38]
seated SAOET/AED [17]
seats SAOETS [18]
second SEBGD [24]
secretary SEBG [38]
see SAOE [46]

seed SAOED [46]
seen SAOEN [46]
seizure SAOEZ/KWRUR [40]
self SEFL [23]
selves SEFLZ [23]
semi SEPL/KWRAOEU [40]
; *semicolon* S -RBGS [17]
sensation SEPB/SAEUGS [24]
sensibility SEPBS/KWREUBLT [33]
sensible SEPBS/KWREUBL [33]
sensitive SEPBS/TEUFB [40]
sensitively SEPBS/TEUFL [40]
sensitivity SEPBS/TEUFT [31]
sent SENT [48]
September SE-FPLT [39]
serve SEFRB [31]
service S-FB [31]
seven SEV [41]
seventeen VAOEN [41]
seventeenth VAOETD [47]
seventh SETD [47]
seventieth SEY/AETD [47]
seventy SEY [41]
seventy-eight SEY/AIGT [43]
seventy-eighth SEY/AITD [48]
seventy-fifth SEY/FITD [48]
seventy-first SEY/FIRT [48]
seventy-five SEY/FAOIV [43]
seventy-four SEY/FOUR [43]
seventy-fourth SEY/FOTD [48]
seventy-nine SEY/NAOIN [43]
seventy-ninth SEY/NAOITD [48]
seventy-one SEY/WUN [43]
seventy-second SEY/SEKD [48]
seventy-seven SEY/SEV [43]
seventy-seventh SEY/SETD [48]
seventy-six SEY/SIX [43]
seventy-sixth SEY/SITD [48]
seventy-third SEY/THIRD [48]
seventy-three SEY/THRAOE [43]
seventy-two SEY/TWO [43]
sew SEFRP [16]
sewage SEFRP/KWRAPBLG [27]
sham SHAPL [17]
shamefully SHAEUPL/TPHRAEFPL [40]
shamelessly SHAEUPL/SHRAEFPL [40]
shawl SHAFRPL [14]
she had SHAEFD [27]
she will SHAEFRP [31]
she would SHAEWD [27]
she'd SHAEDZ [27]
shed SHED [17]
sheer SHAOER [17]
she'll SHAEFRPZ [31]
shine SHAOEUPB [17]
ship SHEUP [15]
shipment SHEUPLT [22]
shirt SHEURT [17]
shone SHOEN [47]
shore SHOR [15]
should not SHOUPB [21]
shouldn't SHOUPBZ [21]
show SHOEFRP [15]
shown SHOUN [47]
shred SKHRED [24]
shrew SKHREFRP [24]
shriek SKHRAOEBG [24]
shrine SKHRAOEUPB [24]
shroud SKHROUD [24]
shrug SKHRUG [24]
shut SHUT [15]
shy SHFPL [15]
sigh SAOEUFD [22]
sight SAOEUGT [22]
sign SAOIN [47]
signature STPHAOUR [38]
silk SEUL/AEBG [39]
silly SEUL/AEFPL [29]
silver SEUL/SRER [29]
sincerely S-Y [43]
sincerely yours S-YZ [43]
sine SAOI/AEN [47]
sing SEUPBG [35]
singe SEUFPBLG [35]
sink SEUFBG [35]
sinned SEUPB/AED [17]

sinning SEUPB/AEG [19]
sister STER [17]
site SAOIT [47]
situate SWAIT [44]
situation SWAIGS [44]
six SIX [41]
sixteen XAOEN [41]
sixteenth XAOETD [47]
sixth SEUTD [47]
sixtieth SEUY/AETD [47]
sixty SIY [41]
sixty-eight SIY/AIGT [43]
sixty-eighth SIY/AITD [48]
sixty-fifth SIY/FITD [48]
sixty-first SIY/FIRT [48]
sixty-five SIY/FAOIV [43]
sixty-four SIY/FOUR [43]
sixty-fourth SIY/FOTD [48]
sixty-nine SIY/NAOIN [43]
sixty-ninth SIY/NAOITD [48]
sixty-one SIY/WUN [43]
sixty-second SIY/SEKD [48]
sixty-seven SIY/SEV [43]
sixty-seventh SIY/SETD [48]
sixty-six SIY/SIX [43]
sixty-sixth SIY/SITD [48]
sixty-third SIY/THIRD [48]
sixty-three SIY/THRAOE [43]
sixty-two SIY/TWO [43]
skimp SKEUPL/AEP [39]
skip SKEUP [18]
skit SKEUT [22]
sky SKFPL [18]
/ *slash* SL-RBGS [29]
sled SHRED [24]
sleek SHRAOEBG
sleep SHRAOEP [24]
sliver SHREUFR [29]
slow SHROEFRP [24]
slug SHRUG [24]
slum SHRUPL [24]
smack SPHABG [16]
small SPHAUL [16]
smart SPHART [16]
smash SPHARB [26]
smear SPHAOER [26]
smell SPHEL [26]
smile SPHAOEUL [16]
smirch SPHEUR/AEFP [39]
smog SPHOG [26]
smoke SPHOEBG [16]
smother SPHOTD/KWRER [37]
smut SPHUT [16]
snag STPHAG [26]
snail STPHAEUL [26]
snake STPHAEUBG [26]
snap STPHAP [26]
snitch STPHEUFP [25]
snow STPHOEFRP [26]
snug STPHUG [26]
so many SOEM [48]
so much SOECH [48]
soapy SOEP/AEFPL [19]
soda SOED/KWRA [40]
soft SOFT [16]
software SOFT/WAER [16]
soil SOEUL [16]
sole SOEL [47]
some are SPH-R [10]
some of SPH-F [10]
some SPH- [10]
some way SPH-FPL [39]
somebody SPH-B [39]
someday SPH-D [39]
somehow SPH-FD [39]
someone SPH-PB [39]
someplace SPH-PS [39]
something SPH-PBG [39]
sometime SPH-T [39]
sometimes SPH-TS [39]
somewhat SWA- [39]
somewhere SPH-FRP [39]
sooth SAOTD [37]
soul SOUL [47]
South Carolina S-FPLT /KR-FPLT [47]
South Dakota S-FPLT /TK-FPLT [47]

South SOUTD [45]
southeast SAOESZ [45]
southwest SWESZ [45]
sow SOEFRP [16]
soy SOFPL [16]
spacial SPAEURBL [25]
spark SPARBG [15]
spasm SPASZ [38]
special SP-RB [25]
specially SP-RBL [25]
specific SPEFK [41]
spicy SPAOEUS/AEFPL [19]
spinelessly SPAOEUPB/SHRAEFPL [40]
spinning SPEUPB/AEG [19]
spirit SPEURT [32]
spray SPRAFPL [32]
spree SPRAOE [32]
sprig SPREUG [32]
sprint SPREUPBT [32]
sprite SPRAOEUT [32]
spurt SPURT [32]
stables STAEUBLZ [18]
stairway STAEUR/WAEFPL [28]
stalk STAUBG [14]
stamp STAPL/AEP [39]
standard STARD [41]
starch STAR/AEFP [39]
starve STAFRB [31]
stash STARB [25]
stayed STAFPLD [17]
steal STAEL [46]
steel STAOEL [46]
steno STEPB/KWROE [40]
stereo STAEUR/KWROE [40]
sterilization STAEURL/SKPWAEUGS [40]
stitch STEUFP [25]
stole STOEL [30]
storms STORPLZ [18]
stream STRAEPL [30]
strike STRAOEUBG [32]
strip STREUP [32]
stripe STRAOEUP [32]
stroll STROEL [32]
strut STRUT [32]
subject SUJ [45]
subtraction SUB/TRABGS [24]
success SES [45]
sudden SUD [31]
Sue KEU-RBGS/SAOU [48]
sue SAOU [48]
suffer SUFR [29]
sufficient SUF [31]
suggest SUG [31]
suite SWAET [46]
Sunday SU-FPLT [33]
sunny SUPB/AEFPL [19]
superintendent SAOUPT [45]
superior SAOUP/KWAOR [40]
supervise SPR-FB [31]
support SUPT [31]
suppose SPOEZ [32]
sure SHAOUR [15]
surely SHAOURL [29]
surf SUFRB [31]
( ) *surround parenthesis* SPR-RBGS [27]
“ ” surround quotes SKW-RBGS [25]
swamp SWAPL/AEP [39]
sweet SWAOET [46]
swerve SWEFRB [31]

T

T- T-FRD [37]
T T-FBG [20]
-T- T-FL [28]
-T T-FLD [37]
t T-FS [24]
T. T-FPD [32]
(T) T-FPS [36]
tables TAEUBLZ [18]
tabs TABZ [18]
taco TABG/KWROE [40]
take TAE [10]
talk TAUBG [14]
talking TAUBG/AEG [19]
tall TAUL [14]
tank TAFBG [35]
task TASZ [38]

tassel TAS/KWREL [29]
taught TAUGT [22]
taxi TAFRPB/KWRAOE [40]
teach TAOEFP [25]
technical T-FP [31]
Ted's TED/AOS [20]
teeth TAOETD [37]
ten TEN [41]
Tennessee T-FPLT /TPH-FPLT [47]
tension TEPBGS [24]
tenth TETD [47]
testify TEF [45]
testimony TEM [41]
Texas T-FPLT /SKP-FPLT [47]
thank THAFBG [35]
thankfully THAFBG/TPHRAEFPL [40]
that are THAR [10]
that is THAS [33]
that THA [10]
that the THAT [10]
that you THAU [12]
that's THAZ [33]
thaw THAUFRP [22]
the -T [10]
theft THEFT [22]
their THEUR [10]
them THEPL [22]
theme THAOEPL [22]
themselves THEPL/SAEFLZ [23]
then THEPB [22]
theoretically THE/RET/KHRAEFPL [40]
there are THR-R [10]
there is THR-S [10]
there THR- [10]
there's THRZ [33]
these THAOEZ [22]
they are THER [10]
they had THEFD [27]
they have THEFB [29]
they THE [10]
they will THEFRP [10]
they would THEWD [27]
they'd THEDZ [27]
they'll THEFRPZ [31]
they're THERZ [25]
they've THEFZ [29]
thick THEUBG [22]
thigh THAOEUFD [22]
thin THEUPB [22]
thing THEUPBG [35]
think THEUFBG [35]
third THIRD [47]
thirteen THAOEN [41]
thirteenth THAOETD [47]
thirtieth THEUY/AETD [47]
thirty THIY [41]
thirty-eight THIY/AIGT [42]
thirty-eighth THIY/AITD [47]
thirty-fifth THIY/FITD [47]
thirty-first THIY/FIRT [47]
thirty-five THIY/FAOIV [42]
thirty-four THIY/FOUR [42]
thirty-fourth THIY/FOTD [47]
thirty-nine THIY/NAOIN [42]
thirty-ninth THIY/NAOITD [47]
thirty-one THIY/WUN [42]
thirty-second THIY/SEKD [47]
thirty-seven THIY/SEV [42]
thirty-seventh THIY/SETD [47]
thirty-six THIY/SIX [42]
thirty-sixth THIY/SITD [47]
thirty-third THIY/THIRD [47]
thirty-three THIY/THRAOE [42]
thirty-two THIY/TWO [42]
this THEU [10]
those THOEZ [22]
thought THOUGT [22]
three THRAOE [41]
throne THROEN [47]
thrown THROUN [47]
Thursday THU-FPLT [33]
thyme T-Y/AEM [47]
tight TAOEUGT [22]
tighten TAOEUGT/KWREPB [27]
~ *tilde* TI-RBGS [41]
time TAOIM [47]

timed TAOEUPLD [17]
timely TAOEUPL/HRAEFPL [29]
tinge TEUFPBLG [35]
To Whom it may concern TWERN [41]
today TOD [27]
toffee TOF/KWRAOE [40]
together TOTD [37]
toil TOEUL [16]
tomorrow TOR [27]
tonight TONT [41]
too many TAOM [48]
too much TAOCH [48]
too TAO [14]
took TAOBG [14]
tooth TAOTD [37]
torch TOR/AEFP [39]
torment TOR/PHAEPBT [22]
total TOELT [41]
tough TUF [22]
tow TOEFRP
town TOUPB
toy TOFPL [16]
traction TRABGS [24]
tractions TRABGS/AEZ [24]
train TRAEUPB [30]
trample TRAPL/PAEL [29]
tranquility TRAPB/KWEULT [31]
transaction TRAPBS/KWRABGS [24]
transactions TRAPBS/KWRABGS/AEZ [24]
transmission TRAPBS/PHEUGS [24]
trap TRAP [30]
tree's TRAOE/AOS [20]
trench TREPB/AEFP [30]
tried TRAOEUD [17]
trifle TRUFL [29]
trip TREUP [30]
trolley TROL/AEFPL [30]
trouble TROUBL [29]
truest TRAOUSZ [38]
truism TRAOU/SKPWEUPL [38]
truly T-Y [29]
truly yours T-YZ [43]
trumpet TRUPL/PET [30]
trust TRUSZ [38]
truth TRAOUTD [37]
trying TRFPLG [19]
Tuesday TU-FPLT [33]
turf TUFRB [31]
tusk TUSZ [38]
tutor TAOUT/KWROR [27]
tweed TWAOED [30]
twelfth TWETD [47]
twelve TWEFL [41]
twentieth TWEY/AETD [47]
twenty TWEY [41]
twenty-eight TWEY/AIGT [42]
twenty-eighth TWEY/AITD [47]
twenty-fifth TWEY/FITD [47]
twenty-first TWEY/FIRT [47]
twenty-five TWEY/FAOIV [42]
twenty-four TWEY/FOUR [42]
twenty-fourth TWEY/FOTD [47]
twenty-nine TWEY/NAOIN [42]
twenty-ninth TWEY/NAOITD [47]
twenty-one TWEY/WUN [42]
twenty-second TWEY/SEKD [47]
twenty-seven TWEY/SEV [42]
twenty-seventh TWEY/SETD [47]
twenty-six TWEY/SIX [42]
twenty-sixth TWEY/SITD [47]
twenty-third TWEY/THIRD [47]
twenty-three TWEY/THRAOE [42]
twenty-two TWEY/TWO [42]
twice TWAOEUS [30]
twilight TWEU/HRAOEUGT [30]
twin TWEUPB [30]
twirl TWEURL [30]
two TWO [30]
type TAOEUP [26]
typo TAOEUP/KWROE [40]

U

U U-FBG [20]
-U- U-FL [28]
-U U-FLD [37]
U- U-FRD [37]
u U-FS [24]

U. U-FPD [32]
(U) U-FPS [36]
U. S. UZ [42]
umpire UPL/PAOEUR [21]
unable UPB/KWRAEUBL [36]
unclear UPB/KHRAOER [36]
un-cola UPB/H-RBGS/KOE/HRA [36]
uncover UPB/KOFR [36]
under TKER [8]
_ *underscore* U-RBGS [41]
understand SDAND [46]
understood SDAOD [46]
undesirable UPB/STKAOEURBL [36]
unforgetable UPB/TPOER/TKPWET/YABL [36]
unite U/NAOEUT [21]
United States NAITS [42]
unity AOUPBT [21]
unless TPH-LS [28]
unnecessary UPB/TPHE [36]
unpack UPB/PABG [36]
until TPH-L [20]
unto UNT [48]
unusual TPHAOURB [31]
unusually TPHAOURBL [31]
unwilling TPH-FRP [28]
upon POPB [28]
uptown UP/AE/TOUPB [28]
used AOUDZ [17]
usual AOURB [31]
usually AOURBL [31]
usurp U/SURP [21]
Utah U-FPLT /T-FPLT [47]
utensil U/TENS/KWREUL [21]

V

V- SR-FRD [37]
V SR-FBG [20]
-V- SR-FL [28]
-V SR-FLD [37]
v SR-FS [24]
V. SR-FPD [32]
(V) SR-FPS [36]
vail VAIL [45]
vale VAEL [45]
veil VAEU/AEL [45]
Vermont SR-FPLT /T-FPLT [47]
very cordially V-BG [43]
very many VEM [48]
very much VECH [48]
very respectfully V-R [43]
very sincerely V-S [43]
very SRE [10]
very truly V-RT [43]
very truly yours VE/T-YZ [43]
victim SREUBGT [28]
view SREFRP [16]
vigor SREUG/KWROR [27]
Virgin Islands SR-FPLT /EU-FPLT [47]
Virginia SR-FPLT /A-FPLT [47]
virtuous SREURT/KWROUS [40]
visa SRAOEZ/KWRA [40]
visible SREUBL [28]
vision SREUGS [24]
volume SROUPL [28]
volunteer SRO [28]
voted SROET/AED [17]
vow SROFRP
vowed SROFRPD [17]

W

W W-FBG [20]
-W- W-FL [28]
-W W-FLD [37]
W- W-FRD [37]
w W-FS [24]
W. W-FPD [32]
(W) W-FPS [36]
wafer WAFR [29]
waffle WAFL [29]
wagon WAG/KWROPB [27]
wait WAIT [45]
waive WAIV [45]
waiver WAEUFR [29]
waken WAEUBG/KWREPB [27]
walk WAUBG [14]
walking WAUBG/AEG [19]
ware WAER [45]

was he WAE [10]
was not WAEPBT [21]
was the WAT [10]
was WA [10]
wash WARB [25]
Washington W-FPLT /A-FPLT [47]
wasn't WAPBZ [21]
wave WAEV [45]
waver WAEFR [29]
way WAFPL [16]
we are WER [10]
we can WEK [10]
we did WAED [10]
we had WEFD [10]
we have WEFB [10]
we WE [46]
we will WEFRP [31]
we would WAEWD [27]
weak WAEK [46]
wealth WETD [37]
wear WAEUR [45]
weather W-TD [37]
we'd WAEDZ [27]
Wednesday WE-FPLT [33]
wee WAOE [46]
week WAOEK [46]
weigh WAEUFD [22]
weight WAIGT [45]
we'll WEFRPZ [31]
we're WERZ [25]
were WR- [10]
were you WRAU [10]
West Virginia W-FPLT /SR-FPLT [47]
West WESZ [45]
we've WEFZ [29]
whale WHAEUL [21]
wharf WHAFRB [31]
what is WHAS [10]
what WHA [10]
what you WHAU [12]
whatever WHAFR [31]
what's WHAZ [33]
wheel WHAOEL [21]
whelm WHEL/AEPL [39]
when are WH-R [10]
when is WH-S [10]
when WH- [10]
when you WHU [12]
whenever WHEFR [28]
where are WHR-R [10]
where is WHRS [33]
where the WHR-T [10]
where WHR- [10]
where's WHRZ [33]
wherever WHR-FR [28]
whether WH-TD [37]
which is WHEUS [10]
which WHEU [10]
while WHAOEUL [21]
whim WHEUPL [21]
whine WHAOEUPB [21]
whiney WHAOEUPB/AEFPL [21]
whisk WHEUSZ [38]
white WHAOEUT [21]
who is WHOS [33]
whole WHOEL [21]
who's WHOZ [33]
whose WHOES [21]
widen WAOEUD/KWREPB [27]
width WEUTD [37]
will he HRE [6]
will HR (-FRP) [6]
will I HREU [6]
will not HR-PBT [10]
will the HR-T [10]
will you HRAU [8]
Wilson WEUL/SOEPB [16]
wing WEUPBG [35]
wink WEUFBG [35]
winning WUEPB/AEG [19]
Wisconsin W-FPLT /EU-FPLT [47]
wisely WAOEUZ/HRAEFPL [29]
wish WEURB [25]
witch WEUFP [25]
with W- [10]
with you WAU [10]

woman WAPB [28]
women WEPB [28]
wonderful WOFL [31]
won't WOEPBZ [21]
work WORBG [15]
worry WOER [28]
would not WOUPB [21]
would WO [10]
would you WAOU [12]
wouldn't WOUPBZ [21]
wrap WRAP [21]
wreck WREBG [21]
writ WREUT [21]
write WREU [10]
writes WREUZ [21]
writing WREUG [21]
written WREUPB [21]
wrong WROPBG [35]
Wyoming W-FPLT /KWR-FPLT [47]

X

X- SKP-FRD [37]
X SKP-FBG [20]
-X- SKP-FL [28]
-X SKP-FLD [37]
x SKP-FS [24]
X. SKP-FPD [32]
(X) SKP-FPS [36]
x-ray SKPRAFPL [30]

Y

Y KWR-FBG [20]
-Y- KWR-FL [28]
-Y KWR-FLD [37]
Y- KWR-FRD [37]
y KWR-FS [24]
Y. KWR-FPD [32]
(Y) KWR-FPS [36]
yawn KWRAEPB [16]
year's KWRAOER/AOS [20]
yes YES [41]
yes, ma'am KWREPL [12]
yes, sir KWREUR [12]
yesterday KWRAFPL [27]
you are UR [12]
you can UBG [12]
you could UBGD [12]
you did UD [12]
you had UFD [12]
you have UFB [12]
you KWROU (U) [12]
you will UFRP [12]
you would UWD [27]
you'd UDZ [27]
you'll UFRPZ [31]
you're URZ [25]
your KWROUR [12]
yours cordially KWR-K [43]
yours resepectfully KWR-R [43]
yours sincerely KWR-S [43]
yours truly KWR-T [43]
yourself YAOUR/SAEFL [23]
yourselves YAOUR/SAEFLZ [23]
youth KWRAOUTD [37]
you've UFZ [29]

Z

Z SKPW-FBG [20]
-Z- SKPW-FL [28]
-Z SKPW-FLD [37]
Z- SKPW-FRD [37]
z SKPW-FS [24]
Z. SKPW-FPD [32]
(Z) SKPW-FPS [36]
zapped SKPWAPD [17]
zero ZROE [41]
zoology SKPWAO/KWROLG [40]

A. BASIC LETTERS AND COMBINATIONS

A-1 The vowel A is written with the left thumb. [2.1]

A-2 The long A is written by striking the A key with your left thumb together with the E and U key using your right thumb. (Long A = A EU) [2.2]

A-3 The initial side B is written by striking the P and W key together using the middle finger of the left hand. (B = P + W) [2.3]

A-4 The final side -B is written by moving the middle finger of the right hand down from its home position P to strike the letter -B. [2.4]

A-5 The initial side C is written by striking the K and R keys together using the ring and index fingers of the left hand. (C = K + R) [2.5]

A-6 The final side -C is written by striking the final side -S and -Z keys together using the ring and small fingers of the right hand. You must move your hand from the home position and strike the last two bottom keys using your last two fingers. (-C = -S + -Z) [2.6]

A-7 The initial side D is written by striking the T and K key together using the ring finger of the left hand. (D = T + K) [3.2]

A-8 The final side -D is written by extending the small finger of the right hand from the home position -T over to the -D. [3.3]

A-9 The vowel E is written with the right thumb. [3.4]

A-10 A long E is written by striking the E key with your right thumb together with the A and O key using your left thumb. (Long E = AO E) [3.5]

A-11 The initial side F is written by striking the T and P keys together using the ring and middle fingers of the left hand. (F = T + P) [4.1]

A-12 The final side -F is written by striking the home position F key with the index finger of the right hand. [4.2]

A-13 The initial side G is written by striking the D keys (TK) together with the B (PW) keys using the ring and middle fingers of the left hand. (G = TK + PW) [4.3]

A-14 The final side -G is written by extending the ring finger of the right hand from the home position -L down to the -G. [4.4]

A-15 The initial side H is written by striking the home position H key with the index finger of the left hand. [4.5]

A-16 The final side -H is written by striking the final side -F and -D keys together with the index and small fingers of the right hand. (-H = -F + -D) [4.6]

A-17 The vowel I is written with the right thumb by combining the letters E and U together in one stroke. (I = E + U) [5.1]

A-18 The long I is written by striking the AO keys with your left thumb together with the EU key using your right thumb. (Long I = AO + EU) [5.2]

A-19 The initial side J is written by striking the four keys SKWR together using the small, ring, middle, and index fingers of the left hand. (J = S + K + W + R) [5.3]

A-20 The final side -J is written by striking the -PB and -LG keys together using the middle and ring fingers of the right hand. (-J = -PB + -LG) [5.4]

A-21 The initial side K is written by striking the K with the ring finger of the left hand. [6.1]

A-22 The final side -K is written by striking the -B and -G keys together using the middle and ring fingers of the right hand. (-K = -B + -G) [6.2]

A-23 The initial side L is written by striking the H and R keys together using the index finger of the left hand. [6.3]

A-24 The final side -L is written by striking the home position -L key with the ring finger of the right hand. [6.4]

A-25 The initial side M is written by striking the home position P and H together using the middle and index fingers of the left hand. (M = P + H) [6.5]

A-26 The final side -M is written by striking the home position -P and -L together using the ring and middle fingers of the right hand. (-M = -P + -L) [6.6]

A-27 The initial side N is written by striking the T, P, and H keys together using the ring, middle, and index fingers of the left hand. (N = T + P + H) [7.1]

A-28 The final side -N is written by striking the home position -P key together with the -B key. Strike the crack between the -P and -B using the middle finger of the right hand. [7.2]

A-29 The vowel O is written with the left thumb by striking the O key. [7.3]

A-30 The long O is written by striking the O key and the E key together using the left and right thumbs. (Long O = O + E) [7.4]

A-31 The initial side P is written by striking the home position P with the middle finger of the left hand. [8.1]

A-32 The final side -P is written by striking the home position -P with the middle finger of the right hand. [8.2]

A-33 The initial side Q is written by striking the K and W keys together using the ring and middle finger of the left hand. (Q = K + W) [8.3]

A-34 The final side -Q is written by striking the -L, -G, -T, and -S keys together. Hit the crack between the -LG and -TS keys and strike all four keys together. (-Q = -LG + -TS) [8.4]

A-35 The initial side R is written by moving the index finger of the left hand from the home position H to the R key. [8.5]

A-36 The final side -R is written by moving the index finger of the right hand from the home position F to the R key. [8.6]

A-37 The initial side S is written by striking the home position S with the small finger of the left hand. [9.1]

A-38 The final side -S is written by striking the -S key moving the small finger of the right hand from its home position -T down to the letter -S. [9.2]

A-39 The initial side T is written by striking the home position T with the ring finger of the left hand. [9.3]

A-40 The final side -T is written by striking the home position -T key with the small finger of the right hand. [9.4]

A-41 The vowel U is written with the right thumb to strike the U key. [10.1]

A-42 The long U is written by striking the U key with your right thumb together with the AO keys using your left thumb. (Long U = AO + U) [10.2]

A-43 The initial side V is written by striking the S and R keys together using the small finger and the index finger of the left hand. Strike both keys at the same time. (V = S + R) [10.3]

A-44 The final side -V is written by striking the -F and -B keys together using the index and middle fingers of the right hand. Strike both keys at the same time. (-V = -F + -B) [10.4]

A-45 The initial side W is written by moving the middle finger of the left hand from the home position P key to the W. [10.5]

A-46 The final side -W is written by striking the -F, -R, and -P keys together using the index and middle fingers of the right hand. Hit the crack between the -FR keys along with the -P key. (-W = -FRP) [10.6]

A-47 The initial side X is written by striking the S, K, and P keys together using the small, ring, and middle fingers of the left hand. (X = S + K + P) [11.1]

A-48 The final side -X is written by striking the -F, -R, -P, and -B keys together. Strike the crack between the -FR and -PB keys, striking all four keys at the same time. (-X = -FR + -PB) [11.2]

A-49 The initial side Y is written by striking the K, W, and R keys together using the ring, middle, and index fingers of the left hand. (Y = K + W + R) [11.3]

A-50 The final side -Y is written by striking the -F, -P, and -L keys together. Strike the keys at the same time using the index, middle, and ring fingers of the right hand. (-Y = -FPL) [11.4]

A-51 The initial side Z is written by striking the S, K, P, and W keys together using the small, middle, and ring fingers of the left hand. Strike the S and K keys along with the crack between the P and W, striking all four keys at the same time. (Z = S + K + PW) [12.1]

A-52 The final side -Z is written by moving the small finger of the right hand from the home position -T to the -Z key. [12.2]

B. GENERAL WRITING PRINCIPLES

B-1 If you make a misstroke while writing on your shorthand machine, strike the asterisk or star key to delete the preceding outline. [3.1]

B-2 Words are written in Realwrite according to the following guidelines: consider how the word is sounded, consider how the word is spelled, and apply any special rules or short forms. [13.1]

B-3 Write a one-syllable word in one stroke by writing the beginning consonant sound(s), the vowel sound(s), and the final consonant sound(s) together. [13.2]

B-4 Write a multi-syllabic word in as many strokes as are necessary to complete the word. [13.3]

B-5 A short form is a quick way of writing a word. A phrase is a series of words written as one short form. All short forms and phrases have three things in common: they are easily and quickly written on the keyboard, they do not change or violate any theory rules, and they are easily recognized for quick read back and transcription. [13.5]

B-6 Write the AE (attached ending) for all derivatives or changes in endings of root words that require a second or subsequent stroke. The AE is written with the ending in the last stroke. [17.4]

B-7 For writing a large number, follow all previous rules regarding numbers. Write the number as you hear it. Use the short forms: PH-L for million; -BL for billion; TR-L for trillion; SKPW-L for zillion. [22.4]

B-8 When two words are separated, use the H-RBGS between the words. [28.3]

B-9 When two words that would normally be separated form a compound word, use the designation AE between the two words to join them together to form one word. [28.4]

B-10 If possible, write multi-syllabic words, one syllable at a time with word endings combined in the same stroke. [40.1]

B-11 If you cannot write a multi-syllabic word in one stroke, write as much of a word as you can in the first stroke, followed by a second and subsequent stroke to complete the outline, combining the word ending in the last stroke if possible. [40.2]

B-12 Where the last stroke of a multi-syllabic word may be confused with the first stroke of the next word, use the AE rule (or an adaptation of the rule) in the last stroke. [40.3]

B-13 Derivatives of words should be written in the same stroke or combined in a second or subsequent stroke. If a separate stroke is required, write the AE before the derived ending. [40.4]

B-14 Some endings or suffixes require the AE to be written between ending consonants. [40.5]

C. WRITING THE FLAGGED ALPHABET

C-1 To write the alphabet in all capital letters, write the alphabetic letter on the initial side of the keyboard along with the final side -FBG (FK). Each letter requires the -FBG. [20.1]

C-2 To write the alphabet in small letters, write the alphabetic letter on the initial side of the keyboard along with the final side -FS in the same stroke. Each letter requires the -FS. [24.1]

C-3 To write the alphabet for letter-by-letter spelling, write the alphabetic letter on the initial side of the keyboard along with the final side -FL (for letter-by-letter) in the same stroke. Each letter requires the -FL. [28.1]

C-4 To write the alphabet in all capital letters with a period after each letter, write the alphabetic letter on the initial side of the keyboard along with the final side -FPD in the same stroke. [32.1]

C-5 To write the alphabet so that it appears with a parenthesis before and after each individual letter, write the alphabetic letter on the initial side of the keyboard along with the final side -FPS (parentheses surround) in the same stroke. [36.1]

C-6 To write the alphabet so that the hyphen appears at the right of each letter, write the alphabetic letter on the initial side of the keyboard along with the final side -FRD (-R for right and -FD for hyphen) the same stroke. [37.1]

C-7 To write the alphabet so that the hyphen appears at the left of each letter, write the alphabetic letter on the initial side of the keyboard along with the final side -FLD (L for left and -FD for hyphen) the same stroke. [37.2]

D. VOWEL SOUNDS

D-1 Write the vowels A and O together for any word that is spelled in English with a "double o" regardless of how the word is pronounced. [14.2]

D-2 Write the vowels AU for any words that contain the "au" sound. If a word is spelled "alk" in English, write AUBG. If a word is spelled "all" in English, write AUL. [14.3]

D-3 Write AWL (AFRPL) for all words that are spelled "aul" or "awl" in English as in "haul," "maul," and "bawl." [14.4]

D-4 Write the AW (AFRP) for words that are spelled with the "aw" regardless of how the word is pronounced as in raw, law, and saw. [14.4]

D-5 Write all multi-syllabic words that begin with a vowel in the final stroke by using the KWR- (initial "y") before the vowel. [14.6]

D-6 Write OW (OFRP) for words that contain the "short o" sound before the "w" as in now (TPHOFRP) and pow (POFRP). [16.1]

D-7 Write the OEW (OEFRP) for words that contain the "long o" sound before the "w" as in row (ROEFRP) and owe (OEFRP). [16.2]

D-8 Write the OUN (OUPB) for words that end in "own" as in town (TOUPB) and drown (TKROUPB). [16.3]

D-9 Write the AW (AFRP) or EW (EFRP) for words that end in "aw" or "ew" regardless of the pronunciation as in law (HRAFRP) and few (TPEFRP). [16.4]

D-10 Write the AUN (AUPB) for words that end in "awn" as in dawn (TKAUPB), lawn (HRAUPB), and fawn (TPAUPB) [16.5]

D-11 Write the OY (OFPL) for words that are spelled "oy" as in toy (TOFPL) and boy (PWOFPL). [16.6]

D-12 Write the AY (AFPL) for words that are spelled "ay" as in say (SAFPL) and ray (RAFPL). [16.7]

D-13 Write the OI (OEU) for one-syllable words that are spelled with the "oi" as in oil (OEUL) and toil (TOIL). [16.8]

D-14 Write the OI (OEU) for two-syllable words that have the sound of "oi" regardless of their spelling as in royal (ROEUL) and lawyer (HROEUR). [16.9]

E. BEGINNING CONSONANT SOUNDS AND COMBINATIONS

E-1 Write words that begin with the sound of "ch" by using the initial side KH together with the remainder of the word. [17.1]

E-2 Write words that begin with the sound of "sh" by using the initial side SH together with the remainder of the word. [17.2]

E-3 Write words that are spelled in English with "wh" by writing WH, even though the "h" is silent. Write words that are spelled in English with "wr" by writing WR, even though the "w" is silent. [21.1]

E-4 Write KL (KHR-) or KM (KPH-) for words that begin with "col" or "com." In some cases, the K- may be used for "com" and combined with a consonant. If it is not possible to write the word in one stroke, write KOL (KOHR) or KOM (KOPH) in the first stroke. [23.2]

E-5 Write words that begin with the "sl" combination by using the SHR; write words that begin with the "shr" combination by using the SKHR. [24.4]

E-6 For all words that begin with the "kn," regardless of the pronunciation, use the STP- to distinguish between words that begin with "n." [32.2]

F. BEGINNING VOWELS AND PREFIXES

F-1 The prefixes or beginnings of words are written with a short vowel. [17.3]

F-2 Use a short vowel for words that begin with the single vowels "a," "e," "i," and "u." Use the long vowel OE for words that begin with the vowel "o." [21.3]

F-3 Use a long or short vowel when a word begins with a vowel that is combined with a consonant in the first stroke. [21.4]

F-4 Write EUPB- for words that begin with "in," write OPB- for words that begin with "on," write EPB- for words that begin with "en." [26.1]

F-5 Write OR- for words that begin with "or," write ER- for words that begin with "er." [26.2]

F-6 Write PRE- for all words that begin with the prefix "pre." Write PRO- for all words that begin with the prefix "pro." [28.5]

F-7 Write the RE- for all words that begin with the prefix "re"; write PWE- for all words that begin with the prefix "be." [28.6]

F-8 Write the TKE for all words that begin with the prefix "de," unless the "de" can be blended or "slurred" together as in words containing the dep (TKP-), dem (TKPH-), or del (TKHR-). [28.7]

F-9 Write the ST- for words that begin with "ext." [30.1]

F-10 Write the SKP- for words that begin with "ex" followed by any vowel or consonant except "ext." [30.2]

F-11 Write EX (E-FRPB) in the first stroke for words that begin with the prefix "ex-" where the hyphen (-) is required between prefix and word.

F-12 Write the EPBT for words that begin with the prefix "enter." Write the EUPBT for words that begin with the prefix "inter." [30.3]

F-13 Write the STK- ("d" and "s" reversed) for words that begin with the prefix "des" or "dis." Combine the STK with a vowel in the first stroke if necessary. If it is necessary to write the "des" or "dis" in a separate stroke, write the TKES or TKEUS. [34.2]

F-14 Write the TPOER at the beginning of words that start with the prefix "fore" or "for." [36.2]

F-15 Write the UPB at the beginning of words that start with the prefix "un." If a hyphen is needed to separate the words, write the H-RBGS between the two words. [36.3]

F-16 Write the TKW- (DW) for words that begin with the"div" or "dev" prefix. If the TKW- cannot be written in the same stroke, write the TKEUFB ("div") or TKEFB ("dev") in the first stroke, followed by the completed outline. [36.4]

F-17 For words that begin with prefixes that could be considered separate words, write them according to the following chart [39.3]:

English	*prefix-*	*word/short form*
down	TKOFRP	TKOUFRP
enter	EPBT	TPHER
fore	TPOER	TP-R
over	OEFR	SRER
post	POESZ	POES
self	SEF	SEFL
super	SAOUP	SPER
under	UPBD	TKER
up	UP/AE	UP
out	OUT/AE	OUT
in	EUPB	TPH-

G. WORD ENDINGS AND COMBINATIONS

G-1 For words that end in "y" or "ey" where a second or subsequent stroke is necessary, write AEFPL (attached ending) in the final stroke. [19.1]

G-2 For words that end in "ee" (double e) or "ie" write KWRAOE (silent "y") in the final stroke. [19.2]

G-3 The final -PLT is used for all words that end in "ment." When possible, write the -PLT in the same stroke. If the -PLT cannot be written in the same stroke, write PHAEPBT in the last stroke. [22.1]

G-4 Words that are spelled in English with "ght" are written with the -GT in the outline. [22.2]

G-5 Write the final H (-FD) for all words that are spelled in English with "gh" and sound like "h." Write the final F for all words that are spelled in English with "gh" and sound like "f." [22.3]

G-6 Write SAEFL in the second stroke for words that end in "self." Write SAEFLZ in the second stroke for words that end in "selves." [23.2]

G-7 Write -GS for all words that end in the "shun" sound, regardless of the spelling. Combine the -GS in the last stroke of the word. Plurals are formed by writing the AEZ in the last stroke. [24.2]

G-8 Write -BGS for all words that end in the "kshun" sound, regardless of the spelling. Combine the -BGS in the last stroke of the word. Plurals are formed by writing AEZ in the last stoke. [24.3]

G-9 Write words that end with the sound of "ch" and "tch" by using the -FP. If it is necessary to write the -FP in a separate stroke by itself, write the AEFP in the last stroke. [25.1]

G-10 Write words that end with the sound of "sh" with the -RB. For words that end in "ish" and require a second stroke, use the "silent y" and write KWREURB. [25.2]

G-11 Use the -RBL for words that end with the sound of "shal," regardless of their spelling. If a separate stroke is required, use SHAEL in the last stroke. [25.4]

G-12 Use the -RBS for words that end with the sound of "shus," regardless of the spelling. If a separate stroke is required, use SHAUS in the last stroke. [25.5]

G-13 Write all multi-syllabic words that begin with a vowel in the final stroke by using the initial "y" (KWR-) before the vowel. [27.1]

G-14 For all words that require a separate stroke for the ending "on," write the designation KWROPB. For all words that require a separate stroke for the ending "en," write the designation KWREPB. [27.2]

G-15 For all words that require a separate stroke for the ending "or," write the designation KWROR. For all words that require a separate stroke for the ending "er," write the designation KWRER. [27.3]

G-16 For all words that end with the "ly" ending, write the -L in the same stroke. If it is necessary to write the -L in a separate stroke, write the HRAEFPL (LAEY) in the last stroke. [29.1]

G-17 If the first syllable of the word ends in the consonant "l" write the AEFPL in the final stroke. [29.2]

G-18 For all words that end with the "le" or "el" combine the -L in the same stroke if possible. If a second stroke is necessary, write the AEL (le) or KWRAEL (el) in the last stroke. [29.3]

G-19 In writing the AEL in the second stroke of words that end in “le” or “el,” it may be necessary to begin the second stroke with a leftover consonant. [29.4]

G-20 For all words that end in "fer" or "ver," write the -FR in the same stroke. If it is necessary to write the "fer" or "ver" in a separate stroke, use FER or SRER. [29.5]

G-21 Write the -T in the same stroke for words that end in "ty" or "ity." If the -T cannot be written in the first stroke, combine the -T in a second or subsequent stroke or write the TAEFPL in the last stroke. [31.3]

G-22 For all words that end with an "rv" or "rf," write the -FRB in the same stroke. [31.2]

G-23 For all words that end with the sound of "able" or "ible," write the -BL in the same stroke or combined in a second stroke. If a separate stroke is necessary, write KWRABL (able) or KWREUBL (ible) in the last stroke. [33.1]

G-24 For all words that end with the sound of "ability" or "ibility," write the -BLT in the same stroke or combined in a second stroke. If a separate stroke is necessary, write KWRABLT (ability) or KWREUBLT (ibility) in the last stroke. [33.2]

G-25 For all words that end in the sound of "ng," write the -PBG (-NG) in the same stroke. [35.1]

G-26 For all words that end in the sound of "nk," write the -FBG (-FK) in the same stroke. [35.2]

G-27 For all words that end in the sound of "nj," write the -FPBLG (-FJ) in the same stroke. [35.3]

G-28 For words that end in "th" write the -TD in the same stroke. If it is necessary to write the -TD in a separate stroke, write the attached ending AETD in the last stroke. [37.3]

G-29 For words that end in "sk" and "sm," write the -SZ in the same stroke. [38.1]

G-30 For words that end in "st," write the -SZ in the same stroke; however, for one-syllable words that contain the vowel "a," use the AE within the same stroke. [38.2]

G-31 For words that end in "ism" and "ist" and require a separate stroke, use the SKPWEUPL for "ism" and the KWREUSZ for "ist." [38.3]

G-32 Final consonants that cannot be written in the same stroke as the root word are written in a separate stroke along with the AE (attached ending). [39.1]

G-33 For words that end with suffixes that could be considered separate words or the beginning of another word, write them according to the following chart [39.2]:

word ending	*suffix*	*word/short form*
-shal	SHAEL	(shall) SHAL
-ment	PHAEPBT	(meant) PHEPBT
-less	HRAES	(less) HRES
-ful (full)	TPAUL	(full) TPUL
-let (lette)	HRAET	(let) HRET
-for (fore)	TPAOR	(for) TPOR
-nette	TPHAET	(net) TPHET
-over	AE/OEFR	SRER
-up	AE/UP	UP
-out	AE/OUT	OUT
-under	AE/UPBD	TKER

G-34 If a final stroke begins with a vowel, write the KWR- before the vowel. [40.6]

G-35 If a word ends in a single vowel, precede the vowel with the KWR, unless the vowel can be written with a consonant. [40.7]

G-36 For words that end in "ier," write KWRAER in the last stroke. [40.8]

G-37 For words that end in "iest," write KWRAESZ in the last stroke. [40.9]

G-38 For words that end in "ior," write the KWRAOR in the last stoke. [40.10]

G-39 For words that end in "ous," write KWROUS, regardless of the pronunciation. [40.11]

G-40 For words that end in "ure," write KWRUR in the last stroke. [40.12]

G-41 For words that end in "ize," write KWRAOEUZ in the last stroke, unless the last stroke can be combined with a consonant. [40.13]

G-42 For words that end in "tiv," write TEUFB. [40.14]

G-43 For words that end in "tivity," write TEUFT. [40.15]

G-44 For words that end in "tively," write TEUFL. [40.16]

G-45 For words that end in "istic," write STEUSZ. [40.17]

G-46 For words that end in "istically," write SKHRAEFPL. [40.18]

G-47 For words that end in "ically," write KHRAEFPL. [40.19]

G-48 For words that end in "lessly," write SHRAEFPL. [40.20]

G-49 For words that end in "fully," write TPHRAEFPL. [40.21]

G-50 For words that end in "ingly," write TKPWHRAEFPL. [40.22]

G-51 For words that end in "zation," write SKPWAEUGS. [40.23]

G-52 For words that end in "ology," write KWROLG. [40.24]

H. ENDING DERIVATIVES

H-1 Write the past tense of a word by adding a -D in the same stroke when possible. If the -D cannot be added in the same stroke, use the "attached ending" rule and write AED in the second or last stroke. [17.5]

H-2 If a one-syllable word ends in "n" do not add the -D in the same stroke; form the past tense by writing the AED in a second stroke. [17.6]

H-3 If the spelling of a word changes by forming the past tense, the new outline should reflect the new spelling. [17.7]

H-4 The plural of a word is formed by writing the final -Z in the same stroke. If a word ends in -T, write the final -TS in the same stroke to form the plural. If a word ends in -S or -Z, write the AEZ (attached ending) in the last stroke. [18.1]

H-5 The final -G is used for all words that end in "ing." When possible, write the -G in the same stroke. If the -G cannot be written in the same stroke, write the AEG (attached ending) in the last stroke. [19.4]

H-6 If a one-syllable word ends in "n," do not add the -G in the same stroke; form the "ing" ending by writing the AEG in a second stroke. [19.5]

H-7 Write the AOS in the last stroke to form the 's for any word, letter or number. Singular possessives are formed by writing AOS ('s) in the last stroke. Plural possessives are formed by writing the A-RBGS (s') in the last stroke. [20.2]

I. BASIC NUMBERS

I-1 Write the number 1 with the small finger of the left hand. Hit the crack between the home position S and the number bar, using the top and flat part of your finger to depress both key and bar at the same time. [3.6]

I-2 Write the number 9 with the small finger of the right hand. Hit the crack between the home position -T and the number bar, using the top and flat part of your finger to depress both key and bar at the same time. [3.7]

I-3 Write the number 2 with the ring finger of the left hand. Hit the crack between the home position T and the number bar, depressing both key and bar at the same time. [5.5]

I-4 Write the number 8 with the ring finger of the right hand. Hit the crack between the home position -L and the number bar, depressing both key and bar at the same time. [5.6]

I-5 Write the number 3 with the middle finger of the left hand. Hit the crack between the home position P and the number bar, depressing both key and bar at the same time. [7.5]

I-6 Write the number 7 with the middle finger of the right hand. Hit the crack between the home position -P and the number bar, depressing both key and bar at the same time. [7.6]

I-7 Write the number 4 with the index finger of the left hand. Hit the crack between the home position H and the number bar, depressing both key and bar at the same time. [9.5]

I-8 Write the number 6 with the index finger of the right hand. Hit the crack between the home position -F and the number bar, depressing both key and bar at the same time. [9.6]

I-9 Write the number 5 with the left thumb striking the vowel A key and the middle finger of the left hand reaching up to strike the number bar, both at the same time. [11.5]

I-10 Write the number 0 with the left thumb striking the vowel O key and the middle finger of the left hand reaching up to strike the number bar, both at the same time. [11.6]

I-11 Write a two-digit number by striking the two numbers together on the keyboard as follows. If the first number is smaller than the second number, write it in one stroke by combining the two numbers together. Write the numbers 10, 20, 30, 40, and 50 in one stroke. [11.7]

I-12 Write any two-digit number where the first number is greater than the second number by writing the two numbers in Inverse order along with the vowel I (EU). The vowel I (EU) indicates that you read and transcribe the numbers in their inverse order. [12.3]

I-13 To double any single-digit number to form a repeated double-digit number, write the single number along with the vowel I (EU) in the same stroke. The vowel I (EU) indicates that you imitate or double the single number. [12.4]

I-14 For numbers beginning with 100, write the first digit(s) in the first stroke followed by the short form H-PBD for hundred. Numbers dictated after the hundreds are written using the same rules you leaned for writing 1 - 99. [16.10]

I-15 For numbers beginning with 1,000, write the first digit in the first stroke followed by the short form TH-Z for thousand. Write the hundreds digit followed by the short form H-PBD. Numbers dictated after the hundreds are written using previous number rules. [18.2]

I-16 For writing a large number, follow all previous rules regarding numbers. Write the number as you hear it. Use the short forms: PH-L for million; -BL for billion; TR-L for trillion; SKPW-L for zillion. [22.4]

J. DOLLARS & CENTS

J-1 To write money amounts in dollars and cents, write the numbers as you hear them, using all previous rules. Write PHE-RBGS or TKHR-RBGS in the first stroke for all money amounts. To indicate dollars, use the -DZ in a separate stroke; to indicate cents, use the -SZ in a separate stroke. [26.3]

J-2 For large amounts of money, write the numbers as you hear them using the following short forms: TR-L for trillion; -BL for billion; PH-L for million. Write PHE-RBGS or TKHR-RBGS in the first stroke for all money amounts. [26.4]

J-3 Very large amounts of money are written as they are said, using all previous number rules. The -DZ for dollars and/or the -SZ for cents are written in the appropriate stroke. Write PHE-RBGS or TKHR-RBGS in the first stroke for all money amounts. [26.5]

J-4 Use the short form TKLAR for dollar, TKLARZ for dollars, KREPBT for cent, and KREPBTS for cents when appropriate. [26.6]

K. PHONETIC NUMBERS, ORDINALS, AND PHONETIC ORDINALS

K-1 Write all phonetic numbers according to the outlines given in Lessons 41-44.

K-2 Write all numeric ordinals according to the outlines given in Lessons 45-46.

K-3 Write all phonetic ordinals according to the outlines given in Lessons 47-48.

L. FRACTIONS

L-1 Write fractions phonetically as you hear them when they are to be transcribed as words. [34.3]

L-2 Write fractions that are to be transcribed using numbers by combining the numerator with the initial R- or final -R in the first stroke. Write the denominator for the second stroke. [34.4]

M. DATES & TIMES

M-1 For all dates that are dictated without any dividing marks between the numbers, automatically write the slash SL-RBGS between the month, day, and year. The hyphen (H-RBGS) may also be used. [30.4]

M-2 For clock time, write the hour figure with the K- or -BG in the same stroke to indicate the colon after the hours, then write the minute figure as dictated. [30.5]

M-3 For clock time, use A-PL for a.m. and P-PL for p.m. in the last stroke. Use AOBG in the last stroke for the word "o'clock" when dictated. [30.6]

N. PUNCTUATION

N-1 Write the symbol for the period (.) by combining the final side -FPLT together in one stroke by using the four fingers of the right hand. [13.4]

N-2 Write the symbol for the comma (,) by combining the final side -RBG-S together in one stroke by using the four fingers of the right hand. [14.1]

N-3 Write the symbol for the question mark (?) by combining the initial side STPH- together in one stroke by using the four fingers of the left hand. [15.1]

N-4 Punctuation marks and special symbols (other than the period, comma, and question mark) are formed by using the initial side to write a one- or two-letter designation together with the final side -RBGS. [15.2]

N-5 The symbol to indicate the beginning of a new paragraph is written PA-RBGS. Write this designation once to indicate the beginning of a new paragraph. [15.3]

N-6 Write K-RBGS to designate the colon whenever it is dictated or as needed within dictation. [17.8]

N-7 Write S-RBGS to designate the semicolon whenever it is dictated or as needed within dictation. [17.9]

N-8 Write the A-RBGS to designate the apostrophe (') whenever it is dictated or as needed within dictation. [19.3]

N-9 Use the KWO-RBGS for "opening" quotes. Use the KWE-RBGS for "ending" quotes. [25.3]

N-10 Use the PRO-RBGS for "opening" parenthesis. Use the PRE-RBGS for "ending" parenthesis. [27.4]

N-11 To write a hyphen, use the H-RBGS. [28.2]

N-12 Write the SKP-RBGS to designate the exclamation point as needed in dictation. [29.6]

N-13 Write the SL-RBGS to designate the slash mark whenever it is needed in dictation. [29.7]

N-14 Write the D-RBGS whenever the dash (--) is needed within dictation. [31.3]

N-15 Write the PW-RBGS whenever the back slash (\ ) is needed within dictation. [31.4]

N-16 Write the DP-RBGS to designate the decimal point whenever it is dictated. [33.3]

N-17 Write the POEU-RBGS to designate the word point whenever it is dictated. [33.4]

N-18 To designate an "initial cap" for a person, place, or thing, use the designation KEU-RBGS before the word. [35.4]

N-19 To designate "all caps" for a word, use the designation KA-RBGS before the word. Each separate word requires a separate designation. [35.5]

O. DAYS & MONTHS

O-1 Write the days of the week using a two- or three-letter designation on the initial side, combined with the -FPLT on the final side. [33.5]

O-2 Write the months of the year using a two- or three-letter designation on the initial side, combined with the -FPLT on the final side. [39.2]

P. CONTRACTIONS

P-1 All contractions are written by adding the final -Z to the short form used to write the root word or phrase. [21.2]

Q. SPECIAL SYMBOLS AND MISCELLANEOUS

Q-1 Punctuation marks and special symbols (other than the period, comma and question mark) are formed by using the initial side to write a one- or two-letter designation together with the final side -RBGS. [15.2]

Q-2 The symbol to indicate the beginning of a new paragraph is written PA-RBGS. Write this designation once to indicate the beginning of a new paragraph. [15.3]

Q-3 To designate an "initial cap" for a person, place, or thing, use the designation KEU-RBGS before the word. [35.4]

Q-4 To designate "all caps" for a word, use the designation KA-RBGS before the word. Each separate word requires a separate designation. [35.5]

Q-5 To designate a Roman numeral, write the special designation RO-RBGS, followed by the regular number using the number bar. [37.4]

Q-6 Write all miscellaneous special symbols according to the outlines given in Lesson 37.

Q-7 Write states and territories of the United States according to the short forms given in Lesson 47.

Q-8 Write all salutations according to the outlines given in Lesson 41.

Q-9 Write all complimentary closing according to the outlines given in Lesson 43.

R. QUESTION AND ANSWER DESIGNATION

R-1 The designation used to indicate a QUESTION is the entire left-hand bank of keys, using the four fingers of the left hand: STKPWHR. Depress the eight keys all at the same time, returning immediately to the home position. [41.1]

R-2 The designation used to indicate an ANSWER is the entire right-hand bank of keys, using the four fingers of the right hand: FRPBLGTS. Depress the eight keys all at the same time, returning immediately to the home position. [41.2]

S. REALTIME WRITING RULES AND CONFLICT ELIMINATION

S-1 In eliminating a conflict between two words that contain the "long a" sound, use the AE for words that contain both the "a" and the "e" in the English spelling. Use the AEU (long a) for all other words. [45.1]

S-2 In eliminating a conflict between two words that contain the "long a" sound, use the AE for words that do not contain the "a" and "i" in their English spelling. [45.2]

S-3 If a conflict cannot be eliminated between two words that contain the "long a" sound by applying all previous rules, write the word in two strokes. [45.3]

S-4 In eliminating a conflict between two words that contain an "a" and "e" in their English spelling, use the AE for the words that have the "ae" in order. Use the long a (AEU) for words that have the "e" before the "a." [45.4]

S-5 In eliminating a conflict between words that contain the "long e" sound, use the AE for all words that contain both vowels "a" and "e" regardless of their order. Use the "long e" for all other words, including words that contain the "double e." [46.1]

S-6 If a conflict cannot be eliminated between two words that contain the "long e" sound by applying all previous rules, write the word in two strokes. [46.2]

S-7 In eliminating a conflict between words that contain the "long i" sound, use the AOEU for all words and make the distinction by writing as close to the English spelling as you can. [47.1]

S-8 In eliminating a conflict between two words that contain the "long o" sound, use the OE (long o) for the word that ends in the silent vowel "e" in the English spelling. Use the O (short o) for all other words in conflict. [47.2]

S-9 In eliminating other conflicts involving the "long o", use the proper English spelling along with other applicable rules. [47.3]

S-10 In eliminating a conflict between two words that contain the "u" sound, write the word as close to the English spelling as possible. [48.1]

S-11 In eliminating conflicts with words that begin with the "s," write the S for words that begin with "s" in the English spelling, write SK for words that begin with "sc," and write KR for words that begin with "c" in the English spelling. [48.2]

S-12 In eliminating conflicts with words that begin with "ex" and "ext," write the SKP for words that begin with "ex" and write the ST for words that begin with "ext." [48.3]

S-13 In eliminating conflicts with one stroke words that begin with a vowel, use the initial Y (KWR) along with the long vowel in order to make a distinction. [48.4]

S-14 In eliminating conflicts with words that end in a double consonant in the English spelling, use the vowels AU for the word containing the double consonant. [48.5]